Acts

TEACH THE TEXT COMMENTARY

John H. Walton
Old Testament General Editor

Mark L. Strauss
New Testament General Editor

Volumes now available:

Old Testament Volumes

Exodus ....T. Desmond Alexander

Leviticus and Numbers .... Joe M. Sprinkle

Joshua .... Kenneth A. Mathews

Judges and Ruth ....Kenneth C. Way

1 & 2 Samuel .... Robert B. Chisholm Jr.

Job .... Daniel J. Estes

Psalms, volume 1 .... C. Hassell Bullock

Ecclesiastes and Song of Songs............ Edward M. Curtis

Jeremiah and Lamentations .... J. Daniel Hays

Daniel.. Ronald W. Pierce

New Testament Volumes

Matthew ....Jeannine K. Brown

Mark ....Grant R. Osborne

Luke ....R. T. France

Acts ....David E. Garland

Romans ....C. Marvin Pate

1 Corinthians .... Preben Vang

2 Corinthians ....Moyer V. Hubbard

James, 1 & 2 Peter, and Jude............................Jim Samra

Revelation.. J. Scott Duvall

Visit the series website at www.teachthetextseries.com.

TEACH the TEXT
COMMENTARY SERIES

Acts

David E. Garland

Mark L. Strauss and John H. Walton
GENERAL EDITORS

ILLUSTRATING THE TEXT

Kevin and Sherry Harney
ASSOCIATE EDITORS

Adam Barr
CONTRIBUTING WRITER

BakerBooks

a division of Baker Publishing Group
Grand Rapids, Michigan

Published by Baker Books
a division of Baker Publishing Group
PO Box 6287, Grand Rapids, MI 49516-6287
www.bakerbooks.com

Printed in the United States of America

Library of Congress Cataloging-in-Publication Data
Names: Garland, David E., author.
Title: Acts / David E. Garland ; Mark L. Strauss and John H. Walton, general editors ; Kevin and
    Sherry Harney, associate editors ; Adam Barr, contributing author.
Description: Grand Rapids : Baker Books, 2017. | Series: Teach the text commentary series |
    Includes bibliographical references and index.
Identifiers: LCCN 2017005297 | ISBN 9780801092299 (pbk.)
Subjects: LCSH: Bible. Acts—Commentaries.
Classification: LCC BS2625.53 .G37 2017 | DDC 226.6/07—dc23
LC record available at https://lccn.loc.gov/2017005297

To my beloved wife, Diana R. Garland
1950–2015

Contents

Welcome to the Teach the Text
  Commentary Series   ix
Introduction to the Teach the Text
  Commentary Series   xi
Acknowledgments   xiii
Abbreviations   xiv
Maps   xvii

Introduction to Acts 1
Acts 1:1–11 13
  Jesus's Resurrection and Ascension: The
  Continuation of the Story
Acts 1:12–26 19
  Replacing Judas among the Twelve
Acts 2:1–13 25
  The Coming of the Spirit
Acts 2:14–47 30
  The Spirit Inspires the Bold
  Proclamation of the Gospel
Acts 3:1–26 37
  The Healing of a Lame Man at the
  Temple Gates
Acts 4:1–31 43
  The Apostles Bold under Fire and the
  Church Fervent in Prayer
Acts 4:32–5:11 50
  Godly Giving and Deadly Lies:
  Barnabas and Ananias and Sapphira

Acts 5:12–42 57
  Signs and Wonders, and Persecution
Acts 6:1–7 63
  The Appointment of the Seven
Acts 6:8–7:50 69
  Stephen's Arrest and Speech
Acts 7:51–8:3 75
  Stephen's Martyrdom
Acts 8:4–25 82
  The Extension of the Mission in
  Samaria
Acts 8:26–40 88
  Philip and the Ethiopian
Acts 9:1–30 94
  Saul's Conversion and Call
Acts 9:31–43 100
  Peter's Ministry in Lydda and Joppa:
  Healing Aeneas and Raising Tabitha
Acts 10:1–48 105
  The Apostle Peter and the Centurion
  Cornelius
Acts 11:1–18 112
  Peter's Report to Jerusalem Believers
Acts 11:19–30 118
  Solidarity between Two Christian
  Communities

Acts 12:1–25 124
James's Death, Peter's Escape, and
Herod's Demise

Acts 13:1–12 132
Resistance and Success in Cyprus

Acts 13:13–52 138
The Expansion of the Gospel in
Pisidian Antioch

Acts 14:1–28 144
Ministry in Iconium, Lystra, and Derbe

Acts 15:1–35 152
The Jerusalem Council: What Is to Be
Required of Gentile Converts?

Acts 15:36–16:15 159
Paul and Barnabas Split Up, but the
Mission Continues

Acts 16:16–40 166
Rocking the Jailhouse

Acts 17:1–15 171
Rejection in Thessalonica and
Acceptance in Berea

Acts 17:16–34 177
Paul's Defense before the Areopagus
Council

Acts 18:1–17 184
Law and Disorder in Corinth

Acts 18:18–19:7 191
Believers Are Strengthened, and
Jews Are Presented with Persuasive
Arguments That Jesus Is the Messiah

Acts 19:8–41 197
The Clash of Gods: Making Waves in a
World of Rival Religiosity

Acts 20:1–16 204
Paul Brings Renewal to the Churches

Acts 20:17–38 210
Paul's Bittersweet Farewell Exhortation
at Miletus

Acts 21:1–14 217
Prepared to Die for the Name of the
Lord Jesus

Acts 21:15–26 222
Paul Meets James and the Elders in
Jerusalem

Acts 21:27–40 228
Paul's Arrest in the Temple

Acts 22:1–30 234
Paul's Defense in the Temple

Acts 23:1–10 241
Paul's Defense before the Sanhedrin

Acts 23:11–35 247
The Vision of God's Purpose for Paul
and the Plot against His Life

Acts 24:1–27 253
The Hearing before Governor Felix in
Caesarea

Acts 25:1–27 260
The Hearing before Governor Festus
and King Agrippa and Bernice

Acts 26:1–32 266
Paul's Speech before King Agrippa

Acts 27:1–28:10 273
Storm, Shipwreck, and Shelter

Acts 28:11–31 281
The Chained Paul and the Unhindered
Gospel

Notes   289
Bibliography   298
Contributors   303
Index   304

Welcome to the Teach the Text Commentary Series

Why another commentary series? That was the question the general editors posed when Baker Books asked us to produce this series. Is there something that we can offer to pastors and teachers that is not currently being offered by other commentary series, or that can be offered in a more helpful way? After carefully researching the needs of pastors who teach the text on a weekly basis, we concluded that yes, more can be done; the Teach the Text Commentary Series (TTCS) is carefully designed to fill an important gap.

The technicality of modern commentaries often overwhelms readers with details that are tangential to the main purpose of the text. Discussions of source and redaction criticism, as well as detailed surveys of secondary literature, seem far removed from preaching and teaching the Word. Rather than wade through technical discussions, pastors often turn to devotional commentaries, which may contain exegetical weaknesses, misuse the Greek and Hebrew languages, and lack hermeneutical sophistication. There is a need for a commentary that utilizes the best of biblical scholarship but also presents the material in a clear, concise, attractive, and user-friendly format.

This commentary is designed for that purpose—to provide a ready reference for the exposition of the biblical text, giving easy access to information that a pastor needs to communicate the text effectively. To that end, the commentary is divided into carefully selected preaching units (with carefully regulated word counts both in the passage as a whole and in each subsection). Pastors and teachers engaged in weekly preparation thus know that they will be reading approximately the same amount of material on a week-by-week basis.

Each passage begins with a concise summary of the central message, or "Big Idea," of the passage and a list of its main themes. This is followed by a more detailed interpretation of the text, including the literary context of the passage, historical background material, and interpretive insights. While drawing on the best of biblical scholarship, this material is clear, concise, and to the point. Technical material is kept to a minimum, with endnotes pointing the reader to more detailed discussion and additional resources.

A second major focus of this commentary is on the preaching and teaching process itself. Few commentaries today help the pastor/teacher move from the meaning of the text to its effective communication. Our goal is to bridge this gap. In addition to interpreting the text in the "Understanding the Text" section, each unit contains a "Teaching the Text" section and an "Illustrating the Text" section. The teaching section points to the key theological themes of the passage and ways to communicate these themes to today's audiences. The illustration section provides ideas and examples for retaining the interest of hearers and connecting the message to daily life.

The creative format of this commentary arises from our belief that the Bible is not just a record of God's dealings in the past but is the living Word of God, "alive and active" and "sharper than any double-edged sword" (Heb. 4:12). Our prayer is that this commentary will help to unleash that transforming power for the glory of God.

The General Editors

Introduction to the Teach the Text Commentary Series

This series is designed to provide a ready reference for teaching the biblical text, giving easy access to information that is needed to communicate a passage effectively. To that end, the commentary is carefully divided into units that are faithful to the biblical authors' ideas and of an appropriate length for teaching or preaching.

The following standard sections are offered in each unit.

1. *Big Idea*. For each unit the commentary identifies the primary theme, or "Big Idea," that drives both the passage and the commentary.
2. *Key Themes*. Together with the Big Idea, the commentary addresses in bullet-point fashion the key ideas presented in the passage.
3. *Understanding the Text*. This section focuses on the exegesis of the text and includes several sections.
   a. The Text in Context. Here the author gives a brief explanation of how the unit fits into the flow of the text around it, including reference to the rhetorical strategy of the book and the unit's contribution to the purpose of the book.

b. Outline/Structure. For some literary genres (e.g., epistles), a brief exegetical outline may be provided to guide the reader through the structure and flow of the passage.

c. Historical and Cultural Background. This section addresses historical and cultural background information that may illuminate a verse or passage.

d. Interpretive Insights. This section provides information needed for a clear understanding of the passage. The intention of the author is to be highly selective and concise rather than exhaustive and expansive.

e. Theological Insights. In this very brief section the commentary identifies a few carefully selected theological insights about the passage.

4. *Teaching the Text.* Under this second main heading the commentary offers guidance for teaching the text. In this section the author lays out the main themes and applications of the passage. These are linked carefully to the Big Idea and are represented in the Key Themes.

5. *Illustrating the Text.* At this point in the commentary the writers partner with a team of pastor/teachers to provide suggestions for relevant and contemporary illustrations from current culture, entertainment, history, the Bible, news, literature, ethics, biography, daily life, medicine, and over forty other categories. They are designed to spark creative thinking for preachers and teachers and to help them design illustrations that bring alive the passage's key themes and message.

Acknowledgments

The crucifixion and resurrection of Christ as recorded in the Gospels have epochal consequence for the salvation of the world, but only Luke of the four evangelists decided that it was also significant to cover the continuation of Christ's work in the Spirit's guiding of the growth of the early church. Studying Acts is not simply an academic, historical exercise so that one can trace the stops of Paul's various journeys on an ancient map. It informs the present life and tasks of the church that continues to carry out Christ's commission to be his witnesses in a world that is often hostile to the gospel. The study of Scripture is always spiritually edifying and challenging, but this project was especially so for me because it was written during my wife's valiant battle with cancer, which she lost. It was also written while I served as interim provost of Baylor University. I am grateful to all who walked alongside us during this time, whose names are too many to mention. I am also grateful to the Regents of Baylor University who, before she died, named the Baylor School of Social Work, of which she was founding dean, in her honor as The Diana R. Garland School of Social Work.

I appreciate the editing of James Korsmo of Baker Books. I am very indebted to my research assistant, Tia Kim, for her invaluable assistance and proofing skill in the production of this volume. She was particularly indispensable in the final editing when I served as interim president of Baylor University. I would also like to thank Mia Casey for her great help during this time. Reading the manifold trials of the various figures in Acts reinforced my view that we are all "interim" in this life and that God always has others ready to take up the baton for the next lap in God's story.

Abbreviations

Old Testament

Gen.	Genesis	2 Chron.	2 Chronicles	Dan.	Daniel
Exod.	Exodus	Ezra	Ezra	Hosea	Hosea
Lev.	Leviticus	Neh.	Nehemiah	Joel	Joel
Num.	Numbers	Esther	Esther	Amos	Amos
Deut.	Deuteronomy	Job	Job	Obad.	Obadiah
Josh.	Joshua	Ps(s).	Psalm(s)	Jon.	Jonah
Judg.	Judges	Prov.	Proverbs	Mic.	Micah
Ruth	Ruth	Eccles.	Ecclesiastes	Nah.	Nahum
1 Sam.	1 Samuel	Song	Song of Songs	Hab.	Habakkuk
2 Sam.	2 Samuel	Isa.	Isaiah	Zeph.	Zephaniah
1 Kings	1 Kings	Jer.	Jeremiah	Hag.	Haggai
2 Kings	2 Kings	Lam.	Lamentations	Zech.	Zechariah
1 Chron.	1 Chronicles	Ezek.	Ezekiel	Mal.	Malachi

New Testament

Matt.	Matthew	Eph.	Ephesians	Heb.	Hebrews
Mark	Mark	Phil.	Philippians	James	James
Luke	Luke	Col.	Colossians	1 Pet.	1 Peter
John	John	1 Thess.	1 Thessalonians	2 Pet.	2 Peter
Acts	Acts	2 Thess.	2 Thessalonians	1 John	1 John
Rom.	Romans	1 Tim.	1 Timothy	2 John	2 John
1 Cor.	1 Corinthians	2 Tim.	2 Timothy	3 John	3 John
2 Cor.	2 Corinthians	Titus	Titus	Jude	Jude
Gal.	Galatians	Philem.	Philemon	Rev.	Revelation

General

cf.	confer, compare	v(v).	verse(s)

Ancient Texts and Versions

LXX	Septuagint

Modern Versions

ASV	American Standard Version	NRSV	New Revised Standard
ESV	English Standard Version		Version
NIV	New International Version	RSV	Revised Standard Version

Apocrypha and Septuagint

2 Esd.	2 Esdras	Jdt.	Judith
1 Macc.	1 Maccabees	Tob.	Tobit
2 Macc.	2 Maccabees		

Old Testament Pseudepigrapha

2 Bar.	2 Baruch	Jub.	Jubilees
1 En.	1 Enoch (Ethiopic Apocalypse)		

Dead Sea Scrolls

1QS	Rule of the Community

Mishnah and Talmud

b.	Babylonian Talmud	Nid.	Niddah
m.	Mishnah	Pesah.	Pesahim
'Abot	'Abot	Shabb.	Shabbat
Naz.	Nazir	Sanh.	Sanhedrin

Other Rabbinic Works

Exod. Rab.	Exodus Rabbah

Apostolic Fathers

1 Clem.	1 Clement	Did.	Didache

New Testament Apocrypha and Pseudepigrapha

Acts Paul	Acts of Paul	Acts Pet.	Acts of Peter

Greek and Latin Works

Apuleius

Metam.   Metamorphoses (The Golden Ass)

Aristotle

Eth. nic.   Nicomachean Ethics

Cicero

Div.   De divinatione
Leg.   De legibus

Demosthenes

Con.   Against Conon

Eusebius

Hist. eccl.   Ecclesiastical History

Homer

Od.   Odyssey

Irenaeus

Haer.   Against Heresies

John Chrysostom

Hom. Act.   Homilies on Acts

Josephus

Ant.   Jewish Antiquities
J.W.   Jewish War

Justin Martyr

1 Apol.   First Apology
Dial.   Dialogue with Trypho

Juvenal

Sat.   Satires

Lucian

Eunuch.   The Eunuch

Ovid

Metam.   Metamorphoses

Pausanius

Descr.   Description of Greece

Philo

Decal.   On the Decalogue
Drunkenness   On Drunkenness

Plato

Apol.   Apology of Socrates

Suetonius

Claud.   Claudius
Nero   Nero
Tit.   Titus

Tacitus

Ann.   Annals
Hist.   Histories

Tertullian

Apol.   Apology
Mart.   To the Martyrs
Praescr.   Prescription against Heretics

Xenophon

Mem.   Memorabilia

Papyri and Inscriptions

CIG   *Corpus Inscriptionum Graecarum.* Edited by August Boeckh. 4 vols. Berlin, 1828–77

IG   *Inscriptiones Graecae.* Berlin: Reimer, 1871–

P.Oxy.   Oxyrhynchus papyri

SIG   *Sylloge Inscriptionum Graecarum.* Edited by Wilhelm Dittenberger. 4 vols. 3rd ed. Leipzig: Hirzel, 1915–24

Maps

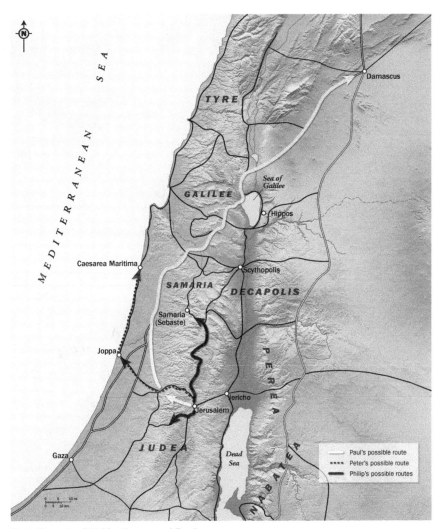

Early Travels of Philip, Peter, and Paul

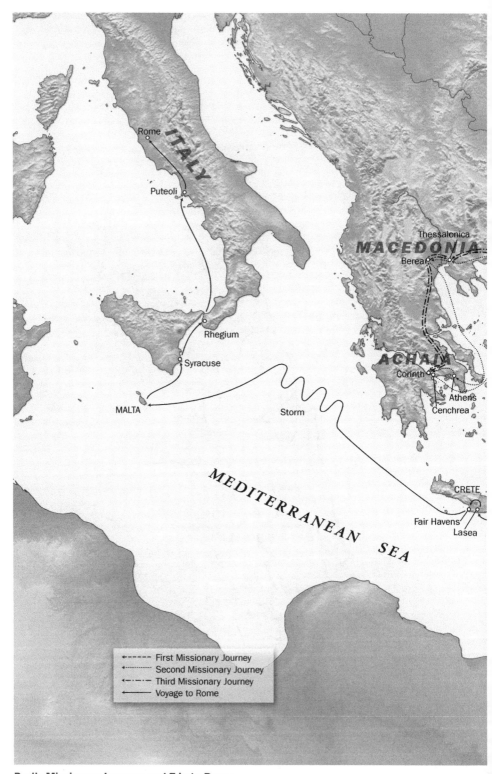

Rome

ITALY

Puteoli

Thessalonica

MACEDONIA

Berea

ACHAIA

Rhegium

Corinth

Syracuse

Athens

Cenchrea

MALTA

Storm

CRETE

MEDITERRANEAN SEA

Fair Havens

Lasea

←----- First Missionary Journey
←·········· Second Missionary Journey
←·–·–·– Third Missionary Journey
←——— Voyage to Rome

Paul's Missionary Journeys and Trip to Rome

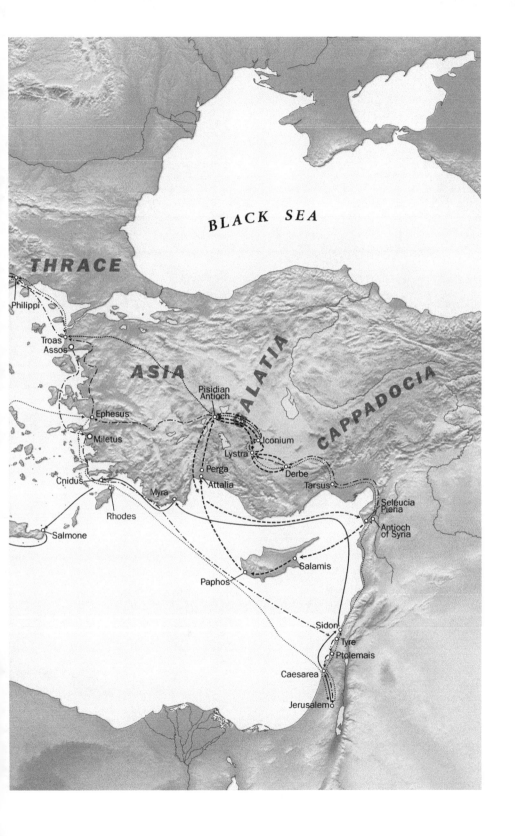

Introduction to Acts

Luke recounts in his second volume the development of the early church after Jesus's ascension. The connection between the Gospel of Luke and Acts easily can be overlooked because, in the order of the canon, Acts falls between the cracks of the Four Gospels and Paul's Letters. The Gospel and Acts can be read with profit quite independently of each other, but it is best to read them in tandem to see the full theological picture that Luke intends to present. Luke is not intent on merely chronicling the past. He recounts and sorts out the past events, "the things that have been fulfilled among us" (Luke 1:1), so that they can inform the present. Acts most often is mined by those seeking models of authentic and vibrant Christianity. But Luke does not intend to provide models of leadership organization, for example, to be duplicated undeviatingly by contemporary churches. He intends to show how God worked in and through the early church to accomplish his will so that Christians, who are often quite powerless according to the world's standards, may understand better that God will continue to work in the world in ways that are mysterious and paradoxical but always powerful.

Luke's purpose in writing, then, is primarily theological, and this historical narrative is undergirded by a theological vision that intends to demonstrate how the epochal significance of Jesus's crucifixion and resurrection and ascension is manifested in the life and preaching of the church. Luke clothes his theological purpose with a history so entertaining that readers sometimes neglect the theology. Acts is not a humdrum registry of events. The story of the gospel's spread throughout the Mediterranean world, beginning in Jerusalem, bristles with enthralling action:

> Where within eighty pages will be found such a varied series of exciting events—trials, riots, persecutions, escapes, martyrdoms, voyages, shipwrecks,

rescues—set in that amazing panorama of the ancient world—Jerusalem, Antioch, Philippi, Corinth, Athens, Ephesus, Rome? And with such scenery and settings—temples, courts, prisons, deserts, ships, seas, barracks, theaters? Has any opera such variety? A bewildering range of scenes and actions passes before the eye of the historian. And in them all he sees the providential hand that has made and guided this great movement for the salvation of mankind.[1]

The history is not intended to be exhaustive. Every event and every character that contributed to the remarkable growth of the Way cannot be covered. The narrator reports, "Everyone was filled with awe at the many wonders and signs performed by the apostles" (2:43). But besides the miracle at Pentecost, only one other miracle, the healing of the lame man (3:1–11), is narrated during these first days of the dramatic Christian advance. Luke intends to show what typically happened. The same is true for the speeches that pepper the text. They vary according to the different occasions but are intended to provide typical examples of the preaching to Jews and gentiles and unveil the scriptural and theological foundations of Christian preaching. The upshot of Luke's selection of events is that his audience should be able to see where and how they fit in the panorama of God's actions to bring salvation to the world through Jesus Christ.

Authorship

The prologues to Luke and Acts indicate a connection between the two works and that they derive from the same author writing with the same purpose. The ending of the Gospel also looks ahead to what happens in Acts. Jesus tells the disciples that the Scriptures foretell that "repentance for the forgiveness of sins will be preached in his name to all nations, beginning at Jerusalem" (Luke 24:47 [cf. Acts 2:38; 3:19; 5:31]). The Gospel ends with the disciples staying "continually at the temple, praising God" (Luke 24:53), but they cannot stay there indefinitely if they are to be witnesses to the ends of the earth (Luke 24:48; Acts 1:8). They obey Jesus's command to stay in the city until they are "clothed with power from on high" (Luke 24:49). That promise is fulfilled in the opening narrative of Acts, and the Holy Spirit thrusts them out into the world. Acts recounts the ascension of Jesus (Acts 1:9–11) from a new and different perspective from what appears at the end of Luke (Luke 24:50–53) to emphasize that it launches a new epoch as the gospel will mushroom from Jerusalem to the ends of the earth until Christ returns.

I have used "Luke" to refer to the author of these two works in accordance with the tradition that has long associated this double work with Luke, a companion of Paul (Col. 4:14; 2 Tim. 4:11; Philem. 24). But the author does not identify himself. The switch from third-person narration to the first-person plural in Acts 16:10–17; 20:5–21:18; 27:1–28:16, now commonly dubbed the "we sections," emerges and then vanishes in such a random manner that it is unlikely that these sections were added simply to make the sea voyages more exciting. Contrary to the argument of some, these sections are not simply a conventional literary device used in travel narratives. They are meant to convey the author's personal experience as one of Paul's occasional fellow travelers.[2] The narrator of the "we sections" is differentiated from Paul's other traveling companions who are specifically mentioned: Silas/Silvanus, Timothy, Sopater, Aristarchus, Secundus, Gaius (of Derbe), Tychicus, and Trophimus. Luke is therefore the most likely candidate and would have been known by Theophilus and his original audience so that he did not need to identify himself.[3]

We know little more about Luke. From his works we can discern that he is thoroughly versed in the Scriptures. In the opening chapters of the Gospel he adopts the style of the Greek Old Testament. He is also at home in the Greco-Roman culture. The preface to Luke "indicates that he was aware of literary customs and self-consciously intended to enter the world of letters."[4] In my view, he was probably a Jew, which would have given him greater authority as an interpreter of the traditions of Jesus, Paul, and Christian history for the wider church.[5] It is possible that he was the unnamed brother famous for proclaiming the gospel in all the churches (2 Cor. 8:18).

Date

Dating a work like Luke-Acts is a highly speculative endeavor. Acts would have been written sometime after the appointment of Festus as procurator (AD 59/60) and before the work is cited by others in the second century. Three viable options for its dating have been proposed: (1) before AD 64, which might explain the abrupt ending; (2) between AD 70 and 94, assuming Luke's dependence on Mark as a source for his Gospel; and (3) between AD 95 and 100, assuming Luke's dependence on Josephus. It is widely held that Luke used Mark as one of the sources he mentions in his prologue (Luke 1:1–3). Mark was written probably in the late 60s or early 70s, near the end or immediately after the Jewish revolt against Rome. Luke-Acts would have been written after Mark's Gospel had circulated, so the second option is most commonly argued. It is difficult, if not impossible, to pin down the timing more precisely. The same applies to where this work was written and its intended audience. Solid evidence for identifying its provenance is wanting.

Purpose

If one believes that Luke-Acts is a unified whole, then it follows that Luke considered the story of Jesus to be incomplete without the story of his church. The second volume follows up on Jesus's ministry, death, and resurrection with the story of the witness to the gospel after Jesus was taken up into heaven. But why does Luke, writing in the 70s or later, end his account in the 60s? Numerous proposals have attempted to ascertain Luke's purpose in writing this history. Only a few will be mentioned here.[6]

1. The promise of the extension of the gospel from Jerusalem to the ends of the earth (1:8) suggests that Luke is concerned with the geographical progress of the gospel. Acts is *not* the story of how the gospel got to Rome. Luke only tells us how Paul got to Rome, since Christians are already in the city and come to greet him (28:14–15). Rome is not "the ends of the earth;" it is the heart of the Roman Empire as Jerusalem is the heart of Judaism. The open-ended nature of the conclusion of Acts suggests that Luke envisions the gospel expanding well beyond Rome. The story, therefore, does not ultimately conclude in Rome but remains open-ended.

2. Luke may be trying to make the case that Christianity should have legal protection from Roman authorities. In Paul's various trial scenes he is found innocent of all the charges brought against him by his malicious opponents (25:8, 18–20, 25; 26:30–32). These scenes make it clear that Christianity is not the latest contrivance of mischief from the East or an aberrant sect of antisocial troublemakers. Christians are law-abiding citizens like Paul, and Christianity is the true fulfillment of Israel's hopes.

The last quarter of Acts deals with Paul's arrest, defense, and arrival in Rome. Even though Paul's defense before Roman officials dominates, Acts was not written to be Paul's defense before official Rome, nor is it written primarily to local authorities as a defense of Christianity. Acts is intended for the church, not the outside world. Vast amounts of Luke-Acts would be totally unintelligible and uninteresting to a non-Christian trying to determine if the Christian faith deserved the same tolerance and legal freedom as that proffered to official Judaism (cf. Gallio's and Festus's reactions to the disputes between Jews and Christians [18:14–15; 26:24]). Theophilus, to whom Luke-Acts is dedicated, is not a high Roman official; he is a Christian, since Luke states his intention to confirm the certainty of the things that Theophilus already "[has] been taught" (Luke 1:4), expressed with a Greek verb (*katēcheō*) that is used in Christian literature only in reference to theological issues. It is most likely that Theophilus is the benefactor who provided the support for the publication of this double work.

Luke primarily has Christian readers like Theophilus in mind. The account of the various trials that Paul endures reveals to these readers the truth of Paul's statement "We must go through many hardships to enter the kingdom of God" (14:22). They also show that even the powerful Roman Empire and the antagonistic power brokers in the various cities that Paul visits are powerless to stop the progress of the gospel.

3. Luke notes that Jesus told the parable of the minas to correct the mistaken belief that the kingdom of God was to appear immediately (Luke 19:11 [cf. 17:20–21; 21:8]). Some suggest that this concern is the primary one that Luke seeks to address. In Acts, after Jesus's resurrection, the disciples ask whether it is now that he is going to restore the kingdom to Israel. Jesus tells them that it is not for them to know the times or seasons (1:6–7). After Jesus's ascension, angels scold the disciples for gazing into the heavens when they needed to be obeying Jesus's command and preparing to bear witness to the gospel (1:10–11). Since Luke writes a history of the early church with a commission to take the gospel to the ends of the earth, he expects the church to be around for a while. But he is not seeking to encourage a church disappointed by the delay of the end-time (cf. 1 Thess. 4:13–5:11; 2 Pet. 3:2–13). The narrative teaches Christians that they are obligated to proclaim Christ to the ends of the earth, wherever the Spirit leads them, until the end of time, whenever that might be.

4. In my view, Luke is primarily interested in showing that Christ's church embodies the fulfillment of the Old Testament promises and the hopes of Israel.[7] His purpose is not so much to encourage Jews to become Christians as to explain to those who are already Christians why so many Jews have not become believers. Luke conveys his view of Israel's status through narrative and speeches, while Paul states his view more directly in a letter, the Letter to the Romans. Paul reminds his readers, "Theirs is the adoption to sonship; theirs the divine glory, the covenants, the receiving of the law, the temple worship and the promises. Theirs are the patriarchs, and from them is traced the human ancestry of the Messiah" (Rom. 9:4–5). Luke underscores this great heritage in the beginning of his Gospel by asserting that promises God made to Israel concerning the Messiah have been realized in the coming of Jesus and his forerunner John the Baptist (Luke 1:67–79; 2:29–35).[8] In writing his history, Luke answers the same questions that Paul raises in Romans 9–11: If the promises were intended for Israel and Jesus was the Jews' Messiah, why do so many Jews not believe and why is the church now dominated by gentiles? If ethnic Jews have not become Christians, what does that mean about the identity of Israel? Do nonbelieving Jews still constitute "the Israel of God" (Gal. 6:16)?

Paul's response is that not all Israelites belong to Israel (Rom. 9:6). Only a remnant that has not persisted in unbelief will be saved (Rom. 9:27). Peter says essentially the same thing in his speech when he reminds his Jewish audience of Moses's prophecy, "The Lord your God will raise up for you a prophet like me from among your own people; you must listen to everything he tells you. Anyone who does not listen to him will be completely cut off from their people" (Acts 3:22–23). Paul issues a similar warning to worshipers in the synagogue: "Take care that what the prophets have said does not happen to you" (Acts 13:40). But every time the gospel is preached to Jews, it creates a divided response. Jesus experienced a similar response to his ministry, a situation that he elaborated on in the parable of the sower (Luke 8:4–8, 11–15). In Acts, the preaching of the gospel meets with neither wholesale repentance nor wholesale rejection. At key points (13:46–47; 18:6; 28:25–28), however, Paul announces that the rejection of the gospel by the Jews entails that he will turn to the gentiles, who will respond. The Acts narrative pictures what Paul states had already happened when he wrote Romans. The Jews' stumbling has resulted in salvation being offered to the gentiles and their acceptance of it (Rom. 11:11). This situation does not mean that God has now abandoned Israel and moved on to a new people. In the Acts narrative, Paul continues to return to the synagogue to preach the gospel, but he soberly recognizes that those Jews who reject it do not consider themselves "worthy of eternal life" (13:46).

When Luke writes, Christianity has separated from Judaism and from the temple, which already has been destroyed by the Romans after the Jewish revolt. Christians are now even more clearly distinguished from Judaism as members of "the Way" (9:2; 19:9, 23; 22:4; 24:14, 22). Luke's purpose in Acts is to show that those Jews and gentiles who believe in Jesus are the real people of God who follow the way of God (18:24–26). The response of faith to what God has done in Christ is what now characterizes God's people, not their ethnic birthright or obedience to Jewish traditions.

Luke does not present the church as a new, replacement Israel composed of gentiles who now supplant the old people of God in salvation history. It is important to recognize that Acts does not depict Jews as a whole rejecting the gospel. The gospel meets with success among many Jews (5:14; 6:7; 13:47; 18:8; 21:20; 28:24 [cf. 4:21; 5:26]). For Luke, this success is vital if the prophecy of Scripture that Israel was to be a light to the nations (Gen. 12:3; Isa. 12:4; 42:6; 49:6; Ezek. 47:22–23) was to be fulfilled. Two Old Testament passages are central for Luke's theological purpose. Paul cites Isaiah 49:6, "I have made you a light for the Gentiles, that you may bring salvation to the ends of the earth" (13:47 [cf. Luke 2:32; Acts 26:23]). This quotation cites the reason God chose and made Israel—namely, for a special task, not for a special status. James cites Amos 9:11–12: "'After this I will return and rebuild David's fallen tent. Its ruins I will rebuild, and I will restore it, that the rest of mankind may seek the Lord, even all the Gentiles who bear my name, says the Lord, who does these things'—things known from long ago" (15:16–18). This quotation implies that Israel will be restored first, and through a restored Israel the gospel will be taken to the gentiles.

Luke portrays the Christian faith as the reconstruction of David's fallen tent, Israel's restoration. It begins as a popular grassroots movement in Jerusalem.

Many Jews are won to the Lord at Pentecost and return to their homelands with the gospel. Even many priests become believers (6:7). Early resistance comes from the temple hierarchy, who, in collusion with the Romans, killed Jesus, the Messiah, but the faith continues to grow among Jews. Persecution in Jerusalem after Stephen's stoning leads to the gospel moving out to and being accepted by Samaritans, regarded by Jews as half Jews at best. Then, it includes an Ethiopian eunuch, someone disqualified by temple Judaism. Through the preaching of Peter, Cornelius and his household, gentile God-worshipers on the fringe of Judaism, believe and receive the Holy Spirit. Through the witness of Paul, the gospel draws in pagans such as the Philippian jailer and his household, who had no interest whatsoever in Judaism.

The obliteration of national, ethnic, and ritual boundaries meets with resistance from both some Christian Jews in Jerusalem and many nonbelieving Jews throughout the Diaspora. The issue is settled for Christians at the Jerusalem Council: gentiles do not need to become Jews in order to be saved, but they cannot remain idolaters (15:5–32). The narrative also shows that Jews do not need to abandon their Jewish heritage when they become Christians. The continued negative Jewish reaction to the gospel and the inclusion of gentiles, however, is part of a long story, which Stephen's speech spotlights (7:2–53): rebellious Jews have consistently resisted God's purposes throughout their history.

The narrative trajectory shows that only after Israel has heard and responded to the gospel is the way fully open to gentiles. This understanding of Luke's purpose in Acts best explains why the narrative ends where it does. After Paul's arrest and the riot at his defense before the Sanhedrin, the Lord reveals to him that as "you have testified about me in Jerusalem, so you must also testify in Rome" (23:11). When the hearings are over and Paul is shipped off to Rome, it may surprise readers that Luke does not describe the outcome of Paul's appeal to Caesar. The officials in Rome are never mentioned. Instead, Luke only reports Paul's encounter with a gathering of the local Jewish leaders (28:16–28). Some respond; others remain skeptical. But Luke's story can end. The gospel has been preached to the Jews throughout the Roman Empire. They have been given a chance to respond (Rom. 10:18), to become what God intends for Israel to be, a light to the nations. Those who reject it are cut off from the people. Those who accept the gospel become the true expression of Israel as part of Christ's church, which now also includes Samaritan and gentile believers.

Luke's Gospel foreshadows this divided response. The angel tells Zechariah that many, not *all*, of the sons of Israel will turn back to the Lord their God (Luke 1:16). Simeon tells Mary that her son Jesus is set for the rise and fall of many in Israel (Luke 2:34). Even one of Jesus's chosen disciples turns away to go to his own place (Luke 22:3–6; Acts 1:25). These do not represent all Israel, and Acts does not recount God's repudiation of Israel for being disobedient. Instead, it shows many Jews repudiating Israel's hope and calling.[9] As a consequence, they cut themselves off from Israel and become merely what Paul calls his "kindred according to the flesh" (Rom. 9:3 NRSV). Their rejection of the gospel explains why the church in Luke's day is increasingly dominated by gentiles who, like wild olive shoots, have been grafted into the rich root of the Israel olive tree (Rom. 11:17–24). Christian Jews are not apostates. They are the remnant of Israel that forms the church that is faithful to the Law and the Prophets and to God and engages in mission to the world. As Paul represents the true Pharisee who believes in the resurrection and believes in Jesus (Acts 26:4–8, 22–23, 29), the church represents the true continuation of Israel that is obedient to God.

This view of Luke's purpose helps us recognize that the promises to Israel were fulfilled. We do not need to resort to views that claim that the promises to Israel are still in reserve or that God has two chosen peoples, the church and a dormant Israel. Israel according to the flesh does not have special status with God as a most favored nation. What became known as Christianity is the fulfillment of Israel's hope and purpose. Christians of whatever ethnic or national stripe should be cautioned by this narrative. If any church is found wanting in its calling to be a light to the nations, it will become Christ's church in name only and will face a similar fate of being cut off (cf. Rom. 11:17–22).

Key Themes

1. Luke's second volume would be more aptly titled the "Acts of God." This theme is most apparent in Peter's sermon in 3:13–26, in which God's actions are highlighted. God made a covenant with Abraham (3:25 [cf. 7:8]). God promised Moses that he would raise up a prophet like him (3:22). God overruled the wickedness of those who put Jesus to death by raising him from the dead (3:15, 26) and glorified him so that healing is done through his name and power (3:16). God will forgive sins (3:19), bless people and turn them from their wickedness (3:26), send times of refreshing (3:19), and restore all things (3:21). This early speech sets the tone. God operates behind the scenes to control the events that are narrated.

In Paul's ministry, the Lord enables him and his companions to perform signs and wonders (14:3; 15:12; 19:11), opens "a door of faith to the Gentiles" (14:27 [cf. 15:3–4, 8; 21:19]), and opens hearts to respond to the message (16:14). Paul and his team routinely preach wherever they go (14:1, 3, 7, 9, 15, 21, 25; 15:35, 36; 16:10, 13, 32), and the report of what happens in each place emphasizes what God has done: how the Lord "confirmed the message of his grace by enabling them to perform signs and wonders" (14:3 [cf. 15:12]); "all that God had done through them and how he had opened a door of faith to the Gentiles" (14:27 [cf. 15:4, 8]); how "the Lord opened [Lydia's] heart to respond to Paul's message" (16:14).

Elsewhere in Acts, other preachers affirm that God created all things (4:24; 14:15; 17:24–28). God directs the course of events and faithfully fulfills the promises (7:17; 13:23, 32–33) to assure the fulfillment of his salvific plan for all people. God anointed Jesus with power to do mighty works (10:38). By God's deliberate plan Jesus was handed over to suffer and die (2:23; 3:18; 17:3; 26:22–23). God then raised him from the dead (2:24, 32; 3:15, 26; 4:10; 5:30; 10:40; 13:30, 33, 37), made him Lord and glorified him (2:36; 3:13; 5:31), and ordained him to be the judge of the living and dead (10:42). God pours out the Holy Spirit (2:17; 5:32; 11:16–17; 15:8), opens hearts and grants repentance (11:18; 16:14), and chooses and calls witnesses and leaders to spread the word (1:8; 2:32; 10:41; 13:17; 15:7; 16:10; 22:14; 26:16). God shows no favoritism (10:34) and looks favorably on the gentiles to include them as part of Israel (15:14). This initiative is authenticated by the mighty works that the missionaries perform among the gentiles (14:27; 15:4, 12; 19:11; 21:19) and their reception of the Holy Spirit (10:47). This list of what God is noted as doing in Acts is not comprehensive. It only indicates how central God is to the plot of Acts.

2. As a corollary to God's dominant role in directing what happens in the story, Acts also emphasizes the work of the Holy Spirit coming at decisive moments in the life of the church. Peter declares that the pouring out of the Spirit at Pentecost is a sign of "the last days" (2:17) and a fulfillment of Joel's prophecy (Joel 2:28–32). It inaugurates a new age when "everyone who calls on the name of the Lord will be saved" (Acts 2:21). Acts does not spell out the fruit of the Spirit in the lives of individual believers (Gal. 5:22–23). Instead, the narrative shows the effects of the Spirit repeatedly filling individuals and the community to accomplish special tasks. The Spirit comes as power to a seemingly powerless community that has gathered together in prayer and unity (2:1). Wind and fire now represent the coming of the Spirit (2:2–3) rather than the gentle descent like a dove (Luke 3:22). The Spirit brings the power to bear witness (2:4; 4:33; 6:8) and to heal (3:12; 4:7; 8:13). The Spirit directs individuals in their mission (8:29; 10:19–20; 11:12; 16:6–7, 9), presides over the church in its decisions (15:28), and guides the church in taking concrete measures on behalf of the poor (4:31–32). The gift of the Spirit is poured out to disciples in such assorted ways that it is evident that the Spirit cannot be controlled or systematized by humans.

3. The apostles, including Philip, Ananias, and Paul, consistently work miracles or "signs and wonders" that are undeniable, visible manifestations of the truth of the gospel. This power is given to them by God and is never

under their control. The purpose and the effect of the miracles are to bring others to faith or to preserve the lives of witnesses so that they can continue their mission to bring others to faith.

4. Jesus chided the disciples on the Emmaus road for being "foolish" and "slow to believe all that the prophets have spoken" (Luke 24:25). Understanding what God has accomplished in Jesus's suffering, death, resurrection, and exaltation and what God is doing in the present (Luke 24:27, 45–48) require knowing the Scriptures. The Ethiopian eunuch expresses it well: "How can I [understand what I am reading] . . . unless someone explains it to me?" (Acts 8:31). The failure of the Jews to recognize Jesus as the Messiah is rooted in their failure to understand the Scriptures or to believe the explanations of the Christian preachers.

The Scriptures figure prominently in the narrative and particularly in the speeches. They unfold the identity of Jesus as the Messiah, show that God had foreordained Jesus's death and resurrection, and reveal that God had ordained the admission of gentiles into the people of God. That is why "the appeal to Scripture was central to the church's apologetic and evangelism and also to the establishment and confirmation of its own identity."[10] Luke is not always specific in citing the Scriptures that validate a point in a speech, and readers are often left to search the Scriptures to discover the references on their own.[11]

Throughout Acts, God also guides believers by means of visions and dreams (9:10–16; 10:9–16, 27–28; 11:5–10; 16:6–10; 22:17–21; 26:13–18). These visions are examined in community, and the Scriptures help to authenticate them.

5. "Word" occurs thirty-three times in Acts, referring to the Old Testament, the word of God, what Jesus has said, or what is said about him. The emphasis on giving witness appears throughout the narrative (1:8, 22; 2:32; 3:15; 4:33; 5:32; 10:39, 41; 13:31; 22:20; 26:16). The church and its message are based on the word of God. It is the church's task to continue to spread the word of God. Christians are not to be stargazing, marking their end-time calendars to calculate the timing of the advent of the end. They are instead to be busy in their mission to the ends of the earth. Persecution against the church always fails to have its intended effect. Rejection leads to the widening of the mission and the spread of the word of God.

6. Acts continues a theme prominent in the Gospel by providing positive and negative examples of the stewardship of money and the right and wrong use of possessions. Judas's reward for his iniquity in betraying Jesus for payment is a gruesome death and going down in infamy as a betrayer (1:18). The perfidy of Ananias and Sapphira, who wanted to keep back a portion of the money that they publicly dedicated to God, results in both of them being struck dead (5:1–11). Simon's offer to buy the rights to the Holy Spirit from the apostles (8:18–20) is met with a sharp rebuke. Human traffickers

who bemoan the loss of money when Paul casts out the spirit from their slave girl (16:16, 19), Ephesian silversmiths who lament the loss of business for their idols (19:24–27), and the governor Felix who expects a bribe from Paul (24:26) serve as negative examples of the obsession with money. These examples contrast with Barnabas, who sold a field and donated the proceeds to help the poor (4:36–37), and with Paul, who did not covet "anyone's silver or gold or clothing" but wholly gave himself over to fulfilling his divine calling (20:33–35). The early church's benevolence toward the poor (2:44–45; 4:32; 9:36) sets the standard for the Christian church.

Jesus's Resurrection and Ascension

The Continuation of the Story

Big Idea

Jesus's resurrection and ascension restore not Israel's kingdom but Israel's vocation to be a light to the nations. The disciples' witness will be empowered by the Holy Spirit and reach to the ends of the earth.

Key Themes

- Jesus does not abandon the disciples to visions and rumors but provides them with evidence that his resurrection is real as he continues to teach them before he is taken up into the divine realm.
- Jesus's resurrection and ascension pave the way for the coming of the Holy Spirit on the disciples, launching a worldwide mission.
- The disciples are powerless on their own and must wait for the Holy Spirit to clothe them with power.

Understanding the Text

The Text in Context

In what Luke calls his first book, the Gospel of Luke, he relates what Jesus "began to do and to teach" (Acts 1:1). This second book is the continuation of that story. In this next phase of salvation history, Luke narrates what Jesus continued to do and teach through the Holy Spirit.[1] The downward thrust of God breaking into human history through the incarnation results in the outward thrust of the gospel, when God's Spirit breaks into the lives of believers. After Jesus ascends into heaven, the Spirit leads the disciples to mission breakthroughs in the world.

Interpretive Insights

1:1–5 *After his suffering, he presented himself to them and gave many convincing proofs that he was alive.* Luke links the life and work of Jesus, recounted in his first volume, to the story of the church and its mission by recalling the dedication to Theophilus (Luke 1:1–4). Theophilus likely was a prominent Christian, and he may have financed the production and dissemination of the two works.

Jesus's forty-day sojourn with the disciples recalls his forty days in the wilderness at the beginning of his ministry (Luke 4:2). "Forty" is a biblical round number used in Jewish writings to refer to a timeframe in which instruction occurs for the work ahead.[2] "Giving instructions" to the apostles "he had chosen" reminds the reader that Jesus chose the apostles; they did not volunteer. He now gives them the mandate to witness (cf. Luke 9:1–2; Acts 9:15). The kingdom of God was the core of Jesus's preaching, and the story in Acts is about the proclamation of the kingdom of God advancing throughout the world (8:12; 14:22; 19:8; 20:25). Proclamation of the kingdom of God brackets the book (1:3; 28:23, 31).

Recalling the water baptism of John the Baptist should also recall his prophecy that one more powerful than he would come to baptize with the Holy Spirit and fire (Luke 3:16). That prophecy will soon be fulfilled.

Jesus's continued table fellowship with his disciples provides irrefutable evidence of his bodily resurrection (Luke 24:38–43). They do not experience mystical visions. It is during this time that he would have appeared "to more than five hundred of the brothers and sisters" and to James, his brother (1 Cor. 15:6–7; Acts 13:30–31), but Luke does not narrate these events. He zeroes in on the disciples' preparation for their mission.

1:6–7 *Lord, are you at this time going to restore the kingdom to Israel?* The disciples' question about restoring the kingdom to Israel puts forward this notion at the very beginning. Perhaps they remember Jesus's promise that they would "sit on thrones, judging the twelve tribes of Israel" (Luke 22:30), and now they assume that this new role is imminent. Or they may think that the coming of the Spirit would be accompanied by the coming of the kingdom (Luke 19:11). Since Jesus does not reprimand the disciples for their question as he did in Luke 22:51 ("No more of this!") or for their lack of understanding as he did in Luke 24:25–27 ("How foolish you are, and how slow to believe"), Luke uses their question to raise an important issue and not to reintroduce their spiritual dullness. The fulfillment of the promises cited in Luke 1:32–33; 2:25, 29–32, 38 is taking place. But they will not be fulfilled in ways that the disciples might expect or prefer. The kingdom of God has nothing to do with establishing Israel as a mighty kingdom that will rule the world with an iron fist as Rome does.

What is most important for Luke is that their query highlights an Old Testament promise: "It is too small a thing for you to be my servant to restore the tribes of Jacob and bring back those of Israel I have kept. I will also make you a light for the Gentiles, that my salvation may reach to the ends of the earth" (Isa. 49:6). The coming of the Holy Spirit will restore Israel's primary vocation to be a light to the nations as the disciples spread the good news of *God's kingdom* (Acts 3:25; 13:47).

The question also gives Jesus the opportunity to remind them that they cannot know the times and seasons when God will restore all things (1:7 [cf. 3:21]). They are not to be concerned about the schedule of history but to be busy about their tasks. God's purposes will be accomplished according to God's timing, which pays no attention to human calendars.

1:8 *But you will receive power when the Holy Spirit comes on you; and you will be my witnesses in Jerusalem, and in all Judea and Samaria, and to the ends of the earth.* Jesus makes two promises: "You will receive power when the Holy Spirit comes on you; and you will be my witnesses." The disciples are not to go off on their own steam, because earlier Jesus had instructed them to wait in Jerusalem "until you have been clothed with power from on high" (Luke 24:49). The success of their witness will be due not to their own strength but to the power of God, because it is God's mission, not theirs.

"Witness" is applied almost exclusively to the Twelve.[3] As eyewitnesses who were with Jesus throughout his ministry, they ensure the certainty of the tradition "handed down to us by those who from the first were eyewitnesses and servants of the word" (Luke 1:2).

The power they will receive from the Holy Spirit is not a power that enables them to conquer and dominate others. Jesus commissions them not to build empires but to confront empires with the truth of the gospel that God is king. They will receive power only to spread the gospel throughout the world. This

---

"To the Ends of the Earth"

The phrase "to the ends of the earth" (Acts 1:8) does not refer to Rome, where Luke's account ends. The mission will not end there. Rome, in Luke's day, is the center of the empire, and all roads lead from it to the ends of the earth.[a] In its westward extent, "the ends of the earth" referred generally to Spain and specifically to the region around Gades, west of Gibraltar.[b] For Luke, however, it signifies the proclamation of the gospel to all people, wherever they may be.[c]

[a] Krodel, *Acts*, 60.
[b] Ellis, "'The End of the Earth.'"
[c] Moore, "'To the End of the Earth,'" 399.

power does not bring a swift victory over the evil kingdoms. Victory will be won through seeming defeat.

1:9–11 *he was taken up before their very eyes.* Jesus's ascension marks the point when the physically resurrected Jesus leaves the disciples. It is the culmination of the resurrection appearances and the prelude to the sending of the Spirit. They are not left in the lurch, having to strike out on their own. If that were the case, they would always fail. Jesus's departure results in the pouring out of the Holy Spirit (2:33), and Jesus can be nearer to them than before because he is no longer limited by a physical body. He goes with each disciple to the ends of the earth until the end of time.

The "cloud" represents the divine presence (cf. Luke 9:34–35), and being taken up into heaven recalls the commencement of Jesus's mission. When Jesus prays at his baptism, the heavens open, the Spirit descends on him, and God declares, "You are my Son, whom I love; with you I am well pleased" (Luke 3:21–22). His ascent in a cloud now confirms his exaltation and his present lordship. The ascension also foreshadows the return of Jesus from heaven to earth (cf. Luke 21:27; 1 Thess. 1:10), when God will restore all things.

"Heaven" may not simply refer to the sky. Luke can use "heaven" as a circumlocution for God (Luke 15:18, 21) or being in association with God (Luke 11:13) or his realm (Luke 15:7; 19:38).[4] It should not be taken so literally that one thinks of Jesus sailing through space to heaven, but it is not simply a symbolic depiction.[5] It is the only language these earthbound eyewitnesses had for describing Jesus's departure to another realm and returning to his Father.[6]

The disciples seem to be rooted to the spot, indulging in a reverie of stargazing, when two men arrayed in white robes call them back to earth to get ready for the task that awaits them. The men's question, "Why?" echoes the question asked of the frightened women at the tomb, except that the women's faces were bowed down to the ground (Luke 24:5). The "two men" are interpreting angels who can explain from a divine perspective what the disciples have witnessed (Luke 24:4–7, 23; Acts 10:30–32). Disciples need to stop looking down or looking up and start looking ahead.

Theological Insights

1. God does not intend to spread the message of salvation through his Son by sending out angels to proclaim it or by writing heavenly messages in the clouds. God chooses to use those chosen by Jesus despite their demonstrable weaknesses. "God's kingdom will be restored to God's people as promised, not at an apocalyptic coming from heaven but rather through the church's Spirit-led mission on earth."[7]

2. The disciples first must be assured of the reality of the resurrection before they can be effective in proclaiming that God indeed reigns.

3. In worldly kingdoms, the ones who do the killing seem to get the power. God's power works in a totally different way and is seemingly powerless. Most of the witnesses in Acts are beaten or killed for proclaiming the gospel, but they possess an unconquerable spiritual power.

Teaching the Text

1. *The disciples have to wait for the power of the Holy Spirit before they can do anything that will be effective.* Therefore, they must wait patiently in prayer. In the modern world, many people hate waiting as a wasteful pause between important things. Instead, waiting can be valued as a time for prayer, reflection, and preparation.

Nevertheless, the disciples are not to sit on their hands waiting forever. When the Holy Spirit comes on them, they must be ready to act. The task of witnessing to a resistant world qualifies as hazardous duty. Acts will narrate their witness to the world in powerful word, in miraculous deeds, and in their caring for one another. It is not surprising, however, that after the disciples have been told what to do, we find them staring up into the heavens. Many Christians today still have their heads in the clouds rather than being engaged in their calling to mission. Mission is not a budget item that the church can outsource. Mission is to the church like air is to fire. Without it, the church fizzles out.

2. *Many Christians today may shy away from evangelism because they think they do not know enough.* One hears excuses such as "I don't know the Bible that well" or "I don't have a theology degree" or "What if they ask me some deep theological question?" God does not call all Christians to be scholars or pastors. It does not take an encyclopedic knowledge of the Bible or a theology degree to tell people—like a witness in court—what you have seen Jesus do for you and for others. It takes openness to the Spirit's leading to speak to others and to communicate the gospel in credible ways.

3. *Jesus's ascension is vital as visible proof of his vindication by God.* The ascension may be confusing to modern readers. The bodily resurrection requires a bodily ascension, and the ascension explains the disappearance of Jesus's physical body. The ascension marks the return of Christ to his Father, provides confirmation of his promised exaltation by God (Luke 22:69; Acts 2:32–35; 7:56), and validates his present lordship in glory.[8] It also assures us of his promised return. Jesus's question, "Did not the Messiah have to suffer these things and then enter his glory?" (Luke 24:26), implies that he had already crossed the threshold of God's glory and has returned to his disciples from glory. His temporary appearances to his disciples after his resurrection will be replaced by his permanent spiritual presence through the Holy Spirit. He

is no longer physically with them, but he will be spiritually within them.[9] His promised return "means that salvation was initiated by the historical Jesus and will be consummated by him at the End."[10]

Illustrating the Text

Waiting demands patience.

Quote: Henri J. M. Nouwen. Nouwen writes, "The word *patience* means the willingness to stay where we are and live the situation out to the full in the belief that something hidden there will manifest itself to us. Impatient people are always expecting the real thing to happen somewhere else and therefore want to go elsewhere. The moment is empty. But the patient dare to stay where they are. Patient living means to live actively in the present and wait there. Waiting, then, is not passive. It involves nurturing the moment, as a mother nurtures the child that is growing in her."[11]

It can be important to tarry before going.

Quote: A. W. Tozer. Tozer writes, "The popular notion that the first obligation of the church is to spread the gospel to the uttermost parts of the earth is false. *Her first obligation is to be spiritually worthy to spread it.* Our Lord said 'Go ye,' but He also said, 'Tarry ye,' and the tarrying had to come before the going. Had the disciples gone forth as missionaries before the day of Pentecost it would have been an overwhelming spiritual disaster, for they could have done no more than make after their likeness, and this would have altered for the worse the whole history of the Western world and had consequences throughout the ages to come."[12]

Witnesses first must be indwelled with the Holy Spirit.

Christian Biography: John Wesley. In 1735, John Wesley went to Savanna, Georgia, to serve as a missionary. During that time, he later acknowledged, he did not yet know what it meant to have a personal relationship with God or to be empowered by the Holy Spirit. He served only out of obligation and duty. He stayed in Savanna for two years; but at the end of that time, his ministry amounted to nothing, and he exited with a romantic scandal. In 1738, back in England, he attended a public reading of Romans and experienced "God [working] in the heart through faith in Christ." He wrote, "I felt my heart strangely warmed. I felt I did trust in Christ, Christ alone for salvation: and an assurance was given me, that He had taken away my sins, even mine, and saved me. . . . I then testified openly to all there what I now felt in my heart."[13] Without the indwelling of the Holy Spirit, John Wesley was an ineffective and powerless witness.

Replacing Judas among the Twelve

Big Idea

Though Jesus chose Judas to be one of the Twelve (Luke 6:13–16) and to abandon everything and follow him (cf. Luke 5:11), Judas chose to abandon Jesus and follow his own path. The disciples now bear responsibility under the guidance of the Holy Spirit to reconfigure the leadership for their mission by choosing a replacement for Judas.

Key Themes

- Peter emerges as the key figure in the early community.
- As eyewitnesses to the ministry and resurrection of Jesus, the apostles are guarantors of the tradition that is passed on to the church.
- Jesus appointed twelve disciples as leaders of the end-time Israel. Judas's betrayal, predicted by Scripture, requires that he be replaced to reestablish this symbolic number.

Understanding the Text

The Text in Context

After witnessing Jesus's resurrection and ascension, the apostles return to the upper room in Jerusalem. In anticipation of the promised gift of the Holy Spirit, they, along with many other disciples, join together in constant prayer. They are guided to find a replacement for Judas to take his position of leadership among the Twelve. Before the events of Pentecost, we find the disciples fervent in prayer, founded in the Scriptures, and guarding the apostolic witness to Jesus's earthly ministry.

Interpretive Insights

1:12–14 *They all joined together constantly in prayer, along with the women and Mary the mother of Jesus, and with his brothers.* The account of the disciples' return to the upper room, where they were staying in Jerusalem, serves as a transition that shows them to be unified before the events at Pentecost.

Despite both Judas's treachery that led to Jesus's death and the dangers that they might face from the authorities, the disciples obey Jesus's command to wait in the city. They do not turn on one another, as they seemed to do at the Last Supper (Luke 22:22–24), but turn to God in prayer. They do not know what will happen next or when, and their fervent prayer strengthens them to deal with this crisis and prepares them for the miracles that take place on Pentecost. Luke reviews the names of the original eleven chosen by Jesus (Luke 6:13–16) who stayed with him up to the end (Luke 22:28) and have now regathered. They are joined by the women who followed Jesus from Galilee (Luke 8:1–3; 23:49, 55), Mary his mother, and his brothers. His earthly family is now included in this spiritual family of followers as "those who hear God's word and put it into practice" (Luke 8:21).

Luke describes them as joined together in prayer. He does not intend to show that a one-to-one correlation exists between prayer and the eventual coming of the Spirit.[1] They have learned from Jesus's example (Luke 5:16; 6:12; 9:18, 28–29; 11:1; 22:31–32, 40–46) that prayer is the attitude that grooms one to receive the comfort of God's presence and the demands of God's marching orders.

1:15–16 *In those days Peter stood up among the believers.* Jesus's assurance that after Peter had been sifted by Satan, his faith would not fail and he would turn back to strengthen his brothers (Luke 22:31–32) comes true when he takes charge as the leader of the group. Peter's mind was opened by Jesus to understand the Scriptures (Luke 24:45), and he interprets Judas's traitorous deed in light of Scripture.

What follows answers two questions: What happened to the traitor? How will Jesus's prophecy that his disciples would "sit on thrones, judging the twelve tribes of Israel" (Luke 22:30) be resolved in light of Judas's defection?

1:17 *He was one of our number and shared in our ministry.* Judas's name was on the roll call of disciples, but he was not a true part of the enterprise. He spurned the gift of being allotted a share in this ministry. Though Satan entered him (Luke 22:3), he is fully responsible for betraying Jesus. He does not simply fall away. He chose to go his own way and wound up in his own place (Acts 1:25)—namely, perdition.

1:18–20 *he fell headlong, his body burst open and all his intestines spilled out.* With the ill-gotten gains from betraying Jesus, Judas bought "an 'estate in the country' or 'farm'" rather than simply a "field."[2] But he never gets to enjoy the spoils of his betrayal. The graphic description of his demise underscores that it is due to divine punishment for his reprehensible deed. Other Jewish stories tie wicked deeds to gruesome deaths: the more wicked the deed, the more gruesome and unhappy the death.[3] While Jesus was taken up to heaven, Judas fell down headlong to his destruction, ironically, in the field that he had purchased with blood money.[4] The property has now become forsaken. Instead of becoming a field of dreams for Judas, it has become a byword as the "Field of Blood." It is named for his wickedness of betraying innocent blood (Matt. 27:4; Luke 11:50 [cf. Deut. 27:25]) that cries out until it is avenged (Gen. 4:10) or for his bloody downfall.

Peter interprets Judas's actions as the fulfillment of Scripture, combining a line from Psalm 69:25, which is found in the midst of an appeal to God to condemn the psalmist's enemies, with one from Psalm 109:8, which is part of a lament psalm that describes the betrayal that the psalmist has experienced. The psalmist's reaction is to call for the utter destruction of the offender and also the offender's family and entire household. The key phrase from Psalm 109, however, is "May another take his place of leadership."

1:21–26 *it is necessary to choose one of the men who have been with us the whole time the Lord Jesus was living among us.* The standard hope of the Jews is that the ten lost tribes will be restored by God in the end time and all Israel will be reunited and reconstituted. The Jews scattered throughout the Diaspora are to be gathered up by God. By having twelve apostles, Jesus and the church are claiming symbolically to be Israel in the remaking. The narrative reveals that God intends for it to be an Israel that would include gentiles as children of Abraham.

Peter offers two criteria for the replacement apostle: to have accompanied the original Twelve as they went around with Jesus during his earthly life and to have been a witness of the resurrection (1:21–22). To convey accurately to the church "the patterns and guidelines by which [Jesus] intends to rule his community"[5] requires having someone who heard Jesus's teaching and witnessed the events.

Two candidates are brought forward: Joseph called Barsabbas (also known as Justus) and Matthias. Both candidates have been with Jesus and probably belonged to the group of seventy(-two) commissioned by Jesus to go on mission to Israel (Luke 10:1–20). They are tested and equally qualified. This ministry position is not a humanly ordained office, so it is not put up for a vote. They use lots, a method sanctioned by God (Lev. 16:8; Num. 26:55; Prov. 16:33; Jon. 1:7–8; Luke 1:8–9), to decide.

They pray to the "Lord" to show them who has been chosen. "Lord" may refer to God or Jesus, but since Jesus is the one who chose the apostles, it is most likely a prayer to him. He is therefore addressed as the one who, like God, knows everyone's heart, the inner person, and their destiny. The lot falls to Matthias, and he falls out of the narrative. One should not take a disciple's absence from the account as an indication that he was unsuccessful in his role as a witness. Luke does not intend to write a comprehensive history of everything every apostle did.

Theological Insights

1. Jesus did not make a mistake in choosing Judas as the one bad egg among the disciples. Every disciple has the potential to betray Jesus and will do so unless remaining earnest in prayer.

2. The community discerns God's will in multiple ways: through the study of Scripture, the memory of Jesus's teaching, the casting of lots, visions, dreams, angels, and ardent prayer. Casting lots belongs to the "old era," before Pentecost, when the Holy Spirit comes upon the community, which explains why this practice does not appear again in the New Testament.[6] After Pentecost, the Christians have a growing sense of the Holy Spirit's presence, which will "guide" them "into all the truth" (John 16:13).[7]

Teaching the Text

1. *Luke interprets Judas's death through the lens of the psalmist (Pss. 69:25; 109:8) and emphasizes the divine punishment that inescapably comes to those who spurn Christ, thirst after riches, and are guilty of a dereliction of duty.* God is a God of mercy, but God is also a righteous judge who admonishes, "You fool! This very night your life will be demanded from you. Then who will get what you have prepared for yourself?" (Luke 12:20).

Divine retribution for sin is not a popular topic today. Most can easily understand the lesson that Judas's country estate provided him no ultimate security, but why did he suffer such a gory death? Luke rehearses Judas's evil fate before the account of the disciples choosing his replacement as a cautionary warning. The sequence raises this question: Who would want this role if desertion and failure lead to such an evil fate? It illustrates another spiritual truth: "From everyone who has been given much, much will be demanded; and from the one who has been entrusted with much, much more will be asked" (Luke 12:48). Accepting Jesus's call to follow requires sitting down and counting the cost (Luke 14:28–32). Discipleship requires renouncing former loyalties, carrying a cross, and giving up everything that one has (Luke 14:26–27, 33). Jesus warns, "No one who puts a hand to the plow and looks back is fit for service in the kingdom of God" (Luke 9:62). Salt (a disciple) that becomes saltless (useless) is not even fit for the manure pile but will be thrown out (Luke 14:34–35). The cost is high; the risks are enormous. But "one should also count the cost of *not* following Jesus."[8]

Matthew's account interprets Judas's death differently through the lens of Jeremiah and Zechariah (Matt. 27:3–10 [cf. Zech. 11:12, 13; Jer. 19:1–13; 32:6–9]) and focuses on blood guilt (Matt. 23:34–35; 27:4, 6, 8). He records Judas first trying to divest himself of this guilt by returning to the priests and confessing. The priests reject any connection with him and essentially confess that they can do nothing to expiate this sin. Since no temple sacrifice washes away this sin, they tell him, "See to it yourself" (Matt. 27:4 NRSV). Like the criminal who prays on the way to the place of his execution, "May my death be an atonement for all my sins" (*m. Sanh.* 6:2), Judas seeks to atone for his guilt under the rules of the old covenant by hanging himself—a life for a life (Num. 35:33). In the new covenant, Jesus's blood is poured out for the forgiveness of sins (Matt. 26:28), and it alone covers all the sins of those who, like Peter, repent and turn to Christ.

2. *In retrospect, Judas's defection fulfilled God's purposes.* Jesus did not make an error in judgment in allotting Judas a share in his ministry. Luke presents what Judas did and his downfall as the fulfillment of Scripture.

Judas is not a helpless pawn, however, in a cosmic battle between Satan and God. Jesus tells Peter, "Simon, Simon, Satan has asked to sift all of you as wheat" (Luke 22:31). The "you" is plural in the Greek. Judas, for his part, succumbs to his own wickedness and allows himself to be overwhelmed by Satan (Acts 1:18).

3. *Another theme in the passage is the significance of the Twelve.* The original Twelve were formed to display symbolically the significance of Jesus's ministry: in the life of Jesus, God is at work, fulfilling his eschatological promise to reconstitute Israel. Losing one from the number "twelve," which symbolized the nucleus of the restoration of the twelve tribes of Israel, might suggest that God's work was somehow compromised or perhaps even defeated. Maintaining the Twelve is about maintaining the integrity of the disciples' witness to Jesus's earthly ministry. The requirement that the one who replaces Judas must have been with them throughout Jesus's ministry recognizes that it takes time for Christian habits to pervade one's life to the degree required for leaders. The church requires leaders who evidence maturity that is visible not just "at work" but in all aspects of their lives.

Illustrating the Text

Replication of the witness of Jesus

Documentary: *Chasing Shackleton* is a documentary that follows five explorers recreating Ernest Shackleton's "epic sea-and-land voyage in a replica of the original explorers' boat, using only the tools and supplies his team used." Shackleton had saved all thirty-one of his men—not one was lost. After the completion of the sea voyage, Seb Coulthard, one of the modern-day explorers, testified, "Personally, I feel it's the closest I've ever been to being immersed in history, where you have taken something that's written word and photographs and you've turned it into reality and you couldn't pick a greater journey than this."[9]

No amount of self-inflicted punishment can atone for our own sins.

Christian Biography: **Martin Luther.** One night when he was in his early twenties, Martin Luther was traveling by coach through a storm and experienced a near-miss lightning strike. He cried out to his patron saint, Anne, promising to become a monk if his life was spared. When his life was saved, Luther kept his word, entering a religious order and immersing himself in the attempt to become holy. If religious works could earn someone a clear conscience, Luther would have had it in short order. The monk spent time in frequent fasting, sometimes for weeks at a time, sleeping only every three or four days. He practiced self-flagellation, whipping himself unconscious, to be found in a pool of blood by his fellow monks. He frequently went to confession, spending so much time listing out his every stray thought and motive that his confessor dreaded the sight of him. All these acts of contrition and self-mortification did nothing to ease Luther's conscience. He found peace only when he realized that God was not looking for him to do something; God wanted him to rest in what Christ already had done.

Christian leaders are not formed overnight; maturity takes time.

Nature: There is a reason why Scripture speaks of Christlikeness as the "fruit of the Spirit" (Gal. 5:22). Fruit is not something that happens overnight. A tree or vine must be planted. It must be cultivated and cared for over time. Eventually, in the right season, fruit springs forth. Christian leaders are called, first and foremost, to have the fruit of Christ in their lives. This takes time. J. Oswald Sanders shares, "Spiritual maturity is indispensable to good leadership. . . . A plant needs time to take root and come to maturity, and the process cannot be hurried. The seedling must take root downward before it can bear fruit upward."[10]

The Coming of the Spirit

Big Idea

The disciples' witness in the world is impelled and empowered by the Holy Spirit.

Key Themes

- The disciples require God's promised Spirit to galvanize them to carry out their assigned mission.
- Speaking in tongues that others understand reveals that the Spirit enables the communication of the gospel to others across cultures and language barriers.
- The list of nations consists of places where Diaspora Jews live and signals the international reach of the gospel.

Understanding the Text

The Text in Context

When Jesus prays at his baptism, the Holy Spirit's descent on him is attended by perceptible phenomena (Luke 3:22). Jesus then launches his ministry, and Luke records his keynote speech in Nazareth (Luke 4:16–30). Similarly, when the Christian community is gathered together in prayer in Acts 2:1, the Holy Spirit descends on them and their baptism in the Spirit (as foretold by John the Baptist in Luke 3:16) is attended by perceptible phenomena. This event launches their public testimony about Jesus, which is summed up in Peter's keynote speech.

Interpretive Insights

2:1 *When the day of Pentecost came.* Pentecost ("fiftieth [day]") is the name given by Greek-speaking Jews to the festival celebrated fifty days after Passover.[1] Pious Jews—like Paul, who bypassed Ephesus so that he might reach Jerusalem by the day of Pentecost (20:16)—were drawn to the temple in Jerusalem from across the world to celebrate the first feast after Passover.[2] Rabbinic texts associate Pentecost with the gift of the law on Sinai.[3] Philo mentions the noise created by God's breath or wind at the giving of the law and also says the voice of God was visible as flames.[4] Luke's account suggests that he "was aware of the association of Pentecost with the renewal of that covenant."[5] The coming of the Spirit marks a new covenant (Luke 22:20), an era defined by faith rather than law (cf. Gal. 3:19–4:6).

2:2–3 *Suddenly a sound like the blowing of a violent wind came from heaven . . . They saw what seemed to be tongues of fire.* The descriptions of a sound like that of a blowing, violent wind and tongues like fire try to express in human language a divine event. Wind and fire are associated with the presence of God.[6] *Jubilees* 1:3 describes the appearance of the Lord "like fire burning on the top of the mountain" where Moses had ascended to receive the tablets of the law. For these first Christians these phenomena are evidence of the Spirit's presence and the inauguration of the new covenant and the beginning of the church.

Although the Spirit came to rest on each one like a nimbus of fire, the emphasis is not on their individual experiences. The Spirit comes on the community gathered together in prayer. Collectively, they become the instruments of the Holy Spirit's power.

2:4 *All of them were filled with the Holy Spirit and began to speak in other tongues as the Spirit enabled them.* Everyone present, which presumably includes about one hundred and twenty followers (1:15), is filled with the Spirit, not just the apostles. They all soon will fill the world with their witness. Luke's Gospel begins with Zechariah tongue-tied in the temple, unable to convey to anyone his encounter with the divine (Luke 1:5–22). He must wait months before the Holy Spirit loosens his tongue, and he then prophesies and praises God (Luke 1:64–79). Acts begins with the disciples passively waiting a much shorter time, but then the Spirit spurs them to action and gives them voice to proclaim the word of God fearlessly and clearly so that all could understand them. Disciples who formerly were only inactive onlookers (Acts 1:11) suddenly become stirring preachers of the word.

2:5–11 *When they heard this sound, a crowd came together in bewilderment, because each one heard their own language being spoken.* The loud noise draws an audience representing worldwide Jewry. The presence of visitors from Rome explains how the gospel had reached that city long before Paul arrived (cf. 28:15). The Greek word translated as "converts to Judaism" (2:11) is usually transliterated as "proselytes." These gentiles would have turned away from their previous polytheism and idolatry to worship the one God of Israel, undergone circumcision, and accepted the obligation to obey all the Mosaic law. They would have been regarded by their former associates as traitors to their ancestral heritage.

The amazed crowd's question, "Aren't all these who are speaking Galileans?" (2:7), might reflect prejudice against Galileans (cf. John 1:46; 7:52). The

Spirit's power in the church will enable persons from different backgrounds and cultures to overcome their biases against others and see them as brothers and sisters in Christ.

2:12–13 *Amazed and perplexed, they asked one another, "What does this mean?" Some, however, made fun of them and said, "They have had too much wine."* The event creates a divided response. Some in the crowd recognize "the wonders of God" and the outpouring of the Spirit (2:11). Others turn up their nose and heckle the disciples as a bunch of gluttonous drunkards (2:13), an accusation previously aimed at Jesus (Luke 7:34). Philo refers to those whose overflowing religious joy is mistaken for drunkenness.[7] The disciples are not guilty of inebriated, slurred speech; they have experienced the joyous ecstasy that the Spirit brings. The Spirit enables them to convey the mighty acts of God in every language. Speaking in tongues in this context refers not to uttering some heavenly angelic language that needed to be interpreted (1 Cor. 14:5, 13, 27) but to the native languages of the people gathered from all over the world.

Theological Insights

What happened at Pentecost is in keeping with the incarnational thrust of the gospel. The gospel is intended to be intelligible at our level and addresses us in the language of our flesh. The disciples are filled to overflowing with the Spirit so as to reach persons from every background. Being filled with the Spirit is not a one-time experience; it recurs in 4:31; 8:17; 10:44–47; 11:15–17; 19:1–6.

Teaching the Text

1. *Acts emphasizes not the Spirit's manifestation in the private, personal lives of individual believers but rather the greater story of the Spirit's empowerment of the community of believers.* The Spirit will push the movement like wind so that it sweeps across the face of the Roman world and beyond. There is danger when we emphasize our individual experiences apart from the community. One may feel that one's personal experiences of the Spirit are so effective and so wonderful that one no longer needs the rest of the congregation or needs to hear about others' different experiences and convictions. This emphasis on private, subjective experiences was the problem for the church in Corinth (1 Cor. 12–14). Some in Corinth came to believe that they had become self-sufficient from their encounters with God and could dispense with fellowship with other Christians since they had met God in the inner sanctum of their souls. The intensity of their personal experiences became a source of pride and inevitably disrupted fellowship.

The Spirit fell on the entire community when they were "all together in one place" (2:1) and praying fervently. This circumstance should not be taken as a magic formula that guarantees the coming of the Spirit. Humans have no control over the Spirit and cannot manufacture his presence. Like the wind, the Spirit blows where he wills, and the effects are not always so dramatic. Sometimes the Spirit is like a still small voice. The church must be alert to and responsive to this divine presence. Presumably, the Spirit can also come when the church is fragmented and at loggerheads, but it is doubtful that the Spirit comes when the church is not living a life of prayer.

2. *The list of nations seems to be random, and it may be intended to evoke the first listing of nations in Genesis 10 that immediately precedes the narrative of the tower of Babel (Gen. 11:1–9).* In that event, God scatters languages in judgment. At Pentecost, "he scatters languages . . . to bring a new cross-cultural *unity* in the Spirit."[8] The catalog of nations reveals the scope of the miracle and symbolizes "the beginning of the gathering of the scattered tribes of Israel (cf. Isa. 66:18) and thus of the restoration of the kingdom to Israel before the parousia (1:6)."[9] The list may also counter Roman political propaganda that boasted of their reign over the entire world.[10] It is God who "made all the nations" (17:26) and who rules over them. The preaching is meant for more than the people of Judea and all who dwell in Jerusalem (2:14); it is meant for the entire world so that all might have an opportunity to turn to God.

3. *The inspiration of the Spirit does not make the disciples excited babblers but enables them to speak so that all those present could understand. Luke presents this phenomenon as speaking in other languages.* The "other tongues" (2:4) are identified by the hearers as "our own tongues" (2:11). They hear their "own language" (2:6), which is further clarified as "our native language" (2:8). The same verb translated as "gave them utterance" (2:4 ESV) is used when Peter "addressed" the crowd (2:14). Luke does not represent this miracle as speaking in the tongues of angels that Paul insists require a spiritual interpreter for anyone to understand and benefit (1 Cor. 14). Rather, they speak intelligible, earthly languages, and the result is that their message edifies and convicts the listeners who understand what they are saying. The miracle of Pentecost is the universal reach of the gospel that can cross barriers of culture and language.

Jesus promises disciples only the power to be witnesses in the world. God is present in power in a seemingly powerless community. Jesus's death and exaltation reveal that God's victory is won through the giving of one's life for others. The community is given the power not to destroy the enemy but to transform the enemy, to win them over rather than simply to win over them. Their primary weapon is the Scripture, as is evident from Peter's speech that follows.

Illustrating the Text

The Holy Spirit comes upon the believers at Pentecost.

Art: *Pentecost*, by El Greco. El Greco's depiction of Pentecost is a gripping display of awe and dependence. In the painting, the disciples, including Mary the mother of Jesus, are gazing heavenward. Some clasp their hands in prayer; others raise them in praise. All have their eyes wide open as glory-light bursts from the top of the canvas and the Holy Spirit descends in the form of a dove. Tongues of fire lick the top of their heads, and one is left with the unmistakable sense that this visitation has followed hard on the heels of intercession. Consider leading a brief moment of reflection on the image: What are some of the different reactions you see? What do the body postures tell us about their response to the Holy Spirit? How does El Greco use the contrast of light and dark to highlight the glory of God's presence? How does the painting agree or disagree with the picture in the Scriptures?

The wonders of God shared in intelligible languages and native tongues can bring good news.

Anecdote: A couple from the United States went to South Korea to adopt their new daughter, Hye-Jin. She was a lovely and active eight-year old, but she spoke only a few words of English. They gestured with their hands and drew simple pictures to communicate with her. When they finally arrived in the United States, they had trouble as they went through customs. In their distraction, they lost Hye-Jin. They began to panic, because they knew that Hye-Jin could not speak enough English to ask for help. The parents ran around, assisted by airport officials, but they could not locate her. Finally, a Korean businessman noticed the trouble that they were having and volunteered to make an announcement over the public address system in Korean. When the announcement was made, Hye-Jin heard the instructions and was reunited with her parents. She had been hiding and scared. She only came out when she heard in her native language the good news that her parents were looking for her and that she could be reunited with them.

The Spirit Inspires the Bold Proclamation of the Gospel

Big Idea

The Spirit leads Christ's followers toward others to proclaim that Jesus is the Lord and that salvation comes in his name. The message demands a response.

Key Themes

- God's purposes, which may seem to be hidden, are revealed in Scripture.
- The crucified Messiah is also the exalted Lord. His death and resurrection belong to God's plan for human salvation.
- The outpouring of the Holy Spirit is a sign that the final epoch of salvation has dawned, and the gospel message requires the response of repentance and baptism.

Understanding the Text

The Text in Context

After witnessing the Spirit's sound-and-light show and the multilingual miracle, the crowd asks, "What does this mean?" (2:12). Peter, who once had cowered on the fringe of the crowd to see what would happen to Jesus and then denied knowing him three times before a small group (Luke 22:54–62), now boldly takes center stage to give the answer. The phrase "with many other words" (2:40) shows that Luke presents only the highlights of Peter's sermon. It is a typical example of what was preached frequently by him and others in the days to come. It is based on the interpretation of Scripture learned from the risen Lord during his sojourn with them before his ascension (Luke 24:44–48).

Interpretive Insights

2:14–16 *Then Peter stood up with the Eleven, raised his voice and addressed the crowd: "Fellow Jews and all of you who live in Jerusalem, let me explain this to you."* Peter will explain to his audience that the spiritual spectacle that they have witnessed is the realization of God's purpose revealed in Scripture. Jesus, whom they saw crucified, is the Messiah, and he has been raised and exalted to the right hand of God as Lord.

2:17–21 *In the last days, God says, I will pour out my Spirit on all people.* The citation from Joel 2:28–32 "outlines the programme that is realized in the next chapters of the narrative."[1] Joel 2:28 says that it will come to pass "afterward." Peter alters the citation slightly by saying that they occur "in the last days" (2:17). This change indicates that he understands this outpouring of the Holy Spirit on Jesus's followers to mean that the final epoch in salvation history has dawned here and now. He also adds "God says" to underscore that it is God's plan.

The phrase "they will prophesy" (2:18) is also inserted into the citation from Joel. The Spirit will inspire indiscriminately old and young, male and female, and slaves (an alternative translation of "servants") to prophesy (cf. 11:28; 19:6; 21:9–11). It reverberates with Moses's yearning, "I wish that all the LORD's people were prophets and that the LORD would put his Spirit on them!" (Num. 11:29). The Spirit is not a new development in God's dealings with humans,[2] but pouring out the Spirit on "all people" (2:17) is. "All people," however, is to be restricted to those who repent and are baptized in the name of Jesus Christ for the forgiveness of their sins (2:38).[3]

The conclusion from Joel, "And everyone who calls on the name of the LORD will be saved" (2:32), stops in midsentence with the positive emphasis on salvation for those who call on the Lord (cf. Rom. 10:13). The prophecy in Joel (2:28–32) continues with an emphasis on the judgment of the nations (3:1–16). The new era focuses on the nations' salvation rather than on their judgment.

The reference to "the LORD" in Joel is taken by Peter to be none other than Jesus. In 2:17, Peter identifies *God* as the one who pours out his Spirit. In 2:33, *Jesus* has received "the promised Holy Spirit and has poured out what you now see and hear."

2:22 *Jesus of Nazareth was a man accredited by God to you by miracles, wonders and signs, which God did among you through him, as you yourselves know.* The wonders and signs (2:19) done by Jesus accredit his extraordinary status and unique connection to God.

2:23 *This man was handed over to you by God's deliberate plan and foreknowledge.* Jesus's death is not a case of tragic injustice; it is part of God's salvation plan, which is a major Lukan theme. It does not relieve the guilt of the persons responsible for his death, but that guilt is not irrevocable. Human wickedness put Jesus to death, but God intends to save the wicked through his death.

2:24–31 *But God raised him from the dead.* Jesus's resurrection and exaltation to God's right hand provide the climax to the story and reveal God's plan to transform the suffering of the cross into salvation and glory. Jesus had interpreted for the disciples how the prophecies of Scriptures were fulfilled in him (Luke 24:27, 32, 45–47). Now that he has departed, the Holy Spirit has come to inspire the apostles to interpret the Scriptures for others.

Peter argues from Psalm 16:8–11 to support Jesus's resurrection. That psalm was thought to be written *by* David, but it cannot be *about* David. His death and well-known tomb eliminate him as the possible subject of the psalm. The "holy one" (Acts 2:27 [cf. Luke 1:35]), therefore, is not David but Jesus, David's descendant (Luke 3:31), who was raised from the dead (Acts 2:24). David functions as a prophet (Luke 24:44) who foresaw the resurrection and exaltation of his descendant, the Messiah.

That God will not abandon him to rot in "the realm of the dead" is "the logical effect, as the only possible outcome, of the love of God for His holy one."[4] Jesus knew that God was with him at every moment in his life, and he knew that God's love would not forsake him in death.

2:32–35 *God has raised this Jesus to life, and we are all witnesses of it.* God has not called the disciples to be brilliant orators to delight crowds. Rather, they are called to give witness to what they have seen God do in Jesus's life, teaching, death, resurrection, and ascension to glory (3:15; 5:32; 10:39; 13:31; 22:15).

2:36 *Therefore let all Israel be assured of this: God has made this Jesus, whom you crucified, both Lord and Messiah.* This proclamation is urgently relevant to all Israel, and the audience consists of "Jews from every nation under heaven" (2:5). They are presumed to have been present during Passover when Jesus was executed and share the guilt for what happened to him (3:13–15). Human wickedness synchronized with God's deliberate plan and foreknowledge so that Jesus's death on the cross, unbeknownst to any of the actors, was only "a stage on the way to glory."[5] God overturned their rejection of the Messiah (2:23) by raising him from the dead and exalting him as Lord (2:24).

Peter does not intend to saddle all the Jewish people with responsibility for Jesus's death, but only those dwelling in Jerusalem and their rulers (13:27–29). The purpose of this indictment is to rouse his fellow Jews from their spiritual stupor so that they can comprehend their guilt and repent.

2:37 *Brothers, what shall we do?* Peter's appeals move the audience emotionally. But emotion is sentiment without action. Those who ask, "What shall we do?" are the most open to guidance that leads to repentance and forgiveness (cf. Luke 3:10–14).

2:38–40 *Repent and be baptized, every one of you, in the name of Jesus Christ for the forgiveness of your sins. And you will receive the gift of the Holy Spirit.* Repentance is a condition of salvation because it entails a change in one's "attitude and orientation that results in a new relation to God and fellow humans."[6] It is often tied to turning to "the Lord" or "to God" (3:19; 9:35; 11:21; 14:15; 15:19; 26:18, 20; 28:27). To bring Israel to repentance is cited as one reason God exalted Jesus to his right hand (5:31). Baptism is not a condition of salvation but follows as the consequence of repentance. Only by breaking with the ways of their wicked generation (cf. Luke 11:29–32; 11:50–51) can the audience escape the coming judgment.

Those who are "far off" are the Jews in the Diaspora (Dan. 9:7; Isa. 57:19; Esther 9:20). Peter thinks of the reconstitution of Israel.

2:41–46 *They devoted themselves to the apostles' teaching and to fellowship, to the breaking of bread and to prayer.* This summary is one of the few places where Luke tells us what happens after people are converted, and it emphasizes key elements of the church's life. They regularly meet together and gather in the temple courts because they could accommodate a large gathering and attract a larger crowd. They pray, teach, break bread together, and support the needy among them. The Spirit has transformed cantankerous disciples (Luke 9:46–48; 22:24–27) into magnanimous believers, unstinting in their care for and generosity toward one another. Their sharing of goods accords with what John the Baptist assumes to be the fruit of repentance (Luke 3:8, 11).

The phrase translated as "enjoying the favor of all the people" is better translated as "having good will toward all the people."[7] Craig Keener notes, "Whereas Peter's preaching leads to many converts on one occasion in Acts 2:41, it is the believing community's *lifestyle* that leads to continuous conversions in 2:47."[8]

Theological Insights

1. Invoking Jesus's name does not work as if it were a magical charm that brings salvation or works miracles (3:6, 16; 4:7, 10, 12, 17, 18, 30; 5:28, 40). Calling on his name means "invoking him in faith."[9] Since anyone can call on his name in faith, anyone can be saved.

2. Jesus's status as Lord is not some new development. God did not transform him into something that he was not before the resurrection. Jesus's resurrection means that humans can now recognize his preexisting identity as Lord despite his rejection and death.[10]

Teaching the Text

1. *Having an impact on others through the Christian message and lifestyle.* The crowd at Pentecost reacted with amazement and perplexity, which can be positive or negative reactions. How should the church amaze others and do so in ways that have positive results? What noises emanate from the church that make people want to come to see what is happening? What is so earth-shattering about what the church does? It should be noted that these first disciples did not focus on producing a spiritual extravaganza to attract and entertain onlookers. Instead, they offered biblical exposition that called for the response of repentance. They also witnessed with more than just words; they presented a distinctively alternative lifestyle.

2. *True repentance requires a change of mind and actions, and it is evoked by a plain-spoken message.* Peter does not try to soft-sell the gospel. Rather, he confronts his audience head-on with the message of the cross: "You crucified him!" This first proclamation of the gospel and call to repent cut the hearers to the heart. Today, the razor-sharp edge of the message is sometimes blunted to make it more palatable and less critical of cultural values and behaviors. Many may resist being included in this accusation that they crucified Jesus. Few like being told that they are doing wrong and deserve God's punishment. Any note of judgment is objectionable to those who are convinced that "I'm OK, you're OK," or maintain that "I am simply expressing who I am."

The call to repent is often made into a cartoon joke with a bearded man flourishing the warning on a sandwich board. As a consequence, that message is as ignored as the flight attendant's instructions on how to fasten the seatbelt. The gospel makes no sense and has no power for people who are not taught the doctrine of sin and are convicted of their sinfulness. Some may also misunderstand what repentance entails. It does not mean just feeling sorry. W. Phillip Keller writes, "True repentance, sometimes called 'godly sorrow,' is seldom seen in our society. This is basically because few of us see that our sins are criminal offenses against a loving Lord. They are what cost Christ the awful agony of Golgotha. It was and always is God's intention to bring people to repentance. The modern church merely brings people to feel sorry for themselves. The two are poles apart!"[11]

3. *The gospel comes with uplifting and inspiring grace.* Peter proclaims that this crowd is blameworthy for crucifying Jesus, the Son of God, but, surprisingly, he also announces that if they repent, they will receive forgiveness. Jesus has been exalted to God's right hand, and he exercises his lordly power with saving grace. Whether one leads with denunciation or with grace depends on the audience and situation. There is a danger, however, in stripping any note of judgment and warning from the message of the gospel. Jesus uttered both beatitudes and woes (Luke 6:20–26). The goal is to bring

about repentance, which means changing directions so that one looks not backward but forward.

Illustrating the Text

The early Christians attracted others to Christ through their authentically transformed lives.

Science: When a metal object is magnetized, it both undergoes change and stays the same. A magnetized object maintains the same size, shape, and weight. But it takes on new properties and interacts differently with the world around it. The Spirit's effects in the lives of humans may be compared to this act of magnetizing. When the Spirit descended on the early church at Pentecost, these Christians would have looked the same as before, but they possessed a new magnetism that drew people to them from different cultures and languages. The church led by the Spirit should be a magnetic place. Not all respond, however. As in the physical world, so in the spiritual realm, some are attracted to a magnetic field; others are repulsed by a magnetic field.

True gospel proclamation must include a conviction of sin.

Quote: C. S. Lewis. "We have a strange illusion that mere time cancels sin. I have heard others, and I have heard myself, recounting cruelties and falsehoods committed in boyhood as if they were no concern of the present speaker's, and even with laughter. But mere time does nothing either to the fact or to the guilt of a sin. The guilt is washed out not by time but by repentance and the blood of Christ."[12]

Baptism is essential to the Christian life.

Movies and Television: Roger Olson notes, "Movies and TV shows have probably included more scenes of baptism than any other distinctly Christian ritual—wedding ceremonies aside." In *The Godfather*, the new mafia boss Michael Corleone stands by his godson's Catholic baptism as his thugs assassinate family foes. In *The Apostle*, Sonny Dewey baptizes himself, now as the Apostle E. F., in a river after fleeing from a murder charge. In *O Brother, Where Art Thou?* the escaped convict Delmar joins a parade of baptismal candidates singing "Down to the River to Pray," and, after he's been dunked, he declares, "The preacher done washed away all my sins and transgressions!" In *My Big, Fat Greek Wedding*, the husband-to-be is baptized by a Greek Orthodox priest in a child's rubber swimming pool. In the television show *All in the Family*, Archie Bunker secretly baptizes his infant grandson when no one else will. Olson asks, "Why is baptism such a popular trope in popular storytelling?" His answer, "Perhaps because it is, or can be, visually dramatic." Baptism has also been divisive: "Almost every Christian denomination has its own twist on baptism." Olson notes, "One response to the multiple views of baptism is to reject or neglect it entirely. Especially in large independent churches, baptism is often relegated to relative unimportance." In the New Testament, there is no such thing as "unbaptized Christians." Olson concludes, "Baptism is requisite for following Jesus in the fullest sense." As dramatic and divisive as it might be, the church needs to wrestle with what it means to be baptized as a Christian.[13]

The Healing
of a Lame Man
at the Temple Gates

Big Idea

God's power continues to operate to bless the people so that they might turn from their wicked ways and turn to Jesus the Messiah.

Key Themes

- The healing of the lame man is an example of the apostles' "many wonders and signs" that filled others with awe.
- The lame man begs for money but gets something far more valuable: physical and spiritual healing.
- The miracle provides an opportunity to preach the gospel to a large temple crowd.

Understanding the Text

The Text in Context

A summary of the early believers' life together, performing "wonders and signs," "[meeting] together in the temple courts," "praising God," and the "Lord [adding] to their number," at the end of Acts 2 appears in capsule form in the story of the healing of the lame man. Although the lame man seeks money, Peter and John give him far more, full restoration to health and salvation in Jesus's name. The lame man's healing is an example of the fulfillment of God's eschatological promises among believers. This "wonder and sign" provides Peter the opportunity to preach to all those gathered in the temple and to persuade more to believe.

Interpretive Insights

3:1 *the time of prayer—at three in the afternoon.* The hour of prayer refers to the *Tamid* service, in which a lamb was offered at 9:00 a.m. and 3:00 p.m.

for the forgiveness of the sins of the people (Exod. 29:38–42; Num. 28:2–8). For the early Christians, the temple is only an ideal venue for preaching and teaching and not a place to offer sacrifices for their sins.

Luke shows that Christianity was cradled in pietistic Judaism among devout and observant Jews (Luke 1–3) until driven out from the synagogue (Luke 4:16–30) and from the temple (Acts 21:26–36) by malicious adversaries. Christianity is neither an apostate fringe sect nor the latest contrivance of mischief from the East; it is the true fulfillment of Old Testament promises.

3:2 *Now a man who was lame from birth was being carried to the temple gate called Beautiful.* The lame, along with others with physical deformities, were barred from entering the temple. Someone who was blemished was not permitted to enter the sanctuary or the presence of God (Lev. 21:17–20 [cf. 2 Sam. 5:8]). The beggar is placed so that he might coax a few coins from those entering the temple complex. All of the gates would have been lined with beggars seeking alms. The gate called "Beautiful" is not mentioned in Jewish descriptions of the temple but may refer to the eastern gate.

3:6–7 *Silver or gold I do not have, but what I do have I give you. In the name of Jesus Christ of Nazareth, walk.* The beauty of the temple's gates and the architectural wonders of its stones and colonnades are useless to this disabled beggar. The temple offers him no healing or help, only banishment. The apostles lack money and insist on eye contact because their interaction with the beggar will not be a degrading exchange of money. They act and speak in the name of the risen Jesus to restore the man to wholeness, both physically and spiritually.

3:8 *He jumped to his feet and began to walk.* Healing the lame is another sign of the fulfillment of eschatological promises (Isa. 35:6; Jer. 31:8; Mic. 4:6–7; Zeph. 3:19; Luke 7:22). His leaping for joy signifies not only his personal joy but also the joy over God acting for Israel's salvation (cf. Luke 1:41, 44; 6:23).[1] Through the name of Jesus, he is "completely healed" (3:16), and his once-wobbly legs begin to whirl him around in joy. His praising God expresses the belief that God's authority and power are at work in Jesus.

The lame man's healing would not have been the only miracle the apostles did. It is chosen because it symbolizes the gift of salvation that the preaching of the gospel offers to all people, particularly those who are marginalized and excluded.

3:11 *While the man held on to Peter and John, all the people were astonished and came running to them in the place called Solomon's Colonnade.* It is unlikely that clutching Peter and John is evidence that the man was not yet confident of being able to walk on his own.[2] He clings "enthusiastically to the men who had brought such a dramatic change into his life."[3]

3:12 *Why do you stare at us as if by our own power or godliness we had made this man walk?* In interpreting the miraculous healing, Peter's speech includes the same themes as his speech at Pentecost. He does not take credit for the healing. The miracle points only to Jesus's power. Peter bears witness to the foundational facts of Jesus's earthly ministry: his death at the hands of his enemies, his resurrection and glorification by the power of God, and the promise of his return.

3:13–15 *The God of Abraham, Isaac and Jacob, the God of our fathers, has glorified his servant Jesus. . . . You killed the author of life, but God raised him from the dead.* Pilate was merely a pawn in the hands of those who wanted to execute Jesus. The audience may not have had a direct hand in Jesus's death, but the guilt of the perpetrators is assumed to be corporate.

Isaiah 53 lies at the forefront of the understanding of Jesus's death as a fulfillment of God's purposes. Identifying Jesus as "servant" and "Righteous One" recalls Isaiah 53:11, and his exaltation, Isaiah 52:13. God undoes what Jesus's mortal enemies did. They inflicted death, but the author of life wondrously transforms it into life for others. Jesus's humiliating death brings the possibility of atonement for their sins. They have a second chance to see the error of their ways and repent. The sin is corporate, but repentance is an individual response.

3:16 *By faith in the name of Jesus, this man whom you see and know was made strong.* The faith is that of the apostles, who trust in the power of Jesus's name, which "represents his divine authority and continuing power to grant the blessings of salvation."[4] The lame man initially expected only alms, but through faith he receives more than alms—the healing of his body.

3:17–18 *Now, fellow Israelites, I know that you acted in ignorance.* Evil deeds may be committed out of ignorance. Ignorance is never a valid excuse for evil.[5] After the resurrection, continued opposition to Jesus and the gospel is deliberate transgression. These Israelites now are informed that Jesus's coming is the fulfillment of the prophetic promises, and Peter asserts that Jesus's death was part of God's plan to restore Israel.

3:19 *Repent, then, and turn to God, so that your sins may be wiped out, that times of refreshing may come from the Lord.* Peter does not condemn the audience without also offering the hope of absolution by returning to God. The "times of refreshing" refers not to the distant, final day of deliverance but to the current time. The coming of the Messiah has brought relief from the cruel bonds of sin.

3:21 *Heaven must receive him until the time comes for God to restore everything.* They currently live during an interim period when Jesus has been received in heaven. He is not going to restore the kingdom to Israel (1:6) but will restore *all things* in due course (cf. 1 Cor. 15:25, 28; Eph. 1:9–10; 2 Pet. 3:10–13).

3:22 *For Moses said, "The Lord your God will raise up for you a prophet like me from among your own people; you must listen to everything he tells* *you.*" Peter affirms in his address that Jesus is none other than the suffering servant Messiah (3:13, 26) of Isaiah 52:13–53:12; the Moses-like Prophet (3:22–23) of Deuteronomy 18:15–20; and the promised seed of Abraham of Genesis 12:1–3 (3:25 [cf. Gal. 3:16–18]).[6] As the long-awaited prophet, Jesus "perfectly embodied the revelation of God and fulfilled all the law and the prophets."[7]

3:23 *Anyone who does not listen to him will be completely cut off from their people.* Luke is interested in confirming for his audience their true identity as the people of God because of their belief in and obedience to Jesus. The prophecies in Scripture that Israel is to become a light to the nations (Gen. 12:3; Isa. 12:4; 42:6; 49:6; Ezek. 47:22–23) will be fulfilled only by those who belong to Jesus. Only they can rightfully claim to be Israel.[8]

3:24–25 *And you are heirs of the prophets and of the covenant God made with your fathers. He said to Abraham, "Through your offspring all peoples on earth will be blessed."*[9] This reference to the promise to Abraham (cf. 3:13) underscores the "continuity between historic Israel and the new Christian movement."[10] It also introduces the idea that the Messiah did not come only for Israel. He will bless all peoples on earth. He came first to Israel to bless Israel and turn them from their ways so that they might bless the nations and turn them from their ways.

3:26 *When God raised up his servant, he sent him first to you to bless you by turning each of you from your wicked ways.* Jews will not partake in the blessings by virtue of their birthright (Luke 3:8). Only those who believe in Christ will be blessed by him to become a blessing to others.

Teaching the Text

1. *The apostles speak the truth to bring repentance rather than seeking to add to their fame.* Christians are not out to win popularity contests and sell-out crowds. As Flannery O'Connor said, Christians are to "push as hard as the age that pushes against you."[11] Peter does not soak up the glory that the crowd showers on him and John for performing this miracle. Instead, he takes the opportunity to confront the crowd with their heinous sin of crucifying the Messiah, the Son of God. They (along with the rest of the human race) are guilty for putting to death the author of life: "You handed him over to be killed, and you disowned him before Pilate, though he had decided to let him go. You disowned the Holy and Righteous One and asked that a murderer be released to you" (3:13–15). Sometimes this message sparks repentance; sometimes it inflames oppression.

2. *People may need to be told that they are sinners, but that cannot be the end of the message.* Now is the time of refreshing with the presence of

the Spirit but also the time of decision when God will no longer pass over ignorance. Guilt can be wiped away by repentance, which entails changing one's mind and one's direction in life. They must be given the opportunity to respond in order to become forgiven sinners so that the past can be put behind them as they open themselves up to God's future. Addressing Jews, Peter insists that those in Israel who do not turn to Jesus will be cut off from the people. Addressing any audience, one may claim that those who do not turn to Jesus will be cut off from salvation.

3. *Jesus is identified as servant, the Holy and Righteous One, the author of life, a prophet like Moses, the Messiah, and the seed of Abraham.* This rich imagery derives entirely from the Old Testament. Scouring the Scripture helps the disciples make sense of what they had seen happen with their eyes. They understand that what happened to Jesus is the pinnacle of the unfolding story of salvation history. It results in a necessary redefinition of who belongs to Israel and who does not. Peter invites his fellow Jews to reaffirm God's calling of Israel and what God has done through Jesus that inaugurates a new epoch while also giving notice of the dire consequences if they refuse to do so.

This healing that takes place in the proximity of the temple complex at the hour of prayer and the sacrifice for the forgiveness of sins puts in vivid relief the temple's ineffectiveness. The leading priests serve only themselves and contaminate the temple with their unrighteousness. The temple with its beautiful gates does not offer life or the forgiveness of sins, since the sacrifices must be continually repeated. It will be supplanted by the church.

Illustrating the Text

Miracles are for gospel proclamation, not self-promotion.

Quote: **F. Olin Stockwell.** Stockwell was a missionary to China in the first half of the twentieth century. He was arrested by the Communist government in 1950. During his imprisonment, he wrote a series of reflections in the margins of his copy of the New Testament. In one of these, he states, "Unless the outward event creates an inner change, it is really no miracle in the New Testament sense. A miracle is that event, either outward or inward, which convinces the participant that God is alive, active and over-ruling in His providential care."[12]

Silver and gold should not hinder the work of God.

History: During the thirteenth century, the church was corrupted by secularism and materialism. Commentator Cornelius a Lapide tells a story of the day that Thomas Aquinas visited Pope Innocent II while he was counting a lot of money. "You see, Thomas," said the Pope, "the church can no longer say, 'Silver and gold have I none.'" "True, holy Father," said Thomas, "and neither can she now say, 'Arise and walk.'"[13]

Choices have consequences.

Object Lesson: One of the most popular toys of the 1980s, the Rubik's Magic Cube, is currently making a comeback. Each side of the cube has nine independent squares moved by an internal mechanism, allowing each row of three squares to be turned on a horizontal or vertical axis. The object of the game is to move each of the color squares, which have been mixed up, so that each side of the cube has squares of only one color. Operating the cube teaches many lessons about the fact that choices have consequences. Each turn of an axis affects the arrangement of the colored squares on other sides of the cube. One twist may bring the colors of one side into alignment, but that twist may lead to greater chaos and confusion for other sides of the cube.

We make choices in life every day, and those choices, including our choice to follow God or to live life apart from God, have consequences. While making choices in an effort to obtain self-righteousness, answers, and satisfaction apart from God might appear to be correct from one's perspective, the choice to reject God has devastating consequences for one's life that may not be seen from this side of eternity. Punishment for rejection of God is an eternal consequence and is a result of one's choice against God. Only when one decides to make choices in line with following God can all aspects of life and death, of salvation and judgment, of righteousness and sin correctly fall into place.

The Apostles Bold under Fire and the Church Fervent in Prayer

Big Idea

The apostles, with no political influence, perform works of power by the Holy Spirit that frighten the Jewish leaders, who refuse to accept what God has done through Jesus.

Key Themes

- God turns the evil intrigues of humans to serve his purposes.
- Boldness to proclaim the gospel in the face of persecution is a divine gift to be prayed for and does not derive from personal courage.[1]
- The early church witnesses through both deeds and words.

Understanding the Text

The Text in Context

The healing of the beggar at the temple gates precipitates a cycle of conflict with the temple authorities. They have witnessed or heard about these events from a cynical distance and try to impose their will to squelch this movement.

Interpretive Insights

4:1–2 *The priests and the captain of the temple guard and the Sadducees came up to Peter and John.* The captain of the temple ranked second behind the high priest in the hierarchy and had oversight over the sacrificial cult. He also served as the chief of police.[2] The temple leaders are irked because they thought that Jesus's crucifixion had eradicated their problem with him. The apostles proclaim that God raised him from the dead and provide convincing proofs through their miracles and teaching from the Scripture.

The Sadducees are mentioned because they are particularly known for not believing in the resurrection of the dead (Acts 23:8; Luke 20:27). Their ranks are composed of members from the aristocratic, priestly families, and Josephus remembers them for being "more heartless than any other Jews."[3] They represent a religious system that promotes an oppressive caste system, keeps down the poor, and kills dissidents. They are never heard from again after the destruction of Jerusalem in AD 70.

4:3–4 *They seized Peter and John . . . But many who heard the message believed; so the number of men who believed grew to about five thousand.*[4] Luke portrays Christianity as a popular grassroots movement. The leaders' attempt to squelch it by arresting its leaders fails, as many continue to be converted.

4:6 *Annas the high priest was there, and so were Caiaphas, John, Alexander and others of the high priest's family.* Annas was high priest during the years AD 6–14. Despite being deposed by the Romans, he apparently retains the title and holds sway as the head of a powerful priestly dynasty. The official high priest is Caiaphas, his son-in-law. Five of Annas's sons would serve as high priest.[5]

4:7 *By what power or what name did you do this?* Jesus too was challenged by the chief priests and scribes, who demanded to know "by what authority" he was "doing these things" (Luke 20:1–2). It is unlikely that they think that the apostles are working by the power of Beelzebul (cf. Luke 11:15, 18). They are disturbed because they have no control over this miraculous act of kindness.

4:8–10 *It is by the name of Jesus Christ of Nazareth, whom you crucified but whom God raised from the dead, that this man stands before you healed.* The Greek word for "healed" can also be translated as "saved," and both meanings apply. The apostles answer that this miracle has come by the power of the name of the one whom the leaders killed but whom God raised from the dead. The command "know this" (4:10) means that the time when ignorance might be excused has now ended. They must believe the message about Jesus or face the consequences of rejecting it.

The contrast between the apostles and the leaders is stark. The apostles are filled with the Holy Spirit. The leaders are filled with only suspicions and fear. The apostles speak with boldness and teach the crowds (4:13). The leaders are sorely troubled (4:2) and can only try to stifle speaking (4:18, 21). The apostles do acts of mercy, which characterized Jesus's ministry (10:38). The leaders threaten those who do good deeds.

4:11 *Jesus is "the stone you builders rejected, which has become the cornerstone."* God salvaged the stone that the builders discarded and built another temple, the end-time temple not made with hands (Ps. 118:22; Luke 20:17). As a spiritual temple, it replaces the leaders' physical temple as the place where God is present among the people.

4:12 *Salvation is found in no one else, for there is no other name under heaven given to mankind by which we must be saved.* The forgiveness of sins that leads to salvation is not to be found in the temple and its cult, which excludes gentiles and blemished Jews; it can be found only in Jesus.

4:13 *they saw the courage of Peter and John and realized that they were unschooled, ordinary men.* The leaders' surprise over the power of Peter's response bears out Jesus's prophecy: "For I will give you words and wisdom that none of your adversaries will be able to resist or contradict" (Luke 21:15). The Greek word translated as "courage" is often translated as "boldness." It refers to confident, frank speech, as opposed to fawning speech that seeks to flatter and placate. It is neither arrogant nor impudent but is marked by earnest conviction. Peter and John are emboldened to proclaim Jesus's exalted status as the resurrected Son of God without fear of the consequences.

The adjectives "unschooled" and "ordinary" mean that the apostles belong to the unexceptional rank and file who are not noted for their learning.[6] They may have no scribal training in the law or skill in public speaking,[7] but Jesus educated them in the Scripture and the Holy Spirit has inspired them.

4:14 *But since they could see the man who had been healed standing there with them, there was nothing they could say.* The undeniable evidence standing before them in the person of the formerly lame man causes their challengers to shrink back into silence. The duration of the man's prior infirmity highlights the miracle's impressiveness.

4:15–18 *"What are we going to do with these men?" they asked.* The leaders are so hardened that they resist every sign from God, and they stand condemned. They do not ask themselves, "What shall we do because we are guilty of Jesus's death and God has vindicated him by raising him from the dead?" (cf. 2:37). Instead, they basically ask, "How do we get rid of these upstarts who are causing us so much trouble?" The apostles' popularity galls them but also causes them temporarily to back down. They had no grounds to punish the apostles and would have aroused the ire of the people. They therefore resort to threats and issue a gag order: no more preaching about Jesus.

4:19–22 *Which is right in God's eyes: to listen to you, or to him?* Peter and John confront them by presuming to ask for their opinion: Who is to be obeyed, God or humans? The apostles already have answered the question for themselves. Whatever the cost, they can obey only the voice of the Lord (cf. 1 Sam. 15:22–23; Jer. 7:22–23).[8] They know that the high court in Israel will be overruled by the higher court of heaven, and they are constrained to proclaim the gospel (cf. Acts 22:15; 1 Cor. 9:16). No earthly authority can silence this proclamation.

4:23–28 *You spoke by the Holy Spirit through the mouth of your servant, our father David.* The church does not complain to God about what happened

Similarities between Jesus's Arrest and Interrogation and the Disciples' Arrest and Interrogation

	Jesus	Disciples
Teaching in the temple before arrest	Luke 20:1–37	Acts 3:1–26
Citation of Psalm 118:22, the rejected stone	Luke 20:17	Acts 4:11
"The captain of the temple"	Luke 22:52	Acts 4:1
"Laid hands on"	Luke 20:19	Acts 4:3; 5:18
Examined by Sanhedrin the morning after the arrest	Luke 22:66	Acts 4:5–6
Challenge: By what authority/power do you do this?	Luke 20:2	Acts 4:7
People prevent leaders from taking action	Luke 19:47–48; 20:19; 22:2	Acts 4:21; 5:26

to Peter and John. Instead, they first turn to Scripture (Ps. 2) to acknowledge God's sovereign authority. The maker of heaven and earth is still in control even when enemies rage against God's people as they did against God's Son.

4:29–31 *Now, Lord, consider their threats and enable your servants to speak your word with great boldness.* Second, the church responds to bitter opposition with ardent prayer. They pray not for vengeance or for safety but for more boldness to preach the word. Their prayers result in a similar Pentecost experience: intense shaking of their meeting place and filling with the Holy Spirit. Their prayers are answered as they continue to preach boldly.

Theological Insights

1. The name of Jesus is as powerful as the name of God (Pss. 20:1–7; 44:4–8; 54:1–7), and that power cannot be stymied by humans (Acts 4:20, 33; 5:39; 6:8).

2. The educational background of those who bear witness to what God has done and is doing in the world has no effect on the power of their testimony. It depends entirely on the power of the Holy Spirit to convict others of its truth and to bring about a positive response.

Teaching the Text

1. *The contrast between Peter and John, who are untrained but who speak with boldness, and the leaders, who presumably are educated, underscores the power of the Holy Spirit to make persons effective witnesses.* These leaders lack the Holy Spirit and are stiff-necked opponents fighting against God and are ultimately powerless (5:39). Having been Jesus's companions places the

disciples under suspicion, but also it offers an additional explanation for their boldness and skill in interpreting Scripture. They have learned from him and read the Scriptures with new eyes.

The cultured despisers of religion often dismiss Christians as ignorant, and Christians often respond in kind by trading insults. These early Christians, however, respond to abuse with prayer. They do not cower before the contempt and threats of others but continue to proclaim the message that God has ordained them to proclaim.

2. *Persecution will become normative for those who proclaim the Christian message to unbelievers.* God does not put them into a witness protection program when the going gets rough. Through the Holy Spirit they continue to do the very things that catch the negative attention of the authorities and unleash their intimidation. Rejection should come not as a surprise but as par for the course. They are proclaiming as Lord and as the cornerstone of God's new temple the one whom the builders had rejected. Jesus cited this verse at the conclusion of his parable about the wicked tenants (Luke 20:9–17). They mercilessly killed the servants whom the owner of the vineyard sent to them to collect the rent and then killed his only son, thinking that they could seize the vineyard for themselves. The disciples do not cite the continuation of the psalm that assures the destruction of those who oppose God: "Everyone who falls on that stone will be broken to pieces; anyone on whom it falls will be crushed" (Luke 20:18). Disciples may be crushed by tyrants and tormenters, but they need not fear them. They can only kill the body. The one to be feared is God, who has the power to throw persons into hell (Luke 12:4–5).

3. *The disciples find God's claim on their lives competing with the claims of the political and religious authorities.* They can allow nothing to compromise Jesus's lordship over their lives. These powerful enemies may seem potent, but Christians know that Christ has disarmed them (Col. 2:15) and therefore they need not fear them (Rom. 8:38–39). Nevertheless, the disciples are highly vulnerable, and the narrative will show that Christians are viewed with suspicion as a sect, libeled as troublemakers, and subjected to shameful treatment without state protection. They are not to invite persecution through open rebellion that would hinder their mission. The Holy Spirit will guide them to know when to resist and when to capitulate to the demands of their rulers and culture (cf. Rom. 13:1–7; 1 Pet. 2:13–17).

Illustrating the Text

Listening to God is a Christian's foremost priority.

Christian Biography: **Caspar ten Boom.** Caspar ten Boom was caught harboring Jews in his home. When the police raided his home on February

28, 1944, they questioned him: "Tell me, what does it say in [your Bible] about obeying the government?" He replied, "Fear God and honor the Queen." He was arrested, because they had the testimony of a snitch who sold out the family for money. But the Gestapo chief had sympathy for the aged man and questioned, "That old man! Did he have to be arrested?" "You, old man!" He whispered to ten Boom, "I'd like to send you home, old fellow. I'll take your word that you won't cause any more trouble." Ten Boom replied, "If I go home today, tomorrow I will open my door again to any man in need who knocks."[9] The chief was so angered by his disobedience that he immediately threw him into prison. Ten Boom would not last one month in prison. He would die on a hospital floor at the age of 84 on March 10, 1944.

Persecution is part of faithful gospel witness.

Christian Biography: **Paul Robert Schneider.** Schneider (1897–1939) was the first Protestant pastor to die in a concentration camp at the hands of the Nazis. His wife, Gretel, wrote his biography, *The Preacher of Buchenwald*, recounting his courage and continual preaching in the camp despite the brutal punishments for disobeying orders to be silent. A fellow prisoner, Alfred Leikam, summarized Schneider's ministry in the camp: "Wholly without fear, he bore witness of his Christian faith to the SS. In this frankness, he was probably unique in Germany. He called the devil by his name: murderer, adulterer, unrighteous, monster. Throughout this witness, in which he presented the grace of Christ together with a call to repentance, Schneider was exposed alternately to severe bodily tortures, humiliations, and agonies."[10] How would you like to be remembered in history and by God: as a commandant of a concentration camp who faithfully carried out orders to murder thousands, or as a witness who faithfully gave witness to Christ and paid the ultimate price? Karl Barth wrote about Schneider in a letter dated August 3, 1939, "His faithful witness has helped many to do and say what is right and God has honoured him in allowing him to suffer. The New Testament speaks of this honour of suffering. It is not for nothing. It is a signpost, pointing up higher, where honour is given and the crown of life will be received."[11]

The bold witness of the disciples is proof of the resurrection.

Quote: *Pensées*, by Blaise Pascal. "The hypothesis that the apostles were knaves is quite absurd. Follow it out to the end and imagine these twelve men meeting after Jesus' death and conspiring to say that he had risen from the dead. This means attacking all the powers that be. The human heart is singularly susceptible to fickleness, to change, to promises, to bribery. One of them had only to deny his story under these inducements, or still more because of possible imprisonment, torture and death, and they would all have been lost. Follow that out."[12]

Even people's evil choices are ultimately used to achieve God's good purposes.

Art: Artist Denny Dent was famous for the live-painting performances that he called a "Two-Fisted Art Attack." Gripping four paintbrushes in two hands, the ambidextrous artist would cover a black canvas with vibrant colors as rock 'n' roll music pumped through speakers and audiences cheered. Dent was driven not only to create amazing art but also to communicate a message: life is art. One of the ways he conveyed this message was by beginning a painting in the usual manner. Part way through the performance, however, the whole thing would look like a mess. Dent would turn to the audience, signal to silence the music and then acknowledge that things appeared to have gone off the rails with this painting. "But things aren't always what they seem." He would then turn, run to the enormous canvas, and spin it 180 degrees. The audience would erupt, realizing he had been painting upside down the whole time. What they thought an irredeemable mess was actually a masterpiece!

Our God is at work in human history. Sometimes, things look like a mess, but we can trust that nothing will stop him from displaying his glory in our story.

Godly Giving and Deadly Lies
Barnabas and Ananias and Sapphira

Big Idea

The Holy Spirit's presence generates the believers' unity and sacrificial giving to care for others.[1] The love of money and status exposes one to Satan's toxic influence.

Key Themes

- The gospel has social ramifications, and spirituality leads to social responsibility.[2]
- Satan contends with the Holy Spirit to try to disrupt the church fellowship.
- The people of God are to have the highest ethical standards.

Understanding the Text

The Text in Context

The chapter division does not serve readers well because the story that begins in 4:32–37 continues in 5:1–11. The two accounts hinge together as panels to provide positive and negative examples of sharing possessions.[3] The selfless generosity of Barnabas sets the stage for the venal duplicity of Ananias and Sapphira. That account reveals that the Christians are not simply victims of persecution. The fearsome power of God resides in their midst. The second account prepares for Gamaliel's warning to the Sanhedrin not to fight against God (5:34–39). Those who are enemies of Christ, the Holy Spirit, and this sacred community place themselves in grave danger of God's judgment.[4]

Interpretive Insights

4:32–35 *All the believers were one in heart and mind. . . . For from time to time those who owned land or houses sold them, brought the money from the sales and put it at the apostles' feet, and it was distributed to anyone who had need.* The community has grown large, but it has its share of poor members.[5] A number of Galileans have taken up residence in Jerusalem, and a common fund is necessary to support all the members of the community. Their needs are not ignored by the church as they try to prevent economic polarization among the members that would disrupt the fellowship. They translate their convictions about caring for their fellow Christians into tangible actions. The wealthier members contribute to a common fund to help the poor. Luke does not say that the apostles solicit the gifts but only that they handle their distribution. Laying their property or the money from the sale of their property at the apostles' feet is a sign of their surrender of their lives wholly to Christ. Because the gifts are presented to the apostles (4:35, 37; 5:2), those who receive help do not become indebted to the individual donors, who otherwise would become their patrons.[6] The recipients are to understand the gifts as God meeting their needs "according to the riches of his glory in Christ Jesus." While they may be thankful for the donors' generosity, they must recognize that their true benefactor is God (Phil. 4:19–20).

4:36–37 *Joseph, a Levite from Cyprus, whom the apostles called Barnabas (which means "son of encouragement"), sold a field he owned and brought the money and put it at the apostles' feet.* The nickname "Barnabas," "son of encouragement," distinguishes him from Joseph called Barsabbas, who was also known as Justus (1:23). Barnabas's bent toward encouraging others is evident in multiple incidents in Acts: his financial gift to help the community, his intercession on behalf of Paul (9:26–27), his exhorting the church in Antioch (11:22–26), and his backing John Mark in the dispute with Paul (15:37).

The field that Barnabas sells recalls the field that Judas bought with the blood money for betraying Jesus (1:18). Barnabas is the antithesis of Judas as one who sacrificially gives up property to serve others. Ananias is Judas's spiritual match as an example of selfishness.[7] As a Levite, Barnabas is also the antithesis to the Levite who ignored the mugging victim on the roadway and passed by on the other side in Jesus's parable (Luke 10:32). He shows compassion to the disadvantaged. Levites were not accorded an allotment in the land (Num. 18:20, 24; Deut. 10:9), but Barnabas's property may have been in his native Cyprus. Regardless of where this property came from, as a Christian, Barnabas fully recognizes that "the LORD is [his] inheritance" (Deut. 10:9), and he does not need this land.

5:1–2 *Now a man named Ananias, together with his wife Sapphira, also sold a piece of property. With his wife's full knowledge he kept back part of* *the money for himself, but brought the rest and put it at the apostles' feet.* The account of Ananias and Sapphira divides into two equal parts (5:1–6, 7–11), and the space devoted to this incident shows that it must have special significance for Luke. The church has threats not only from without but also from within. Ananias and Sapphira conspire to hold back a portion of the proceeds from the piece of property that they sold when they had vowed that the entire proceeds would be devoted to communal use.[8]

5:3–4 *Ananias, how is it that Satan has so filled your heart that you have lied to the Holy Spirit . . . ?* Peter's questions show that the issue is not between him and this couple but between the Holy Spirit and Satan.[9] Satan contends with the Holy Spirit in multiple ways to try to destroy the church. Persecution has failed, and now Satan employs a subtler but more poisonous method by using money to coax individuals in the church to do evil. That is why Jesus consistently warned about the dangers of riches (Luke 6:24; 12:13–34; 16:1–14, 19–31). Peter emphasizes that giving the money from the sale of their property over to the apostles was purely optional.[10] Satan entered Ananias's heart, as he did Judas's (Luke 22:3 [cf. John 13:27]). Judas decided to defect; Ananias decided to defraud. The Greek term translated as "kept for yourself" implies that he pilfered the money by skimming off the top (cf. Titus 2:10).

5:5–6 *When Ananias heard this, he fell down and died. And great fear seized all who heard what had happened.* Peter formally charges Ananias with an offense that places him under divine judgment. The charge is not simply that he defrauded the community but that he lied to the Holy Spirit. The motivation seems to be that he sought honor from the community for bestowing such a gracious gift, while hanging on to some of the money. Since Peter does not condemn him (or Sapphira) to death, their sudden deaths must be attributable to God's reckoning.[11]

5:7–10 *About three hours later his wife came in.* Peter gives Sapphira a chance to confess and repent, but she continues the deception. The two summaries of the couple's sin (5:4, 9) reveal its gravity. They have lied to God and put the Spirit to the test.

5:11 *Great fear seized the whole church and all who heard about these events.* The term "church" appears for the first time in Acts. "Great fear" refers to holy awe that recognizes the hand of God in these events.[12]

Theological Insights

God works many signs and wonders through the apostles (5:12), and God also works judgment through the words of the apostle Peter. Peter does not simply inform Ananias and Sapphira what they already know but formally charges them with an offense that places them under divine judgment. The account reveals that the "same hand which stretches out to heal the diseased and disabled (4.30) might suddenly turn and strike down a pretentious disciple."[13] One cannot trifle with God with impunity. Elsewhere in Acts, the consequences of sin are vividly depicted. Judas dies in a gory heap (1:18–20); Herod Agrippa I is struck down and eaten by worms (12:21–23); and the Jewish magician and false prophet Bar-Jesus (Elymas) is struck blind (13:6–12). The consequences of unrepented sin are not always "so instantaneous or so visibly drastic,"[14] but they are inescapable.

Teaching the Text

1. *Christians should be generous with their money.* Barnabas follows the admonitions of Jesus in Luke's Gospel (12:33; 14:33; 16:9, 13 [cf. 18:28]). He divests himself of mammon (money) that would hinder his devotion to Jesus. Andrew Murray's sermon "The Holy Spirit and Money," explains that when Christ takes possession of us, the Spirit takes possession of our money and belongings. He states, "Money is the great symbol of the power of happiness of this world, one of its chief idols, drawing men away from God; a never-ceasing temptation to worldliness, to which the Christian is daily exposed. It would not have been a full salvation that did not provide complete deliverance from the power of money. The story of Pentecost assures us that when the Holy Spirit comes in His fullness into the heart, then earthly possessions lose their place in it."[15] Any Christian whose life can be reduced to a six-word story, "All I ever wanted was more," has been seduced by Satan's bait and has put trust in worthless material things rather than Christ.

2. *Was God's judgment of Ananias and Sapphira overly harsh?* Modern readers may be troubled that Ananias and Sapphira both drop dead suddenly with no due process of a trial and no sympathy extended to the bereaved family.

We may not judge their dishonesty to be an offense serious enough to warrant the death penalty. It could be dismissed as a "relatively small deceit."[16] The key phrases for interpreting the passage are in 5:5, 11, 13. Breaking the sanctity of a vow was a serious breach. One cannot renege on a promise to God without serious consequences (cf. Num. 30:1–2; Deut. 23:21–23). In the Greco-Roman world, Demosthenes said, "If I swear truly, may many blessings be mine, and may I never again suffer such an outrage; but if I am forsworn, may I perish utterly, I and all I possess, or ever may possess."[17] The first-century audience would recognize Ananias's and Sapphira's sin as a case of grave impiety. This view is represented in epigraphic evidence: "If I keep this oath may it go well for me, but if I forswear may I perish, myself and all that is mine."[18] Ananias and Sapphira characterize the failure to fear divine retribution by assuming that God did not hear their vow or did not care enough to do anything to punish its violation.[19]

Since Peter couches their offense as lying to and testing the Holy Spirit, it does not bode well for the temple leaders and their followers whom Stephen accuses of "forever opposing the Holy Spirit" (7:51 NRSV). They too inevitably will face divine wrath.

3. *Luke intends for the story to have an impact on insiders and outsiders and to establish that Christians have high ethical standards.* The early Christians are concerned about the poor and will make sacrifices for their economic welfare. Care for the poor is what is to be expected of ideal Israel (Lev. 25:35–38; Deut. 15:4). Christians also fear God and observe the solemnity of their oaths. They are not immoral or corrupt and do not condone impiety in their midst but root it out. They are not money-mad and grasping. They do not feign piety to gain honor and prestige.

Illustrating the Text

Faith may be measured by a believer's attitude toward money.

Quote: **François-Marie Arouet.** François-Marie Arouet, better known as Voltaire, was a French writer, philosopher, and historian, and a staunch atheist. He was against the established Catholic Church, because he could not see any difference that religion had upon the individual or the world. He stated, "When it is a question of money, everybody is of the same religion."[20] One of the distinguishing factors of the early believers was their willingness to sell their "property and possessions to give to anyone who had need" (2:43–44). Joseph Barnabas laid his money and possessions before the feet of the apostles for the sake of the poor (4:36–37). On the other hand, Ananias and Sapphira cherished money more than the vow that they had made before the Lord and the church, and God would not turn a blind eye. Today's world, driven as it is by materialism, superficiality, and greed, must see that Christians are driven by extravagant generosity and unselfish stewardship.

Relinquish privilege and possession for the sake of the gospel.

Christian Biography: Selina Hastings. Countess Selina Hastings (1707–91) was a person of privilege and status. Her father was the second earl of Ferrers; her grandfather was the speaker of the House of Commons; and she married the earl of Huntingdon. After her husband passed away when she was only thirty-nine, she fully committed her life to service. Rather than enjoying the luxury and status of an aristocrat's life, she used all her wealth, sold all of her jewelry and valuable possessions, and moved to a more modest home to support more than sixty chapels, a seminary, and the work of George Whitefield.[21]

Christians, of all people, must maintain high ethical standards.

News: As the summer of 2015 drew to a close, a major scandal erupted in the United States. A group of internet hackers had broken into the now notorious Ashley Madison website. This website had been designed to allow people to arrange extramarital affairs anonymously. By breaking through the security systems on the site, these hackers had discovered the true identities of those who had registered to be part of the "adultery pool" available for illicit hookups. The names and identities were published on the internet and became instant fodder for the kind of public shaming possible only in this age of social media. Heartbreakingly, it soon became clear that way too many of the names on the Ashley Madison list were those of pastors and ministry leaders (some sources claiming as many as four hundred pastors). A few very high-profile Christians were "outed" as well.

Our personal ethics are anything but private. As Christians, what we do speaks volumes about the authenticity of our message. We are called to be people of character so that the gospel is never mischaracterized by the failure of our witness.

Satan seeks to break Spirit-forged fellowship in the Christian community.

Human Metaphor: Those who live in cold-weather states know the frustration of winter ice storms and power outages. A serious storm can weigh down tree branches, leading to broken power lines. The result? The flow of electricity is interrupted, and whole communities can go days without it.

Satan loves to break the connection between believers in community. When he can achieve that, the flow of the Holy Spirit's power can be interrupted. The energy of a church on mission can be shut down, leaving the world around it dark.

Acts 4:32–5:11

Only the church that confronts great sin and its devastating consequences will survive.

Quote: **Dietrich Bonhoeffer.** Dietrich Bonhoeffer explains that the church cannot live in a "dream world" but that God is a God of truth. He challenges, "Only that fellowship which faces such disillusionment, with all its unhappy and ugly aspects, begins to be what it should be in God's sight, begins to grasp in faith the promise that is given to it. The sooner this shock of disillusionment comes to an individual and to a community the better for both. A community which cannot bear and cannot survive such a crisis, which insists upon keeping its illusion when it should be shattered, permanently loses in that moment the promise of Christian community. Sooner or later it will collapse."[22]

Signs and Wonders, and Persecution

Big Idea

All heavy-handed attempts to curb the spread of the gospel are doomed to fail.

Key Themes

- Divine power continues to work through the apostles.
- Obedience to God opens one up to persecution from human authorities.
- Angelic intervention illustrates God's control over a situation that seems to jeopardize his plans. Those who oppose the church are on a collision course with God.

Understanding the Text

The Text in Context

This text contains the third and last summary statement (5:12–16) recounting the remarkable success of the early church (cf. 2:42–47; 4:32–35). Signs and wonders win public acclaim for the apostles, but the divided response also continues. Many are drawn to the church; others are cautious. The temple leaders are jealous, which continues to feed their open hostility and attempts to suppress the movement.

Interpretive Insights

5:12 *many signs and wonders among the people.* Joel's prophecy, cited by Peter in 2:18–19, that the outpouring of the Spirit would lead to signs and wonders continues to be fulfilled. The phrase "signs and wonders" should remind the reader that the disciples do not work them through their own power but must rely entirely on the Holy Spirit for any success. The group that has gathered around the apostles has grown so that they now meet regularly in Solomon's Colonnade (cf. 3:11). It was a portico consisting of a roof supported by a row of double columns placed at regular intervals. It ran along the eastern wall of the temple and opened into the outer court. People could gather there in view of the sanctuary. It had nothing to do with Solomon's original temple, since nothing of that building survived, but the legendary connection to Solomon and the expensive architectural touches gave this space a sacred aura.

5:13–14 *No one else dared join them . . . Nevertheless, more and more men and women believed in the Lord and were added to their number.* Many increasingly recognize that becoming too closely associated with the church invites trouble from the authorities, who are becoming more and more nervous about the growth of this movement. Luke notes that people now keep the believers at arm's length but continue to admire them from a safe distance. It may be that their fear of the divine power in their midst (cf. 5:5, 11) also kept them at bay. Luke seems to contradict himself by saying that "no one else dared join them" and then that "more and more men and women believed in the Lord and were added to their number." Those who dare not associate too closely with the church are those afflicted by faintheartedness. They shrink from any commitment that might endanger their safety. Those who do join are willing to risk everything and to take up their cross and follow Jesus (Luke 14:27).

5:15–16 *people brought the sick into the streets and laid them on beds and mats so that at least Peter's shadow might fall on some of them as he passed by.* Even Peter's shadow becomes a conduit for God's healing power. Later, Luke will tell of the healing power working through Paul and how in extreme cases "that even handkerchiefs and aprons that had touched him were taken to the sick, and their illnesses were cured and the evil spirits left them" (19:12). Luke does not intend to convey that Peter's shadow possessed magical properties. During his ministry, Jesus called the Twelve together and gave them power and authority to drive out all demons and to cure diseases (Luke 9:1 [cf. 10:9]). That power and authority did not evaporate when Jesus ascended to heaven. This summary reveals that the same power that worked through Jesus to heal the crowds of people who came to hear him and be healed of their sicknesses (Luke 5:15; 6:18; 7:21) continues to work in and through his apostles. God heals those whom God wills through them. These healings should be interpreted through the lens of a similar miracle performed by Jesus. The woman with a hemorrhage for twelve years who touched the fringe of his garment was immediately healed (Luke 8:44). Jesus clarifies that it was her act of faith, not the enchanted power of the fringe, that made her well (Luke 8:48 [cf. 8:50]). It is the faith of those bringing their friends to Peter, not the magical properties of the shadow, that brings healing (cf. Luke 5:20).

5:17–18 *filled with jealousy.* The Sadducean cabal of high priests forms the heart of the opposition to Christians in Jerusalem. Since one is not jealous of someone contemptible, the leaders' envy ironically concedes the apostles' superiority. Putting Peter and John in prison overnight is an effort to tarnish their status with the people. Had these leaders not tried to mislead the people, even more would have responded favorably to the gospel. They are the blind leading the blind into the bottomless pit (Luke 6:39).

5:19–21 *an angel of the Lord opened the doors of the jail and brought them out.* The irony of this angelic breakout is that the Sadducees did not believe in angels (23:8).[1] The great escape does not mean that the apostles can scamper off to safety. They are set free only to fulfill their task to teach and preach (cf. Jer. 26:2) about the "new life" (5:20). "New life" is another synonym for "salvation." God will not allow this redemptive message to be throttled by religious or secular despots, spiritual powers, or maximum security prisons.

5:22–26 *The men you put in jail are standing in the temple courts teaching the people.* The captain of the temple guard and the chief priests are mystified by this escape and wondering what might grow out of it. They are so blinded that apparently it never occurs to them that this breakout was the work of God, that they are opposing God, and that they cannot resist God's word from breaking loose into the entire world.

The apostles do not try to give the authorities the slip and retreat to a hideout; instead, they return to teach in the temple courts in obedience to the angel's directive. They have no regard for their own safety, since the temple guard could easily find them and recapture them.

5:27–33 *We must obey God rather than human beings!* The apostles have a rematch with the Sanhedrin. Peter's speech emphasizes obedience, and the clear implication is that these religious leaders are *not* obeying God. Deuteronomy 28:1–14 contains a list of blessings for those who obey God, and then the text switches to a much lengthier list of curses for those who do not obey God (Deut. 28:15–68). The list of blessings generally has to do with material well-being. The greatest gift for believers who realize that they are living in the last days is the gift of the Holy Spirit bestowed on those who obey. Their obedience to God requires them to evangelize, and the Holy Spirit inspires them to do so boldly and without fear of the consequences.

The temple overseers have flouted God's commands, and the threat in Deuteronomy 28:20 will come true: "The LORD will send on you curses, confusion and rebuke in everything you put your hand to, until you are destroyed and come to sudden ruin because of the evil you have done in forsaking him." They defied God by executing his Son, but their intrigues were futile. Hanged on a tree, Jesus is not accursed of God as his enemies assumed (Deut. 21:22–23; Gal. 3:13). God overruled their villainy by exalting Jesus to his right hand. Jesus's death, not the temple sacrifices, offers the forgiveness of sins to those who call on him as their Savior (Acts 2:21, 38). The temple, which serves as the headquarters for the leaders' iniquity, will be destroyed, as will they themselves. It is not only a necessity to obey God rather than human authorities; it is a much wiser choice.

5:34–39 *if their purpose or activity is of human origin, it will fail. But if it is from God, you will not be able to stop these men; you will only find yourselves fighting against God.* Gamaliel, a well-respected expert in the law and a Pharisee, has a hunch that Jesus's followers might be doing the will and work of God. He admonishes his colleagues with a lesson from recent history and ends with the theological axiom that those who resist God's will meet their downfall. Luke is not interested in Gamaliel's motives for defending the apostles, only this theological assertion. The Greek verb for "fail" in the phrase "it will fail" is in the passive voice and can be translated "it will be overthrown" (ASV). God is the implied agent who will overthrow the enemies.

5:40–42 *The apostles left the Sanhedrin, rejoicing because they had been counted worthy of suffering disgrace for the Name.* Jesus had warned that his followers would be subject to scourging (Mark 13:9), and the flogging presumably was the thirty-nine lashes administered to those deemed to be rebellious (cf. 2 Cor. 11:24). This brutal punishment does not have the desired effect. The disciples do not become despondent over their ill-treatment but rejoice over the privilege of suffering on behalf of Christ (cf. Luke 6:23). Their proclamation now extends beyond the temple and goes house to house.

Teaching the Text

1. *The futile plotting of opponents of the gospel will always come to nothing even though the proclaimers of the gospel may suffer grievously.* The fuming leaders are primarily concerned with politics, not theology, and want to murder rather than ponder. Their rage contrasts with the apostles' calm in the face of deadly threats. A prison cannot keep the gospel in check. Even threatening God's messengers with death cannot stymie the spread of the gospel.

2. *Gamaliel's open-mindedness may seem to be commendable, but when one is confronted with the gospel, a wait-and-see approach is dangerous.* If one waits too long, it will be too late. Gamaliel is not a secret disciple. He "studiously" avoids the name of Jesus,[2] and his pupil Saul (22:3) does not wait and see but zealously joins the persecution of the church (8:1–3; 9:1–2). The purpose of Gamaliel's speech for Luke is to make the following points. First, as one who is held in honor by the people, Gamaliel's advocacy adds weight to the apostles' high esteem among the populace.[3] Second, the reader can infer from the reference to the abortive rebellions against Roman rule led by Judas the Galilean and Theudas that Jesus is not another failed revolutionary prophet. Christianity's continued success confirms that it is not a flash in the pan that will soon die out but is from God.[4]

3. *The opponents of the Christian faith do not recognize that they hang by a precarious thread.* In seeking to destroy Christians, they lay the groundwork for their own destruction. When assaulted by those seeking to destroy them, true Christians do not back off or bemoan their fate but rejoice over being counted worthy to suffer for Jesus. They will obey God rather than human tyrants, no matter the cost, because the cost of not obeying God is infinitely greater. It is difficult for humans to regard the pain of tribulations as a reason to rejoice. The community's joy flows from a changed perspective, knowing that the Lord tests the hearts of his people in the same way that gold and silver are tested in a crucible (Prov. 17:3). God's remnant will be purified through their difficulties (Isa. 48:10–11), and their redeemer will carry them through the fire of troubles and bring them out to a place of abundance (Ps. 66:12).

Illustrating the Text

Believers can rejoice in suffering.

Church History: Dietrich Bonhoeffer wrote, "Satan knows that the flesh is afraid of suffering." But empowered by the Holy Spirit, the disciples do not ask, "Why is this happening to us?" They rejoice instead (cf. James 1:2–4). One man who endured severe persecution in a South American torture cellar said that all Christian doctrines disappeared then. The only thing that sustained him during this time was the knowledge that Jesus had also been on the wrong side of a whip and that Jesus was with him.[5]

God is willing to use regular people to achieve supernatural results.

Television: Have you ever watched the X Games or *American Ninja Warrior*? It is incredible to watch these extreme athletes do things that seem simply impossible. Some drive dirt bikes off thirty-foot-high ramps, turning backflips, clicking heels, letting go and simply flying through the air with the bike beneath them. The "ninja warriors" throw themselves off trampolines, catch ropes, climb walls that appear nearly flat, and hop across shaky platforms with frigid water waiting below. It all looks impossible, but they do it.

In the kingdom of God, we are invited to be part of something more amazing than anything accomplished in these extreme sports: the transformation of lives. We're invited to be part of seeing people who are spiritually dead begin to live and breathe again. It's an astonishing privilege to live a life that can only be explained by God! Major Ian Thomas, founder of Torchbearers Bible schools, challenged, "The Christian life can be explained only in terms of Jesus Christ, and if your life as a Christian can still be explained in terms of *you—your* personality, *your* will-power, *your* gift, *your* talent, *your* money, *your* courage, *your* scholarship, *your* dedication, *your* sacrifice, or *your* anything—then although you may have the Christian life, you are not yet living it!"[6]

Obedience to God, even in the face of imprisonment, persecution, and suffering

Church History: The Japanese took control over Korea in 1937. During the time of Japanese occupation, many Korean Christians endured harsh persecution if they maintained their allegiance to Christ. Esther Ahn was a music teacher who was imprisoned and tortured for her Christian beliefs. When she was questioned by the superintendent of the Pyongyang police station, he demanded to know what she thought about the state and the worship at the shrine. Knowing that she could be immediately killed for her beliefs, she testified, "I shall never break His commandment, even if I might be killed for it. Because His commandments reveal His love for us, I can't offend God. The law of God stands above the law of any state." She later reflected, "I was excited. If I should be sentenced to death for this, it would mean that the task of my life was accomplished. I had only to speak boldly, calmly, freely, and clearly, as Jesus would have done." After being punished for her beliefs, she "began to think that life might be worth living in this time of persecution. It might even be a truer picture of the believers to agonize, to suffer, to be hated and tortured, and even to be killed in obeying God's words rather than to live an ordinary, uneventful life."[7] Eventually her life was spared, and she was freed.

The Appointment of the Seven

Big Idea

The Holy Spirit resolves dissension in the church as its leaders act to restore unity that is essential to its growth.

Key Themes

- No one is to be overlooked as unimportant, and all are to be cared for in the church fellowship.
- Those who are chosen to be leaders should understand themselves to be servants of the community.
- The preaching and teaching ministry is not limited to the Twelve. Others, led by the Spirit and attested by the church, can preach and teach as well.

Understanding the Text

The Text in Context

This unit is set off by an emphasis on the church's growth with the verb "increase" appearing at the beginning in 6:1 and at the end in 6:7. The increased membership brings new problems. Luke has emphasized the togetherness as a crucial aspect of the community's life from the beginning (2:42–47), and one can assume that he presents it as a model for his readers to emulate. The enormous response to the apostles' preaching means that the growing church no longer is composed of those who came from the same area, socioeconomic background, and linguistic heritage. Greek culture had penetrated the Palestinian world since the conquests of Alexander. Nearly all Jews during this period spoke some Greek, but the Hellenistic Jews from the Diaspora spoke *only* Greek and did not know Hebrew or Aramaic, the mother tongue of the disciples. It is possible that the "'hellenists' probably found participation in the (Aramaic) worship of the original disciple-group difficult, and started to develop as a more independent community."[1] The church's togetherness comes under threat. The tightly knit group is beginning to show signs of unraveling.

This clash, under God's providence, leads to the transfer of authority to new figures who will play a significant role in the growth of the church's mission. The solution for maintaining the church's unity by commissioning Hellenist deacons to assist the apostles provides an impetus to the gentile mission. This passage serves as preparation for the story to move to the next stages in the narrative, from the mission in Jerusalem to the mission into Samaria and into the gentile world.

Interpretive Insights

6:1 *the Hellenistic Jews among them complained against the Hebraic Jews because their widows were being overlooked in the daily distribution of food.* Luke portrays widows as particularly prone to be destitute and defenseless (Luke 2:36–38; 7:11–17; 18:1–8; 21:1–4), and they along with orphans and resident aliens belong to a group that God commands be given special protection (Deut. 16:11; Mal. 3:5). Hellenistic widows were likely to be doubly in need of support, cut off from their former kinship networks or family members who may have rebuffed them when they became believers. Goods have been laid at the feet of the apostles for distribution to those in the community who are in need. The church's joyful unity and generous sharing of resources are temporarily interrupted when murmurings arise over inequities in the assistance of Hellenistic widows.

Luke does not explain why or how they were overlooked. It is unlikely that it was rooted in theological differences or prejudice over cultural differences. They may not have been integrated in the daily distribution because they were part of an autonomous community of worshipers that had not developed the same level of organization to help their needy. The apostles are not so preoccupied with teaching and preaching that they ignore widows (9:36–43), but they need additional help to carry out all of their tasks (cf. Exod. 18:13–23; Deut. 1:9–18) and to minister to an increasingly diverse church.

6:2–4 *So the Twelve gathered all the disciples together and said, ". . . choose seven men from among you who are known to be full of the Spirit and wisdom."* The apostles take action to redress the concerns. Believers are described as "disciples" for the first time in Acts so that the term is expanded beyond those who followed Jesus during his earthly ministry. Luke does not intend to imply that waiting on tables was beneath the Twelve (cf. Luke 22:26–27) but emphasizes that the apostles were specifically called to the ministry of preaching and teaching (1:8) and to underscore the vital importance of that task.

6:5–6 *They chose Stephen, a man full of faith and of the Holy Spirit; also Philip, Procorus, Nicanor, Timon, Parmenas, and Nicolas from Antioch, a convert to Judaism.* The church body, not the apostles, chooses these men, discerning that they are full of the Spirit and wisdom. The number "seven" has no special significance here and serves only as a round number (cf. Josh. 6:4; Esther 1:14; Jer. 52:25). Their names reveal that they were Hellenists. Ostensibly, they were chosen to serve tables, but Stephen and Philip are singled out in the narrative to follow for playing a key role in the next stage of the church's expansion. Nicolas is identified as a proselyte, a convert to Judaism, which prepares the way for those who were not born Jews to join the church. That he hails from Antioch is important. The church there is started and endorsed by people from Jerusalem. It would become the bridgehead for the mission into the gentile world and later commission Paul and Barnabas along with others for this ministry.

The laying on of hands in this context is not a formal rite of ordination into an office but a commissioning for a task.[2] The Greek text could imply that the apostles or the whole group laid hands on the men.[3] It did not transfer apostolic power so much as publicly ratify the choice of these men and confer on them the apostles' blessing.

6:7 *So the word of God spread. The number of disciples in Jerusalem increased rapidly, and a large number of priests became obedient to the faith.* The Greek verb for "increased" also appears in 6:1, and its usage enfolds this account and reveals its emphasis. "The word of God" is portrayed as a dynamic power that grows of its own accord. The gospel's growth is no longer due solely to the preaching of Peter and John and other members of the Twelve; the seven men and many others, who remain anonymous, extend its impact.

The "priests" who become believers are not the Sadducean priests, who belong to the wealthy aristocracy that violently opposes the movement. They come from the large number of poorer priests, like Zechariah (Luke 1:5–23), who lived in the area.

Theological Insights

The church cannot be allowed to break up into different caucuses. If the problem was caused by discrimination, the church learns to be tolerant of cultural differences. If the problem was caused by a language barrier, the church addresses it through setting up a stronger administration of the charity (cf. 1 Tim. 5:3–16).

Teaching the Text

1. *All who believe in Christ receive unconditional acceptance in the fellowship of believers.* The earliest church experienced growth problems, and Luke describes the leaders quickly taking action to find solutions. It is easy for those who speak a different language and come from a different culture to

be ignored because these differences create communication difficulties. That problem is compounded if they worship in a different setting. This incident reveals how the Christian community is sensitive to the danger of creating second-class members who may be out of sight and therefore out of mind. The church solves this problem through prayer and the Spirit-led discernment of the entire fellowship.

The apostles recognize that they cannot meet all the demands on their time and energy. They understand that successful ministry requires a team effort and a division of labor. An effective, principled infrastructure is vital to the spread of the gospel. This account is often appealed to in services related to the ordination of deacons. It does not, however, describe the origin of the diaconate. The noun "deacon" (*diakonos*) does not occur in the text, only the cognate noun "service" (*diakonia*), which is translated as "distribution" (6:1), and the cognate verb "serving" (*diakoneō*), which is translated as "wait on" (6:2). The task that was given to these seven men did not have a "formal name" and was not a formal office.[4] The account portrays the corporate recognition of leadership gifts and the spiritual depth of these men and a commissioning of them to exercise those gifts within the church, in this case, performing a charitable service on behalf of the congregation. Their authority and spiritual power reside not in official titles or offices but in their effective ministry to others. They also are servants not of the church members but of Jesus Christ who serve others in obedience to him.

2. *The apostles convey authority to other significant leaders in the church.* The church body as a whole chose these men, and the apostles laid hands on them to bless them for this ministry. A similar commissioning occurs in the church at Antioch, where the church, with no apostles present, chose men who were already involved in prophecy and teaching and proven in their ministry. They "placed their hands on them and sent them off" to new fields of mission (13:1–3). Their apostolic power springs from the Holy Spirit, not from human institutions, however sanctified they might be.

The men are singled out for being "full of the Spirit and wisdom" (6:3), but the church does not have a spiritual Geiger counter to detect these vital attributes. Churches can gain spiritual discernment in choosing leaders only through prayer, worshiping together, and observing persons in action.

3. *Serving the word of God is contrasted with waiting on tables, but Luke does not intend to create a dichotomy between preaching the word and caring for the poor.* Luke emphasizes that the church feeds the hungry and takes care of the needs of the poor, but it does not do this to the exclusion of preaching the gospel. Good preaching cannot stand alone; it also requires good administration and good shepherding, such as caring for widows. Likewise, social ministry cannot stand alone. In the narrative that follows, two of the appointed

seven, Stephen and Philip, do exactly what the apostles do: they devote themselves to the ministry of the word (6:4). They are known not for their table service but for their evangelizing. Service to the poor in helping with the daily distribution does not rule out preaching to others. Peter exhorts Christians to exercise their gifts as good managers of God's diverse gifts: "Whoever speaks must do so as one speaking the very words of God; whoever serves must do so with the strength that God supplies, so that God may be glorified in all things through Jesus Christ" (1 Pet. 4:11 NRSV). Having the gift of speaking does not exclude one from also having the gift of service, and vice versa. From what follows in the narrative in Acts, it is clear that Stephen also had a powerful gift of speaking. The manifold gifts that God gives to individuals in the church gave rise to the development of specialized responsibilities and positions in the church, and the goal is solely to bring glory to God.

The Hellenists are an interesting force in the movement of the gospel. They were fully aware of God's presence and power outside the nationalistic confines of the temple and Jerusalem. They were possibly more liberal in their approaches to mission as the first to break through the boundaries that had been erected between Jews and other peoples. In doing so, they received the greatest hostility. With fewer local ties to shield them, they were soon hounded by their fellow Jews.

Illustrating the Text

Dealing with conflict is part of leadership.

Applying the Text: Most ministers are ready for success and growth, but few are prepared for breakdown and opposition. No matter how successful a ministry is, the minister will have to deal with conflict and division at one time or another. A. W. Tozer advises, "Church difficulties are spiritual also and admit of a spiritual answer. Whatever may be wrong in the life of any church may be cleared up by recognizing the quality of the trouble and dealing with it at the root. Prayer, humility and a generous application of the Spirit of Christ will cure just about any disease in the body of believers."[5]

Empowering those closest to a problem often provides the best solution.

Quote: Dennis Bakke. Bakke is a former CEO who advocates for egalitarian structures in the workplace that encourage worker autonomy and allow for collective self-supervision. He observes, "There is an intrinsic organizational assumption that mistakes or problems could be avoided if high-ranking people made all the decisions. But more often than not, lower-ranking people are closer to the problem and better positioned to come up with a solution, especially if they seek advice from their colleagues"[6]

There are no unimportant people in the church.

Classic Sermon: "No Little People, No Little Places," by Francis Schaeffer. In this sermon, Schaeffer uses Moses's staff as an eloquent metaphor for what every life can be. He describes Moses carrying this six-foot piece of wood around with him in the wilderness, the most mundane and taken-for-granted possession that he had. Yet when Moses, standing before the burning bush, wondered how in the world he would be able to convince Pharaoh to let God's people go, God asked, "What is that in your hand?" (Exod. 4:2). For the rest of his life, Moses's simple staff was simultaneously *God's* staff. Schaeffer concludes: "Consider the mighty ways in which God used a dead stick of wood. . . . Though we are limited and weak in talent, physical energy, and psychological strength, we are not less than a stick of wood. But as the rod of Moses had to become the rod of God, so that which is *me* must become the *me* of God. Then I can become useful in God's hands. The Scripture emphasizes that much can come from little if the little is truly consecrated to God. There are no little people and no big people in the true spiritual sense, but only consecrated and unconsecrated people. The problem for each of us is applying this truth to ourselves."[7]

Future leaders always begin as faithful servants.

Christian Biography: Hudson Taylor. Taylor was summoned to visit the home of an impoverished family. He was faced with a poor man who had a sick wife and six small children, including an infant who was only two days old. Taylor was called to pray for the ill wife, but he had difficulty praying because he was unwilling to give his own money to help the family. The father was desperate, and he was disappointed by the lack of help from God and from this man of God. Later, the father approached Taylor again, begging for help, "If you can help us, for God's sake, do!" Taylor was convicted by God to surrender his last coin to save this family. Years later, he reflected that this one experience helped him to be a great leader even during times of great trial. He confesses, "If we are faithful to GOD in little things, we shall gain experience and strength that will be helpful to us in the more serious trials of life."[8]

Stephen's Arrest and Speech

Big Idea

Throughout Israel's history God has been at work salvaging good from the evil deeds of a disobedient people and rescuing them from disasters, yet they continue to rebel.

Key Themes

- God's dealings with Israel are marked by promises and fulfillments, but also by turning away because of the people's disobedience.
- The people have always been divided between those who respond obediently to God's chosen servants and the disobedient who repeatedly oppose, persecute, and murder them.
- God's reign is universal, and worship of God cannot be confined to the Jerusalem temple.

Understanding the Text

The Text in Context

Stephen's speech and martyrdom mark the transition from the mission to the inhabitants in Jerusalem to the mission to those outside of Jerusalem, starting with the Samaritans. It is the longest speech in Acts as Stephen does not rebut the accusations against him but turns the prisoner's dock into a pulpit in which he upbraids his accusers. His speech levels the ground theologically for the inclusion of gentiles into God's people.

Interpretive Insights

6:8–13 *Stephen, a man full of God's grace and power, performed great wonders and signs among the people. Opposition arose, however.* The miracles done by Stephen do not provoke opposition, but his teaching, presumably in this particular synagogue, does. "Freedmen" were those who had been set free from slavery by their masters, and the term also might be applied to their sons. Unlike the church in Jerusalem, which strives to be united, the synagogues in Jerusalem apparently were organized and divided along provincial, social, and cultural lines. As devout Jews who returned from various points in the Diaspora to live in Jerusalem, they would be particularly upset at Stephen's message challenging the validity of the temple. These Hellenistic Jews are united in their militant opposition to Stephen and now begin to stir up hostility against him.

Jesus promised that he would give words and wisdom to his followers that their opponents could not refute (Luke 21:15). Stephen's antagonists can only misrepresent his teaching and accuse him of blasphemy, punishable by death (Lev. 24:11–16). They suborn false witnesses who claim that they heard him attacking the core values of Jewish life and its heritage. He is brought up on charges of denigrating Moses, God, the temple, and the law and subverting Jewish customs.[1]

6:15 *the face of an angel.* Luke intends to picture Stephen as radiating not a sweet, cherubic visage but one that is aflame from being so near to God's presence. His face reflects God's glory (cf. Exod. 34:29–35), and he speaks with the blistering voice of a prophet.

7:1–6 *The God of glory appeared to our father Abraham while he was still in Mesopotamia.* Inspired by the Spirit, Stephen rehearses crucial junctures in Israel's history that are tied to individual persons beginning with Abraham, the principal recipient of God's promises.[2] God first revealed himself in full glory to Abraham in Mesopotamia, *outside* the promised land, to call him, and Abraham obediently answered. It led him to become a rambler moving from one place to another, but God was with him and continued to reveal his plans to him. God promised a son to childless Abraham and land to landless Abraham. The first promise was fulfilled during Abraham's lifetime, though so late it seemed impossible. The second promise was not fulfilled during his lifetime. The promise of land was just that, a promise, and it seemed to have been breached when the patriarchs landed in Egypt. His descendants would become aliens, oppressed and enslaved for four hundred years in a country not their own. But as John Polhill comments, "The real goal of God's promise to Abraham was not the land at all. It was instead the freedom to render true worship and devotion to God. Stephen would go on to show that even the temple had not realized this purpose. The promise remains yet unfulfilled. It is only fulfilled in Christ."[3]

7:7 *they will come out of that country and worship me in this place.* The phrase promising that they will come to worship God "in this place" as the goal of the exodus derives from Exodus 3:12. It is affixed to a quotation from Genesis 15:13–14 that alters its emphasis. Genesis 15:14 ends with the promise "they will come out with great possessions." Instead of coming out with great possessions, they came out with a greater purpose to worship God at a certain place. In the context of Exodus, "this place" refers not to Mount Zion but to this mountain, Mount Sinai. It conveys that at the most significant stage of Israel's history, when God gave them the law, they worshiped God without a temple. In fact, they worshiped God for around four hundred years without a temple.

7:8 *Then he gave Abraham the covenant of circumcision.* God fulfilled the promise to Abraham with the birth of Isaac and sealed it with the covenant of circumcision when he was still transient and outside the promised land.

7:9–16 *Because the patriarchs were jealous of Joseph, they sold him as a slave into Egypt.* The mention of Joseph and the patriarchs marks the second epoch and continues the theme of the wandering people of God (conflating Gen. 23:1–20; 25:9–10; 33:19; 50:13). Joseph was rejected by his jealous brothers (cf. Acts 17:5) in the promised land, but God did not abandon him. While he was in Egypt, God worked mightily through him, and he acted to save his brothers when famine struck. This unit mentions four trips away from the promised land to Egypt and concludes with the burial of all the patriarchs with Abraham in Shechem, in the land of the hated Samaritans near Mount Gerizim, their sacred temple. This detail sets up the inclusion of Samaritans who respond to the gospel in the next chapter.

7:17–37 *This is the Moses who told the Israelites, "God will raise up a prophet like me from your own people."* These verses cover three forty-year phases of Moses in Egypt and Sinai: Moses's birth and time in Egypt (7:17–22), Moses's rejection by the people and his flight to Midian (7:23–29), and God's appearance to him in Midian that sends him back to Egypt to redeem the people (7:30–38). The emphasis falls on Israel's rejection of Moses (7:27–29, 35, 39).

A christological theme emerges in 7:37, which reminds the audience that God promised to "raise up for you a prophet like [Moses] from your own people" (cf. Deut. 18:15). Stephen interprets it as a reference to Jesus. He assumes that Moses pointed beyond himself and the revelation that came to him to another whom God would raise up in the future. Israel must give heed to that one and cannot "limit divine revelation and redemption to the confines of the Mosaic law."[4] Stephen also expresses christological content by referring to the coming one with the titles "ruler and deliverer" (7:35), "Righteous One" (7:52), and "Lord" (7:59–60).

7:38–43 *our ancestors refused to obey him.* Despite their deliverance from Egypt and the miracles at Mount Sinai, the people doubted their leader, yearned for the good old days of slavery back in Egypt, and ordered Aaron to make them a golden calf to lead them. Stephen does not ask how they could shift so quickly from the one who redeemed them to outright pagan idolatry, but he implies that it follows a depressing pattern and sets the stage for the exile in Babylon. He implies that his accusers are the spiritual heirs of these wayward Israelites and face the same danger that God will turn away from them.

7:44–50 *However, the Most High does not live in houses made by human hands.* The tabernacle was built according to the pattern God showed to Moses on Sinai, and it symbolized God's presence during the conquest of the promised land. Joshua, David, and Solomon are mentioned in a brief summary. The building of the temple by Solomon would seem to be the culmination of the promises. Stephen subverts this milestone by citing the prophet Isaiah: God does not dwell in houses "made by human hands." This phrase is used to condemn pagan idols (7:41).[5] The temple is likened to an idol and could not be the fulfillment of God's promise. God cannot and will not be sequestered in some human edifice.

Theological Insights

Stephen daringly attacks the fatal theological delusions of his audience. He undermines the importance of the holy land and the national shrine, the temple, by affirming that God can get along fine without either and that he has done so. The quotation from Isaiah 66 emphasizes that God's hands have made everything and also implies that the whole world is in God's hands. Therefore God cannot be confined to one people, one land, or one cultic worship center.

Teaching the Text

1. *Stephen's outline of Israel's history teaches about God's true dwelling place.* He concentrates on Israel's experience of God's presence outside the land of Judea, the period prior to the settlement in the promised land and before Jerusalem became the national and religious capital. This addresses important questions: Where did God's glory appear (7:2)? Where does God dwell (7:48)? The answers require a proper reading of the Scriptures, which reveals that God never had been rigidly bound to the land, Jerusalem, or the temple. The implication is that the current movement of God's Spirit will also not be bound to the land, to Jerusalem, or to the temple.

2. *In rehearsing biblical history, Stephen highlights that when God works a mighty work, the family of Israel divides between those who are open to God's pioneering spirit and those who want to circle the wagons.* One segment of the people has consistently rejected those selected by God to lead them. A direct line of apostasy is drawn from Israel's rejection of Moses for the tangible idolatry of the golden calf (7:39–41) to the worship of planetary powers resulting in the exile (7:42–43) to the present idolatry of the temple (7:48–50). Stephen attacks his nemeses as belonging to the

camp that rejects the work of God's hands and reveres instead the work of their own hands.

3. *Stephen contrasts the tabernacle with the temple.* The tabernacle was used in the time of the wilderness when the congregation received the living oracles and the angel of the presence was with them (7:38). It provided no permanent place of worship during Israel's golden age (7:46). The conclusion is that God does not have a resting place like a temple, a static edifice, which has become an immovable, petrified tent.

This text should cause us to reexamine the institutions we regard as sacrosanct. Is it all show, all leaves and no fruit (cf. Mark 11:13–14)? Are the leaders corrupt, intent on furthering their own careers and reputations and feathering their own nests? Does it offer people a false security? Does it allow people to get away with ritual repentance that never affects the heart and how they live? Has it become a source of pride, fostering the belief that the people have a monopoly on God? Is it something that separates us from others and bestows special status only on the elite? If the gospel is to reach to the ends of the earth, sacred cows that hinder God's often surprising purposes must be cast aside.

Illustrating the Text

Christians do not have the right to remain silent.

Scenario: In the United States, the law requires that anyone who has been arrested be read his or her "Miranda" rights by the police, a process often dramatized in the media. A police officer nabs a culprit and runs through the litany of rights: "You have the right to remain silent. . . ." When Christians are delivered up for their faith, they do *not* have the right to remain silent. Instead, they have the privilege of speaking the truth to their persecutors. The episode of Stephen's stoning shows how dangerous that can be.

Jesus warned his disciples that they would be hated by all for his name's sake and would be handed over for trial. He comforted them that when this happens, they need not worry about what to say. He encouraged them not to fret about giving a feeble testimony by assuring them that he would give them "words and wisdom that none of [their] adversaries [would] be able to resist or contradict" (Luke 21:15). Stephen's sermon in the face of a lynch mob is a perfect example of the fulfillment of Jesus's promise.

The history of the Jewish people serves as background for the good news of Jesus Christ.

Bible: Many people skip over the genealogy in Matthew 1:1–17. They quickly glance at the long list of names and begin their meditations with the story of

Jesus's birth, which begins in the second half of the chapter. But people fail to recognize the spiritual value and lesson of carefully examining the names listed in the genealogy. The record of the genealogy tells the story of God's faithfulness to the Jewish people that led to the birth of their Messiah. God upheld his covenant with the patriarchs—Abraham, Isaac, and Jacob (1:2–3). He honored the faithfulness of Tamar, Rahab, and Ruth (1:3, 5). He upheld his promises to Kings David and Solomon (1:6–7). Despite the exile to Babylon (1:12) and evil kings, God did not forget or abandon his people and sent the Messiah. A retrospect of Jewish history is the background for the coming of Jesus and the call to turn to him.

Stephen's Martyrdom

Big Idea

The enraged crowd stones Stephen to death, and a deadly campaign of persecution follows.

Key Themes

- Mob passion rears its ugly head to stone Stephen.
- Stephen imitates Jesus in his death in asking God to forgive his murderers and uttering a final cry for God to receive his spirit.
- Saul/Paul is introduced as supporting Stephen's execution and carrying out a crusade to destroy the church.

Understanding the Text

The Text in Context

Stephen had been charged with speaking against this holy place, the temple, and his accusers' holy theology with all of its implications. He does not retract his proclamation of the truth but instead goes on the attack, connecting almost every major episode in Israel's history to his criticism of the current state of affairs. His enemies who combat his message are "fighting against God" (5:39) and are not the true heirs of God's promises. His denunciation results in this lynch mob boiling over with rage. Stephen is killed, but his death leads to the movement of God's Spirit beyond Jerusalem.

Interpretive Insights

7:51–53 *You stiff-necked people! Your heart and ears are still uncircumcised. . . . You always resist the Holy Spirit!* In contrast to the other sermons in Acts, Stephen's speech ends in an indictment rather than an invitation. Stephen nails his audience for being "stiff-necked," those who reject God's will (Exod. 32:9; 33:3, 5); being "uncircumcised" in heart and ears, those who ignore God's word (Lev. 26:41; Jer. 6:10); resisting the Holy Spirit, those who reject God's leading (Isa. 63:10); assassinating the prophets sent to them; and worse, murdering the promised Righteous One, Jesus (Luke 23:47; Acts

Angels and the Law

A widespread view in Judaism was that the law was delivered by angels (7:38, 53; Heb. 2:2; *Jub.* 2:1; Josephus, *Ant.* 15.5.3 §136). Paul uses this belief to argue that God does not use brokers or mediators to accomplish his great works and that the law represents a compromise situation. Therefore, the promise is more significant than the giving of the law (Gal. 3:19–20).

3:14). They may revere the customs of Moses as given by angels, but they do not keep the law (7:53).

Throughout his speech, Stephen speaks of "our ancestors" (7:2, 11, 12, 15, 19, 38, 44, 45). Now, he divorces himself from the audience when he accuses them of being like those who murdered the prophets and killed the Righteous One. All sinners, not just this generation of Jews, are guilty of Jesus's death, and the only way to escape the consequences of this shame is to become his follower.

7:54 *When the members of the Sanhedrin heard this, they were furious and gnashed their teeth at him.* The reaction to Stephen's harangue is venomous. Those who gnash their teeth are the wicked who resist God and God's messengers (Pss. 35:16; 37:12; 112:10; Lam. 2:16). If they continue to be impenitent, they will gnash their teeth again when they see Abraham, Isaac, and Jacob, all the prophets, and people from east and west and north and south feasting together in the kingdom of God but they are barred from this banquet (Luke 13:28–29).

7:55–56 *But Stephen, full of the Holy Spirit, looked up to heaven and saw the glory of God, and Jesus standing at the right hand of God.* Stephen, filled with the Holy Spirit, sees the Son of Man standing at the right hand of God. This vision of God's glory carefully balances with the glory of God at the beginning of the speech in 7:2 and marks it off as a unit. Stephen's vision confirms his point that God dwells not in temples made by human hands but in heaven. It also reveals that "worship of the God of glory from now on includes worship of Jesus standing beside him as risen lord, the vindicated Son of Man, fulfilling the vision of Daniel" (cf. Dan. 7:13–14).[1]

7:57–58 *they . . . dragged him out of the city and began to stone him.* Stephen's broadside against his accusers does not cut them to the heart as Peter's sermon to the Pentecost crowds did (2:37). Instead, their hearts are filled with rage (cf. 5:33). They cover their ears that Stephen had just described as "uncircumcised." They haul him out of the city (as was done to Jesus at his crucifixion) to stone him. The lynch mob ironically substantiates the accusation that they are of the same ilk as their ancestors who persecuted and murdered the prophets.

7:59–60 *Lord, do not hold this sin against them.* Peter and John were almost killed; Stephen does not escape being killed. In the throes of death, Stephen imitates Jesus even as he worships him. He echoes Jesus's actions and words as he faced death. He kneels down to pray as Jesus did in Gethsemane (Luke 22:41). His prayer for God to receive his spirit parallels Jesus's prayer at his death (Luke 23:46). He cries out in a loud voice as he dies as Jesus did on the cross (Luke 23:46), and he pleads for the forgiveness of his killers as Jesus did (Luke 23:34). Stephen models what it means to follow Jesus (Luke 9:23; 14:27). His killers take up stones to take life. Stephen is an example of one who hates "even their own life" and is willing to take up a cross as Jesus's disciple (Luke 14:26–27).

8:1–3 *On that day a great persecution broke out against the church in Jerusalem.* Stephen's martyrdom affords an introduction to Saul, a young law student from Tarsus in Cilicia (21:39) who approvingly witnesses his death. He is introduced in the narrative so abruptly that Luke must assume that his audience already knows who he is. They would know that through the transformative power of the Spirit, he would turn into a great missionary spreading the gospel far and wide. Ironically, he will face the same bitter hostility from a mob in Jerusalem that Stephen faced (21:26–30). Before that occurs, his fanatic loyalty to the law leads him to try to destroy what he regards to be an insidious blasphemy that proclaims a crucified man as the Messiah of Israel and the Son of God. Perhaps he belongs to those from Cilicia along with those from Cyrene, Alexandria, and Asia who stood up to argue with Stephen but could not "stand up against the wisdom the Spirit gave him as he spoke" (6:9–10). This new movement undermines the distinctive features of Jewish national and religious identity that make Jews God's most-favored people. They cannot beat him with arguments, so they overpower him with this violent attack. The later miraculous transformation of Saul from persecutor to missionary reveals that they are up against a far greater divine power that never resorts to violence to prevail. The church will not be destroyed, and Jesus's promise, like the promises of God throughout Scripture, will not fail. The witness to the gospel will spread beyond Jerusalem throughout Judea and Samaria and to the ends of the earth (1:8).

Theological Insights

After his resurrection, Jesus pledged that his disciples would soon receive power. Stephen is described as being "full of God's grace and power" (6:8), but that did not make him invincible. He had only the power to preach in the worst of circumstances with him staring death in the face and the power to forgive those pelting him with stones.

Teaching the Text

1. *Challenging those who are stiff-necked and callous is dangerous but necessary.* When such people get riled, they inevitably strike back. Most persons therefore would prefer to play it safe by avoiding them altogether or by giving them innocuous, candy-coated sermons that will not rouse their fury. Love does not turn away from the hard-hearted or cower before their wrathful opposition. God's herald must confront them with their sin even though doing so may result in death. Stephen speaks fearlessly in hopes that some might be won over. Perhaps there is a Paul in the audience who, though breathing threats and murder, may yet submit to God.

Luke notes that when a great persecution arose against the church, all were scattered except the apostles. Why did the apostles not leave or have to leave? Was it because they were less offensive? Hardly. Peter and John have been threatened with death. James will be executed, and Peter again imprisoned. This instance of persecution was specifically directed against the Hellenists, but the apostles stayed in the city even when it was dangerous so that they might continue to teach. It is possible that they were mindful of the prophetic confidence that the nations would march to Jerusalem[2] and worship there.[3] Any influx of natives from foreign lands to Jerusalem would find faithful Christians present who could teach them the gospel, and they could return to their homes, as the Ethiopian eunuch did (8:39), with the gospel.

2. *Stephen's concluding words, "You stiff-necked people! Your hearts and ears are still uncircumcised," do not seem to be the best way to end a sermon.* The vitriol strikes one as unloving. Stephen is not demonizing his opponents, but, like the prophets before him, he tries to give his audience a wake-up call using the strongest language. As life ebbs from his battered body, Stephen cries out to God to forgive these hard-hearted murderers for this deed. He dies a seemingly powerless death, but his assailants could not repress the power of his testimony. After every violent attack on the Christians for their preaching, they get up to continue their preaching, or, if they do not get up again, others show up to take their place. It is a strange proof of the power and resilience of the gospel that will not be suppressed.

Can everyone whose violent death stems from his or her religious convictions be labeled a martyr? In our day, we have seen those who commit violent acts of terrorism called "martyrs" by their coreligionists. In dying for their cause, they try to kill as many other innocent people as possible and are hailed as laudable martyrs who will receive special rewards in the afterlife for their sacrifice. But these deaths are not noble deaths. Stephen's death gives a true picture of what martyrdom means from a Christian perspective. Stephen did not cower before his enemies or comply with their demands, but neither did he strike out against them with physical force resulting in carnage. Instead, he confronted his enemies, as Jesus had, nonviolently, with the powerful words of the gospel. He was willing to accept death at their hands rather than yield to their hostile threats. What is distinctly Christian about his martyrdom is that he prays for God to forgive those who have wronged him and will kill him. The door remains open for them to repent.

3. *Striking parallels exist between the Synoptic accounts of Jesus's trial and death and the accounts in Acts of Stephen's trial and death.* The narrative of Stephen's trial in Acts has many similarities with the Markan account of Jesus's trial. Both are tried before the high priest and Sanhedrin (Mark 14:53; Acts 6:12; 7:1). The high priest demands an answer (Mark 14:61 [cf. Matt. 26:63]; Acts 7:1). False witnesses give testimony (Mark 14:56–57 [cf. Matt. 26:60–61]; Acts 6:13). Charges of blasphemy (Mark 14:64 [cf. Matt. 26:65]; Acts 6:11) and threats against the temple (Mark 14:58 [cf. Matt. 26:61]; Acts 6:14) emerge. Jesus tells the high priest and his cohorts that they will see the Son of Man sitting at the right hand of God, and Stephen shouts at his death that he sees the heavens open and the Son of Man standing at God's right hand (Mark 14:62; Acts 7:56). Luke's account of Jesus's death on the cross parallels the account of Stephen's death. Both commit their spirit to God (Luke 23:46; Acts 7:59), and both intercede for their enemies' forgiveness (Luke 23:34; Acts 7:60). The difference is that Jesus prays to his "Father," but Stephen prays to Jesus as "Lord." These parallels do not single Stephen out as exceptionally holy. What he does is what anyone who takes up his or her cross and follows Jesus must do and can do when empowered by the Holy Spirit.

Illustrating the Text

Believers are called to an uncompromising, fearless, peaceful proclamation of the gospel, regardless of the consequences.

Christian Biography: **Dietrich Bonhoeffer.** Bonhoeffer, a pastor, theologian, and writer, was viewed as a political enemy of the state for his views against Adolf Hitler and the Third Reich of Germany. During his studies in the United States, his friends attempted to persuade him to stay longer and not return to Germany, because they knew the dangers that lay in wait for him there. But he refused and returned to his homeland because of his commitment to lead and to support the church. Eventually he was arrested and imprisoned in the Tegel military prison in April, 1943. He would be transferred many times to Gestapo prisons in Berlin, Buchenwald, and Schöenberg. He was finally moved to the Flossenbürg concentration camp, where he would remain until his death on April 9, 1945. One of the English officers who was imprisoned with him shared, "Bonhoeffer always seemed to me to spread an atmosphere of happiness and joy over the least incident and profound gratitude for the mere fact that he was alive. . . . He was one of the very few persons I have ever met for whom God was real and always near. . . . On Sunday, April 8, 1945, Pastor Bonhoeffer conducted a little service of worship and spoke to us in a way that went to the heart of all of us. . . . He had hardly ended his last prayer when the door opened and two civilians entered. They said, 'Prisoner Bonhoeffer, come with us.' That had only one meaning for all prisoners—the gallows. We said good-by to him. He took me aside, 'This is the end, but for me it is the beginning of life.' The next day he was hanged in Flossenbürg."[4]

Understanding the zeal of the Jews, including Saul

Church History: William Willimon writes,

> Stephen's speech ...is a recollection of troubles within a family. Stephen begins with the promises to Abraham "our father." The subsequent history of Abraham's family is the history of the unfolding of God's promise to bless. But it is, in Luke's hands, also a story of conflict within the family, reminiscent of Joseph's jealous brothers who sold him into slavery, of Moses' rejection by his own brothers and sisters (Acts 7:23–29). There has always been trouble within God's family, says Stephen.
>
> . . . Acts reminds us that, in any age, there are believers who would rather kill those who do not share their faith than to trust their truth claims to stand or fall on their own.[5]

Forgiveness for one's enemies is one example of how Christians are like Jesus.

Testimony: On October 2, 2006, a man with a gun walked into an Amish school house. After the teacher fled to summon help, the man ordered all the children to lie down on the floor at the front of the class below the blackboard. He then allowed all of the boys to leave and shot all the girls before shooting himself to death. Five girls out of the ten survived that horrible day. News traveled slowly in the community, which shuns telephones, but families and friends soon started to gather around the school house that was now being examined by the police and other investigators. Within hours, the Amish community proclaimed that they forgave the shooter, and many, including family members of those who had lost their young children on that day, went to visit his wife with food and words of consolation and forgiveness. Ten years after the event, one newspaper wrote, "There have been many mass shootings across America in the 10 years since the shooting in the tiny village of Nickel Mines, some with much higher death tolls. But the Amish school shooting still strikes a chord. The attacker preyed on the most innocent and defenseless members of a determinedly bucolic and pacifistic religious community. Within hours, the Amish announced they had forgiven him."[6] The whole world came to know of grace and forgiveness because of the actions and attitudes of the Amish community, and even ten years later, the impact is not lost.

Christians can display Christlike forgiveness in the face of terrible persecution.

Missions: In her book *Through Gates of Splendor*, Elisabeth Elliot tells the story of Operation Auca, when she joined her husband and five other families to reach the remote Huaorani tribe of Ecuador in the 1950s.[7] Their hope was to take the good news to this unreached people group. Gradually the missionaries attempted to establish contact and build trust with the Huaorani people. In time they felt they were making headway. The five men flew in and made camp close to the Huaorani and were encouraged by their initial contacts. A short time later, a group from the tribe attacked and killed the men. But even after her husband's body was found floating downstream, Elisabeth resolved to be part of reaching the people who had killed her husband. In time, she lived among them and shared the good news of Christ's atoning work. Her confidence in the gospel gave her the capacity to forgive.

Even in death, God does not abandon his witness.

Missions: In 1989 Olive Fleming-Liefeld, the widow of Pete Fleming, one of the five missionaries who were killed by the Auca Indians, returned to the place where they were martyred. This time, she returned with Dawa, one of the Aucan Indians who witnessed their deaths and later became a Christian. Dawa shared about the misunderstandings that led to the killing of the five missionaries, the decisive action of the missionaries, who had guns in their possession, not to kill their attackers, and one story that no one had previously known. Rachel Saint, sister of Nate Saint (another one of the five missionaries), translated the story: "After the men were killed, Dawa in the woods and Kimo on the beach heard singing. As they looked up over the tops of the trees they saw a large group of people. They were all singing, and it looked as if there were a hundred flashlights. . . . This is the only word for 'bright lights' that they know." Fleming, Saint, and the others who heard this story could not believe their ears, but they recalled the hymn that the five men sang the day before their death, "We Rest on Thee." The hymn concludes, "We rest on Thee, our Shield and our Defender! Thine is the battle, Thine shall be the praise; When passing through the gates of pearly splendor, Victors, we rest with Thee, through endless days," and they concluded that they had indeed passed through the gates of pearly splendor and were greeted by an angelic choir.[8]

The Extension of the Mission in Samaria

Big Idea

The persecution that disperses the early believers means not that God has abandoned them but that the gospel will be spoken in new circumstances as they fan out to new places.

Key Themes

- The blessings of salvation available in Christ will be offered to those on the distant margins of Judaism.
- Turning to the Samaritans with the gospel is intended not to create independent communities of Samaritan Christians but to include Samaritans within the Jewish messianic community.
- Miraculous signs combined with the proclamation of the good news electrify those who "pay close attention" to the message.

Understanding the Text

The Text in Context

In Acts 1:8, Jesus foretold the coming of the Holy Spirit and of the disciples' witness in Jerusalem, Judea and Samaria, and to the ends of the earth. The day of Stephen's martyrdom not only marks the beginning of the great persecution of the church but also the scattering of the believers and the word of God from Jerusalem to Judea and Samaria (8:1–3 [cf. 11:19–20]). Stephen, one of the seven chosen to serve in the ministry of the distribution of food (6:3–6), becomes the first martyr, and Philip, also one of the seven, begins proclaiming the Messiah to everyone he encounters in Samaria.

Interpretive Insights

8:4 *Those who had been scattered preached the word wherever they went.* Following Stephen's martyrdom, a storm of persecution broke out against the church. Church members were driven out of town and chased down. One might think that they would lie low for a while until everything blew over or change their tactics so that they were less offensive. Instead, they keep on doing the exact same things that caused the persecution in the first place. They boldly proclaim the word, fearing nothing, and the persecution results in the gospel expanding into Judea and Samaria.

8:5 *Philip went down to a city in Samaria and proclaimed the Messiah there.* Philip is the first who is recorded preaching beyond Jerusalem, fulfilling what Jesus said would happen (1:8). Nevertheless, "The holy city remains in the reader's rear view mirror—always in sight but now left behind."[1] Samaritans and Jews hated one another though they shared a common heritage (2 Kings 17:24–41), worshiped the same God, and read versions of the same books of Moses. The Samaritans, however, worshiped not in Jerusalem but on Mount Gerizim (John 4:20). The incident in Luke 9:52–56 reveals the animosity between the two groups. A Samaritan village turned Jesus away because he was going to Jerusalem. James and John are so irked by this rebuff that they ask Jesus, "Lord, do you want us to call fire down from heaven to destroy them?" (9:54). Had their request been granted, there would have been no chance for the gospel in Samaria. The Samaritans embraced the Jewish Christians fleeing Jerusalem and accept Philip's message about the Jewish Messiah.

8:6–8 *When the crowds heard Philip and saw the signs he performed.* Philip performs the same signs that the apostles did (2:43), which validates his mission and wins the joyous attention of the Samaritans whose afflicted are healed. The joy is an expression of their acceptance of the message (cf. Luke 24:52).

8:9–11 *Now for some time a man named Simon had practiced sorcery in the city.* Simon is identified as a sorcerer, someone who practices black magic for personal gain. Worse, he accepts the people's adulation of him as a divine figure, which from the Christian perspective would make him satanic. Justin Martyr, "himself a Samaritan, reports . . . that nearly all his countrymen revered Simon as the highest god. It is clear from the history of his movement that 'the great power' was a Samaritan designation for the supreme deity."[2]

Magic

Eckhard Schnabel clarifies, "In the ancient world, magic—what today we would call witchcraft, sorcery, or the occult—was based on the view that human beings, gods, demons, and the visible world are all connected by sympathies and antipathies in ways that can be influenced by rituals involving incantations and the manipulation of objects. Its purpose was to overcome public or private problems. Usually magic was defensive, harnessing the powers of gods or spirits in order to gain protection against diseases and demons."[a]

[a] Schnabel, *Acts*, 407.

Acts 8:4–25

8:12–13 *But when they believed Philip as he proclaimed the good news of the kingdom of God and the name of Jesus Christ, they were baptized . . . Simon himself believed.* The narrative of Acts begins with the resurrected Jesus preaching about the kingdom of God to his disciples (1:3). It ends with Paul proclaiming the kingdom of God as a prisoner in Rome (28:23, 31). Philip's preaching about the kingdom of God shows that "the missionaries of the early church effectively carry on Jesus' work."[3]

The Samaritans expected their own messianic prophet (John 4:25), and to believe that Jesus was the Messiah meant they had to forgo their own misdirected expectation and expand their horizons. They had to believe that the fulfillment of their hopes was to be found in the Jewish Messiah, Jesus, and in the Jewish prophetic Scriptures (John 4:22). They also had to abandon their superstitious trust in sorcery as a viable answer to problems.

The people's submission to the gospel demonstrates its superiority over demonic wizardry, and even the "great" sorcerer Simon is attracted to it. His astonishment at the impressive signs and miracles that come from the power of the Holy Spirit is not repentance but may become the first step toward repentance.

8:14–17 *When the apostles in Jerusalem heard that Samaria had accepted the word of God, they sent Peter and John to Samaria.* The apostles' arrival from Jerusalem and participation in Philip's mission show that any chasm between Samaritans and Jewish Christians has been bridged. Samaritans, baptized and regenerated by the Spirit, take their place alongside Jews in the people of God.

8:18–21 *When Simon saw that the Spirit was given at the laying on of the apostles' hands, he offered them money.* Simon has substantial means amassed from his unsavory career as a sorcerer and essentially bids to purchase the license that will give him the territorial rights to distribute the Holy Spirit in Samaria. His motivations are similar to Elisha's avaricious servant Gehazi, who wanted to exploit God's power to make money (2 Kings 5). This foolish attempt to buy off the apostles underscores the fact that the enchantments of Simon's conjuring are nothing compared to the matchless experience of the Holy Spirit.

8:22–25 *Repent of this wickedness and pray to the Lord in the hope that he may forgive you.* Some regard Simon as only pretending to have been converted in receiving baptism. Nothing suggests that he was insincere, but his attempted "simony," a word derived from this incident to refer to buying or selling of church offices or powers, suggests that his conversion was incomplete. Peter's demand that he repent indicates that Simon has not done anything unpardonable and still can be redeemed. Simon's plea for Peter to pray for him is an admission of his guilt and a sign of his renewed penitence.

Theological Insights

The Holy Spirit is purely a gift of God, and that is made clear by the fact the apostles prayed first and then laid their hands on the people. The gifts of the Spirit are not for sale and cannot be franchised. "The Holy Spirit can be and is used by God to confirm the word proclaimed by God's servants, but it cannot be used to bring glory to an individual."[4] The Spirit cannot be directed by humans; instead, the Spirit's role is to direct the lives and activities of humans.

Teaching the Text

1. *Signs and wonders can be from God or from Satan.* Philip performed signs and wonders, and so did Simon the sorcerer. Both attracted crowds. One, however, belonged to God; the other, to Satan's lot. Philip's motives were pure; Simon's were purely self-serving. The obvious difference was that Simon did it for the money and elicited public adulation and even self-deification. Philip healed people for free and directed all praise toward God by preaching of the kingdom of God. It was his preaching the word, not his miracles, that was the foundation of the Samaritans' faith. It is important to recognize, "Before any miracles are reported, Philip's preaching is highlighted along with the fact that the crowds 'listened eagerly to what was said' by him (8.6a). When the Samaritans' belief is mentioned, it is directly connected to Philip's 'proclaiming the good news about the kingdom of God' (8.12)."[5] Two summaries that emphasize the preaching of the word and testifying about Jesus also enfold the text (8:4–5, 25). Preaching is therefore the key to conversion. Signs and wonders and the gift of the Spirit validate the conversions.

2. *There is one church led by one Spirit made up of diverse people.* After the Samaritans had believed and been baptized, why was it necessary for Peter and John to pray and lay hands on them for them to receive the Holy Spirit? The laying on of hands is also connected to the reception of the Holy Spirit in the case of Saul/Paul (9:17) and the Ephesian disciples (19:6), but Luke has no interest in describing a set pattern by which one receives the Spirit. Luke does not intend to portray the laying on of hands as a special ritual that channels the Spirit.

Luke's purpose in describing this incident is twofold. First, the apostles' intervention and laying on of hands are intended to show that the expansion of the Christian mission must be appraised and confirmed by the apostolic witness to Jesus's life and ministry. Second, Peter and John also prayed for and laid hands on the seven Hellenists (6:6). When they do the same thing for the Samaritans, it is a sign of "acceptance and solidarity" that acknowledges them "as members of the people of God."[6] Their preaching the gospel in many Samaritan villages on their way back to Jerusalem (8:25) further confirms their desire to convert and accept Samaritans as fellow believers. The apostles' involvement reveals that old cleavages are not to be perpetuated in the new, reconstituted Israel. The church is not to be divided into various ethnic splinter groups. The church might be scattered, but believers, whether Hebrews or Hellenists, Jews or Samaritans, are unified by the same Spirit and the same message.

3. *Repentance is always an option.* Did Simon truly repent from his wickedness when he was baptized? Some think that he would believe anything if it was to his advantage. According to one interpreter, Simon, when confronted by Peter, "resembles a cornered criminal, frightened at the prospect of punishment although not obviously remorseful over his crimes."[7] In later apocryphal tradition, he becomes the fountainhead of all heresies.[8]

This interpretation is excessively cynical. The account simply reveals that many who will come to believe and be baptized, particularly those living in a culture where they meet pagan sorcery at every turn, will need to grow in the faith. Repentance is not a once-for-all occurrence that never needs repeating. Surrendering to the cross and its call to self-renunciation as a way of life may take time. Old sins also can regain their attractiveness and reclaim persons. Christians can relapse. Those who have leadership positions in the church are also at risk of faltering and of, for example, "making their own persons the theme of their preaching, with the intention of making financial gain."[9] Lapsing Christians are always offered the option of repenting and remaining in the community. Whether they should hold office again is another matter.

Illustrating the Text

Christian commitment to share the word of God requires trust in and obedience to the Holy Spirit, not a clearly marked road.

Biography: **David Livingstone.** Livingstone was a Scottish medical missionary to Africa. He was approached by a South African aid society that had men whom they wanted to send to serve under his leadership. They asked, "Have you found a good road to where you are?" Livingstone wrote back, "If you have men who will come only if they know there is a good road, I don't want them. I want men who will come even if there is no road at all."[10]

Simony corrupts the church.

Etymology: According to *Merriam–Webster's Collegiate Dictionary*, the term "simony" refers to "the buying or selling of a church office or ecclesiastical preferment" and attributes the origin to Simon the sorcerer.[11] The anonymous author of the pamphlet *The Anatomy of Simon Magus, or, the Sin of Simony Laid Open* wrote in 1700, "There is no corruption more dangerous; nor is there more need of watching against any Evil, than to preserve the Church from the Impurity of this *Simoniacal* Malady. . . . If [the Church] be corrupt, then all Faith and Religion withereth and decayeth."[12]

Philip and the Ethiopian

Big Idea

The gospel is offered to all comers, requiring no preconditions and permitting no artificial barriers to bar them from being accepted as part of God's people when they repent and believe.

Key Themes

- Christians must be ready to interpret the Scriptures to those drawn to the Bible but bewildered by it.
- Nothing hinders any converted believer from being baptized and included in the household of God, which provides a home for the homeless and a family for those without family.
- Nothing can hinder the spread of the gospel, because the Spirit, not humans, is in control.

Understanding the Text

The Text in Context

Philip continues his evangelistic ministry to those who are excluded or marginalized in Judaism. The gospel breaks through another barrier as Philip redeploys. After leading Samaritans to believe, he now converts an Ethiopian eunuch.

In this incident, two complete strangers, Philip and an Ethiopian eunuch, are brought together by the Spirit. The Ethiopian has a religious stimulus from reading the prophet Isaiah but fails to comprehend fully its meaning. An angel instructs Philip to go south to the road that goes down from Jerusalem to Gaza. He is not told why. Only when he crosses the path of the Ethiopian does he understand what God has arranged. Only when he asserts himself and communes with this high-ranking traveler do their individual, private experiences become clarified. The result from following the Spirit's leadership is that a new, totally unforeseen kinship is created. This pattern will recur as Ananias seeks out Saul (9:1–19) and Cornelius seeks out Peter (10:1–11:18). The pattern is modified in this last instance: instead of a disciple obeying a divine command that leads him to reach out to another and deliver a divine message, a nondisciple obeys a divine command to seek out a disciple to ask for spiritual help. In each case, artificial human barriers are shattered as God expands the community of believers. The Ethiopian eunuch, Saul, and Cornelius are devoutly pious, though in Saul's case quite misdirected, and are open to receive God's revelation that changes their lives.

Interpretive Insights

8:26 *Now an angel of the Lord said to Philip, "Go south to the road—the desert road—that goes down from Jerusalem to Gaza."* An angel of the Lord spoke to Moses in guiding him (7:30, 35, 38), and an angel also appears to Philip directing his mission. The angel's appearance affirms that God is behind this new initiative. In Luke-Acts, angels make birth announcements (Luke 1:11–2:15), strengthen Jesus (Luke 22:43), rescue apostles (Acts 5:19; 12:7–11), give directions related to mission (Acts 8:26; 10:3, 7, 22; 11:13), strike down the wicked (Acts 12:23), and appear in visions (Luke 24:23; Acts 27:23–24).

8:27 *he met an Ethiopian eunuch, an important official in charge of all the treasury of the Kandake (which means "queen of the Ethiopians"). This man had gone to Jerusalem to worship.* An Ethiopian would have been regarded as an exotic foreigner, from far distant, black (cf. Jer. 13:23) Africa, what today is Sudan and is called Cush in Scripture (Esther 1:1; 8:9; Ezek. 29:10; Zeph. 3:10). He is branded by his condition as a sexless person, and this condition is mentioned five times in the passage (cf. Jer. 38:7–12 and the references to Ebed-Melek, an Ethiopian eunuch). He had been physically castrated either to punish him or to make him safer to serve in the royal court (Esther 2:3, 14–15). He has since risen to become a high official in the court. Connected to power in the service of the queen, he is wealthy enough to travel in a chariot and to

---

Eunuchs

In the ancient world, "Eunuchs are the marginal group par excellence: not only have they no social identity by background, but their inability to found a family means that even if freed, their only social link would be to their master."[a] Lucian of Samosata has a character report a declaration made about a philosopher reputed to be a eunuch: "Such people ought to be excluded . . . not simply from all [the rewards of philosophy] but even from temples and holy-water bowls and all the places of public assembly, and he declared it an ill-omened, ill-met sight if on first leaving home in the morning, one should set eyes on any such person. He had a great deal to say, too, on that score, observing that a eunuch was neither man nor woman but something composite, hybrid, and monstrous, alien to human nature."[b]

[a] Wiedemann, "Slavery," 584.
[b] Lucian, *Eunuch.* 6–11.

Acts 8:26–40

own a scroll of Isaiah. Despite his lofty rank, he would have been despised and derided as effeminate.

The Ethiopian made a pilgrimage to worship in Jerusalem despite the restrictions in Deuteronomy 23:1 that barred him from entering the temple. These restrictions also may have prevented him from becoming a proselyte. Luke intends for this incident to show that God will gather the remnant from every nation in fulfillment of Isaiah 11:11, which refers to those from Cush among other nations (cf. Ps. 68:31). It also shows that those who were formerly disqualified by the law can be received into the full fellowship of Jesus's followers with no strings attached. They will not be delegated to second-class status in the community of believers.

8:28–30 *was sitting in his chariot reading the Book of Isaiah the prophet.* The man is intrigued and puzzled by the Scripture as he studies it for illumination and hope. Deuteronomy 23:1 excludes him as someone impaired and polluted. The story that he is reading from Isaiah, however, is about one who also was humiliated, slaughtered, and shorn (cut) but was regarded as God's servant. The Scripture captures his imagination, but its full meaning escapes him. People did not read silently in the ancient world, so when Philip came alongside, he could hear him reading and identify the passage. Philip does not hesitate, immediately interrupting to ask if he understands what he is reading.

8:32–34 *He was led like a sheep to the slaughter.* The text (Isa. 53:7–8 LXX) is ambiguous. To whom does it refer? Does Isaiah lament the Suffering Servant's lack of descendants, something that a eunuch would resonate with, or marvel at their number despite a humiliating death?

8:35 *Then Philip began with that very passage of Scripture and told him the good news about Jesus.* The phrase "began with" is the same phrase that appears in Luke 24:27 when Jesus, "beginning with Moses and all the prophets," explained to his disciples "what was said in all the Scriptures concerning himself." The Scriptures testify to the divine necessity that the Messiah must suffer and then enter his glory (Luke 24:26), and this account makes clear that Isaiah 53 would have been one of the key passages Jesus used.[1] Philip explains that Jesus is the suffering figure who was abused and died a shameful death. His death on a cross, however, was not the end of the story. The good news is that God raised him from the dead and exalted him in glory ("His life was taken from the earth"). Because of God's action, he is destined to have countless numbers who will belong to his spiritual family. It describes a "radical social reversal" as "shame is replaced by honor."[2]

8:36–38 *What can stand in the way of my being baptized?* Two questions have been answered: How can I understand unless someone guides me? and Who is the prophet talking about? Luke does not narrate the answer to the second question, which must have been lengthy because it leads to the man's third question, What prevents me from being baptized? In this first-century context, some would answer that his mutilated condition and ethnic background would prevent him. Philip, however, joins him in the water to baptize him.

8:39–40 *When they came up out of the water, the Spirit of the Lord suddenly took Philip away, and the eunuch did not see him again, but went on his way rejoicing.* Philip is miraculously and precipitously carried away and finds himself in Azotus, twenty miles north of Gaza, where he had been. The Ethiopian goes on his way joyfully, unconcerned with Philip's disappearance. Philip continues on to Caesarea, and his preaching prepares the way for Peter where he will encounter Cornelius. One can presume that the eunuch will preach the good news when he arrives in Ethiopia as the gospel continues to spread.

Teaching the Text

1. *The Bible is not always a self-interpreting text.* Understanding the Scripture requires more than being able to give out information about it. To unlock its spiritual meaning requires being thoroughly grounded in Scripture and being guided by the Spirit. Luke understands that the Old Testament must be read in relation to Jesus (cf. 2 Cor. 3:12–18). This tenet is clear from the account of Jesus's interpretation of Moses, the Prophets, and the Psalms to explain the meaning of his crucifixion (Luke 24:26–27, 44–47).

2. *The incident with the Ethiopian eunuch highlights that God is no respecter of persons and that Jesus died and was raised to save all and enfold them into his greater family.* Prevented from becoming a proselyte to Judaism, the eunuch is led by Philip to understand that baptism serves as a symbolic ritual signifying his identification with Jesus's death, his cleansing, and his incorporation into the Christian family. This event adds further evidence of the universal thrust of the gospel. As J. B. Lightfoot remarks, the gospel will receive "all comers, asking no questions, allowing no impediments, insisting on no preliminary conditions, if only it were found that the petitioner 'feared God and worked righteousness.'"[3] Since God, through Jesus's sacrificial death, bestows grace on persons without regard to their worth and without distinction, membership in the people of God will know no bounds.

3. *The passage is about a man who cannot have a biological family but who can become a member of God's great family.* Prevented from becoming a proselyte to Judaism, the eunuch read Isaiah probably wondering what hope it could offer him. He thought that he was hopelessly alienated, but Philip teaches him that because of Jesus's death and resurrection those who had

been excluded from Judaism could not be excluded from the renewed Israel. He can be included in the household of God, which provides a home for the homeless and a family for those without family (Luke 18:29–30). The point applies today that the gospel is for all and is good news particularly for the broken, disadvantaged, and aliens. It is the great challenge of the church today to be the good-news family that Jesus promised to those journeying on lonely downhill roads and wondering who this lamb is who died and what it means for them. The Ethiopian eunuch's shameful condition was public, and despite his rise in the chain of command of the queen's entourage, that shame would have seared his soul. Its stain would have seemed enduring. The truth is that everyone has secrets that they regard as shameful, that are not public, and that they wish to hide. Shame can become like a cancer that eats away at the soul. Persons can become deadened by fear of exposure to the prejudices of others and the judgment that they are worthless being broadcast far and wide. In his humiliating, shameful death on the cross, Jesus takes on the shame of those who have been shamed and removes it. All who put their faith in him are renewed and can begin again as they trust in him who makes all things new.

Illustrating the Text

The gospel message may be personalized for each person.

True Story: Duke K. McCall, the president of the Southern Baptist Theological Seminary from 1951 to 1982, told of visiting China and exchanging gifts, according to custom, with the premier. He told the premier that he was offering the most precious gift that he could give. Against normal practice, the premier opened the present and discovered a beautifully bound Bible with his name printed on it. He said, "I have a Bible, but this one has my name on it. I will read it." The Bible has our name written in it, as the Ethiopian eunuch discovered reading Isaiah. If the eunuch continued reading in Isaiah, he would find his "name" in Isaiah 56:4–7:

For this is what the LORD says:

> "To the eunuchs who keep my Sabbaths,
>   who choose what pleases me
>   and hold fast to my covenant—
> to them I will give within my temple and its walls
>   a memorial and a name
>   better than sons and daughters;
> I will give them an everlasting name
>   that will endure forever.

And foreigners who bind themselves to the LORD
     to minister to him,
to love the name of the LORD,
     and to be his servants,
all who keep the Sabbath without desecrating it
     and who hold fast to my covenant—
these I will bring to my holy mountain
     and give them joy in my house of prayer.
Their burnt offerings and sacrifices
     will be accepted on my altar;
for my house will be called
     a house of prayer for all nations."

The encounter with Philip teaches the eunuch that he is no longer cut off, a "dry," fruitless tree, and an outsider; instead, he is someone included in God's family.

Church is a family for those who have none.

Personal Story: In 2005 Christmas day fell on a Sunday. Many churches decided to shutter their doors on Sunday morning so that their ministry staff might spend time with their families. I (David) heard the young wife of a minister at a large church that had decided to hold services on Christmas morning lament that it was not fair for the ministers and staff to have to come to church and miss this precious time with family. She said, "No one will be there. The only people who will come are the singles and the old people without families." A single adult who was not involved in a church herself overheard this remark and was shocked. "I thought the church was to be the place where those without families could go and find a home," she said later. "Isn't the church supposed to be the home for the homeless, the family for the family-less?"[4] The church should be a family, especially for those who have none.

Saul's Conversion and Call

Big Idea

The risen Jesus appears to Saul on his way to apprehend Christians and commissions him to proclaim his name among gentiles and Jews.

Key Themes

- The risen Lord identifies himself with his churches and their suffering.
- The appearance of the risen Lord to Saul produces an about-face in his life from persecutor to proclaimer.
- The spread of Christianity into the world is accompanied by the suffering of those who proclaim Christ's name.

Understanding the Text

The Text in Context

As the opening scenes began with Jesus's resurrection appearances in Jerusalem (1:3) and with the disciples waiting in prayer (1:14), this next stage of the Christian mission that will lead eventually to Rome begins with a resurrection appearance and Saul waiting in prayer.

Interpretive Insights

9:1–2 *Saul was still breathing out murderous threats against the Lord's disciples.* For the first time, we find that the Lord's disciples are identified as "the Way" (cf. 19:9, 23; 22:4; 24:14, 22). The name may stem from the quotation from Isaiah 40:3, "Prepare the way of the Lord" (Matt. 3:3; Mark 1:3; Luke 3:4), from Jesus's statement in John 14:6 that he is "the way" to salvation, or from the idea of following Jesus on "the way" of discipleship. Christians also are identified in this passage as "the Lord's disciples," "your holy people" (9:13), and "all who call on your name" (9:14).

"Saul, who was also called Paul" (13:9), later wrote that his zealotry for the traditions of the fathers had caused him to persecute intensely "the church of God" and to try "to destroy it" (Gal. 1:13–14 [cf. Phil. 3:6; 1 Cor. 15:9]). Phinehas, who slew a Jewish defector and the gentile woman who led him astray (Num. 25), was celebrated for his zeal (Ps. 106:30). Saul had the same kind of zeal and probably was driven to violence against Christians because they were breaking down the walls separating Jews from the pagan nations.

The letters that Saul carried sought the extradition of Christians to be punished according to Jewish law (cf. 1 Macc. 15:21). The high priest must have secured this authority to seize unorthodox Jews outside of his Jerusalem jurisdiction from the Romans, since Damascus belonged to the Roman province of Syria.

9:3–5 *suddenly a light from heaven flashed around him. He fell to the ground and heard a voice say to him, "Saul, Saul, why do you persecute me?"* A dazzling light, falling to the ground, double naming (cf. Gen. 22:11; 46:2; Exod. 3:4), and a voice identifying itself are elements that frequently occur in Scripture when a divine being appears to humans. Christ reveals himself to Saul in terms of the church he was persecuting. It reveals the intimate relationship between the two. Saul can only conclude that if Jesus is speaking to him, he must be alive. If the light shines from heaven, then he must be glorified.

9:6–9 *Now get up and go into the city, and you will be told what you must do.* This resurrection appearance of Jesus is the only one in the New Testament that occurs after Pentecost, and Paul says he appeared to him "last of all" (1 Cor. 15:8). Jesus appears to Saul not to prove him wrong but to give him a commission (cf. 1 Cor. 9:1; Gal. 1:12). That explains why his companions could hear the voice of Saul but could not see or understand the one with whom he was speaking. It was intended only for Saul. The mighty persecutor, broken by the blinding light, will learn how blind he had really been after he is led by the hand to Damascus.

9:10–14 *The Lord called to him in a vision, "Ananias!"* Ananias responds differently than Saul did to the Lord's call. Instead of asking, "Who are you?" he stands ready to obey, "Here I am, Lord" (9:10 ESV). Like some of the prophets of old, however, he raises objections to a divine commission that seems so unwise. Saul's dangerous reputation precedes him. Ananias's initial "Yes, Lord" becomes, in essence, "No, Lord": surely not Saul, the Christians' archenemy. Ananias learns that even the most hardened and dreaded enemy cannot be written off. Confronting his own fears, he must be obedient to God and trust God's grace to transform even the most intransigent foe. He will relent because Saul also receives a vision that Ananias will come to restore his sight.

9:15–16 *Go! This man is my chosen instrument to proclaim my name to the Gentiles and their kings and to the people of Israel.* Saul does not hear about his role directly from the Lord but from Ananias. The Lord has singled out Saul not simply for salvation but for a special mission (cf. 13:47; 20:24; 22:14; 26:16). Paul highlights in his letters that he is the "apostle to the Gentiles" (Rom. 1:5; 11:13; Gal. 2:7–9), and that role is mentioned here first. But he will also preach to Jews in their synagogues, in the temple, and before the Sanhedrin and King Agrippa (25:23–26:29).

Saul went to Damascus to get his hands on some Christians; he ends up having a Christian lay hands on him instead. Soon, the tables will be turned. He will be on the receiving end of persecutions (cf. 2 Cor. 11:23–28). The Lord does not assure him of success in his mission, but only that he will suffer.

9:17–19 *Brother Saul, the Lord—Jesus, who appeared to you on the road as you were coming here—has sent me so that you may see again and be filled with the Holy Spirit.* Luke understands "the Lord" to be Jesus. The disciples on the road to Emmaus had their eyes opened spiritually (Luke 24:31). Saul had his eyes opened both spiritually and physically.

9:20–22 *At once he began to preach in the synagogues that Jesus is the Son of God.* The "at once" emphasizes Saul's immediate and unhesitating obedience to the Lord's commission. The old Saul, who once was filled with hatred and breathing threats, is now filled with the Spirit and preaching the gospel of love and forgiveness, proclaiming that Jesus is the Son of God, the Messiah, and the Lord (9:28). He does not ruminate over what this call might mean or go on a retreat to rethink things in light of this dramatic event. He immediately discharges his call before ever meeting with the apostles in Jerusalem to receive their approval or instruction. He applies his training in Scripture to show that Jesus is the Messiah and the Son of God (cf. 2 Tim. 3:16).

9:23–25 *there was a conspiracy among the Jews to kill him.* The one who formerly pursued Christians is now the pursued. Preaching the gospel continues to stir up deadly animosity but also wins over many. These new Christians are determined to protect Saul from harm to help him evade a dragnet. He later describes this incident as an ignominious escape in connection with his weakness (2 Cor. 11:32–33).

9:26–30 *Barnabas took him and brought him to the apostles.* The disciples remain suspicious of Saul as a possible mole and shun his overtures to join them. Barnabas comes to his defense by recounting his heroic evangelization in Damascus. Every attempt by the Jewish leaders to stifle preaching the name of Jesus in Jerusalem has failed, and now their former henchman is preaching freely and boldly in the city. Once again, the ferocious resistance of Hellenistic Jews boils over, and Saul must be slipped out of the city to save him from certain death.

Theological Insights

Saul did not decide after long deliberation to switch sides and volunteer to become a Christian missionary. It is wrong to think that the death of Stephen was etched on his mind as he journeyed to Damascus and that he finally broke under the pangs of conscience. The only explanation for Saul's dramatic transformation is that Christ intervened directly to call him.

The calling had a purpose. The final object of the appearance of Christ to Saul was not his own personal salvation but to give him the mandate to preach salvation to others. The declaration that Saul "must" suffer in carrying out his commission evokes Jesus's statements about the necessity of his own suffering to accomplish his divine mission (Luke 9:22; 17:25; 24:26). Jesus's followers will share the sufferings of their crucified Lord (Rom. 8:17; Phil. 3:10; Col. 1:24).

Teaching the Text

1. *This incident should be understood as depicting both Paul's conversion and call.* In Galatians 1:15–16, Paul pictures his dramatic change in direction as a prophetic call similar to that of Isaiah (Isa. 49:1–6) and Jeremiah (Jer. 1:5).

If we understand conversion to mean a personal encounter with the risen Lord that produces a transformation of the values and self-understanding that previously governed one's life, then Paul indeed was converted. This does not mean that he changed from the Jewish religion to the Christian religion. He acknowledged his sinful condition and that he had no resources within himself to attain righteousness or salvation. He did not convert from a rigorous Jew to a lax one. Instead, he changed parties within Judaism. He changed from being a Pharisee, zealous for the traditions of the fathers, to a believer in Jesus as the Messiah and a follower of "the Way." He changed lordships, now serving Jesus as the risen Lord. He remained a faithful Jew as he fulfilled his mission to both the Jews and the gentiles (cf. 16:3; 20:16; 21:26; 24:11, 14, 17; 25:8). He changed his basic assumptions about God, righteousness, and how gentiles might also be saved and included as recipients of the promises to Israel.

2. *Paul's encounter with Christ is narrated three times in Acts (9:1–9; 22:1–21; 26:1–23), which reflects its great importance for Luke and for Paul.* We can detect its effect on numerous theological matters that appear in Paul's Letters. Paul now understood that Jesus was his Lord and that he was Jesus's slave. He saw that the one who died accursed on a cross (Deut. 21:23) was exalted in glory by God. He understood God's grace in a new light. He says, "I . . . do not even deserve to be called an apostle, because I persecuted the church of God. But by the grace of God I am what I am" (1 Cor. 15:9–10). As one who had experienced a violent break in his life, he understood that God alone had worked this transformation. He better understood the treacherous nature of sin. In persecuting the church, Paul thought he was doing what was pleasing to God. Despite his pious intentions, doing what he thought was the will of God, his persecution of the church turned out to be the cause of his greatest guilt. When it came to zeal, Paul testifies that he was exceedingly zealous

(Gal. 1:14; Phil. 3:6), as are the Jews (Rom. 10:2). He realized that God is not concerned about muzzle velocity, only accuracy. As one who made a radical about-face in his theological orientation, he was better able to see the negative side of his own past (Phil. 3:5–10). He saw the dangers of creeping legalism in Christianity as no one else did. Christ's appearance to him also confirmed his hope in the resurrection. He met the risen Lord, whom he considers to be "the firstfruits of those who have fallen asleep" (1 Cor. 15:20).

3. *The early church faced a seemingly hopeless situation in being hounded by fierce persecutors like Saul.* They chose to believe in Christ knowing full well that others would consider them to be pariahs and that they would be hunted down and suffer for their faith. They did not simply believe in Christ; they submitted their lives to him as Lord, leading to a new way of life. They recognized, as Saul soon would, that suffering for the faith was a sign not of their abandonment by God but of a special grace granted to them (Phil. 1:29). Paul helps the Philippians to understand their suffering and his sharing in Christ's sufferings, becoming like him in his death (Phil. 3:10–11).

In a self-help, quick-fix culture few want to hear that the Christian life can be one of painful endurance. Many mistakenly believe that the gospel should be summed up this way: "God loves you and has a wonderful plan for your life." Most take it to mean that God intends only for believers to prosper and to be happy. This attitude is no different from the ancient pagan attitude toward religion. Persons sacrificed to their various gods so that the gods would protect them and give them what they wanted. If that did not happen, they would switch to other, more accommodating gods.

These new Jewish Christians would have a different perspective, inspired by and anchored in Scripture. They were blown not by the winds of culture but by the wind of the Spirit, and they turned their world upside down. They had deeply repented, surrendered themselves to Christ's lordship, and engaged in fervent prayer together. It was recognizable that they were following a new Way. As for Paul, he knew he had been chosen, as Israel had been, to suffer for God in carrying out the mission to the world. The purpose of the suffering was not to prove his mettle or to make him sturdier; rather, it was the consequence of spreading the gospel and helping other Christians to grow in faith (1 Thess. 2:2).

Illustrating the Text

Suffering is not a sign that we have been abandoned.

Quote: **Elaine Prevallet.** "Suffering is an invitation to surrender the course of our lives to God. . . . Suffering offends not only our human pretension to control what happens, but even more, our capacity to comprehend. That life should be reasonable—more, that we should be able to grasp its rationality is a demand deeply entrenched within our humanity. Yet, with suffering, we brush up against a life-process that we did not create, would not choose, and cannot comprehend."[1]

Salvation can transform any person into a proclaimer.

Christian Biography: Chuck Colson. In 1973 the American press and political world were shocked to find out that President Nixon's "hatchet man," Chuck Colson, had given his life to Jesus Christ. The *Los Angeles Times* headline read, "'Tough Guy' Colson Has Turned Religious," and the *New York Times* announced, "Colson Has 'Found Religion.'" His conversion was met with skepticism. According to *Time* magazine (December 17, 1973), "Of all the Watergate cast, few had a reputation for being tougher, wilier, nastier or more tenaciously loyal to Richard Nixon than onetime Presidential Advisor Charles W. Colson."[2] He was embroiled in the Watergate scandal and would eventually plead guilty to obstruction of justice. The years that followed proved Colson's confession true. He would devote his life to Christ, to prison ministry, and to the defense of the Christian worldview. His Prison Fellowship Ministry and his Breakpoint Ministry are still active even after his death.

It is a privilege to have a brother or sister who will defend you.

Testimony: After the news broke that Chuck Colson had accepted Christ, he was met with much cynicism and disbelief. He knew that many people, especially his political enemies, would not believe that his decision was true; however, he met a strong supporter in a most unlikely man. Harold Hughes was the thirty-eighth governor of Iowa (1963–69) and a US senator (1969–75). According to Colson, Hughes was put "high on the [Nixon White House's] 'enemies' list" due to his liberal causes and position against the Vietnam War,[3] and they were on opposite ends, politically speaking. But when Chuck Colson shared his testimony with him, Hughes encouraged him and shared, "That's all I need to know. Chuck, you have accepted Jesus and He has forgiven you. I do the same. I love you now as my brother in Christ, I will stand with you, defend you anywhere and trust you with anything I have." Colson reflected, "I was overwhelmed, so astonished, in fact, that I could only utter a feeble, 'Thank you.' In all my life no one had ever been so warm and loving to me outside of my family. And now it was coming from a man who had loathed me for years."[4]

Peter's Ministry in Lydda and Joppa
Healing Aeneas and Raising Tabitha

Big Idea

God's saving power continues to be evident as the gospel spreads into Judea.

Key Themes

- Fear of the Lord is the foundation on which the church is built and advances.
- Jesus Christ's miraculous power continues to work through Peter.
- The miracles of healing are signs of God's salvation in the world.

Understanding the Text

The Text in Context

Luke returns to an account of Peter's ministry in a long unit, 9:32–11:18. These first two incidents are relatively brief and focus on his miraculous ministry among Jews outside of Jerusalem who came to faith in the Lord. The common pattern in Luke's Gospel of linking together two separate stories, one involving a male and one a female, appears here with the healing of two devout believers, Aeneas (9:32–35) and Tabitha/Dorcas (9:36–43).[1] The pairing indicates that females in the church are as important in their service as males. The next account is a lengthy two-part episode (10:1–11:18) that records the conversion of the centurion Cornelius, a gentile sympathetic to Judaism.

Interpretive Insights

9:31 *Then the church throughout Judea, Galilee and Samaria enjoyed a time of peace and was strengthened.* Paul has departed for the relative safety of Tarsus to proclaim the gospel there, and the church continues to thrive and grow among Jews in Judea. "Peace" does not refer to an absence of persecution, because that is not the case. The church is still under threat. Peace refers to a sense of security that comes from responding with faith to the good news from God (Isa. 52:7) that creates a harmonious relationship among Christians.

The Greek word translated as "strengthened" also means "built up," and it is attributable to the church's fear of the Lord. The Holy Spirit in their midst gives them encouragement and the power to speak persuasively to win new converts and to continue to work miracles.

9:32 *As Peter traveled about the country, he went to visit the Lord's people who lived in Lydda.* Peter did not stay only in Jerusalem, but, like Jesus, he travels widely as an itinerant minister across Judea (1:8). After preaching with John to the Samaritan villages (8:25), he leaves Jerusalem for Lydda (the "Lod" of the Old Testament [1 Chron. 8:12]), which is located southwest of Jerusalem. The translation "visit" may be misleading because the Greek verb says only that he "came down." Presumably, he goes to Lydda to preach to those who have not heard the gospel and to instruct believers. Leaving Jerusalem, he will have closer contact with gentiles.

9:33–35 *a man named Aeneas, who was paralyzed and had been bedridden for eight years.* This miracle is similar to the one worked by Jesus in healing a paralyzed man (Luke 5:18–26), but there are also major differences. No mention is made of friends bringing Aeneas to Peter because of their faith in Peter's power to heal. Also, Peter does not announce that the man's sins have been forgiven. If he is a believer, his sins already have been forgiven. Luke gives no indication, however, that Aeneas is a believer, nor does he tell us how Peter learns about him. Also, Aeneas makes no appeal to Peter for healing. It then may come as a surprise to the onlookers, but not to the readers, that Peter, like Jesus, tells Aeneas, "Get up." What is decisive in this healing is the statement before this command that "Jesus Christ heals you." Peter continues the healing miracles of Jesus Christ only through the power and authority of Christ. Peter's command that Aeneas roll up his mat implies that he does not need to be carried any more but can stand up and walk. Those who witness a man formerly bedridden for eight years ambling about the city respond with awe and also become interested in learning the source of this miracle. They do not believe in Peter as a great miracle worker but put their trust in the Lord in whose name Peter pronounces the man's healing.

"Sharon" refers to a fertile plain north of Lydda, not a particular town. Inhabitants of that area saw the results of this miracle when they visited Lydda and wondrously turned to the Lord.

9:36–40 *In Joppa there was a disciple named Tabitha.* The next miracle occurs in the coastline city of Joppa and parallels Jesus's miracle in which he raises

Jairus's daughter to life (Luke 8:40–41, 49–56). "Tabitha" means "gazelle" in Aramaic, and Luke translates it for his Greek readers with the name "Dorcas." Raising Tabitha back to life after she had died is a far more dramatic miracle than the healing of Aeneas. Luke identifies her as a "disciple," the only occurrence of the feminine form of the Greek word in the New Testament. Tabitha used her means and skillful needlework to provide material support for the poor, a regular practice among the first believers (cf. Luke 8:2–3).

The illness that led to her death is not specified, nor is the reason why the disciples in Joppa summoned Peter from nearby Lydda. He has a reputation for working miracles but not for raising the dead. Tabitha's body had been washed in preparation for burial, so it does not seem that they expected him to raise her from the dead. The widows, who have been helped by her handmade clothing, have gathered to mourn her death (cf. Luke 8:52). Presumably, Peter goes to ease their grief and to fortify them with his teaching (cf. 1 Thess. 4:13). The summons for Peter to come and his quick response prepare for the summons from Cornelius for Peter to come to him (10:17–23). In both cases, an unexpected miracle occurs. Tabitha is raised to life; the gentile Cornelius and his household believe, the Holy Spirit comes on them, and they are baptized.

9:40–42 *"Tabitha, get up." She opened her eyes, and seeing Peter she sat up.* Peter knew what to do because Jesus had sent the disciples out with the marching orders to heal the sick and raise the dead (Matt. 10:8). He also had witnessed Jesus raising the daughter of Jairus, the leader of a synagogue. In this miracle, Peter does what Jesus has done (cf. Luke 7:11–16; 8:49–56). Like Jesus, who took the young girl by the hand and commanded, "My child, get up!" (Luke 8:54), Peter takes Tabitha by the hand after commanding, "Tabitha, get up." Peter has no power of his own to reverse death but must rely solely on the power of God through prayer. The miracle is also reminiscent of those done by Elijah (1 Kings 17:17–24) and Elisha (2 Kings 4:32–37) and portrays Peter as a prophetic miracle worker like these two prophets.

9:43 *Peter stayed in Joppa for some time with a tanner named Simon.* Tanners were spurned by fastidious Jews because their work, dealing with carcasses, rendered them ritually unclean (Lev. 11:24). They usually lived away from a town because of the foul smells that their work emitted. Dwelling with Simon leads into the next story (10:6, 17), but it also prepares for its emphasis on the issue of who and what, under the gospel, are to be regarded as clean and unclean. The gospel makes no distinction.

Teaching the Text

1. *The conversions of the people in Lydda, Sharon, and Joppa were triggered by two significant miracles.* They "saw" Aeneas (9:35), and Tabitha's return

to life "became known" (9:42). Luke does not narrate the preaching of the word that would have prepared for and accompanied these conversions. One can assume that the pattern narrated in Acts 3, whereby the miracle of healing the lame man is accompanied by Peter's sermon that points to Jesus as the fulfillment of God's promises in the Scripture, also occurred in these instances. Miracles can grab people's attention, but conversions require preaching and teaching for the converts to understand fully how the miracles are tied to Jesus and God's salvation through his death and resurrection. Otherwise, they may only be attracted to spectacles and have only a superficial faith that quickly erodes when suffering arises. The account of the cleansing of the lepers in Luke 17:11–19 reveals that miracles do not always produce faith or gratitude. But in these instances in Acts, the miracles do spark faith in the Lord.

2. *Miracles point to Jesus, not the human agent.* It is important to note that Peter does not take credit for the miracles. He says not "I heal you" but "Jesus Christ heals you." All credit and glory must go to Christ when his merciful power brings healing. The goal is to bring about faith in Christ as Lord, not to bring acclaim to the one through whom Christ's power is made manifest. Key phrases occur at the end of each account emphasizing conversions. When news of the two miracles spreads in the respective towns, "all . . . turned to the Lord" (9:35) and "many people believed in the Lord" (9:42). They do not turn to Peter and hail him as "the Great Power of God," which the people of Samaria did in celebrating Simon Magus (8:10). Ministers who seek to win a personal following may be able to do so, but by feeding their vanity, their ministry will be in vain. If persons lift up the minister rather than the Lord, then they have not truly turned to God.

3. *Miracles do not always happen regardless of how righteous persons who are deathly ill might be or how fervently faithful people might pray for them.* Miracles depend entirely on God's power and God's will, and humans cannot control God's will nor can they always discern why it is that some are healed and others not.

Likewise, miracles, when they do happen, do not always turn people to the Lord. Everything depends on the will of God, which is so often inexplicable to humans. In these two particular cases, God used the healing of the paralyzed Aeneas and the resuscitation of Tabitha to advance the gospel in these locations. One cannot insist that God should always work miracles. On the other hand, one also should not rule out that God might work miracles. In this mortal vale, Christians can have faith that God will work the ultimate miracle of resurrection, "when the perishable has been clothed with the imperishable, and the mortal with immortality, then the saying that is written will come true: 'Death has been swallowed up in victory'" (1 Cor. 15:54).

Illustrating the Text

In times of peace, we must not lose the fear of the Lord.

Church History: John Calvin comments about times of peace:

> For as we are wont to riot and exceed in time of peace, the Churches are more happy, for the most part, amidst the tumults of war, than if they should enjoy what rest they would desire. But and if holy conversation, and the consolation of the Spirit, whereby their state doth flourish, be taken away, they lose not only their felicity, but they come to nought. Therefore, let us learn not to abuse external peace in banqueting and idleness; but the more rest we have given us from our enemies, to encourage ourselves to go forward in godliness whilst we may. And if at any time the Lord let loose the bridle to the wicked to trouble us, let the inward consolation of the Spirit be sufficient for us. Finally, as well in peace as in war, let us always joyfully go forward toward him who hath a reward for us.[2]

Miracles direct our attention to Jesus.

Quote: **Martin Luther.** Luther stated, "Miracles are recorded for us, who are chosen. . . . We are edified, when we learn and believe by them, that in Christ we have a gracious, meek, loving, beneficent Lord, who is able and knows how to help us."[3]

Miracles and salvation are both the work of God.

Classic Sermon: **"A Revival Promise," by Charles Spurgeon.** In this sermon Spurgeon pled with his congregation to realize that apart from the Holy Spirit's work, they were impotent to work true ministry. Preaching from Isaiah 44:3–6, he reminded the congregation of the deep need to seek God's presence for ministry:

> I pray that you who teach in the Sunday school, you who visit the poor, you who work in any way for God may acknowledge your impotence for good and look for power from on high. To our hands the Holy Spirit is the force, to our eyes He is the light. We are but the stones and He the sling, we are the arrows and He the bow. Confess your weakness and you will be fit to be strengthened. Acknowledge your emptiness and it will be a preparation for receiving Divine fullness. . . . Without the Spirit of God we can do nothing![4]

The Apostle Peter and the Centurion Cornelius

Big Idea

Salvation through Christ is not just for Israel but for all people. God is not a tribal deity and shows no partiality.

Key Themes

- God reveals his will to humans through prayer.
- If there is to be a gentile mission, insistence on categorizing people according to laws of ritual and dietary purity must be abandoned.
- Because Peter undergoes a transformation of his views of gentiles, a Roman centurion and his household are converted to Christ.

Understanding the Text

The Text in Context

Jonah retreated to Joppa to avoid preaching to gentiles (Jon. 1:3). Peter is prodded to leave Joppa to go preach to gentiles. Peter, Simon bar Jonah (Matt. 16:17), is very much like Jonah in his resistance to bringing God's message to gentiles, who are considered by pious Jews to be tainted.

Interpretive Insights

10:1–2 *At Caesarea there was a man named Cornelius.* Roman soldiers were drawn from a variety of backgrounds. Originally, the Italian Cohort, an auxiliary unit, was distinguished from others because it included Roman citizens, but later it enlisted recruits from other nationalities.[1] Centurions commanded eighty to one hundred men. A centurion is known as one who issues commands that are obeyed because he serves a greater power, the Roman emperor (Luke 7:8). Cornelius would have risen to this high echelon in the ranks as a model of the esteemed virtues of self-discipline and obedience to authority.

Charity

In Greco-Roman society, charity toward strangers was not regarded as a virtuous act or as something to be divinely rewarded.[a] Giving to others was intended to win oneself honor and prestige. Aristotle wrote, "Honor is the due reward for virtue and beneficence."[b] In this cultural context, people gave only to those who were capable of giving something in return, either repayment in kind or public praise. Cornelius's almsgiving is governed by the ideal Jewish perspective, espoused by Jesus, that almsgiving is to be selfless and that God alone rewards it (Matt. 6:2–4).

[a] Peterman, *Paul's Gift from Philippi*, 156.
[b] Aristotle, *Eth. nic.* 8.14.2.

Luke's portrayal of him defies the stereotype of a representative of Roman imperial power. Soldiers were united by a religious devotion to their group's standards (flags). Tertullian remarked, "The religious system of the Roman army is entirely devoted to the worship of the standards; oaths are sworn by the standards, and the standards are preferred to all deities."[2] Cornelius, however, is noted for honoring and praying to the God of the Jews and giving alms to the poor.

10:3–8 *Your prayers and gifts to the poor have come up as a memorial offering before God.* Three o'clock is the set time for the evening daily sacrifice in the Jewish temple for the forgiveness of sins. Cornelius is portrayed as praying regularly at that hour when suddenly an angel of God appears to him (cf. Ps. 141:2; Dan. 9:21; Jdt. 9:1). The angel announces that God has heard his prayers (cf. Luke 1:11–13) and has taken note of his alms. Though he does not know why he must send for Peter, he immediately obeys and dispatches men to fetch him.

10:13 *Then a voice told him, "Get up, Peter. Kill and eat."* Peter too receives a revelation from God while praying. Something like a sheet descended from heaven containing all kinds of animals, including reptiles and birds. Leviticus 11:1–47 and Deuteronomy 14:3–20 catalogue all the animals that Jews are forbidden to eat, which include reptiles (Lev. 11:29–38) and birds of prey (Lev. 11:13–19). The command to eat goes back to Genesis 9:3: "Everything that lives and moves about will be food for you."

10:14 *Surely not, Lord! . . . I have never eaten anything impure or unclean.* Peter's protest echoes Ezekiel 4:13–14, where the prophet insists that he has never defiled himself by eating ceremonially unclean food and never would do so. Since God commands, "You are to be holy to me because I, the LORD, am holy, and I have set you apart from the nations" (Lev. 20:26), food laws epitomized the separation of the people of Israel from the unwashed hordes who flout God's commands and eat what is "common" ("impure" in the

NIV). Daniel was a hero precisely because he would not defile himself with the pagan king's rich food and wine. Because of his devotion, he was delivered by God (Dan. 1:8–16). Tobit too was a hero because of his scrupulous concern for food laws: "After I was carried away captive to Assyria and came as a captive to Nineveh, everyone of my kindred and my people ate the food of the Gentiles, but I kept myself from eating the food of the Gentiles. . . . I was mindful of God with all my heart" (Tob. 1:10–12 NRSV). Judith's scrupulous observance of dietary laws helped her to win a victory over the enemy (Jdt. 10:5; 12:19). Those martyrs who resisted the orders of Antiochus Epiphanes to forsake their customs and eat swine's flesh were celebrated (2 Macc. 6–7). Eating kosher was the way to show devotion to and love for God.

Jewish dietary prohibitions made any association with gentiles problematic because of their presumed defilement. Their food was likely to be prohibited, sacrificed to an idol (Exod. 34:15; 1 Cor. 10:28), and prepared improperly (Exod. 23:19). In *Jubilees* 22:16, Isaac says to Jacob, "And you also, my son, Jacob, remember my words, and keep the commandments of Abraham, your father. Separate yourself from the Gentiles, and do not eat with them, and do not perform deeds like theirs. And do not become associates of theirs. Because their deeds are defiled, and all their ways are contaminated, and despicable, and abominable." Preserving those prohibitions clearly would deter any mission endeavors to the gentiles.

10:15–16 *The voice spoke to him a second time, "Do not call anything impure that God has made clean."* This divine announcement is truly revolutionary. That the vision occurs three times conveys how hard it is to change deeply ingrained perceptions of the world that are buttressed by religious embargoes but also how important it is. The purpose of the command is to open the doors for a gentile mission that will invite uncircumcised, unkosher gentiles into the faith.

10:17–23a *the Spirit said to him, "Simon, three men are looking for you."* Cornelius is described by his emissaries as a "righteous [upright] and

God-Fearers

"God-fearer" was a quasi-technical term to refer to non-Jews who were sympathetic to Judaism. They "did not submit to circumcision or observe the Torah in its entirety, but . . . did agree with the ethical monotheism of the Jews and attended their synagogue services."[a] There was no such thing as a semi-Jew, however. Jews continued to deem them as gentiles "unless they went over to Judaism completely through circumcision and ritual baptism."[b]

[a] Fitzmyer, *Acts*, 449–50.
[b] Hengel, *Acts and the History of Earliest Christianity*, 89.

God-fearing man." His righteousness fits Jewish categories in observing the ethical injunctions in the Mosaic law. That is why he is "respected by all the Jewish people," a rarity for centurions. Like the Jewish envoys of the centurion in Luke 7:4–5, the two servants commend Cornelius's works, but it is God's revelation, not Cornelius's reported righteousness, that convinces Peter to heed their request to come. That Peter extends hospitality to these gentile couriers reveals that he has put two and two together from the vision and so his prejudice against gentiles has softened.

10:23b–26 *As Peter entered the house, Cornelius met him and fell at his feet in reverence.* Cornelius shows excessive homage to Peter. Peter's protest asserts the truth that the gospel's messengers do not dispense salvation; they only proclaim it. Reverence is to be directed only to the source of salvation, the Lord.

10:27–33 *You are well aware that it is against our law for a Jew to associate with or visit a Gentile. But God has shown me that I should not call anyone impure or unclean.* Peter's greeting to the assembled crowd is an odd way to begin a sermon, but it reiterates the issue with which he and the church must grapple. How can one preach the gospel to those with whom one is unwilling to associate? Cornelius's account of his angelic encounter clarifies Peter's own vision. Peter understands that it was not simply about labeling food as impure or unclean but about labeling people that way.

10:34–35 *I now realize how true it is that God does not show favoritism.* Peter has learned that those who were not acceptable to him are in fact acceptable to God. He is not to use his former prejudice as a stick to drive others away from God.

10:36–43 *You know the message God sent to the people of Israel, announcing the good news of peace through Jesus Christ, who is Lord of all.* Peter preaches the same message that he preached to the Jews in Jerusalem (2:23, 36; 4:10), except he presents a more detailed picture of Jesus's ministry, death, and resurrection. God's anointing of Jesus with the Holy Spirit and with power alludes to Jesus's baptism (Luke 3:21–22). Verse 36 expresses the fundamental theological perspective of Luke-Acts: "The messianic Lordship of Jesus, which brings peace to the Jewish people in fulfillment of scriptural promises, applies to all peoples, for they are invited to share with Israel in this messianic peace."[3] "Peace" harkens back to Luke's birth narrative (Luke 2:14, 29–32) and is another word for the salvation (Luke 19:42) that is brought by God's action in Christ.

10:44–46 *While Peter was still speaking these words, the Holy Spirit came on all who heard the message.* Are the Jewish believers astonished that the Holy Spirit would come on gentiles or that the gentiles were able to manifest the same gifts of the Holy Spirit that the Jewish believers had experienced?

At Pentecost, Peter quoted Joel's prophecy that "everyone who calls on the name of the Lord will be saved" (Acts 2:21). Now, they are witnessing that prophecy coming to pass in the lives of gentiles.

10:47–48 *Surely no one can stand in the way of their being baptized with water. They have received the Holy Spirit just as we have.* The Greek word translated as "stand in the way" appears also in 8:36 when the Ethiopian eunuch asks what prevents him from being baptized. The NIV translation captures the emphasis of the Greek grammar, "Surely no one." The ritual of baptism signifies both that persons have been made new creations in Christ and that they are now incorporated into the body of Christ. Peter has caught on to a glorious theological truth that God's sovereign action in bestowing the Spirit on these gentiles means that God has accepted them.

The Holy Spirit does not come on people in any systematically regimented order. In this case, the people present receive the Spirit *before* they are baptized, which confirms that there is nothing that hinders them, as far as God is concerned, from being baptized. As John Stott puts it, "How could the sign be denied to those who had already received the reality signified?"[4] The issue is not simply whether they could be baptized. Their baptism is not narrated so that the emphasis falls on Peter and his companions accepting the hospitality of these new Christians, which implies eating their food (cf. 11:3). By doing so, these Jewish Christians acknowledge them as their brothers and sisters in Christ.

Theological Insights

What God has declared to be "OK," humans have no right to insist is not "OK." Peter's vision and the experience in Cornelius's house emphasize that no one should be barred from the opportunity to hear the gospel and receive salvation. In Judaism, the uncircumcised Cornelius can be, at best, only a "God-fearer." As a Christian, he does not have second-class status; he is fully accepted as a brother in Christ.

Teaching the Text

1. *Christ requires one's ultimate loyalty.* Cornelius, as a centurion in the Roman army, had pledged his absolute loyalty to Caesar. This incident shows the gospel going head to head with a member of the Roman imperial forces, a seemingly indomitable adversary. At stake is who will provide the predominant structures and values in the world. If one of Caesar's finest is converted, then anyone can believe. If a centurion believes that the God of Israel and the Lord Jesus Christ are more powerful than all other so-called powers and

must be obeyed above all others, then Caesar's God-denying world is in danger of collapsing. It will be defeated not by a more powerful army but by the all-powerful gospel.

2. *Cornelius is "devout," generously charitable, "God-fearing" (10:2), and "righteous" (10:22), yet he still needs to be saved (11:14).* Peter's vision affirms that all are "clean" (10:28). God "accepts from every nation the one who fears him and does what is right" (10:35). But this cleanliness does not mean that they are saved.[5] It means that they cannot automatically be written off as beyond the pale. Being acceptable to God refers to being in "an acceptable state (of repentance) to hear and receive the message of salvation and release from sins."[6] The characters who are converted in Acts are not what many would regard as horrible sinners. The Ethiopian eunuch was devout; Saul persecuted because of his zealous devotion to the law and was not a wanton sinner; and Cornelius's prayers, which served as a "memorial" before God (10:4), and his almsgiving (10:31) reveal that he, like the Ethiopian eunuch and Saul, had a relationship with God before his conversion. When Peter relates that the angel told Cornelius to send for Peter in Joppa because "he will bring you a message through which you and all your household will be saved" (11:14), this indicates that Cornelius is not saved. Simply being good and pious does not earn salvation. That Cornelius feared God and did what was right (10:35) indicates only that he was someone who might be receptive to the message of God's grace.

Salvation and the forgiveness of sins come from a believing response to the message (10:42–43), repentance, and submission to Jesus as the Lord of all (10:36), not from being a good person doing good deeds. The latter may win commendation from humans but not salvation from God. Cornelius's full response to the message resulted in his receiving the Holy Spirit and baptism, which confirmed his salvation in God's eyes.

3. *In Luke-Acts, "prayer is the means by which God makes the divine will known for new departures in the unfolding of His plan for history (cf. Luke 3:21–22; 6:12–16; 9:18–22; 9:28–31; 22:39–46; Acts 1:14; 13:1–3)."*[7] Revelations from God came to Cornelius and Peter, one in a vision, the other in an ecstatic trance, when both were engaged in intense prayer. Such prayer should be cultivated by Christians, who too often allow the busyness and business of the day to jettison prayer time. Private visions, however, are incomplete on their own and must be clarified in community. Paul and Ananias had divine encounters that they did not fully understand until they came together and shared them. In the same way, Cornelius and Peter have divine revelations they had to share with others for the revelations to make sense. Christians are called not to be isolated mystics but rather to live with others in community in which they share revelations to instruct and encourage others who in turn weigh what is said to discern the Spirit (cf. 1 Cor. 14:26–31).

Illustrating the Text

Possessing a good character, moral lifestyle, and even spiritual sensitivity are not the same thing as saving faith.

Testimony: Corrie ten Boom wrote about Hans Rahms, a caseworker in Scheveningen prison, where she and her sister, Betsy, were interrogated and interned. He showed kindness to Corrie and Betsy: he destroyed evidence that would have incriminated their family and allowed Betsy to pray for him during their interrogation times. He was impressed with the witness exemplified by Corrie and Betsy, but he was not a Christian. She shared, "There were many things for which I needed to thank Mr. Rahms, for it was he who helped free my friends and some of my family from prison. Because he did many good deeds for people, it was difficult for him to see that he needed a Saviour."[8]

Prayer in community is a vehicle for divine guidance.

Quote: **Dietrich Bonhoeffer.** In his discussion about Christian fellowship, Dietrich Bonhoeffer writes,

> The Body of Christ is praying, and as an individual one acknowledges that his prayer is only a minute fragment of the whole prayer of the Church. He learns to pray the prayer of the Body of Christ. And that lifts him above his personal concerns and allows him to pray selflessly. . . . There are two voices, bringing the same concern to God. . . . Is this not an indication that prayer is not a matter of pouring out the human heart once and for all in need or joy, but of an unbroken, constant learning, accepting, and impressing upon the mind of God's will in Jesus Christ?[9]

Peter's Report to Jerusalem Believers

Big Idea

God directed Peter to preach to gentiles and to baptize them. The church must submit to God's will and not erect artificial barriers that exclude others who are different.

Key Themes

- The Holy Spirit enables the Jewish believers to see that Israel was chosen to be a light to the gentiles, not sentries keeping them out in the darkness, and creates a church dedicated to spreading the gospel to all people.
- The mission to the gentiles is not a human initiative but is generated by God and certified by the Holy Spirit.
- The church's mission is to be the voice and action of Christ so that repentance and forgiveness of sins should be preached in his name to all nations.

Understanding the Text

The Text in Context

The events surrounding the conversion of Cornelius and his household are rehashed when some take exception to Peter's table fellowship with uncircumcised gentiles. In Luke, Jesus faced similar censure from the Pharisees for eating with Jewish tax collectors and sinners (5:30; 7:34; 15:1–2; 19:7). In Acts, not all Jewish believers object to Peter's intermingling with gentiles, but it does provoke a controversy among some that must be resolved if the church is to remain unified and the witness to the gentiles is to move forward.

Interpretive Insights

11:1–3 *the circumcised believers criticized him and said, "You went into the house of uncircumcised men and ate with them."* Peter apparently does not have unchallenged authority in the Jerusalem church, and these scandalized "circumcised believers" call him on the carpet to defend his actions in

The Significance of Circumcision

When Antiochus IV prohibited Jews from circumcising their sons, the rite of circumcision acquired confessional significance. Later rabbinic literature emphasizes the atoning power of the blood of circumcision, the performance of which even overrides the Sabbath.[a]

[a] b. Shabb. 132a.

Caesarea. Since all male Jews would have been circumcised (Luke 1:59; 2:21; Acts 7:8), the designation "the circumcised believers" may single out those who see their circumcision as a key to their religious identity that accords them special status with God. It does not refer to a "party," since those who were with Peter and witnessed the gift of the Holy Spirit being poured on gentiles are also identified as "circumcised believers" (10:45).

The lesson that God accepts all persons and seeks to enfold them into Israel was a hard pill for many Jews to swallow. The same Greek word translated as "criticize" appears in 10:20 and is translated as "hesitate." The angel commands Peter not "to hesitate" to go with Cornelius's messengers. The criticism is driven by the same mistaken scruples that Peter had about associating with gentiles. Some of Christ's followers are still programmed by the beliefs and practices of a rigid, legalistic Judaism and continue to believe that gentiles, even God-fearers, are impure. They insist on preserving a strict separation of the races. They find this new reality that God shows no partiality and saves gentiles without their first becoming full-fledged Jews to be something against nature and God's laws. A lack of discrimination, they assume, could only lead to accommodation with idolatry, the loss of Jewish heritage and identity, and a church filled with the off-scourings of humanity. Such qualms would scuttle taking the gospel to the gentiles.

Clashes over this particular issue will continue to haunt the church (Acts 15:1–2) and particularly Paul's ministry. His blistering Letter to the Galatians testifies to how heated the exchange became.

11:4–10 *Starting from the beginning, Peter told them the whole story.* Peter does not defend his actions with a theological exposition but simply relates what happened. He recounts the visions, God's command, and the amazing results of his obedience. This repetition of the highlights from the previous account serves to underscore their importance in understanding the movement of God's Spirit.

11:11–14 *He will bring you a message through which you and all your household will be saved.* The "household" could also include any slaves. The same Greek word appears in 10:2 and is translated as "family": "He and all his family were devout and God-fearing." This statement indicates that the household members who were baptized "were of an age to do so consciously."[1] Speaking the word of the Lord to them (10:44) assumes that they could understand the speech and respond by praising God (10:46).

11:15–18 *As I began to speak, the Holy Spirit came on them as he had come on us at the beginning.* Peter defends his actions by basically saying, "Don't blame me, blame God. Who was I to resist God?" He then recalls what the resurrected Jesus had promised would happen. They would be baptized with the Holy Spirit, and filled with the Spirit they would be his witnesses beyond Judea and Samaria to the ends of the world (Acts 1:8 [cf. Luke 3:16]). What occurred in Cornelius's house makes it clear that the disciples are to be witnesses to the ends of the world to both Jews and gentiles. The outpouring of the Spirit on Cornelius and his household validated this enlargement of the mission. It was a gentile Pentecost.

The conflict is not resolved by Peter's exercise of authority, eloquence, or wisdom. He simply relates what happened. Notably, Peter shifts from the issue of table fellowship with gentiles to their salvation.[2] If God saves them in the same way God saves Jews, through faith in Christ, it should put an end to the disputes about table fellowship. The Jerusalem church concludes that they must defer to the Holy Spirit's initiative.

Theological Insights

1. Luke conveys his theology through narrative and does not attempt to systematize the aspects of conversion and salvation. The various elements related to salvation appear in random order in the accounts in 10:1–11:18, but they are present: faith (10:43; 11:17); forgiveness (10:43); the gift of the Holy Spirit (10:45–47; 11:15–17); and repentance (11:18). The community affirms that God granted these gentiles "repentance that leads to life" (11:18). This statement confirms that salvation is not something that persons earn by their good works or even by their repentance, for which they can take credit. It comes as an "incongruous" gift from God without regard to the recipients' worth; it means that "there is no possible limit on the membership of this people, no ethnic frontier that would keep some nations out."[3]

2. "The message God sent to the people of Israel, announcing the good news of peace through Jesus Christ, who is Lord of all," (10:36) is the same message that God directs Peter to bring to gentiles "through which [they] will be saved" (11:14). This incident is a fulfillment of the prophecies in Scripture that Israel was to be a light to the nations (Gen. 12:3; Isa. 12:4; 42:6; 49:6; Ezek. 47:22–23), which is a prominent theme in Acts (13:47; 26:23 [cf. Luke 2:32]). The gospel is mediated to gentiles through the witness of the faithful believers in Israel.

Teaching the Text

1. *The reception of the Holy Spirit is a sign of salvation.* As the gentiles were hearing the gospel message, they received the Holy Spirit. It shocked those Jews who accompanied Peter: "The circumcised believers who had come with Peter were astonished that the gift of the Holy Spirit had been poured out *even* on Gentiles" (10:45). Facts were facts, and they could not be denied. The narrative shows that this event was not an aberration. God intends for gentiles to be incorporated in the people of Israel through their conversion to Christ. We are not the gatekeepers who decide when, where, and to whom the Holy Spirit speaks.

The coming of the Holy Spirit, like the blowing of wind, is apparent only from its discernible effects. It cannot be compelled, manipulated, or regulated. In this case, it is evident that the only precondition for receiving the gift of the Spirit is the readiness to hear and accept God's words (10:44). And God has worked behind the scenes in preparing hearts to respond in faith.[4]

2. *The harmony of the church is disrupted when dissension emerges over the gentile issue.* It was no small matter, since it could split the church into Jewish and gentile factions. Those who objected to Peter's mixing with gentiles presumably did not expect the inclusion of gentiles in the church unless they became full Jewish proselytes and therefore "clean." They may have thought that Christ accepts all who are circumcised, or they may have had no problem with gentiles becoming believers as long as they kept their place—segregated from Jewish believers. Peter himself was not eager to go to preach to gentiles. God had to prod him to do what he did. He was not like Philip, who ran up, without objection, to the chariot of the Ethiopian eunuch. It took Cornelius's men one day to travel from Caesarea to Joppa (10:9). It took Peter three days to get to Cornelius, as he rounded up witnesses to go with him, perhaps to protect his own reputation, fearing the criticism that surely would follow. It is often the case that believers are slow to understand God's purposes and quick to allow their personal prejudices to interfere.

The passage reveals that Jewish believers must not insist that gentile believers become Jews before they are acceptable to God. It is one thing to assent to the principle that God has cleansed everything, however; it is another to apply it to real life and to real people. It will take more than this one incident and one church decision for this truth to sink in. It took time for the early Christians to understand and accept that the gospel united people with different customs from different cultures and races through their common confession of faith. The new wine of the gospel will rip the old wineskin of the basic precepts and traditions of Judaism. This new wine requires new wineskins (Luke 5:37–38). Robert Wall observes, "We typically learn God's will over time through a series of 'aha' experiences."[5] Luke's account conveys that Jesus's death on the cross and his resurrection marked the beginning of a new era in salvation history, and the new creation in the Spirit eliminated any advantage created by the covenant of circumcision (cf. 1 Cor. 7:19; Gal. 5:6; 6:15; Col. 3:11). As Paul writes, "For we were all baptized by one Spirit so as to form one body—whether Jews or Gentiles, slave or free—and we were all given the one Spirit to drink" (1 Cor. 12:13). Every person who has faith in Christ is purified.

The embarrassing record of racial hatred and segregation that infiltrated the church in America and elsewhere in the world throughout history reveals that prejudice continues to be a plague that Satan uses to drive a wedge between believers. There have always been those who complain, "Why are you associating with them?" or "Don't think that you can bring them in here with us!" We might ask who we might consciously or unconsciously label as unclean and insist should become like us before they can be accepted by God.

3. *Baptism and the reception of the gift of the Holy Spirit do not follow a single, set pattern in Acts.* Peter does not mention the baptism of Cornelius's household in this second account, and it reflects an inconsistency in Acts regarding the relationship of baptism to the gift of the Holy Spirit. In 2:38, Peter would seem to contend that the two are inseparable: "Repent and be baptized. . . . And you will receive the gift of the Holy Spirit." In Samaria, however, the new believers had only been baptized in the name of the Lord Jesus, and they received the Holy Spirit when Peter and John laid hands on them (8:16–17). No mention of Spirit is made when the Ethiopian eunuch is baptized (8:36–39). Is it implied? The Spirit comes on Cornelius's household while Peter is preaching *before* they are baptized (10:44–48). In 16:32–34, the Philippian jailer and his household receive baptism, but no mention is made of the Spirit. In 19:1–6, the disciples of John the Baptist were baptized in the name of the Lord Jesus, but the Holy Spirit came on them and they spoke with tongues and prophesied only *after* Paul had laid his hands on them. Clearly, no set pattern exists relating to baptism and receiving the Holy Spirit.

Being a Christian and being baptized is taken for granted in the New Testament. The mode and meaning of baptism have long been a point of dispute among Christians. Perhaps, hoping to avoid theological controversy, some Christians today have ignored baptism as an inconsequential issue. For the New Testament, baptism is the visible confirmation of justification by faith, and it should not be passed over.

Illustrating the Text

Our prejudices can hinder those whom God is calling to him.

Biography: **Helen Roseveare.** Roseveare was an English medical missionary to Congo. She served the people of Congo from 1953 to 1973. At one point during her time there, she lost her temper and cursed one of the patients in fluent Swahili. One of her first students, a medical assistant, timidly approached and admonished her, "I don't think the Lord Jesus would have spoken like that." Due to this incident, she began to struggle about herself and her relationship with God and the people whom she was serving. During her sabbatical, her spiritual mentor, Pastor Ndugu, challenged her, "Helen, why can't you forget for a moment that you are white? You've helped so many Africans to find cleansing and filling and joy in the Holy Spirit through the blood of Jesus Christ. Why don't you let Him do for you what He has done for so many others?" She was horrified and confessed how racial prejudice was a hidden area in her heart, and she repented that her racism hindered others from coming to know God.[6]

We are sometimes slow to follow where the Lord leads.

Bible: **Jonah.** The Lord came to Jonah with the command to preach to the great city of Nineveh. The city of Nineveh was the capital of Assyria, a long-time enemy of Israel. Due to a history of animosity and his personal prejudice, Jonah was unwilling to obey God and attempted to flee by ship from Joppa to Tarshish. Thwarted by a great storm and trapped within the belly of a huge fish, Jonah reflected and prayed to God with words of repentance, "What I have vowed I will make good. I will say, 'Salvation comes from the LORD'" (Jonah 2:9). The Lord commands the great fish to spew out the slow-to-move and slower-to-understand Jonah, and Jonah successfully preaches to Nineveh, causing everyone, from the least to the greatest, to repent, fast, and pray to the Lord for salvation from their impending destruction. It's not up to us to draw lines on where we should or should not preach the gospel or who can or cannot receive it.

Nature: Gardeners who want to be successful in planting spend a good deal of time testing the soil. They'll move about their property, identifying the ideal place to sink the spade, turn the earth, and plant seed. In other words, they exercise prudence and discrimination, determining the fit and unfit places for planting. If the soil is unacceptable for planting, they may have to spend a fair amount of time and money adding new things to the soil so that it's ready to receive the seed.

Working in the garden of God's kingdom, however, we are not allowed to be so discriminating or deliberate when it comes to sowing. Jesus told the parable of the sower who scattered seed everywhere (Luke 8:4–8). After sharing the parable, Jesus declared, "*Whoever* has ears to hear, let them hear" (8:8). The book of Acts teaches us that we should never make judgments about who is or isn't ready to receive. Our call is to sow the gospel widely while we still have energy to labor in God's garden.

Solidarity between Two Christian Communities

Big Idea

The church grows as the power of the Holy Spirit impels believers to teach from the word, fashion disciples, witness to the gospel beyond their boundaries, and selflessly attend to the needs of other Christian communities.

Key Themes

- Antioch becomes the hub for missionary work in the gentile world.
- The disciples are distinguished from other Jewish groups as "Christians."
- Barnabas and Paul become the new lead figures in the narrative for spreading the gospel.

Understanding the Text

The Text in Context

The opening words of this section (11:19) recall 8:4 and the scattering of the Greek-speaking Jewish Christians because of the persecution that broke out when Stephen was killed. They have taken the gospel beyond the boundaries of Israel. Their enterprise was not planned and organized by the Jerusalem church, but Luke focuses on the relationship between the church in Jerusalem and the church in Antioch. The account makes clear that even though disciples are scattered far and wide, the church remains unified in its teaching and bonded together by its members' mutual commitment to Jesus as Lord.

Interpretive Insights

11:19–21 *Some of them, however, . . . began to speak to Greeks also, telling them the good news about the Lord Jesus.* The next chapter in the church's mission begins by repeating the report of the aftermath of Stephen's martyrdom in 8:4. Persecution had the unintended effect of causing the gospel to spread as disciples fleeing from Jerusalem to safer climes continue to share the good news about Jesus with other Jews. Cyprus is mentioned twice in the list of territories perhaps because Barnabas hails from there (4:36). It prepares for his reentrance into the picture and the first missionary journey. Cyprus had a large settlement of Jews, and Barnabas and Paul will begin their work together there (13:4–12).

Antioch on the Orontes River was the third-largest city in the Greco-Roman world after Rome and Alexandria and was the capital of the Roman province of Syria. A seismic shift in the church's outreach occurs here. For the first time, Luke records that "some" Jewish believers, who come from Cyprus and Cyrene, share God's word with non-Jews who are idol worshipers and not sympathetic to Judaism. Greek-speaking believers could communicate the gospel message best to a Greek-speaking audience. Fittingly, they refer to Jesus not as "Messiah" (cf. 2:36; 5:42; 8:5; 9:22), which would be incomprehensible to non-Jews, but as "Lord." The goal is to have them turn from false gods to the one true Lord (Acts 14:15; 26:18, 20; 1 Thess. 1:9). It is noteworthy that they do not require the converts to become circumcised.

Luke uses a biblical phrase, "the Lord's hand,"[1] to attribute the conversion success to the Lord's power. The phrase is often used to refer to amazing deeds worked through God's power (1 Kings 18:46; 2 Kings 3:15), and its usage here presumes that the conversion of gentiles in Antioch is an amazing deed that can be explained only as an act of God. Christianity gains such a strong footing in Antioch that it becomes the center of the church's mission into the Greco-Roman world.

11:22–23 *News of this reached the church in Jerusalem.* The Jerusalem church had sent Peter and John to Samaria to confirm and affirm the converts there (8:14). Now, they send Barnabas to Antioch at news of conversions there. His dispatch should not be taken to mean that the Jerusalem church was suspicious of successful evangelism outside of their immediate orbit and wanted to control it. Instead, Barnabas goes as a kind of ambassador. His presence links the two communities and verifies that God's word spreading throughout the world is unified and based on the original apostolic witness. Though Barnabas is known as the "son of encouragement" (4:36), the Greek verb translated here as "encouraged" (11:23) implies more than cheering on these new Christians. The verb implies that he "exhorts" them through his Spirit-filled teaching to remain true to the Lord with steadfast purpose so that they do not lose their way. The result of his teaching was the addition of even more converts.

11:24 *He was a good man, full of the Holy Spirit and faith, and a great number of people were brought to the Lord.* Stephen is described in a similar way (6:5). Beverly Gaventa notes that "faith and being filled with the Holy Spirit are not traits of an individual personality but signs of God's presence."[2] This verse is tied to the previous verse grammatically and explains why Barnabas rejoices upon witnessing what the grace of God has done in Antioch and has not become suspicious or begrudging: he is a good man. He successfully exhorts them because he is full of the Holy Spirit.

11:25–26 *Then Barnabas went to Tarsus to look for Saul.* Barnabas knows that God has called Paul to proclaim the gospel to gentiles (9:15) and that Paul has preached boldly in Damascus (9:19–20, 27) and Jerusalem (9:28). Presumably, Paul has not been idling away the time when in Tarsus but continues to preach there. As an ex-Pharisee, trained in and zealous for the law, a Hebrew of Hebrews, a well-traveled Roman citizen, an experienced preacher of the gospel, and at home in the Greek-speaking world, he has a unique background that makes him ideal as a special envoy of Christ to the gentiles in Antioch.

That the disciples are first "*called* Christians" in Antioch suggests that this label originates with outsiders (cf. 1 Pet. 4:16) and is not the believers' self-designation. It is possible that proclaiming Jesus as Lord has sparked unrest among the Jewish community, and the Roman authorities have blamed it on the Christ-followers as distinguished from other Jews. Or it may be that so many gentiles have joined the church that outsiders regard them as so different from a Jewish ethnic group that they have given believers the name to differentiate them. Luke has no interest in explaining the origin of the name and includes this note only because it implies that the believers have split off from the Jewish community that rejects faith in Christ. What is important is that this name emphasizes their identification with Christ, and this identification is noticeable in all that they did.

11:27–30 *One of them, named Agabus, stood up and through the Spirit predicted that a severe famine would spread over the entire Roman world.* Prophets are not always predictors of the future, but in this instance Agabus, the prophet from Jerusalem, foretells a severe famine that will affect the entire Roman world. The mention of Claudius's reign as emperor reminds the audience that salvation history is happening in world history. The famine relief effort coordinated in Antioch for believers in Jerusalem exhibits the harmony in the church that crosses geographical and ethnic borders. The Antioch church emulates the Jerusalem church in sharing resources with the needy (2:44–46; 4:32–37; 6:1–6) because the same Holy Spirit is working in their midst. Barnabas has already modeled the generous sharing of goods, and he and Paul will deliver the gifts. They do not attempt to help everyone in the area but only their Christian brothers and sisters. Paul will take on helping the poor of the saints in Jerusalem as a major project later in his ministry (Rom. 15:25–31; 1 Cor. 16:1–4; 2 Cor. 8–9).

"Elders" appear for the first time in Acts and serve alongside the apostles (15:2, 4, 6, 22–23; 16:4) in authoritative roles. In this instance, they undertake a role that would be similar to what the Hellenist deacons shouldered (6:1–6) in distributing funds to the needy.

Teaching the Text

1. *The successful mission beyond Jerusalem was the result not of the church's carefully thought-out mission strategy but of Christians being scattered throughout the area after Stephen's murder.* Reggie McNeal writes, "We don't have to manufacture the work of God in ourselves or in the world. God is doing the heavy lifting! . . . We can quit trying to drum up a breeze by generating a lot of frenetic church activity and instead hoist our sails to catch the breeze that's already blowing."[3] Planning mission strategies is not to be minimized, but much of what happens in Luke's account of the church's witnessing effort was completely out of the believers' control—for example, the sudden coming of the Spirit, the hostile persecution, the angel's appearance to a gentile centurion. Also, the Christian message is spread through anonymous, individual Christians traveling across the empire and sharing the gospel in informal ways. The church experienced amazing growth without the benefit of impressive buildings or high-powered programs and while experiencing harsh persecution. We can learn from their example. The church grows when every believer becomes a gospel teller.

2. *The gift of prophecy is a gift of the Holy Spirit that is not given to all and is to be used in the service of the church to build up the church (cf. 1 Cor. 14:4).* Agabus shows no interest in promoting his own prophetic gifts or feathering the nest of his own economic welfare. He is interested in serving the welfare of the Christian community. Paul lists "prophets" between "apostles" and "teachers" (1 Cor. 12:28) and insists that apostles and prophets form the foundation of the church with Jesus Christ the chief cornerstone (Eph. 2:20). Agabus makes a prediction that will save many in the church from famine, but predicting the future (cf. 21:10–11) is not the only role of the prophets. Prophets also persuade and teach (13:1). Often those who claim a gift of prophecy in our current age provide fear-mongering entertainment for their own personal financial gain. The money that they collect is rarely if ever used to relieve the suffering of the destitute. The early church tried to address the problem of discerning false prophets from true. The *Didache* (or *Teaching of the Twelve Apostles*), which dates from the second century, offers very specific conditions for identifying a false prophet (*Did.* 11:1–8): prophets are to be welcomed unreservedly and their message received, but if they stay for more than three days, ask for money as a reward, or their conduct does not match their words, they are to be rejected as false prophets.

3. *Generosity to the poor.* The Christians in Antioch pass a spiritual acid test by being generous with the poor. Their generosity toward their fellow believers in Jerusalem is a sign that God's grace indeed works powerfully in them as it did among the Jerusalem Christians (4:33). The difference is that the Christian community in Antioch shares with people who live far away and may be of a different ethnicity. Their sharing reveals that the unity of the early believers in Jerusalem, who were "one in heart and mind" (4:32), now reaches across racial and geographical divides. The Christians are not rich. Resources are limited. But the church is growing because they are rich in love and care for one another.

Illustrating the Text

The church's resources cannot be quantified on a spreadsheet.

Informational: What should we make of the fact that the church is growing more rapidly in the developing world, where financial resources are limited, than in cultures where resources are far greater? One recent report notes,

> The Church has seen dramatic and explosive growth in Asia, Africa and South America. The growth of the African Church in particular is jaw-dropping. In 1900 there were fewer than 9 million Christians in Africa. Now there are more than 541 million. In the last 15 years alone, the Church in Africa has seen a 51 percent increase, which works out on average at around 33,000 people either becoming Christians or being born into Christian families each day in Africa alone.[4]

The Christian community is wealthy when it is filled with Christlike love and generosity.

News: Syria has been embroiled in a brutal civil war. It is home to a historic Syriac Orthodox Christian community, and these Christians have not been spared from the violence. But even amid the destruction and suffering, Christians in Midyat have reached out to their Christian brothers and sisters who have become refugees. They set up the Tur Abdin Syriac Christian Committee to provide needed support to those who are fleeing violence. Father Ishak Ergun, the priest of Mor Barsaumo Syriac Orthodox Church and a member of the committee, detailed, in an interview, the material and spiritual care that the committee provides. When one family fled to Midyat, he helped them secure an apartment at a reduced rate. But in addition to logistical care, the committee also emphasizes pastoral care. "'We pray for them,' Ergun says. Not long ago, the community held a three-day fast to 'call upon God to stop the pressure and to show a peaceful way forward.' Ergun had just counseled a family that had trouble sleeping because of 'the death, murder that they faced in their eyes,' he says. He provided a Bible in Arabic and encouraged them to read the Lord's Prayer before bed. 'After they read the Bible,' he says, they started to find some comfort."[5]

Fruit of faithfulness may not be visible until much time has elapsed.

Christian History: In 1929, Dr. William Leslie left his mission work among the tribal people in the Democratic Republic of Congo. He was discouraged because he left the tribal people on bad terms and considered his ministry of seventeen years a failure, bearing no fruit. He died in 1938 without any knowledge of his impact. In 2010, a minister named Eric Ramsey returned to the area to find "a network of reproducing churches hidden like glittering diamonds in the dense jungle across the Kweilu River from Vanga, where Dr. Leslie was stationed." It was discovered that Leslie had been sharing the gospel and teaching the tribal children in this area to read and write. "He felt like he was there for 17 years and he never really made a big impact, but the legacy he left is huge."[6]

James's Death, Peter's Escape, and Herod's Demise

Big Idea

Peter miraculously escapes from prison and is driven from Jerusalem, and James, the brother of the Lord, becomes a key figure in the Jerusalem church.

Key Themes

- Nothing stops the advance of God's word even when tragedy strikes and Jesus's followers are put to death or imprisoned.
- The leaders of the church are not irreplaceable, and God will raise up their successors.
- No matter how lauded or deified those who oppose God's people might be, ultimately they will be destroyed.

Understanding the Text

The Text in Context

While Barnabas and Paul are meeting and teaching the church at Antioch (11:25–26) and completing their mission there (12:25), King Herod arrests and persecutes some of the believers in Jerusalem. James the brother of John is put to death with the sword, and Peter is imprisoned but is eventually freed by an angel of God. God remains ever in control. King Herod, taking on the trappings of a divine figure, meets a miserable death. The word of God is not stopped by this tormentor but continues to spread and flourish.

Interpretive Insights

12:1–2 *It was about this time that King Herod . . . had James, the brother of John, put to death with the sword.* "King Herod" refers to Herod Agrippa I, the grandson of Herod the Great and the son of Aristobulus IV and Bernice I. He was born 9–10 BC, brought up in Rome, and had influential Roman friends who became emperors, Gaius (Caligula) (AD 37–41) and Claudius (AD 41–54). His sister was the infamous Herodias, whose marriage to her husband's half brother, Herod Antipas, was denounced by John the Baptist and led to John's beheading (Mark 6:14–29; Luke 3:19–20; 9:7–9). Agrippa I reigned during the years AD 37–43. He received Herod Philip's tetrarchy (Luke 3:1) in 37, added Galilee and Perea in 39 when Herod Antipas was sent into exile, was given Judea and Samaria, which formerly had been under the control of Roman prefects, and was granted the title "king" by the emperor Claudius in 41. His kingdom was almost as large as that of his grandfather, Herod the Great, but his rapid rise was fleeting and ended when he died in 43. Josephus describes him positively as beneficent, mild in temperament, humane to foreigners, careful in his observance of the law and appointed sacrifices, and close to the Pharisees.[1]

He is not normally identified as "Herod" in secular sources, and Luke's use of the name is intended to recall the murderous Herod Antipas (Luke 13:31). The disciples' success has again attracted the threatening notice of another treacherous Herod, and he does what we normally expect of petty tyrants. He lays violent hands on the disciples.

James the son of Zebedee, whom Jesus assured would drink the cup that he drank (Mark 10:39), is executed by the sword, which probably means that he is beheaded. It is a scandalous death for Jews because it was reserved for apostates who are then thought to have "no share in the world to come."[2]

12:3–5 *When he saw that this met with approval among the Jews, he proceeded to seize Peter also.* Agrippa I sought to cultivate the favor of the Jewish authorities who probably called his attention to the Christian apostles and instigated his persecution of them. When they welcomed the beheading of James, he thought that he had hit on the means to increase their backing and planned the same fate for Peter. Luke does not narrate what happened to change the people's attitude toward the disciples in Jerusalem. It is possible that the word "Jews" (cf. 12:11) refers to the religious leadership and their supporters rather than the general population. One can surmise that their hostility stemmed from a combination of the Christians' world-shattering preaching about Jesus as the resurrected Lord and, as they gained converts, the political threat that they posed to the religious establishment.

Peter was arrested during the season of Passover, as was his Lord. The Feast of Unleavened Bread overlaps the Passover festival in that leavened bread was removed prior to the day of Passover (14 Nisan), and unleavened bread was eaten for seven days after Passover. Luke uses the term "Passover" to refer to the entire festal period. The Greek verb translated as "bring out" (12:4) in a judicial context was used for sentencing someone.[3] Like Jesus's trial (Luke 22:66–71), this public trial of Peter was intended not to determine his guilt or innocence but to establish the charges by which he could be executed. Agrippa planned a trial that would be followed by an execution.

12:6–11 *Peter followed him out of the prison, but he had no idea that what the angel was doing was really happening.* This event is the second account of Peter being divinely rescued. This last-minute deliverance in the dead of night saves his life. The four squads consist of ten men each who serve three hours during the four watches of the night. Two are chained to Peter as he sleeps, and two guard the cell door. Escape was impossible and could not occur through natural means.

With his fate hanging in the balance, Peter is fast asleep. He is so sound asleep that the angel has to strike him on the side to wake him up. The roles are reversed from when the disciples frantically tried to awaken Jesus when raging waters from a squall threatened to swamp their boat (Luke 8:22–25). Peter now possesses the same tranquility in the face of danger that Jesus had, knowing that everything is in the hands of God, who raises the dead.

Though Peter knew the biblical stories of angels rescuing the people of God (Exod. 14:19; Num. 20:16; Dan. 3:28) and already has been rescued by an angel (5:19–20), when he is delivered, he does not believe it. He thinks that it might be a dream or a vision as he slips away from his captors and drowsily waltzes through an impregnable iron gate that miraculously opens.

12:12–17 *he went to the house of Mary the mother of John, also called Mark.* It is unusual that Mary is introduced by her relation to Mark, who has not yet appeared in the narrative. It suggests that her son is the better-known figure to the original audience. It is quite possible that he is known as the author of the Gospel of Mark and not simply as the mission companion of Paul and Barnabas. Mary must have been wealthy enough to have a home that has an outer gate and is large enough to house a segment of the church for the prayer meeting. Possibly, they belonged to a Cypriot family that settled in Jerusalem, since Paul identifies Mark's cousin as Barnabas who comes from Cyprus (4:36; Col. 4:10).

Peter did not believe that his escape was real, and the church that is at that moment praying for his deliverance does not believe it either. The scene becomes comic when Rhoda, a serving girl, is so overcome by joy that she neglects to open the door for Peter to enter.[4] Then, the people inside dismiss her as mad when she says that Peter is at the door. They do not have faith that God would answer their prayers and set Peter free. Their response is similar to the disciples' response to the women who announced Jesus's resurrection: they "did not believe the women, because their words seemed to them like nonsense" (Luke 24:11). These believers presume that Rhoda saw Peter's guardian angel or some kind of celestial double. Instead of going back to get Peter to provide proof, she argues with them.

When Peter finally is let in, he relates the story of his release and then goes underground. Luke does not tell us where he went, and he drops out of the narrative until he reappears in chapter 15. James is now mentioned for the first time, with no introduction, which indicates that the original audience is familiar with him as the brother of the Lord (Mark 6:3) and knows of his leadership role in the Jerusalem church, which becomes most obvious in chapter 15.

12:18–19 *After Herod had a thorough search made for him and did not find him, he cross-examined the guards and ordered that they be executed.* The guards are executed for what is to be presumed to be a dereliction of duty or complicity in the escape. Herod leaves for the luxury of his palace by the sea in Caesarea.

12:20–25 *Immediately, because Herod did not give praise to God, an angel of the Lord struck him down, and he was eaten by worms and died. But the word of God continued to spread and flourish.* Luke provides an abbreviated account of the context of Herod Agrippa's demise. Presumably, he quarreled with the regions of Tyre and Sidon over the supply of foodstuffs. He is not openhanded with them and "blocked shipments of food, perhaps grain from Galilee exported to southern Syria."[5] The delegation to Agrippa apparently is successful, and he gives a speech that wins their applause. They laud him as if he were a divine being.

Josephus gives a similar account of Agrippa's speech and subsequent death.[6] In Josephus's report, Herod is decked out like a god. In Acts, he sounds like a god. Though he may perceive himself as deified, he is only a mortal who goes the way of all flesh. He is eaten by worms and then dies. Jewish tradition reports that other tyrants who persecuted God's people were consumed by worms (Jdt. 16:17; 2 Macc. 9:9). The angel of the Lord can come as a destroyer (Exod. 12:23; Ps. 78:49) as well as a rescuer, and he destroys the one who thinks that his judgment, rather than God's, is decisive.

Teaching the Text

1. *Those earthly leaders, no matter how powerful they imagine themselves to be and how lauded they are by others, will receive retribution for claiming honor and glory that belongs only to God.* Herod Agrippa I curried the favor of the Jews, basked in the favor of pagans, and in the end lost the favor of God.[7] His plan to decimate the leadership of the Christian movement failed because he thought that this movement could easily be crushed through violence. The crusades of Theudas and of Judas the Galilean disintegrated when these rebel leaders were killed and their followers took flight (5:36–37). The movement led by Jesus's apostles, however, is different. It is of God, and Herod

does not recognize that he is "fighting against God" (5:39), not simply against humans. History is littered with tyrants who, as John Stott observes, "may be permitted for a time to boast and bluster, oppressing the church and hindering the spread of the gospel, but they will not last. In the end, their empire will be broken and their pride abased."[8] The death of Herod Agrippa I recalls Ezekiel's message to the ruler of Tyre: "This is what the Sovereign Lord says: 'In the pride of your heart you say, "I am a god; I sit on the throne of a god in the heart of the seas." But you are a mere mortal and not a god, though you think you are as wise as a god'" (Ezek. 28:2). The point is that history is in the hands of God, not those who think that they can compete with God and strut on the world's stage and exploit others without remorse. They think that they are in control, but if even the gates of hell cannot withstand the gospel (Matt. 16:18), the iron gates of tyrants are nothing.

Herod Agrippa I is not the first or the last ruler whose dazzling oratory and theatrical rallies deceive a nation and cause its people to deify their leader. Grandiloquence has a demonic ability to mesmerize the masses and instigate mass destruction. That is why the gospel is not based on "eloquence or human wisdom" or "persuasive words" that glorify the speaker rather than point to the cross (1 Cor. 2:1–5).

2. *Miracles, no matter how fervently prayed for, are not always forthcoming.* Peter is miraculously delivered from prison twice (5:18–20; 12:6–10). Paul and Silas will be rescued from a Philippian jail (16:22–26). James, however, was not liberated and was martyred. Luke does not seek to answer why Peter was rescued and James was not. God does not always rescue. Christians trust in God, who says, "I am the Lord, and there is no other. I form the light and create darkness, I bring prosperity and create disaster" (Isa. 45:6–7). What matters is not the individual believer's prosperity and safety but committing one's life entirely to God whatever may come. Christian martyrs through the ages have joined Shadrach, Meshach, and Abednego in saying to a tyrant, "If we are thrown into the blazing furnace, the God we serve is able to deliver us from it, and he will deliver us from Your Majesty's hand. But even if he does not, we want you to know, Your Majesty, that we will not serve your gods or worship the image of gold you have set up" (Dan. 3:17–18).

Our responsibility as Christians is not to come up with explanations for why things happen but to respond in trust regardless of what happens. To want to have all of the answers is to want to become gods, as Herod Agrippa I did. Both James and Peter heard Jesus's teaching that they should not fear those who can only kill the body (Luke 12:4). After enemies do their worst, they are through, but God is not. God has the power to throw persons into hell, but God will not abandon to hell those whose hairs are numbered and who believe in Jesus (Luke 12:4–12). The resurrected Jesus identifies with those who are persecuted (Acts 9:4–5), and the liberation of Peter from a jail cell and a death sentence is only a foreshadowing of a far greater liberation from an eternal death sentence.

3. *God's miraculous deliverance often catches believers off guard, even when they pray for it.* Peter's trancelike state when the angel escorts him from prison and the church's denial that it could be Peter knocking at their door reveal that Christians are often dumbfounded in the face of liberation. Christians may engage in intercessory prayer but are sometimes surprised when their prayers are answered. Christians should pray with confidence that God hears their prayers and answers them. That is quite different from praying with certainty that God will give the answers that we desire. It does not mean that we should have a blithe confidence that all will work out as we plan simply because we prayed. The word "confidence" derives from Latin and means "with faith." Faith stands amazed in the presence of God's miraculous power and remains steadfast in the presence of tragedy and disappointment knowing that God's power ultimately will triumph.

Illustrating the Text

Earthly power cannot save us from God's judgment.

Church History: The Borgia pope Alexander VI was a notorious pope whose time in office was said to be characterized by nepotism and licentiousness (he acknowledged having four children by a mistress). He was also thought to have poisoned many rivals. The pope and one of his illegitimate sons, Cesare, whom had been made an archbishop at seventeen, were both taken ill with fever after dining with a cardinal. Cesare eventually recovered, but the pope, who was much older, did not. According to the diary of a leading member in the pope's household, the pope's stomach became swollen and turned to liquid, while his face became wine colored and his skin began to peel off. Finally, his stomach and bowels bled profusely. After more than a week of intestinal bleeding and convulsive fevers, and after receiving the last rites and making a confession, the despairing Alexander VI died on August 18, 1503, at the age of seventy-two.[9]

History: From July 1979 until April 2003 Saddam Hussein was the president of Iraq, wielding absolute power over that oil-rich, historically significant nation. Rising from life as a peasant child, he made his way to the top through a combination of daring action, coalition building, and cunning political maneuvering. Along the way, he suppressed freedom movements by Shi'a and Kurdish groups and built up a reputation as an absolutely ruthless dictator. In 1980 he invaded Iran, leading Iraq into a deadly eight-year war that ended in stalemate. In 1986 he launched an attack against his own citizens, the Kurds, killing as many as 182,000. During this campaign, Hussein used mustard gas and nerve agents to kill at least 5,000 civilians and maim 10,000 more. In 1990 he invaded Kuwait, thirsty for its oil reserves and the prospect of paying off debts accrued in the war against Iran. He was driven out in 1991, but he retained power for the next decade, fighting off various insurgencies and attempts at his life (including a 1995 CIA attempt at assassination).

Hussein believed himself to be an unshakable leader, someone who was destined to wield power. Hadn't his longevity proven his invincibility? All that changed in 2003 when a coalition led by the United States overthrew Saddam's government. The powerful dictator went into hiding, and the man who had caused the death of many was eventually found inside a hole in the ground on December 13, 2003. After a guilty verdict and death sentence, upheld by Iraq's Supreme Court of Appeals, Saddam Hussein was hanged.

We might think that we are above justice. We might believe that we can run from justice, but we can be sure that justice will fall one day. Whether in this world or the next, we cannot hide from God's justice.

Prayer supports our fellow believers in hardship and suffering.

Poem: "Believe Me," by Irina Ratushinskaya. Ratushinskaya, a Russian dissident and poet, wrote about her time in prison, often in solitary confinement. She was arrested for being outspoken against the Russian government. In the poem "Believe Me" from her book *Pencil Letter*, she writes about the support from the prayers of thousands of Christians who knew of her trials, including a "sudden sense of joy and warmth" that brought assurance that others were praying for her. She writes of her gratitude for those who faithfully prayed for her and the likelihood that she would not have endured, had it not been for those prayers.[10]

Serving God does not serve as a guarantee against persecution.
Suffering is not outside of the will of God.

Biography: Helen Roseveare. Roseveare, an English medical missionary to Congo, found herself brutally beaten and raped in the midst of Congo's civil war in the 1960s. She shares, "At the moment of restoration I am in His present will for me. . . . I have found this to be a most liberating and glorious truth. If it were not so, who among us would not live his life in an atmosphere of continual regret? The night I was first taken captive by the rebel soldiers He worked that liberation for me in the midst of all the horror and anguish! . . . I was 'acceptable before God' [1 Peter 2:20], and this could only mean that I was in the centre of His will. Certainly this could be no 'second-best.'"[11]

Angelic intervention illustrates God's control over a situation.

Testimony: Corrie and Betsie ten Boom were imprisoned at Ravensbrück, a German concentration camp, for harboring Jews during World War II. When they first entered the prison, they were instructed to surrender all of their worldly possessions, but they did not want to be separated from their most treasured possession, the Bible. Corrie hid the Bible in her underwear, but the Bible was bulging and apparent. She "asked the Lord to cause his angels to surround her so that the guards would not see her." Each woman had to pass several inspection points, but at each point Corrie was not checked and her Bible was never found. "Bolstered by the angelic intervention, Corrie prayed with joy in her heart: 'O Lord, if thou dost so answer prayer, I can face even Ravensbrück unafraid.'"[12]

Resistance and Success in Cyprus

Big Idea
The Holy Spirit instills a vision in the church in Antioch to send out witnesses into the world.

Key Themes
- A praying church becomes a witnessing church under the guidance of the Holy Spirit.
- The gospel continues to be resisted by ethnic Jews who embody a false Judaism that is of the devil and perverts God's righteous ways.
- The gospel begins to make inroads into Roman high society.

Understanding the Text

The Text in Context

Formerly, the ministry to the gentiles was at the spur of the moment and unplanned, as with Peter's encounter with Cornelius. Now, the Holy Spirit directs the church at Antioch to engage in an organized outreach to the gentiles. The church commissions, among others, Paul, who was called to proclaim Jesus's name "to the Gentiles and their kings and to the people of Israel" (9:15), to fulfill that calling in partnership with Barnabas. The gospel continues to meet resistance but also meets success with the belief of a prominent Roman proconsul.

Interpretive Insights

13:1 *Now in the church at Antioch there were prophets and teachers: Barnabas, Simeon called Niger, Lucius of Cyrene, Manaen (who had been brought up with Herod the tetrarch) and Saul.* The "teachers and prophets" demonstrated spiritual gifts in these areas that made them stand out. Their diversity, which is becoming a mark of the Christian movement that is reaching out into the wider world, is striking. Barnabas is a Levite from Cyprus. Saul is a Pharisee educated under Rabbi Gamaliel. Simeon called Niger (the Latin word for "black") is most likely a black man;[1] Manaen was a boyhood friend of Herod Antipas, the son of Herod the Great and tetrarch of Galilee during Jesus's ministry. Manaen probably would have been in his midsixties.[2] Thus far in the narrative, when leaders' names are listed in pairs—Peter and John (1:13), Stephen and Philip (6:5)—the first-named leader plays the primary role in the narrative that follows. It is odd then that Barnabas is listed first but Saul appears last. What follows in the narrative suggests that the last will become first as Saul dominates the story.[3]

13:2–3 *Set apart for me Barnabas and Saul for the work to which I have called them.* The next phase of the church's outreach with the gospel, outlined in 1:8, is not the consequence of persecution that drives believers out and into the world but is a result of the Holy Spirit's specific instruction and assignment. God is the driving force in the church's venture, and the Holy Spirit is the sending agent. The church becomes receptive to the Holy Spirit's leadership through communal prayer and fasting, which are mentioned twice (cf. Luke 5:33–35). Laying hands on those who are chosen to be set apart marks the conferral of a blessing for their future mission enterprise. It does not confer power or ordain them to the office of missionary.

13:4–5 *The two of them . . . sailed from there to Cyprus. When they arrived at Salamis, they proclaimed the word of God in the Jewish synagogues. John was with them as their helper.* The mission is never conceived as only a mission to the gentiles. Synagogues are a natural place to start to preach the gospel to Jews and to encourage them to fulfill the Old Testament promises for Israel to become a light to the nations. The preachers would also find as part of the audience gentiles sympathetic to and interested in Jewish monotheism and ethics.

John is John Mark (12:25). The Greek term translated as "helper" to describe his role was used in the papyri for "a man who handles documents and delivers their contents" to others.[4] He may have "served Barnabas and Paul with material that aided them in their preaching activity."[5] The same term is used in Luke 1:2 to refer to the "servants of the word" (cf. Acts 26:16), and he may also have engaged in preaching and teaching.[6]

13:6–8 *they met a Jewish sorcerer and false prophet named Bar-Jesus, who was an attendant of the proconsul, Sergius Paulus.* Saul and Barnabas are identified as "prophets and teachers" (13:1) and are sent by the Spirit, which sets up the skirmish with Bar-Jesus, who is identified as a false prophet who perverts "the right ways of the Lord" (13:10; literally, "the straight paths of the Lord" [cf. Luke 3:4–5]). Bar-Jesus probably opposes these Jews as "unwelcome competitors."[7] The incident recalls Peter's earlier encounter with the sorcerer Simon (8:9–24) but also Moses's battle with Pharaoh's sorcerers (Exod. 7–8) and Elijah's clash with the priests of Baal (1 Kings 18).

Bar-Jesus is identified twice as a "sorcerer" (the name "Elymas" is defined as meaning "sorcerer" in 13:8). In the context of Acts, it brands him as a huckster and a fraud. An intelligent Roman proconsul, however, was unlikely to have in his entourage a sorcerer, and Bar-Jesus probably served as his astrologer, foretelling the future and interpreting dreams and signs. Though Cicero called astrology "inconceivable madness"[8] and astrologers were occasionally expelled from Rome for unsettling the people or creating political rivalries, astrology exercised considerable influence in imperial times. Many believed that their destinies were written in the movement of the stars, and Sergius Paulus would have wanted someone to give him guidance to identify propitious times to take actions and to safeguard him from taking ill-advised actions. Those from the East were considered to be particularly gifted in this kind of divination. His role as an astrologer best explains the unusual description of Bar-Jesus's becoming blind: he was not able "to see the light of the sun" (13:11). The sun's position was crucial for astrological calculations.[9]

Bar-Jesus's name means "son of Jesus" (Joshua), which is ironic. Not only is he not a follower of Jesus, but also he is a paganized Jew who opposes Jesus and is really "the child of the devil," the chief slanderer (13:10 [cf. John 8:44]). Nevertheless, Sergius Paulus probably learned something about the Jewish worship of God from Bar-Jesus, which made him receptive to the preaching of Barnabas and Paul.

13:9 *Then Saul, who was also called Paul, filled with the Holy Spirit.* Though Barnabas appears to be the senior partner in their mission venture, Paul now becomes the prominent figure in the rest of the narrative. To this point, Paul has been identified as Saul, his Hebrew name by which Jesus addresses him in his call (9:4; 22:7; 26:14). Paul counts his belonging to King Saul's tribe of Benjamin as one of his former boasts (Phil. 3:5), and he did not change his name at his conversion. It is unlikely that he adopted the name of Sergius Paulus to honor his prominent Roman convert. Paul (*Paulus*) was his Latin surname that probably stemmed from his family's history, now lost to us, when his father or grandfather became a Roman citizen. Others in the New Testament with both a Jewish name and Roman name are John Mark, Joseph Justus (1:23), and Jesus Justus (Col. 4:11). Silas is known by his Hebrew

Proconsul

A proconsul was appointed by the Roman Senate to serve for one year to govern a senatorial province. These provinces were well within the outer borders of the empire and not judged likely to be attacked or to rebel, so they did not require a military presence.

name in Acts (15:22) and by his Latin substitute name, Silvanus, in the letters (1 Thess. 1:1). Identifying Saul now by his other name, Paul, reflects the shift of the narrative's mission focus to the Roman world.

13:10–12 *You are a child of the devil and an enemy of everything that is right!* Elymas recognizes that if Sergius Paulus turns to faith, Elymas himself would be turned out of office. He resists the Holy Spirit with a satanic spirit, and it is no contest. Once again, a Jew tries to frustrate the plan of God and becomes an enemy of all righteousness. God visits crippling punishment on those who stand in the way of the mission.

Sergius Paulus is impressed by Paul's miraculous power and believes. Luke shows the gospel continuing to infiltrate the Roman imperial power structure: first a centurion, and now a proconsul. Defeating a son of the devil and winning over a high Roman official to the faith, however, do not mean that it will be smooth sailing from here on. Victories are often followed by setbacks.

Theological Insights

Prayer is always necessary for receiving the Holy Spirit's guidance. In fasting one humbles oneself and withdraws "in the highest degree from the influence of the world and makes oneself receptive to commands from heaven."[10]

Teaching the Text

1. *Bar-Jesus and Saul share a common past in opposing the gospel.* Saul tried to thwart the work of the church before his encounter with Christ. Bar-Jesus tries to do the same. Both were temporarily blinded, and both had to be led about by the hand (9:8; 13:11). Susan Garrett notes, "Bar Jesus is a 'son of the devil,' and Paul—like the devil—has 'authority to bind' (9:14), tries to make Christians blaspheme (26:11), and repeatedly casts them into prison. The parallels suggest that Luke saw Paul, too, as a one-time servant of the devil."[11] That is where the parallels end. Paul was blinded by "a light from heaven" (9:3); Bar-Jesus was blinded by "mist and darkness" (13:11). Both can amaze gentiles with their powers, but Bar-Jesus is the exact opposite of Paul. He misrepresents the one true God and is a false prophet, a sorcerer, a child of the devil, "an enemy of everything that is right," "full of all kinds of deceit and trickery," and a perverter of "the right ways of the Lord" (13:10).

As a Jew, Bar-Jesus is supposed to be part of Israel's calling to be a light to the nations, but he is filled with darkness. In a similar vein, the greatest enemies of the gospel sometimes are those who know the traditions of the faith but misrepresent them and lead others astray for their own financial gain.

2. *Miracles underscore the message and can inspire faith.* Elymas is temporarily blinded as Paul had been, but the question remains whether he will ever gain spiritual sight, as Paul did. The period of blindness gives him a chance. What would lead to his repentance? The punishing miracle caused Sergius Paulus to believe, but Luke makes sure to add that it was not just a miracle that is behind his faith. He was amazed at the teaching of Paul and Barnabas (13:12). Miracles are momentary attention getters, but it is only through the abiding word that convicts and transforms that Christianity will progress. This abiding word can transform even an archenemy like Elymas if he would listen.

3. *Throughout history the church has fought distortions of the true faith and believers' attraction to append non-Christian and anti-Christian elements to their faith and practice.* Most notably, astrology has infected the faith of many and undermined faith in God's providence. Many examples could be cited. John Dee, a mathematician and an astrologer, chose the date of Queen Elizabeth I's coronation in 1559 after consulting his star charts to determine the most auspicious day. People may think that they are adding extra insurance and greater security in this life by consulting various fortune-telling gurus. In reality, they endanger their lives to come by manifesting their lack of complete trust in God.

Illustrating the Text

Our times of prayer may lead us out into mission.

Bible: In chapter 6 of his Gospel, Luke tells of Jesus choosing the twelve apostles. Matthew and Mark record the same event. However, Luke alone recounts that before choosing these twelve men who would serve alongside him in ministry, Jesus spent the entire night in prayer. For Jesus, prayer was essential.

Biography: **Jonathan Goforth.** Goforth was appointed by the Canadian Presbyterian Church to start a new mission in the province of Honan, China. Before he and his wife, Rosalind, went to China, Hudson Taylor wrote to them, "We understand North Honan is to be your field. . . . Brother, if you would enter that province, you must go forward on your knees." They committed to pray for God's certain direction to the mission in Honan, and Taylor's exhortation became the motto of the North Honan Mission. Rosalind Goforth would write, "Our strength as a mission and as individuals, during those years so fraught with dangers and difficulties, lay in the fact that we did realize the hopelessness of our task apart from divine aid."[12]

Quote: **Samuel Zwemer.** Zwemer, a scholar and missionary to Busrah, Bahrain (1891–1905), said, "The history of missions is the history of answered prayer."[13]

Sometimes, the greatest enemies of the gospel are those who were once members of the faith.

Biography: Ryan Bell. Bell used to be a pastor. In fact, for nineteen years he served a Seventh-Day Adventist congregation. Over his time in ministry, however, he began to have doubts. He became increasingly active in political and social causes. Eventually his involvement in controversial issues led to a loss of his credentials in his denomination. At this critical pivot point, Bell determined to try something out and launched a "Year Without God." Bell describes this experiment as an effort to answer the question an atheist friend had once asked him, "What difference does God make?" By the time his "Year Without God" came to an end, Bell's faith had as well. He now leads an organization called "Life After God." They describe their mission:

> Life After God exists to empower people and communities to live deeply into the space after God. This in-between world is lonely and uncharted. Our mission is to create safe, hospitable space for people to explore their doubts, recalibrate their "moral compass," and create new friendships. . . .
>
> We do this through personal and group coaching, retreats and online resources. We also consult with organizations that want to better understand the challenge of post-theism and grow their capacity to serve.[14]

Miracles can grab attention, but only preaching brings conviction.

Popular Culture: The statement "Seeing is believing" is often used when someone makes a claim that's hard to accept. Especially in today's modern culture, people want to see the photograph, the video clip, or the scientific proof. We feel much safer if we have some kind of evidence that we can trust. The problem, though, is that seeing is not always believing. Jesus did numerous signs and miracles in the presence of the people, but still many of them refused to believe. Even with the greatest miracle of all—Jesus's death and resurrection—some people would not believe. We often see what we want to see or explain away what we do not want to see. Preaching brings a message of truth, which is either accepted or rejected, and although signs can help point to or substantiate the message, it is the message itself that is needed. Preaching is what brings that message and what compels someone to make a decision, to come to a conviction one way or another.

The Expansion of the Gospel in Pisidian Antioch

Big Idea

The arc of the gospel extends to include gentiles. Since God chose them to be a light to the nations, Jews who resist this advance of the gospel cut themselves off from the people of God.

Key Themes

- God chose Israel to be a light to the nations.
- God fulfilled his promises by sending the Savior Jesus and raising him from the dead.
- The law cannot save. God conquers sin and death through Jesus's death and resurrection. Salvation comes through faith in him.

Understanding the Text

The Text in Context

Paul's impromptu inaugural sermon is similar to Peter's initial sermons in Jerusalem. His speech begins with a historical reminder of God's initiative to choose and save Israel (vv. 16b–25). A summary of Jesus's death and resurrection capped by scriptural proofs (vv. 26–37) follows, and it concludes with an exhortation to accept the forgiveness of sin offered through faith in Jesus (vv. 38–41). The episode closes with the synagogue inviting Paul and Barnabas to speak again on the next Sabbath so that the congregation might hear more. The next visit ends badly. When the audience swells to include gentiles who are neither proselytes nor God-fearers, it provokes resistance from the Jewish leaders.

Interpretive Insights

13:13 *John left them to return to Jerusalem.* Luke offers no reason to explain why John Mark left Barnabas and Paul, and it is fruitless to try to determine his motives.[1] His departure is noted only to set up the cause for the breakup of the team of Paul and Barnabas later (15:36–41).

13:14–15 *From Perga they went on to Pisidian Antioch.* Going from Perga to Antioch of Pisidia requires an arduous trek over the Taurus Mountains. Maps of the missionary journeys in Acts do not convey the physical exertion that such travel demanded.

Brothers, if you have a word of exhortation for the people, please speak. Paul and Barnabas begin their preaching in a well-established synagogue, which allows them to reach both Jews and gentile God-fearers. Paul has become the chief spokesman, and he is invited to add interpretation and exhortation to the customary reading of the Law and the Prophets in the service.

13:16–20a *Fellow Israelites and you Gentiles who worship God, listen to me! The God of the people of Israel chose our ancestors.* In recounting Israel's history, Paul emphasizes God's redemptive acts. God is the subject of all the verbs. God chose Israel (Deut. 4:37; 10:15). God caused them to prosper in Egypt and led them out of Egypt through his mighty power (Deut. 4:37).[2] The people's disobedience in the wilderness for forty years is quickly passed over so that the emphasis falls on God's patience with them during that time (Deut. 1:31; 29:5). God then "overthrew seven nations in Canaan" (cf. Deut. 7:1) in order to give the land "to his people as their inheritance" (cf. Exod. 6:8; Josh. 14:1–2).

13:20b–23 *From this man's descendants God has brought to Israel the Savior Jesus, as he promised.* The emphasis stays on God's sovereign control as God works throughout the sweep of Israel's history that leads up to the coming of the "Savior." God gave "judges" and a king and then removed that unfaithful king (Saul) to install a king who would do his will (David). Paul assumes that his audience knows Scripture, and he stitches together portions from four different texts (Ps. 89:20; 1 Sam. 16:1; 13:14; Isa. 44:28) to describe David. He then draws on the widespread assumption in this era that the Messiah was to come from the Davidic line, but he uses the term "Savior" instead (cf. Luke 1:47; 2:11). As Peter did (5:31), Paul boldly identifies "Jesus" as Israel's promised deliverer.

13:24–25 *Before the coming of Jesus, John preached repentance and baptism to all the people of Israel.* The next stage in Paul's argument offers the verification for his assertion about Jesus. He assumes that they already know about the ministry of John (cf. 18:25) and declares that he was not the promised rescuer (cf. Luke 3:15–16) but instead prophesied about Jesus's coming.

13:26–31 *The people of Jerusalem and their rulers did not recognize Jesus, yet in condemning him they fulfilled the words of the prophets that are read every Sabbath. . . . But God raised him from the dead.* Paul offers a brief summary of Jesus's death and stresses that it fulfilled prophecy. Luke offers only a synopsis of Paul's speech, and one can imagine that Paul identified specific prophetic passages that were fulfilled. What is important in Luke's summary is the emphasis on God fulfilling his purposes. God took action to reverse the actions of the rulers in Jerusalem and of Pilate, who had Jesus executed. God raised him from the dead.

Jesus's death and resurrection sum up the message of salvation. God has sent that message to "our people," "fellow children of Abraham," but Paul adds that "God-fearing Gentiles" are also included. The inclusion of gentiles will become a sticking point in the events to follow.

13:32–37 *What God promised our ancestors he has fulfilled for us, their children, by raising up Jesus.* Paul insists that the promise refers to Jesus's resurrection, and it has been fulfilled for "us." He cites a string of Scripture passages that make it clear that these promise-filled texts (Ps. 2:7; Isa. 55:3; Ps. 16:10) could apply only to Jesus. David "served God's purpose in his own generation," and that statement could serve as a noble epitaph on his tombstone. Such an epitaph reveals that he was not the decisive fulfillment of God's promise. His reign was limited to his generation. Jesus has no epitaph because the tomb (13:29) and death's pitiless tendrils could not hold him.

13:38–39 *Therefore, my friends, I want you to know that through Jesus the forgiveness of sins is proclaimed to you.* Paul's argument about Jesus, whom he identifies as Savior, God's Son, God's Holy One, and the one whom God would not allow to see death's decay, reaches its high point and defines what it means that Jesus is "Savior." What happened with Jesus is not simply one more in the series of divine events in Israel's history; rather, it is *the crowning event* to which everything pointed. His resurrection is tied to God's offer of grace, forgiveness, and justification. It establishes a new order in God's interface with Israel and the gentiles ("everyone").

13:40–41 *Take care that what the prophets have said does not happen to you.* Paul's last Scripture citation (Hab. 1:5) sharpens the invitation to salvation in Christ with a warning of judgment if they refuse to believe. The context in Habakkuk 1:1–11 reveals that God designs also to save gentiles.

13:42–43 *When the congregation was dismissed, many of the Jews and devout converts to Judaism followed Paul and Barnabas, who talked with them and urged them to continue in the grace of God.* Some in the congregation go on their way after the sermon; others follow Paul and Barnabas to continue the conversation. That Paul urges them "to continue in the grace of

God" suggests that they are converts. Devout converts to Judaism are also included and now become converts to a Judaism that is based on grace and not the law of Moses (13:39).

13:44–47 *On the next Sabbath almost the whole city gathered to hear the word of the Lord.* Since they invited Paul and Barnabas back, the synagogue was not put off by the sermon. When "the whole city," implying a large crowd of gentiles, shows up at the next Sabbath, the mood changes to hostility. This swing in attitude is reminiscent of the reaction to Jesus's sermon in the Nazareth synagogue: they "all spoke well of him and were amazed at the gracious words" until he mentioned gentiles in a favorable light, at which point they tried to kill him (Luke 4:22–29). Now, the "Jews" in the Antioch synagogue are filled with jealousy, which causes many to turn away from an offer of grace that would embrace gentiles on equal terms. The references to the unfaithful wilderness generation, the judges being supplanted by Saul, and Saul supplanted by David establish the idea that God can and will supplant even those in Israel. Those Jews who reject the gospel cut themselves off from the people of God and will be supplanted by others. The task of being a light to the nations will continue without them.

13:48–52 *When the Gentiles heard this, they were glad and honored the word of the Lord; and all who were appointed for eternal life believed.* In response to the positive reception by many gentiles of the gospel, the Jewish leaders incited the God-fearing women of high standing and the leading men of the city. Paul and Barnabas will work among the gentiles. That does not mean that they have abandoned preaching to Jews. In the next city, they again go first to the Jews to announce the fulfillment of the promises, and again they get kicked out. The continuing theme of joy in the midst of persecution is attributed to their recognition of the power of the Holy Spirit that prevents the light of their witness from ever being extinguished.

Theological Insights

1. Paul's absolute conviction that only faith in Christ can save leads him to the recognition that the law cannot save. The law cannot produce righteousness, only demand it. It cannot lead to justification—being made right with God—because it cannot transform the commands into actions. In fact, the law specifically rules out the justification of the ungodly that is so central to the gospel: "I will not acquit the wicked" (Exod. 23:7 ESV). The law serves to make people aware that they are transgressors and sentences them for being transgressors, but it offers no remedy for transgressions. A do-it-yourself religion is doomed to plunge the adherent into an abyss. If God's purpose is to save humanity, then it cannot happen through the law. Justification transpires only through faith in Christ.

2. The statement that all the gentiles "who were appointed for eternal life believed" (13:48) reinforces the point that God is in control. As God chose Israel (13:17), God chooses these believing gentiles. The believer does not elect God; God elects the believer.

Teaching the Text

1. *Paul's review of Israel's history reveals that the movement toward the inclusion of the gentiles in God's people was not happenstance; God had planned it (cf. Luke 24:47)*. Christians are often in danger of a myopic focus on their own current issues and problems and never think about their place in God's metahistory, which arches beyond them. God is not the God simply of ancient history. God is the God of the living and continues to do mighty deeds. But God is also the God of the future. Failing to know and understand what God has done in history as revealed in Scripture can blind one from seeing what God is doing now and what God might do in the future that defies our expectations.

One might ask if the people living during the various epochs that Paul covers in this passage understood what God was doing at the time and where it would lead in the future. I suspect that most would have been utterly astonished to learn the rest of the story. According to Luke, even Jesus's own disciples did not expect that he would be crucified, let alone be resurrected, and that this fulfilled God's purposes. They could understand it only when Jesus taught them from the Scriptures (Luke 24:27, 44–46). The same principle applies today. Understanding God's work in history helps us to interpret what is happening today and to recognize that God's purposes extend far beyond our own little worlds.

2. *The Jewish rejection of the gospel will not thwart its advance in the world*. It is important to recognize, however, that every time the gospel is preached to Jews, it meets with neither wholesale repentance nor wholesale rejection. It creates a divided response. This division was prophesied. Many of the people of Israel, but not all, will turn to the Lord their God (Luke 1:16; Rom. 11:2–6). Jesus's coming will result in "the falling and the rising of many in Israel" (Luke 2:34).

Paul cites Isaiah's prophecy (Isa. 49:6) that Israel was chosen by God to be "a light for the Gentiles, that you may bring salvation to the ends of the earth" (13:47 [cf. Gen. 12:3; Isa. 12:4; 42:6; 49:6; Ezek. 47:22–23]). This promise would be unfulfilled if it were true that the mission to the gentiles depends on the Jews' wholesale rejection of the gospel. Gentiles come to Christ through Jewish mediation. All the missionaries in Acts are Jews! Paul's coworker Titus, an uncircumcised gentile, is never mentioned in Acts. Paul will have his future companion and coworker Timothy circumcised (Acts 16:3). The witnesses in Acts, like Paul, represent what is truly Jewish, and they carry on Israel's vocation.

The rejection of the gospel by some of the Jews in this account and elsewhere in the narrative is understandable. They perceive themselves to possess high status as God's chosen people, and "High status groups carefully restrict access into their circle and their benefits, otherwise, the status they possess would be diluted and their social power lessened."[3] Though they hear the Scriptures every Sabbath, they do not understand them. They do not know that the Scriptures prophesy that God wills for gentiles to turn from their idols to the Lord and receive the forgiveness of sins through faith in Jesus. They fail to accept that they were chosen for this special duty and not because God honored them as special.

Illustrating the Text

The good news of Jesus Christ is open to all.

Testimony: Lamin Sanneh, professor of missions, world Christianity, and history at Yale University, learned that "an ancient faith need not hew to its antiquarian roots to blossom under present conditions." He writes that "world Christianity overcame obstacles local and foreign to surge with the primal impulse of the gospel: as a source of renewal and hope, the movement should challenge us to overcome our cultural shibboleths and bring us into our true ecumenical inheritance."[4] Sanneh grew up as a Muslim. He only knew of Jesus as the one who was persecuted and crucified by his own people, and he felt pity and sympathy for him. But he eventually came to know Christ: "Christianity was not what I was looking for, yet Christianity's slain founder had risen from the grave and was threatening to pursue me in my thoughts. . . . My devout bid to treat Jesus' tragedy as an illusion was a barrier against recognizing my part in his death, placing me in need of God's exoneration, too. I didn't need a complicated theology to appreciate that our hates for God need God to forgive."[5]

We serve a God who often defies our expectations.

Testimony: David Chansky is a Jew who came to follow Jesus Christ. He reflected, "I have returned to Judaism. True, it was not the return that opposers of Y'shua were hoping I would make. But I have been grafted back into the tree planted by our God when he made that first promise to Abraham. The fact that so many Gentiles have accepted the Messiah and were grafted into our tree shows God's goodness, and I am glad. The fact that our Messiah came for Jews and Gentiles affirms my Jewish identity, for God promised Abraham that we would be a light to the nations."[6]

Ministry in Iconium, Lystra, and Derbe

Big Idea

The missionaries' preaching follows the pattern of a divided response, a favorable reception by some Jews and gentiles and stiff and sometimes violent opposition by others.

Key Themes

- The gospel's globalization reaches into places that have never heard of God's loving care.
- Preaching the gospel and even powerful miracles inevitably result in acceptance by some and rejection by others.
- Miraculous signs and wonders are not limited to Israel and do not always generate conversions (2:22 [cf. Exod. 7:3]).

Understanding the Text

The Text in Context

The gospel emissaries continue their travel southeast along the Via Sebaste, the paved road that Augustus built to connect the military colonies in the region to Iconium and Lystra. They then take an unpaved byway to Derbe.[1]

Interpretive Insights

14:1–2 *At Iconium . . . a great number of Jews and Greeks believed. But the Jews who refused to believe stirred up the other Gentiles and poisoned their minds against the brothers.* Although Paul is known from his letters as the apostle to the gentiles (Rom. 1:5; Gal. 2:9), Acts portrays him as engaging in a mission to reach Jews. The synagogue continues to be the base of evangelism. Once again, some Jews who are disturbed by the message and its effectiveness stir up gentiles against the missionaries. These Jewish opponents want to do more than turn public opinion against them; they want to do them violence and enlist the help of gentiles.

14:3 *So Paul and Barnabas spent considerable time there, speaking boldly for the Lord, who confirmed the message of his grace by enabling them to perform signs and wonders.* The "so" may be better put as an adversative, "nevertheless."[2] Despite the attempts by Jewish opponents to do them in, they refuse to retreat from persecution. Greater opposition kindles greater boldness.[3] They counter this opposition with "the message of his grace"—shorthand for the story of Jesus's life, death, and resurrection, which resulted in the offer of the forgiveness of sins to both Jews and gentiles—and with "signs and wonders" that the Lord performs through them. The signs and wonders performed by the original apostles (5:12) and continued by Stephen (6:8) in Jerusalem are also done here and in the gentile world by Paul and Barnabas (cf. 15:12).

14:4–5 *The people of the city were divided . . . There was a plot afoot among both Gentiles and Jews . . . to mistreat them and stone them.* The divided response to the gospel message is not limited to Jews. Gentiles too are not always "glad" and do not always "honor the word of the Lord" (cf. 13:48) when it is presented to them.

14:6–7 *But they found out about it and fled to the Lycaonian cities of Lystra and Derbe.* The witnesses do not recklessly dig in their heels in the face of murderous antagonism; instead, they take flight to another area with the message. They are called not to be martyrs but witnesses. Their departure is driven by the urgency to spread the gospel far and wide (cf. Matt. 10:23). Ironically, witnesses often become victims, transforming the meaning of the term "martyr," which in the original Greek means "witness."

14:8–10 *In Lystra there sat a man who was lame. . . . Paul looked directly at him, saw that he had faith to be healed and called out, "Stand up on your feet!" At that, the man jumped up and began to walk.* The encounter with a lame man in Lystra parallels Peter's healing of a lame man (3:1–10, 16). The setting is similar, the gates of a temple, as is the severity and length of the disability, lame from birth. Both men were dependent on handouts to survive. Both Peter and Paul look intently at the men and raise them up. Both leap up when they are healed, which results in passionate praise from the onlookers.

The man obeys Paul's command to stand up on his feet. He could have said, "I can't. I'm lame." This incident presents faith in action as the immobilized lame man does something that he had never done in his entire life.

14:11–13 *The gods have come down to us in human form!* The crowds are agog over this miracle, but they interpret it through the lens of their own religious mythology, which is all that they have to go on. They credit these strangers with divine attributes and are ready to worship Barnabas as the embodiment of Zeus, the chief god of the Greeks. Paul is presumably the chief speaker and is venerated as Hermes, the messenger god. A priest prepares to adorn bulls with wreaths for a religious procession to the temple, where they will be sacrificed. This reaction may strike modern readers as over the top, but the pervasiveness of tales from Homer in which the gods appear frequently in human guise would have conditioned the citizens to associate miracles with the presence of gods.[4] According to local folklore, Zeus and Hermes had previously visited the area disguised as humans. Only an elderly couple welcomed them into their humble cottage, and they were richly rewarded and made priests in the temple of Zeus while those who were unreceptive were punished.[5]

14:14–15a *But when the apostles Barnabas and Paul heard of this, they tore their clothes and rushed out into the crowd, shouting: "Friends, why are you doing this? We too are only human, like you."* The apostles do not understand the local Lycaonian dialect, but when they are fully informed, they respond vigorously to put a stop to the sacrifice (cf. 10:26). Tearing one's clothes was a Jewish response of horror to perceived blasphemy (Mark 14:63 [cf. Acts 22:23]). Unlike Herod (12:21–23), they will not accept adoration and glory that belong only to the Lord. The Lord, not Paul and Barnabas, caused the miracle.

14:15b–18 *We are bringing you good news, telling you to turn from these worthless things to the living God.* Paul and Barnabas do more than try to stop this miscarriage of worship; they condemn the people's traditional religious beliefs and practices as worthless and futile. Their response reveals that idolatry and Christianity are irreconcilable and cannot coexist.

Paul cannot appeal to the testimony of Scripture as he might in the synagogue, so he starts with a message that his audience can understand: the goodness of creation that gives them pointers to transcendence. Zeus was believed to send thunder and rain, which nourished the crops.[6] Their counterfeit gods have no power to bring rain, let alone heal. Gentiles have also benefited from "the sustaining goodness of the universal creator," the God of Israel.[7] They do not need to add another name to their pantheon but rather to discard their false gods and turn to the one true living God (cf. 1 Thess. 1:9).

14:19–20 *Then some Jews came from Antioch and Iconium and won the crowd over. They stoned Paul and dragged him outside the city, thinking he was dead.* One moment the crowd is ready to offer sacrifice to them as gods; the next moment they are ready to stone them. We may only guess the reasons for this change of heart. It is likely that they were incensed by the blunt appraisal of their traditions as worthless and the insistence that they must turn away from them. Paul attacks the foundations of their society. The arrival of a posse of malicious Jews from Antioch and Iconium pours fuel on the flames to rally public opinion against them.

Paul (no mention is made of Barnabas) is left for dead on the side of the highway after being stoned (cf. 2 Cor. 11:25; Gal. 6:17; 2 Tim. 3:11). His stoning is an ironic reversal of Stephen's stoning, in which Paul was a willing accomplice. Disciples encircle him, perhaps gathering to bury him, but he rises up and will continue his ministry. The incident underscores Paul's "indefatigable faith and loyalty."[8] Despite his injuries, he will persist in preaching the gospel in the face of opposition (cf. 2 Cor. 4:6–14) because of his deep devotion to Christ who saved him and commissioned him.

14:21–23 *Then they returned to Lystra, Iconium and Antioch, strengthening the disciples and encouraging them to remain true to the faith.* The missionaries circle back to the towns where they had been, despite the dangers, in order to encourage their converts. A battered Paul, still nursing his wounds, continues winning disciples with the message that "believers will *inevitably* pass through . . . trials."[9]

14:24–28 *they sailed back to Antioch . . . they gathered the church together and reported all that God had done through them and how he had opened a door of faith to the Gentiles.* They return to home base in Antioch with good news about their work that is received with joy. The grace of God not only offers forgiveness for sins (13:38) and creates opportunities for people to hear the message and respond (11:18) but also brings the missionaries safely home. It is rare, however, that a door of opportunity is opened by God that is not also accompanied by a wall of opposition, which surfaces in the next episode.

Theological Insights

It seems as though the witnessing in Lystra was for naught, and all that Paul got for his trouble was a severe bruising. But one of the converts from the city would be Timothy (16:1–3; 2 Tim. 3:11), whom he identifies as his "beloved and faithful child in the Lord" (1 Cor. 4:17 NRSV), who slaved in the gospel with him (Phil. 2:22). It is evidence "that in all things God works for the good of those who love him, who have been called according to his purpose" (Rom. 8:28).

Teaching the Text

1. *The baton continues to be passed on to others who become witnesses to the foundational facts of the gospel and carry on the work.* Paul and Barnabas are identified as "apostles" even though they do not meet the strict qualifications of an apostle outlined in 1:21–22. The phrase "to the ends of the earth" in 13:47 echoes the commission given to the eleven apostles in 1:8, and this same commission is given to Paul and Barnabas. They preach the same message

that the original apostles passed on to them. They work the same signs and wonders that the apostles did (5:12; 14:3 [cf. 2 Cor. 12:11–12]).[10] They make disciples (14:21) as the original apostles were commanded to do (Matt. 28:19). In particular, Acts presents Paul as having the same power and authority as Peter even though he was not one of the Twelve. He thwarts a sorcerer as Peter did (8:9–14; 13:6–12). He will be an instrument to convey the Holy Spirit to others as Peter was (8:14–17; 19:1–6). He also receives divine visions or dreams directing him to do something related to mission (10:10–16; 16:9), will be miraculously delivered from prison (5:18–25; 12:6–11; 16:24–26), and will raise a dead person to life (9:35–43; 20:9–12). His person also has miraculous powers: Peter's shadow (5:15), Paul's aprons (19:12).

2. *Paul finds common ground with his audience to communicate the truth about God.* The reaction to the miracle by the priest of Zeus who wants to offer sacrifices to Paul and Barnabas seems more reassuring than the harsh reaction of the Jerusalem priests who seized Peter and John and threw them into jail (4:1–22). However, the priest of Zeus is afflicted with the same benighted ignorance that held sway over the Jewish priests. His and his compatriots' ignorance of God is more excusable, however (cf. Rom. 3:17). How does one make a breakthrough with people who have no familiarity with Scripture? Peter could resort to Scripture to interpret what the miracle meant, but Paul cannot do so when addressing a pagan, polytheistic audience that lives in a world of superstition and is prone to mistake messengers from God as gods.

We live in an age when many do not know the biblical tradition, have an uninformed contempt for the Christian faith, and are influenced by traditions from other religions and misrepresentations in the media. What can we learn from this incident about preaching in a nonbiblical milieu? First, we see that Paul does not begin by condemning his audience as worthless sinners who must repent. Instead, he tries to find common ground and begins with the goodness of the transcendent God as evident in the handiwork of nature. Paul subtly argues from the biblical tradition (cf. Pss. 145:15–16; 147:8–9; Jer. 5:24) but uses images that his audience can apprehend and appreciate.

Second, he does not simply try to win their good opinion; he also confronts them with the truth and with the error of their ways. They worship false gods. He exhorts them to turn to the sovereign living God, who has made himself known to them through the world he has created. Only the living creator God can bring life. The divine and the universe are not identical, contrary to what pantheism assumes. God is the sovereign creator.

What is striking is that Paul says nothing about Jesus. The foundation of faith is belief in the one God. If one does not believe in the one God, then the story of Jesus makes no sense.[11] Not mentioning Jesus in this context does not mean that Paul thinks that gentiles can be saved by simply turning to God without also turning to Christ. If Paul could persuade them to believe in the one God who is gracious to all, the next step would be to teach them how this gracious God gave his only Son so that they might have life everlasting (cf. 17:16–34).

Paul also would teach that bringing a good harvest, however, is not the sum total of what God does. As Robert Wall states it, "The aim of their witness is not hearts gladdened by a full stomach occasioned by a bountiful harvest but hearts gladdened by the Holy Spirit occasioned by forgiveness (see 13:52)."[12]

3. *Believers will face opposition and oppression.* The sufferings of Christ (Luke 24:46–47; Acts 13:27–29) are carried on by his apostles (Acts 9:15–16) and by believers (Luke 9:23–27). One therefore cannot coast into the kingdom. "We must go through many hardships to enter the kingdom of God" (Acts 14:22). Those who understand the rewards of Christian faith in terms of material abundance on earth do the gospel message a disservice. They may attract "short-term buyers—but then when life unfolds in its usual messy, joyful, sad, tragic, up-and-downway, those buyers realize they were sold a bill of goods."[13] The sufferings that Paul has in mind are not simply related to the unfolding of life; they are afflictions that will come to Christians precisely because of their commitment to Christ. If they are not deeply rooted in the faith, they will fall away in the times of testing that are sure to come (Luke 8:13).

One can say that those whose faith costs them nothing will ultimately pay for what they get. Those who are faithful through the many afflictions will receive their reward from God.

This teaching is difficult to put across. Paul and Barnabas cannot stay to do it. They do not ask for volunteers to be leaders and teachers in the churches that they establish, but instead select the elders through prayer and fasting. Since no criteria are listed for their appointment, one can only infer that the apostles chose those who accepted the tenet that they too "must go through many hardships to enter the kingdom of God."

Illustrating the Text

To reach a pagan/post-Christian culture, we must speak a language they understand.

Missions: *Peace Child* tells the story of Don and Carol Richardson and their mission to the Sawi people of New Guinea. The Sawi were a tribe that deeply admired someone who could draw a person in, convince them of true friendship, and then stab them in the back (quite literally). This point was driven home to the Richardsons when, over the course of several tellings, they conveyed the story of Jesus. They were shocked when the tribesmen began cheering at the point in the story when Judas betrayed Jesus. They regarded the betrayer as the hero! Over time, however, the Richardsons also learned that the tribe had a way to overcome enmity between warring factions. One party must be willing to give a son to the other tribe. As long as the child was loved and cared for, they would have peace. The Richardsons used this cultural communication point to represent the gospel to the Sawi, with Christ being God's peace child, sent for our redemption.

As Christians living in a post-Christian culture, we cannot simply sit back and wait for the world to come to us. We cannot simply resent the reality that the culture no longer speaks our language. We must become bridge builders who can span the communication gaps and share the good news.

Simply identifying with lost people is not enough; we must call them to repent and believe.

Human Experience: Anyone who's had a doctor with a poor "bedside manner" knows how difficult that can be. This kind of doctor can leave you feeling like a car at the mechanic's shop. Even so, a good bedside manner is no replacement for medical competence. Just because a doctor can connect and make you feel heard doesn't guarantee that you will get an accurate diagnosis and be cured.

Christians are called to show love, understanding, and acceptance. We are also compelled to share the truth that people must repent and believe the gospel.

Quote: Amy Carmichael. Carmichael prayed, "*IF* I am afraid to speak the truth, lest I lose affection, or lest the one concerned should say, 'You do not understand,' or because I fear to lose my reputation for kindness; if I put my own good name before the other's highest good, then I know nothing of Calvary love."[14]

The necessity of repentance

Essay: "Evangelism and Repentance Ethics," by René Padilla. In this paper presented before the Lausanne Congress in 1974, Padilla wrote, "This new reality places men in a position of crisis—they cannot continue to live as if nothing had happened; the Kingdom of God demands a new mentality, a reorientation of all their values, repentance. . . . Repentance is much more than a private affair between individual and God. It is the complete reorientation of life in the world—among men—in response to the work of God in Jesus Christ."[15]

The gospel mission involves suffering.

News: On February 15, 2015, the Islamic State (ISIS) released gruesome video of the beheading of twenty-one Orthodox Coptic men in Libya by Islamic State affiliates. On that same day Egypt's Coptic Catholic Church celebrated the consecration of its first-ever church in Sinai, in the community of Sharm

El-Sheikh. The church is known as Our Lady of Peace. The brutal execution hung like a cloud over Egypt's Christian community, but the Coptic Catholic bishop Youssef Aboul-Kheir of Sohag told the international Catholic charity Aid to the Church in Need, "The Church in Egypt has been strengthened by the murder of our brothers in Libya." The guest workers in Libya "suffered a holy death with prayers on their lips. They went to their deaths just like the early Christians."[16]

The Jerusalem Council
What Is to Be Required of Gentile Converts?

Big Idea

Community tension stemming from not requiring gentiles to be circumcised is confronted head on by the church leaders. It is resolved through testimonies about God's work among gentiles, the application of Scripture, and the guidance of the Holy Spirit.

Key Themes

- The Holy Spirit leads the church to break through the barrier of Jewish ethnocentricity so that a universal mission can continue.
- Gentiles are saved as gentiles and do not need to become Jews to be saved.
- The church cannot make a test of fellowship what God does not make a condition of salvation.

Understanding the Text

The Text in Context

The rosy report of the evangelistic success among gentiles breeds a controversy over what is required for gentiles to be saved and to have fellowship with Jewish Christians. This incident appears in the center of Acts and serves as a fulcrum that looks back on the movement of the Christian witness beyond Jerusalem and forward to Paul's continuing mission leading to Rome.

Interpretive Insights

15:1–3 *Certain people came down from Judea to Antioch and were teaching the believers: "Unless you are circumcised, according to the custom taught by Moses, you cannot be saved."* Allowing gentiles full membership in the church without requiring them to be circumcised causes consternation among some well-meaning Jewish Christians who presumably belong to the mother church in Jerusalem. They question how the church can still regard itself as the true Israel if it disregards the commandment about circumcision that is linked to God's covenant with Israel (cf. 7:8; Gen. 17). Their insistence that gentiles need to be circumcised and become Jews to be saved flies in the face of Peter's quote from Joel in his Pentecost sermon: "Everyone who calls on the name of the Lord will be saved" (2:21). They resist the new state of affairs that has arisen in salvation history.

15:4–6 *The apostles and elders met to consider this question.* The welcome of Barnabas and Paul indicates that the church is not bitterly divided over this issue, which bodes well for a harmonious resolution. Paul already preaches that salvation does not come through the law of Moses (13:38–39), and under the Spirit's guidance the apostles and elders in Jerusalem will confirm the eternal truth of that message.

15:7–9 *God, who knows the heart, showed that he accepted them by giving the Holy Spirit to them, just as he did to us.* Peter testifies again about his firsthand experience with Cornelius. Without first consulting Peter or anyone else in the church, God showed that believing gentiles were accepted as they were by pouring out the Holy Spirit into their hearts. This divine outpouring of the Spirit was identical to what happened to the disciples at Pentecost (11:15). God has spoken decisively about the acceptance of Gentiles who believe in the Lord Jesus Christ (11:17).

15:10–11 *Now then, why do you try to test God by putting on the necks of Gentiles a yoke that neither we nor our ancestors have been able to bear?* Peter decries the attempt to blackball those whom God has accepted and to put God to the test by adding the burden of obedience to the law (cf. Luke 11:46) for gentiles that even Jews cannot shoulder (cf. Gal. 6:13). Putting God to the test is a grave offense, since that is what the wilderness generation did (Heb. 3:9), what Ananias and Sapphira did (Acts 5:9), and what the devil continues to try to get persons to do (Luke 4:2). If they impose the law as a means of salvation, it dooms the gentiles to failure. Jews have failed to obey it themselves (7:53). Worse, it makes faith in Christ insufficient for salvation and nullifies God's grace because it requires that one do something more before receiving full acceptance by God.

15:12 *The whole assembly became silent as they listened to Barnabas and Paul telling about the signs and wonders God had done among the Gentiles through them.* Barnabas and Paul testify from their mission experience and reconfirm that the Spirit has been working among the gentiles. The signs and wonders worked by God should leave no doubt that God has accepted and blessed gentiles.

15:13–14 *James spoke up.* James is not identified as "the Lord's brother" (Gal. 1:19). He speaks as the leader of the Jerusalem church, though Luke does not narrate how this transition transpired (12:17). No one questions his commitment to the Jewish heritage, and he proposes the pivotal ruling.

"A people for his name" possibly refers to Zechariah 2:11. God has taken "a group of people out of the Gentile nations," and that group "now belongs to God in the same way as Israel does."[1]

15:15–18 *I will return and rebuild David's fallen tent. . . . I will restore it, that the rest of mankind may seek the Lord, even all the Gentiles who bear my name, says the Lord.* James refers to the prophets but specifically cites Amos 9:11–12 to affirm that God's purpose from the beginning was to include gentiles into the people of God.[2] Amos's prophecy is being fulfilled as God overhauls Israel and adds gentiles to God's people.

Rebuilding "David's fallen tent" does not mean that God restores the Davidic line to temporal power. It refers to the Messiah and his community and the eschatological temple, where God now dwells and where gentiles are included in worship.[3]

15:19–21 *It is my judgment, therefore, that we should not make it difficult for the Gentiles who are turning to God.* While the preaching of Moses in the synagogues hindered gentiles, the preaching of Jesus, however, has been successful. The final decision on whether to impose the law of Moses on gentiles and require them to be circumcised is not put up for a vote such that whoever packed the audience might win the day. James, led by the Holy Spirit, renders the apostles' and elders' decision but adds a stipulation: gentile Christians may remain gentiles, but they cannot remain idolaters.

15:22–26 *decided to choose some of their own men and send them to Antioch with Paul and Barnabas.* To deliver the news of the decision they send a letter with envoys. Identifying themselves and the recipients as "brothers" in the salutation of the letter indicates that they affirm gentiles as members of the Christian family. Those they send with the letter have not simply praised the name of the Lord but have also actually risked their lives for the name of the Lord.

15:27–29 *It seemed good to the Holy Spirit and to us not to burden you with anything beyond the following requirements: You are to abstain from food sacrificed to idols, from blood, from the meat of strangled animals and from sexual immorality.* The decision to accept gentiles as gentiles was made by the Holy Spirit. The addition of the so-called apostolic decree is not offered as a compromise that urges gentiles to avoid offending Jewish sensibilities on certain matters. Rather, these restrictions are related to idolatry and are nonnegotiable. As Christians, the gentiles may no longer be involved in anything related to their former idolatry.

15:30–35 *The people read it and were glad for its encouraging message.* The decision inspires comfort not simply because gentile converts are not forced to be circumcised but because the unity between Jewish and gentile Christians is sustained. Jewish leaders—Judas, Silas, Paul, and Barnabas—will continue to preach and teach Jews and gentiles a gospel that is free from requiring Jewish identity markers as prerequisites to salvation and edifying for all of God's people.

Theological Insights

Requiring circumcision for gentile converts will not purify their hearts (15:9), draw them closer to God, make them more righteous, or cause the Holy Spirit to flow more abundantly into their hearts. All it would do is make them Jewish proselytes, and second-class Jews at that. More significantly, if circumcision and obedience to the Mosaic law were still necessary for salvation, it would imply that Christ's death and resurrection had not changed a thing.

Teaching the Text

1. *Well-intentioned, zealous believers can be fatally wrong and can unintentionally sabotage the church's mission.* These opponents assume that Israel must be faithful to its covenant with God and that the covenant promises to Abraham are operative only for the sons of Abraham and those who make themselves sons of Abraham through circumcision. Therefore, they contend that gentiles need to become Jews if they are to be a part of God's covenant people. They also assume that the failure to require circumcision is a slippery slope that inevitably will erode the identity of God's people. They worry that this open-door policy regarding gentiles (14:27) will only open the doors to apostasy like that committed in Maccabean times when some Jews stopped circumcising their children and tried to remove the marks of circumcision to assimilate into the culture of their gentile oppressors (1 Macc. 1:11–15).

The church always must guard against those who imply that faith is fine as far as it goes, but it does not go far enough. They want to add asterisks to the message that one is saved by faith. The asterisks append other salvation requirements in the fine print. Those extra requirements add burdens that weigh persons down and cancel out the grace that can lift them up. In teaching the text, one can ask persons to fill in the blank from what they may have heard others say or thought themselves: "Unless you *also* _____, you cannot be saved." One should ask, "Is this condition congruent with the gospel?"

2. *The principle that emerges from the council is not to add things that are unnecessary burdens (15:28), but the requirements in 15:20, 29 seem to do just that.* These obligations are difficult for modern readers to understand. They are not designed to find a middle ground for gentile Christians to have fellowship with Jewish Christians. Some point to the requirements of Leviticus 17–18 as the background, but this is misleading if it is interpreted to mean, for

example, that gentiles must use only Jewish butchers and buy kosher meat. If it were true that the decree was simply a "concession to the law-oriented consciences of Jews who want the Gentiles to meet them halfway as a means of expressing cultural sensitivity and thereby promoting unified table fellowship," then why not also ask them not to eat pork in the presence of Jews?[4]

The Greek word translated as "food sacrificed to idols" (15:29) is the key, and it is best to interpret all of these prohibitions as connected to the pervasive idolatry in the pagan world.[5] The council's rejection of the requirement of circumcision, which separated Jewish Christians from gentile Christians, does not entail rejection of restrictions involving idolatry, which separated Christians, who are exclusively tied to the one true God, from idolaters, who relate to many gods and lords. The prohibitions are intended to prevent gentile converts from being sucked back into the vortex of idolatrous influences.[6] The Corinthians thought that it was harmless to eat meat offered in sacrifice to pagan idols because they knew that the gods did not exist. In a lengthy rebuttal, Paul addresses the issues related to idol food in 1 Corinthians 8–10 and insists that Christians must "flee from idolatry" (1 Cor. 10:14). He refers to pagan temple feasts as partaking of "the cup of demons" (1 Cor. 10:20–21). "Blood" refers to the ritual drinking of the sacrificed animals' blood, and what is "strangled" (a word that does not appear in Lev. 17) refers to the animals that are ritually strangled for a sacrifice to an idol.[7] "Sexual immorality" covers all illicit sexual sins, but why stipulate that gentiles need to refrain from sexual immorality as a minimal requirement to have fellowship with Jewish Christians? Chastity is not optional for Christians. It is required of both Jews and gentile Christians (cf. 1 Thess. 4:1–8). In this case, however, "sexual immorality" more likely refers to any associations with temple prostitution (cf. Rev. 2:20–21).

The prohibitions may seem irrelevant in our culture, but the principle behind them is valid. There are some behaviors that Christians cannot do and still claim to be Christian. For example, is one's sexual behavior a matter of indifference? Does the church have the right to interpose prohibitions on members' behavior that might otherwise be considered acceptable according to cultural mores? Also, many people today no longer bow down to idols in pagan temples, but what other forms of idolatry threaten to compromise the Christian gospel to which the church must say no?

3. *The early church regarded members as a family of brothers and sisters.* Like any family, the early church experienced its share of fights, particularly as the gospel reached across the world and included brothers and sisters from unfamiliar places and cultures. How does the church resolve disputes when both sides draw opposite conclusions from their sincere reading of Scripture? In this case, the apostles based their decision on the interpretation of Scripture

that was informed by their own story of God's Spirit working among them and fundamental principles extrapolated from a gospel of grace. They conferred not behind closed doors in a backroom but in a completely transparent process. They define and limit the problem and gather information from worthy leaders. They also recognize that as leaders in the church they will accomplish little if they try to make everyone happy. They must choose what they believe to be the right path knowing that some may resist the decision. They then take action and seek to communicate clearly the decision and how it is to be applied to all concerned.

Illustrating the Text

The church must guard against any teaching that asserts that something more than faith is required.

Government: In order to vote in an election, you don't need money, status, fame, or power—you only need to be a registered voter. Prior to 1964, some local governments and even states forced people to pay a "poll tax." In other words, one could not get into the voting station without bringing some kind of payment. This was eventually outlawed by the Twenty-Fourth Amendment, which says, "The right of citizens of the United States to vote in any primary or other election . . . shall not be denied or abridged by the United States or any State by reason of failure to pay any poll tax or other tax."

Christians come to God with faith alone—nothing else. Nothing else can bring us to God—not money, status, fame, or power. Any other presumed conditions for acceptance have been "outlawed" and rejected by God. All believers enter God's kingdom in the same way and on the same basis: by grace through faith in Christ.

The call to holiness is not legalism.

Philosophy: Consider the phrase "He used his blade expertly." Taken in isolation, it's impossible to know exactly what is indicated by this sentence. Context will determine meaning. For instance, imagine you read the phrase in a novel about pirates. Or you read the phrase in a crime thriller, where a detective is looking down at the victim of a knife attack. Or you're reading a novel whose main character is a surgeon. Or it could occur in a story in which a character has a cruel way with words. Each context elicits a different meaning for the same sentence. Context drives meaning.

The word "holiness" when used in a context of law-oriented legalism can sound harsh, a matter of externals and reputation. When used in a grace-permeated setting, "holiness" becomes a beautiful word. It points us toward Christlikeness. It means drawing closer to our Father. It indicates a life filled with the Holy Spirit. Holiness, when defined by a gospel context, is one of the most beautiful words in the Christian vocabulary.

The church today may not identify with carved idols, but we still must identify and throw away idolatry.

Object Lesson: The idea of bowing down to a carved statue may seem ridiculous to the modern person. Idols are not limited to graven images, but to any person, possession, purpose, or pursuit that takes priority and precedence over God. Take out a credit card and bow down to it. Take out a laptop or smart phone and bow down to it. Take out a sports jersey or toy car and bow down to it. The picture may seem silly and absurd, but we can challenge, "How many of us live our lives idolizing these very things? How many of us give more of ourselves—our minds, our resources, our time, our attention spans, and our hearts—to these items than to God?"

Paul and Barnabas Split Up, but the Mission Continues

Big Idea

The split between Paul and Barnabas does not hinder the continuing mission into gentile lands. Barnabas takes Mark. Paul takes Silas, and Timothy joins Paul's company.

Key Themes

- The decision by the Jerusalem Council promotes understanding and unity in the church, but disagreements may still arise among Christians.
- Jews who become followers of Christ do not have to abandon their Jewish identity. While Jews may not insist that gentiles be circumcised to be saved, they may continue that practice as part of their own cultural heritage and identity.
- The offer of Christian hospitality turns strangers into brothers and sisters.

Understanding the Text

The Text in Context

A potentially ruinous breach in the unity of the church over the gentile issue is averted by the Jerusalem Council, but a rupture over a different issue does occur in Paul's relationship with Barnabas. The two missionaries go their separate ways, each taking different coworkers as they continue their work in different regions.

Interpretive Insights

15:36–39a *Barnabas wanted to take John, also called Mark, with them, but Paul did not think it wise to take him, because he had deserted them in Pamphylia.* Paul wishes to return to the churches that he and Barnabas founded to check on their progress. He balks at Barnabas's desire to take Mark with them again on this return trip. The NIV translation interprets Mark's earlier leave-taking (13:13) as desertion. Luke does use the verb elsewhere to mean "to fall away" (Luke 8:13), but he uses it more frequently in a neutral sense to mean "to depart" (Luke 2:37; 4:13; Acts 12:10; 19:9; 22:29). In the context, Paul presumably considers Mark unfit for the task and refuses to take him again. Barnabas interprets Mark's departure quite differently. Their sharp disagreement results in a split.

15:39b–41 *Barnabas took Mark and sailed for Cyprus, but Paul chose Silas . . . He went through Syria and Cilicia, strengthening the churches.* Barnabas and Mark head off to Cyprus and drop out of Luke's story at this point, as does Peter. We might like to know more, but Acts is about the spread of the gospel into the world, not a profile of individual missionary lives, no matter how notable they were.

Paul's new coworker, Silas, is one of the leaders of the Jerusalem church (15:22) and belonged to the delegation of men "who have risked their lives for the name of our Lord Jesus Christ" (15:25–27) sent to confirm for the church in Antioch the decision to accept gentiles as full members without having to be circumcised. These brief comments disclose three qualities that must have commended Silas to Paul for his next missionary venture. Silas had risen in the Jerusalem church to become one of its leaders. He had demonstrated his willingness to sacrifice his life for the gospel. He shared Paul's theological conviction that gentiles need only to repent and believe in Christ to be saved and grafted on to Israel.

Commending the missionaries to the grace of the Lord involves more than sending them off with prayers and best wishes; they are sent off with material support.

16:1–3 *Paul came to Derbe and then to Lystra, where a disciple named Timothy lived . . . Paul wanted to take him along on the journey, so he circumcised him because of the Jews who lived in that area, for they all knew that his father was a Greek.* Timothy and his mother were converted probably during Paul's first journey to the area. Since that visit, Timothy developed a good reputation among believers, perhaps also taking a leadership role. Although his mother is Jewish, her Greek name, "Eunice" (2 Tim. 1:5), which means "conquering well," is associated with mythological figures. It suggests her family's assimilation to Greek culture. Timothy has been schooled in the Scriptures from his youth but had not been circumcised. The obligation to circumcise a son belonged to the father, and Timothy's father was not a Jew. Before taking him on the mission, Paul takes over that paternal role (cf. 1 Cor. 4:17; 1 Tim. 1:2; 2 Tim. 1:2) and has Timothy circumcised, a painful surgery for an adult (cf. Gen. 34:24–25).

Having Timothy circumcised may seem unnecessary and at odds with the decision of the apostolic council recounted in Acts 15. His circumcision, however, establishes his Jewish identity (Rom. 3:1–2). Paul considered him to be a Jew. An uncircumcised gentile was one thing; an uncircumcised Jew was quite another. This measure shows the later accusation that Paul teaches "all the Jews who live among the Gentiles to turn away from Moses, telling them not to circumcise their children" (21:21) to be totally unfounded.

16:4–5 *So the churches were strengthened in the faith and grew daily in numbers.* The missionaries relay to the new church-starts the formal decree that gentiles need not be circumcised but must abandon their heritage of idolatry. They provide grounding through preaching and teaching that both strengthens and grows churches.

16:6–8 *Paul and his companions traveled throughout the region of Phrygia and Galatia, having been kept by the Holy Spirit from preaching the word in the province of Asia. . . . they tried to enter Bithynia, but the Spirit of Jesus would not allow them to.* When the missionaries have completed their primary objective to revisit and strengthen the churches, their initial plans to expand their preaching in Asia and then in Bithynia are twice vetoed by divine embargoes.[1] God has different ideas. The account emphasizes that divine guidance, rather than human strategy, directs the mission. They are to embark on an unplanned advance into Macedonia (Europe).[2]

Luke narrates Paul and his companions hurtling from Derbe, Lystra, and Iconium to Troas. The itinerary conveys "some impression of the irresistible sweep of events that took Paul to Macedonia."[3] Like Jesus's journey to Jerusalem in Luke (13:33), the missionaries also travel under a divine necessity.

16:9–10 *During the night Paul had a vision of a man of Macedonia.* This vision is the second of six that Acts records Paul experiencing (9:1–9; 18:9; 22:17–21; 23:11; 27:23–24). Luke's presentation of God's communication and direction reveals their power and absence of ambiguity. This vision is quite different from the others. It involves a cry for help for a land and people that lack the gospel. It promises receptivity to the preaching of the gospel. The Scripture affirms that only God can answer this cry for help and provide salvation (cf. Gen. 49:25; Exod. 18:4; Deut. 33:26; Ps. 10:14).

Luke introduces "we" to his narration. The "we sections" (16:10–17; 20:5–16; 21:1–18; 27:1–28:16) suggest that Luke has now joined Paul's company. These passages possibly derive from a log that he kept. Luke "does not wish to make a great deal of his own personal participation in these events, especially since he seems only to have been an observer and recorder of the actions and words of others, and so he quietly and subtly includes the 'we' material, without fanfare, and thus without introduction."[4] If Luke teamed up with them about the time Paul suffered the malady mentioned in Galatians 4:13–14, he may have served as Paul's physician (cf. Col. 4:14).

16:11–12 *From there we traveled to Philippi, a Roman colony and the leading city of that district of Macedonia.* They do not dawdle but set out immediately for Europe and wind up in Philippi. It was established as a Roman colony and populated by veterans to commemorate the decisive victory of Octavian (later Caesar Augustus) there in the civil war against those who assassinated Julius Caesar. Rome created colonies to relieve congestion in the city and to propagate Roman values across the world. The city would have had political organizations and institutions similar to Rome. Going to Macedonia is in some way a preparation for Paul to go to Rome.

16:13 *On the Sabbath we went outside the city gate to the river, where we expected to find a place of prayer. We sat down and began to speak to the women who had gathered there.* It is often argued that Philippi had too small a Jewish population to have the ten men required for a synagogue (*m. 'Abot* 3:7), but "place of prayer" is a term also used for a synagogue. It is possible that only women were there because the men and women met at different times.[5] Worshiping by the river makes ceremonial washings with running water easier. As a foreign cult, Jews would not have been allowed to establish a worship center within the city walls, which explains why the missionaries looked for them outside the city gates.[6]

16:14–15 *a woman from the city of Thyatira named Lydia.* Lydia is a merchant of purple goods and hails from Thyatira, a city famous for its dyeing industry. The rich dressed in purple (Luke 16:19; Rev 17:4), and presumably she is well-off from her trade. Apparently, she is without a husband and is the head of her household.

The identification of Lydia as a "worshiper of God" indicates that she had converted from her pagan past to Judaism (cf. 17:17). God had already been working in her life. She belongs to the ranks of gentiles who readily accept the message about the Lord Jesus when they hear it. Once again, the agent of her faith is the Lord, who opened her heart to believe. When she is baptized, she offers hospitality to the traveling missionaries. She has the resources to do so but is also persuasive in prevailing on them to stay with her. Her hospitality to Jews and their acceptance of it underscore that Jewish regulations concerning clean and unclean have become irrelevant. The gospel is offered to all and creates a bond among believers.

Theological Insights

The Holy Spirit prevents the missionaries from preaching in Asia (probably a reference to Ephesus, since Paul usually confined his mission efforts to major cities). Then, the Spirit of Jesus does not allow them to enter Bithynia. Luke does not distinguish between the Holy Spirit and the Spirit of Jesus, which reflects Luke's high view of Jesus's divinity. "The Spirit of Jesus" is also the same as "the Spirit of the Lord" (Luke 4:18; Acts 5:9; 8:39).

Teaching the Text

1. *God works through human disputes.* Luke has no interest in examining the causes of the disagreement between Paul and Barnabas but uses it for its theological implications. He may use this clash to portray the sovereignty of God working through human weakness[7] or to show that even division between leading missionaries cannot ultimately hinder the mission.[8] The gospel will not be stopped.

Luke does not record the breakup between Paul and Barnabas to vilify Mark any more than the Gospel accounts of Peter's denial of Jesus were recorded to disparage Peter. Luke does not narrate Paul's reconciliation with Mark because his account of the spread of the gospel is not interested in providing biographical sketches. We know only from the Pauline Letters that Mark must have redeemed himself in Paul's eyes. Mark is included in the greeting to the Colossians and is identified as the cousin of Barnabas (Col. 4:10), which may explain Barnabas's commitment to Mark. He also is mentioned in the greeting to Philemon (Philem. 24) and identified with Aristarchus, Demas, and Luke as Paul's fellow workers. In 2 Timothy 4:11, Paul asks Timothy to get Mark and bring him along "because he is helpful to me in my ministry." In 1 Peter 5:12–13, Silvanus (the Greek form of "Silas") and Mark are mentioned together as serving with Peter. In giving greetings to the recipients, Silvanus is identified as "a faithful brother," through whom the letter was written, and Mark is distinguished as "my son."

One can only guess what may have transpired in the rest of the story about Mark. It does suggest that although one may let down others at various points in one's life, those failures need not be irredeemable, which is the message of the gospel of grace. Barnabas is often hailed as living up to his name as an encourager (Acts 4:36) in this situation. Paul is sometimes regarded less favorably as difficult and demanding. But the work of taking the gospel to the world is demanding, and one cannot be sentimental in making choices about personnel and whether they are fit for a task. Jesus's warning in Luke 9:62 about those who put a hand to the plow and look back supports Paul's decision.

2. *Keeping the doors open to preach the gospel.* Paul has Timothy circumcised so that he can continue preaching in Jewish venues with Timothy at his side. Becoming a Christian does not mean that one ceases to be a Jew or a non-Jew. Timothy's full Jewish identity is established by his circumcision. Paul outlines his mission strategy to win as many people as possible from

various backgrounds in 1 Corinthians 9:19–23. He writes, "To the Jews I became like a Jew, to win the Jews. To those under the law I became like one under the law (though I myself am not under the law), so as to win those under the law" (1 Cor. 9:20).

On the other hand, the missionaries in Acts represent what is truly Jewish. All of them are Jews![9] Acts portrays the spread of the gospel not as a simple progression "first to the Jew, then to the Gentile" (Rom. 1:16), but rather first to the Jew (Acts 10:36) and then *through* the Jew to the gentile. Paul's trusted coworker Titus, an uncircumcised gentile (Gal. 2:1–5), is never mentioned in Acts. This fact supports the view that Luke intends to show that Jewish missionaries are fulfilling the prophecy of Isaiah 49:6. Timothy represents another who is restored to the tribes of Jacob who serves as a light for the gentiles to bring God's salvation to the ends of the earth.

3. *Discerning God's will is often a group decision.* Paul shares with his companions his vision to go to Macedonia so that they can help him discern what they should do. He does not dictate to them what the new plan will be. The rest of his group helps to interpret its meaning and decide what they should do. They conclude that "God had called us" (16:10). Good leaders learn that it is not all about them and their personal visions. Others must also discern that a particular direction is indeed *God's* calling, not an individual's deluded egotism or self-interest.

Illustrating the Text

God can use our setbacks to further his mission.

Bible: The story of Joseph shows us what it looks like when God takes our tragic and insufferable setbacks and uses them to advance his purposes. Joseph undergoes a series of setbacks. Yet God is moving Joseph's life unerringly toward the exact place he will need to occupy in order to save the lives of God's chosen people, Israel. What Joseph experienced as tragedy was actually part of God's plan. He tells his brothers who betrayed him, "You intended to harm me, but God intended it for good to accomplish what is now being done, the saving of many lives" (Gen. 50:20). When we experience difficulty and setbacks, we can rest in the plan of the sovereign God, who works all things together for good.

Despite division, the mission continues.

Quote: A. W. Tozer. Tozer instructs, "In a fallen world like ours unity is no treasure to be purchased at the price of compromise. Loyalty to God, faithfulness and truth and the preservation of a good conscience are jewels more precious than gold of Ophir or diamonds from the mine. . . . Power lies in the union of things similar and the division of things dissimilar. Maybe what we need in religious circles today is not more union but some wise and courageous division. Everyone desires peace but it could be that revival will follow the sword."[10]

Preaching the gospel trumps personal comfort.

Television: In the 1990s television show *Quantum Leap*, the main character, Dr. Sam Beckett, is a brilliant physicist who has developed a machine that will allow time travel. When it looks like the government is about to shut down his project, Sam leaps in and is thrust into a time-travel odyssey that would last five years. In each episode, Sam is thrown somewhere new in time, inhabiting the body of another person. Sam's job is to help each person by navigating him or her through a difficult life situation, changing the future and "setting right what once went wrong." The job is never easy. But it is his mission.

As believers, we're called to put ourselves in another's shoes and discover how best to reach them with the news that they desperately need to hear. It might not be easy or comfortable, but it is our mission.

Quote: **Gladys Aylward.** Aylward, a British missionary to China, wrote to her parents: "Life is pitiful, death so familiar, suffering and pain so common, yet I would not be anywhere else. Do not wish me out of this or in any way seek to get me out, for I will not be got out while this trial is on. These are my people, God has given them to me, and I will live or die for Him and His glory."[11]

Discerning God's call is a team effort.

Theological Reference: How do we know what God wants us to do? This question can apply to a small decision such as "Am I supposed to go on this mission trip?" It can apply to a trajectory-altering decision such as "Should I step out of my current job, go to seminary, and become a pastor?" How do we know what to do in this situation?

Theologians refer to the "internal" and the "external" calls of God. These terms typically are applied to those called into a specialized ministry, such as pastor or missionary, but they are relevant for anyone seeking God's will. The internal call is our inner sense of purpose, dictated by the word of God and through prayer, where we sense that God is directing us. The external call is the affirming voice of other believers, confirming what we have seen God doing in our lives. We cannot simply follow the life plan that someone else may give us if we do not sense the internal call of God. Likewise, we should never ignore the voices of those who might confirm or question our direction, God's external call.

Rocking the Jailhouse

Big Idea

The missionaries suffer hardships, but God protects them.

Key Themes

- The gospel has an impact on immoral business. Persons profiting from human trafficking are shut down by the power of Jesus's name.
- Persecution does not dampen the believers' joy.
- Conversion results in concrete actions of mercy and hospitality.

Understanding the Text

The Text in Context

The gospel cuts across the spectrum of society in Philippi, and Luke notes changes in the lives of three persons. The first is a respectable businesswoman and devout God-fearer. The second is a slave girl ruthlessly exploited by her masters. The third is a jailer from the lower class, perhaps a civic slave.

Interpretive Insights

16:16 *a female slave who had a spirit by which she predicted the future.* The girl is said to have, literally, a "Python spirit." It was associated with the oracles delivered at Delphi, where, in the cult's mythology, the god Apollo had killed the dragon that protected the sanctuary. Apollo then became the deity of the sanctuary. The spirit possessing the girl was not considered to be a malign one but was presumed to enable persons to predict the future. Her owners used her soothsaying to hustle gullible clients.

16:17–18 *These men are servants of the Most High God, who are telling you the way to be saved.* The slave girl's spirit of divination publicizes the missionaries. The notice that it attracts is unwelcome to Paul because her declarations are likely to mislead observers. Most people imagined a kind of organizational flow chart for the various gods with their roles and powers, and many cults recognized a "most high god" in their hierarchies. Those who heard her yells were likely to think not of the one God of the Old Testament but of their own highest god, which might be Zeus or another pagan deity.[1]

There also is no definite article in the Greek text before "way of salvation," and so it may be understood as referring to "*a* way of salvation," not "*the* way of salvation." "Salvation" also may be understood only as "well-being, bodily health, deliverance and preservation."[2] Finally, from what follows, her shouts may be construed as an accusation and a warning: "These men are proselytizing Jews."

She is right that the missionaries are "slaves" ("servants") of God (cf. Gal. 1:10; Phil. 1:1). They serve the one and only God and proclaim the one and only way of salvation, not one option among many.[3] Paul silences her and drives out the spirit in the name of Jesus, who is dominant over all.

16:19–22 *they seized Paul and Silas and dragged them into the marketplace.* The owners are unimpressed with the exorcism of a powerful spirit and only see their source of income evaporating. Paul has sabotaged their business. To her owners, the slave girl was only a meal ticket, and they treated her as if she were little more than an organ grinder's monkey.

The missionaries are accosted not as Christians but as Jews who are spreading Jewish propaganda. This charge would have been relevant in a Roman colony. The expulsion of Jews from Rome by the emperor Claudius (c. AD 49/50) to suppress riots in the city (Acts 18:2) was well publicized.[4] The owners mention nothing about the exorcism or loss of business, which would not hold up in court, but bring religious and political charges to the magistrates, who are charged as the guardians of order and of the "Roman religion in the colony."[5] Both sedition and proselytizing are serious charges. Conversion to Judaism was a punishable offense in Roman law, though this was not always enforced.[6] Monotheism from a pagan perspective is tantamount to atheism because it denies the existence of the gods (cf. Acts 19:27) and requires abandonment of the state cult.

The plaintiffs have a higher legal and social status as "Romans" and are recognized local residents. The accused therefore have three strikes against them from the outset: they are outsiders, Jews, and poor itinerants with no one of lofty status to vouch for them. They are guilty until proven innocent. Crowds normally assembled to observe open-air trials and are not necessarily unruly. By siding with the accusers, they seal the defendants' fate.

16:23–24 *After they had been severely flogged, they were thrown into prison.* It was forbidden for Roman citizens to be flogged, but it was a different story for those considered to be low-life felons accused of disturbing the peace. The severe flogging with rods left open wounds that are not cleansed until much later (16:33). Paul mentions undergoing this ordeal three times (2 Cor. 11:25).

The officials have Paul and Silas securely fastened in stocks (an additional cause of pain in itself) in an inner cell. As with Peter's earlier maximum-security imprisonment (12:4–6), escape seems impossible.

16:25–26 *Suddenly there was such a violent earthquake that . . . everyone's chains came loose.* Rather than being disheartened by their treatment, Paul and Silas sing hymns and voice aloud their prayers to God for all the other prisoners to hear. The chains do not stop the gospel from being proclaimed. Then, an earthquake interrupts. It should be interpreted not as a lucky happenstance but as a response to their prayers. Jews would interpret such tremors as evidence of God's sovereignty. Pagans were likely to interpret them as an expression of a deity's anger and an omen of more evil to come.[7]

16:27–34 *The jailer woke up, and when he saw the prison doors open, he drew his sword and was about to kill himself . . . "Sirs, what must I do to be saved?"* The jailer assumes either that all the prisoners have escaped and a death sentence awaits him for dereliction of duty (cf. 12:19) or that the deity behind this event would severely punish him. He opts for suicide, but a greater miracle confronts him when Paul shouts that all the prisoners are present and accounted for. Paul stops the jailer's suicide and guides him to life in Christ.

Paul's shout, "We are all here!" suggests that the prisoners were jammed together "into a single secure cell."[8] That explains why the other prisoners could listen intently to Paul and Silas. The jailer's call for lights indicates that they are secured in utter darkness. In his terror, the humbled jailer addresses them with respect and cries out, "What must I do to be saved?" The answer is simple: have faith in Jesus Christ; no sacrifices are needed to appease the gods' wrath; and no penitential labors are required. What it means to have faith in Jesus will be elaborated by Paul's teaching from Scripture and the story of Jesus.

16:32–34 *Then they spoke the word of the Lord to him and to all the others in his house.* The earthquake does not set free the imprisoned missionaries but results in the conversion of a jailer and his household. The jailer's conversion represents a common pattern. He is intrigued by the virtuous actions of Christians. He asks a universal question, "What must I do to be saved?" He receives instruction, and his acceptance of the message is demonstrated in concrete actions. He is baptized, shows compassion by tending to the wounds that he had previously disregarded, offers hospitality to Paul and Silas, and rejoices over salvation.

16:35–40 *When it was daylight, the magistrates sent their officers to the jailer with the order: "Release those men." . . . But Paul said to the officers: "They beat us publicly without a trial, even though we are Roman citizens, and threw us into prison. And now do they want to get rid of us quietly? No! Let them come themselves and escort us out."* The magistrates may have thought that the earthquake was an act of divine retribution by the Most High God, whom the missionaries serve, and want to be rid of them. We learn more about the background of Paul and Silas. Both are Roman citizens. Perhaps that is another reason why Paul selected Silas. Normally, Roman citizenship would bring some privileges—a more orderly trial process and no humiliating treatment before conviction. Rather than seeking amends for themselves, Paul demands an official apology, which he may have hoped would protect their converts in the city from future harassment.[9]

Teaching the Text

1. *Hope for those without hope.* Many people in the ancient world felt a sense of dislocation, spiritual rootlessness, and purposelessness. They sensed that they were adrift in the vast sea of humanity, where one was a nonentity. They did not feel at home or secure in the world and longed for some word of assurance. A fortune-teller might offer some sense of security, however flimsy. The possessed slave girl and her handlers are essentially hucksters dealing snake oil and can at best offer only demonic support.

One might think that Paul would appreciate the free advertising that he was getting from the girl, but Paul does not want testimony that is demonic. He also does not want to gain benefit from her demonic possession the way her masters do. This nameless girl is like so many who are victimized by heartless masters. Nowadays, they would put her in the sex trade. The church must use the power of Christ to help eliminate all forms of human trafficking. The text does not say, but one might hope that this slave girl who has been liberated from her demon joined Lydia's house church, where she could hear the gospel and be redeemed. It would have resulted in a God-fearing purple merchant, a jailer, and a Pythoness being united in Christ.

2. *One should not imagine the missionaries as being confined in anything like a modern jail with separate cells.* Brian Rapske gives a grim description of normal conditions. The prisoners would be crammed together in the dark. Their wounds from any flogging would be untended. With no circulation, a stench would fill the air. Their necks would be in collars and their feet and arms manacled. A length of chain running through their fetters prevented any hope of escape and probably any hope of restful sleep.[10] How can anyone sing hymns in these conditions? But joy pervades the missionaries' lives, and sing they do. Tertullian wrote, "The leg does not feel the chain when the mind is in the heavens."[11]

3. *Relinquishing privileges for the sake of the gospel.* Paul's Roman citizenship could offer many privileges. Why, then, does Paul announce their status *after* he and Silas have been released? It surely was "a carefully considered choice."[12] First, trying to establish proof of citizenship could have resulted in protracted litigation that would have delayed the mission work. Second, it implies submission to the emperor and commitment to his preeminence rather than to Christ. For Paul, the only citizenship that matters is one's heavenly citizenship (Phil. 3:20). Third, potential converts who were not Roman citizens

might think twice about becoming Christians. If they were to become believers in Christ, what would protect them from suffering at the hands of the state? How could Paul convince others, "We must go through many hardships to enter the kingdom of God" (Acts 14:22), when he had a "get out of jail free" card? The Thessalonians knew that Paul "had previously suffered and been treated outrageously in Philippi" and "dared" to continue to preach the gospel "in the face of strong opposition" (1 Thess. 2:2). They recognized that it was through God's help that he did so, not because of his Roman citizenship. They committed themselves to the faith knowing that though they were destined for persecution along with Paul, "God did not appoint us to suffer wrath but to receive salvation through our Lord Jesus Christ" (1 Thess. 5:9).

Illustrating the Text

The gospel of liberation should lead to real-world action.

Informational: The FBI website describes the real-world situation of human trafficking in the United States:

> Here in this country, people are being bought, sold, and smuggled like modern-day slaves, often beaten, starved, and forced to work as prostitutes or to take jobs as migrant, domestic, restaurant, or factory workers with little or no pay. Over the past decade, human trafficking has been identified as a heinous crime which exploits the most vulnerable in society.[13]

Joe Carter, an editor for the Gospel Coalition, notes the tragic reality that there are "more slaves today than were seized from Africa in four centuries of the trans-Atlantic slave trade. In fact, there are more slaves in the world today than at any other point in human history, with an estimated 21 million in bondage across the globe."[14] Shared Hope International, which seeks to eradicate sex trafficking, notes that in the United States at least 100,000 juveniles are victims of this heinous practice each year.[15] You can take action.

Our imprisonment can lead to others' freedom.

Biography: **Saeed Abedini.** Pastor Abedini, a former Muslim, was used by God to help found more than one hundred house churches in thirty cities in Iran, with more than two thousand members. He and his wife were forced to move from Iran to the United States in 2005 when Mahmoud Ahmedinejad rose to power and the situation became much more dangerous. While visiting family in Iran in 2012, Abedini was arrested and thrown into prison, where he underwent horrific torture and isolation for three years. But even then, God had a plan. During his first year in prison, Abedini led ten inmates to Christ.[16]

Rejection in Thessalonica and Acceptance in Berea

Big Idea

The preaching of the gospel in two Macedonian towns threatens Jewish opponents who vigorously harass Paul and force him to flee.

Key Themes

- Teaching from the Scriptures is an essential part of evangelism.
- The gospel continues to evoke a divided response.
- Prominent persons in society also come to faith.

Understanding the Text

The Text in Context

Paul has answered the call to go to Macedonia, and he now comes to Thessalonica, its capital. As in Philippi, his mission meets with bitter opposition from jealous Jews (cf. 1 Thess. 2:14–16) who inflame gentiles to join them in a mob action against the Christians. Paul's first letter to the community reminded them of the "strong opposition" when he preached (1 Thess. 2:2) and that they received the message with joy "in the midst of severe suffering" (1 Thess. 1:6). Paul's retreat to Berea finds a community more receptive to the gospel, but the Jews from Thessalonica continue to hound him, forcing Paul to withdraw under the cover of darkness to Athens.

The Jewish opponents are emphasized in this unit, but they are not the only foes of the gospel. During this trip, Jews will twice accuse the missionaries of being troublemakers (17:5–7; 18:12–13). Gentiles also take action against them twice (16:22–24; 17:8–9). The door of faith is open for gentiles (14:27), but the persistent intimidation confirms the truth that Christians "must go through many hardships to enter the kingdom of God" (14:22).

Interpretive Insights

17:1–3 *they came to Thessalonica, where there was a Jewish synagogue.* Thessalonica served as the seat of the Roman governor of Macedonia. It was well situated as a seaport on the Via Egnatia, the road the Romans constructed from Byzantium to the Adriatic Sea. Thessalonica was granted the status of a "free city" and was ruled by its own local "politarchs," a term that Luke accurately uses to refer to the civic officials.[1]

The city also had a large Jewish community. On three Sabbaths Paul spoke in a synagogue trying to persuade them of the truth of his beliefs about Jesus Christ. He is not asked to speak but contributes to the conversation about the interpretation of the Scriptures. His stay lasts longer than three weeks, since Paul reports that he worked to earn his own keep while there (1 Thess. 2:9) and also received financial help from the Philippians more than once (Phil. 4:16). He probably was ousted from the synagogue and continued to engage others while working in the marketplace. His first letter to the Thessalonians assumes that most in the church had been former pagans who had "turned to God from idols to serve the living and true God" (1 Thess. 1:9).

The Scriptures that Paul argued from are not specified, but they would have to do with those passages that speak "about the coming Redeemer and Savior of Israel."[2] It is necessary to explain how someone who was crucified could possibly be the Messiah. Paul's teaching accords with that of Jesus, who taught his disciples, "Did not the Messiah have to suffer these things and then enter his glory?" (Luke 24:26). Such a message would be shocking and incomprehensible to many Jews. To some, it is so offensive (cf. 1 Cor. 1:23) that it sparks a violent reaction.

17:4 *Some of the Jews were persuaded and joined Paul and Silas, as did a large number of God-fearing Greeks and quite a few prominent women.* The preaching, as one has come to expect from reading Acts, creates a divided response. Both verbs in the phrase "some of the Jews were persuaded and joined Paul and Silas" are in the passive voice in Greek. It underscores that it is not the teachers' arguments decked out in clever and persuasive finery that convince the audience. The persuasion comes about from God's mediation through the Spirit.

"Quite a few" accurately translates the phrase that literally reads, "not a few." Luke frequently uses this figure of speech (litotes) that employs understatement to emphasize a point. It does not mean "a few," but states things in the negative to underscore a positive. In this context, it indicates that many prominent women belonging to higher social circles were persuaded. Acts consistently points out the significant role that women play in the church's growth (cf. 1:14; 5:14; 8:3, 12; 9:2; 12:12; 16:15, 40; 17:12, 34; 18:2, 18, 26; 21:9). Two men who became believers in Thessalonica, Aristarchus and Secundus, will travel with Paul on his last, fateful journey to Jerusalem (20:4). Aristarchus will also accompany him to Rome (27:2).

17:5-7 *But other Jews were jealous; so they rounded up some bad characters from the marketplace, formed a mob and started a riot in the city.* Resistance from some Jews has occurred in almost every city. Luke identifies the chief root of their hostility as jealousy (cf. 5:17). The conversion of prominent women troubles them because it means the potential loss of wealthy and influential supporters of the synagogue and a corresponding loss of their influence. One is not jealous of someone who is pitiful, and it basically acknowledges the Christian missionaries' superiority. This jealousy turns nasty when they rally the opposition and incite the rabble to take action against the Christians.

The ministers of the gospel are again accused of fostering un-Roman beliefs, but now they are also accused of "turning the world upside down" (17:6 NRSV) with their preaching. The charge that they claim there is another king is high treason from a Roman point of view. Ironically, the Jewish leaders are the ones disturbing the peace by whipping up mob violence in the city.

17:8-10a *Then they made Jason and the others post bond and let them go. As soon as it was night, the believers sent Paul and Silas away to Berea.* Jason's hospitality toward the missionaries is interpreted as harboring a nest of treasonous lawbreakers. It is most likely that the charges relate to "the imperial laws repressing Graeco-Roman voluntary associations."[3] Jason is held responsible for any group meeting in his house, and he is subsequently required to post bond, which would be forfeited if another violation were to occur.[4] The onslaught against him shows that believers share in the persecution of the missionaries. Paul and Silas are sped off to Berea during the night to avoid any further trouble.

17:10b-11 *Now the Berean Jews were of more noble character than those in Thessalonica.* The synagogue functioned not simply as a house of worship but also as a house of study in which people could investigate the Scriptures every day. This study group allows Paul to explore the Scriptures with them to verify his teaching. They treat Paul "as a highly respected rabbi or teacher of Scripture" and "[evaluate] his teaching based on his answers to the questions they put to him in light of their own prior knowledge and understanding of the Scriptures."[5] From Luke's perspective, they represent true Jews. They examine the Scripture for the truth and recognize that what Paul says is true.

17:12-14 *As a result, many of them believed . . . the Jews in Thessalonica . . . went there too, agitating the crowds and stirring them up.* The gospel meets with rejection but also with success. As in Thessalonica, many prominent women and Greek men believe, but Jewish harassment continues. Paul is sent away for his safety and health, since he would still be nursing his wounds from Philippi (16:22–23). He does not completely abandon the new believers, as Silas and Timothy remain to continue the instruction.

Teaching the Text

1. *Paul represents another king and another kingdom.* Opposition to the gospel remains unremitting and comes from both Jews and Romans. The charge that would catch the attention of the Roman magistrates is that Paul and his companions are rabble-rousers intent on causing social unrest throughout the world as enemies of Roman law and order (16:20–21). More grave is the accusation that they show disrespect for the surpassing might and majesty of the Roman emperor and the Roman people by claiming that there is another greater king and kingdom.

No Roman official who investigates the charge that Paul and his companions are mischief makers gives it any credence. The charge that they are turning the world upside down, however, is truer than the accusers realize, though they are wrong in attributing these world-shaking consequences to the missionaries. Beverly Roberts Gaventa writes, "The shaking of heaven and earth takes place in this story, but it does so entirely because God is the actor—not Rome, not the apostles, nor their opponents."[6] It is only God, not Rome, who controls and rattles the world and the heavens because God is the maker of heaven and earth and the maker of nations (17:24–26).

The second charge, that the missionaries claim that there is another king, Jesus, is true. As the Son of God, Jesus is the true king, and as the one who died and was raised and exalted by God, he is the only king worthy of worship and allegiance. The chief priests manipulated Pilate to obtain a sentence of death by crucifixion for Jesus and declared, "We have no king but Caesar" (John 19:15). This declaration is apostasy for a Jew. The calling of Israel was to testify to the world that "the Most High is sovereign over all kingdoms on earth" (Dan. 4:32). The claim that Christ alone reigns and all earthly kings and kingdoms are subordinate to him will only invite trouble for Christians. Christians in the second century "were executed because they refused to swear an oath of allegiance to the emperor."[7]

2. *Scripture undergirds and confirms Paul's message.* He utilizes every means to convey the gospel, from proclamation to dialogue over the meaning of Scripture, and persuading other Jews and gentile God-fearers through the interpretation of the Scripture is vital to his success. Luke does not cite the scriptural proofs Paul employed in Thessalonica and Berea, since he has already given examples that Christian preachers used in 2:22–36 and 13:16–41. New truths from Scripture would also come to light in the discussions as the missionaries are led by the Spirit to respond to queries and to what they may

have heard from other teachers. Paul did not have the advantage of carrying around a Bible that could be easily and quickly referenced. He had to know the Scriptures backward and forward in his head and heart to be ready to make his case and to answer any question. Intimate knowledge of Scripture is essential to all Christian apologetics.

3. *Paul does not try to win people over through crafty speechifying or glib answers.* He tells the Corinthians that he "did not come with eloquence or human wisdom as I proclaimed to you the testimony about God" (1 Cor. 2:1) and that he did not speak "in words taught us by human wisdom but in words taught by the Spirit, explaining spiritual realities with Spirit-taught words" (1 Cor. 2:13). These statements apply to his ministry everywhere. He states the facts: Jesus is the Messiah, who was crucified and raised by God from the dead. He cites the Scriptures that support this outcome as God's purpose for the Messiah and the salvation of humanity. Christ's death and resurrection are the keys for opening up the meaning of the Scripture. After explaining the Scripture and its connection to Jesus, Paul leaves it to God's Spirit to do the persuading.

Jesus talked about scattering the seeds of God's word in various soils. When they land in good soil, they inevitably produce a harvest (Luke 8:5–8). The Berean Jews prove to be good soil. The identification of them as being of "more noble character" redefines the meaning of nobility. Their nobility is one of mind and spirit and not of birth. It is manifest in being fair-minded in their "eagerness to learn about God, to discern how he is working, and to evaluate it in light of the written revelation."[8]

Illustrating the Text

Christians preach a revolutionary message.

History: The twentieth century was one of radical revolutions. The Russian Empire became the USSR. The Chinese, long ruled by an emperor, were introduced to the "joys" and horrors of rule by "the people." The spread of communist revolution into Korea, Vietnam, and Cuba made it seem as if a red tide would deluge the world. In many ways the century was defined by the geopolitical realities ushered in by these changes. But these apparently "world-shaking" revolutions were really just the replacement of one fallen, sinful system of government with another. Every one of them failed to keep their promises or live up to their ideals. As Christians, we proclaim revolutionary good news: the suffering, death, and resurrection of the Messiah, salvation and righteousness offered through grace rather than by good works, and the mission that requires the laying down of our lives so that others may live.

Modern-day Bereans seek the Scriptures in their quest to know Jesus.

Biography: **Ruth Orr.** Orr was a creator of Bible curriculum for World Bible School. She was invited to Takoradi in Ghana to follow up with students who were seeking to know God and to find out the truth of the gospel. Prior to going to Ghana, she contacted her potential students. They were so eager to learn about the Bible that they made plans to meet with her. "On the night of the group's arrival, four of her students were waiting for her. Three had come over 600 miles to see their WBS teacher. Other students had ridden buses and vans for 10 to 12 hours to meet their teacher and receive more teaching. In all, 43 of Ruth's students came to the special campaign and stayed for three or four days to continue their study. Thirty-eight were converted during the campaign."[9]

The mission and message must be grounded in Scripture.

Lesson: Scripture provides the evidence for the veracity of the claims of the gospel. In modern times, police often examine all the evidence in such a thorough manner that they are able to discover the truth; however, there are cases when the investigators refuse to look at evidence and go with a gut feeling, unreliable witnesses, and assumptions, mistakenly convicting a person who is actually innocent.

Scripture is not the end but leads us to Jesus.

Sermon: **"The Higher Faith," by George MacDonald.** MacDonald, a Scottish minister, author, and poet, preached: "But herein is the Bible greatly wronged. It nowhere lays claim to be regarded as *the* Word, *the* Way, *the* Truth. The Bible leads us to Jesus, the inexhaustible, the ever-unfolding Revelation of God. It is Christ 'in whom are hid all the treasures of wisdom and knowledge,' not the Bible, save as leading to Him."[10]

Paul's Defense before the Areopagus Council

Big Idea

As creator, God places a claim on all people. God's purpose for humankind is for all to be in a worshipful relation with their creator, and he will hold all accountable for their willful ignorance and rejection.

Key Themes

- Human life is surrounded by and sustained by God. Religious quests search for God, but God remains unknown to many whose ignorance leads them astray. The truth is now revealed only in Jesus Christ, whom God has raised from the dead.
- God has overlooked human ignorance for a time but will not do so forever. Judgment looms on the horizon.
- Many possess superficial curiosity about religious matters but do not accept the ideas of repentance, judgment, and the resurrection of the dead, which require a radical change in their lives.

Understanding the Text

The Text in Context

After his ministry in Thessalonica and Berea, Paul journeys to Athens. The city, awash in idols, greatly perturbs him. By trying to appease every possible god with altars and temples, the people of Athens affront the one true God. Paul makes his case before the Areopagus and the people of Athens that "there is no longer room for altars dedicated to an unknown god because God has now made himself known."[1] This one true God will no longer overlook their ignorance but commands all people everywhere to repent.

Interpretive Insights

17:16–17 *he was greatly distressed to see that the city was full of idols.* Athens represents the golden age of Greece and the birthplace of Western philosophy, theater, and government. Illustrious figures such as Socrates, Pericles, Aristophanes, Aristotle, and Plato are associated with the city.

Paul is not in a cultural sightseeing mood, and his spirit is agitated by the proliferation of idols. He does not bide his time waiting for his coworkers to arrive; he proclaims the gospel to Jews in the synagogue and to pagans in the town square. His preaching leads to hot debates.

17:18–20 *A group of Epicurean and Stoic philosophers began to debate with him. . . . Then they took him and brought him to a meeting of the Areopagus.* Paul is not outgunned by learned but cynical philosophers who are practiced in debate, even though some view him as only a "babbler." This epithet refers to one who scrounges for scraps of ideas and fools himself and others into thinking he is educated. They regard Paul as a pseudointellectual with no substance.

The charge of introducing foreign gods is serious. Socrates was executed on the grounds that he rejected the gods who were the guardians of the state and introduced new deities.[2] Paul is brought before the "Areopagus," which refers not to a location but to the high court of appeal for criminal and civil cases.[3] The phrase "they took him" (cf. 16:19) suggests a trial scene.[4] Paul's preaching has again "drawn the attention of the authorities," and he must defend himself against this new charge.[5]

17:21–22 *All the Athenians and the foreigners who lived there spent their time doing nothing but talking about and listening to the latest ideas.* To say that these gadflies are interested only in the new and the now is a biting criticism. While many in our modern culture are convinced that "new" implies improved, the rage for the latest thing was not the dominant view in the Hellenistic age. New truth was considered to be a contradiction. The ancient age of a religion authenticated it and made it deserving of honor because it had passed the test of time. Consequently, greater respect was accorded to what was old and established. Christianity would be easily dismissed if it was perceived as a brand new development. Acts shows, however, that the Christian faith springs from the purposes of God from the beginning of time.

Paul's supposed compliment that opens his speech, that the members of the council are "extremely religious," will become part of his defense. It reveals that the ancient world was not a blank tablet waiting for an apostle to come to offer people something to believe in. A bewildering assortment of religious cults and beliefs competed for attention and claimed to offer something: a popular philosophy for coping with life, a saving knowledge, a transforming ritual, magical spells and concoctions that offered protection or granted one's wishes. The religiosity of the people is reflected in the abundance of idols and temples dotting the city—many with good Greek names such as Zeus, Hermes, and Athena, and others with foreign names such as Isis, Serapis, and the Phrygian Mother Goddess. Immigration into the urban areas resulted in the blending of various religious beliefs and practices. What were formerly local cults became internationalized and reinterpreted in a new culture.

Though Paul opens his speech with a compliment, from his perspective Athens was a wasteland of idolatry. The Greek word translated as "religious" can mean "devout" but also "superstitious." The ambiguity is probably deliberate on Paul's part. As a Jew, he believes that gentiles will worship anything that they think gives them an advantage.

17:23–25 *an altar with this inscription:* TO AN UNKNOWN GOD. Paul's first point parries the allegation of introducing novel deities. He argues that he is speaking not about a new god but about the true God, whom they do not know. Their altar to an unknown god tries to cover their bases: "To whatever god we do not know to honor: please do not hold it against us." The altar, however, bears witness to their ignorance. The one whom Paul preaches is this unknown God, whom he identifies as the creator of the universe (14:15; Gen. 1–2; Isa. 45:18–25). The cosmic creator God is independent of the world and needs no shrine in the prime real estate of the Athens public square. Everything in existence depends on this one God, who cannot be confined to shrines and spurns human religious oblations and idols.

17:26–29 *From one man he made all the nations, that they should inhabit the whole earth . . . Therefore since we are God's offspring, we should not think that the divine being is like gold or silver or stone—an image made by human design and skill.* Paul's second point is that God shapes human affairs and the destinies of nations (cf. Gen. 10–11; Deut. 32:8), whether they acknowledge this fact or not.[6] The third point is that God created humankind and wills for persons to be in relationship with him. Many believed that the higher deities rarely involved themselves in the affairs of average people and were likened to the emperor, who, at the top of the heap, rarely if ever came into direct contact with ordinary persons. As a result, most tried to curry favor with the lesser deities that they believed were more directly involved in the affairs of life related to fortune, love, and illness. Paul argues that the true God is not an impassive, absentee God but is near at hand. He cites a famous quotation from the poet Aratus[7] but interprets its meaning from a biblical framework. God is the sustainer of humankind, not some foreign deity, and has always been intimately involved in human life.[8] At best, however, humans have only fumbled after this unknown God and as a result have manufactured false gods.

His fourth point is that as God's offspring, humans, the created, exist in radical disparity with their creator. God is nothing like what humans imagine with their finite minds and liken with images made with their hands.

17:30–31 *In the past God overlooked such ignorance, but now he commands all people everywhere to repent.* God's mercy toward ignorance does not give persons license to persist in it. Paul changes tack and summons them to repent, which entails turning away from the unenlightened worship of idols to the one, true God. This appeal is made urgent by the coming judgment that will be carried out by the one whom God raised from the dead. Paul has moved from the creation to the consummation. He does not specify that the one whom God has appointed to bring judgment to all is the crucified and resurrected Jesus, just as he has not named Adam, the one ancestor of all. His audience knows neither name. He also does not define what constitutes "righteousness." They can learn what it means if they want to hear more.

17:32–33 *When they heard about the resurrection of the dead, some of them sneered, but others said, "We want to hear you again on this subject."* The mention of resurrection meets with confusion and incredulity from some. They may think that Paul is talking about two new gods: a male deity, Jesus, and his female consort, Resurrection. *Anastasis* is the Greek word for "resurrection," and "Anastasia" was a Greek feminine name. If that is the case, Paul says one thing, and they understand another.

17:34 *Some of the people became followers of Paul and believed. Among them was Dionysius, a member of the Areopagus, also a woman named Damaris, and a number of others.* The two named persons may be the source for this account. Paul's defense was not a total failure. Some were converted.

Teaching the Text

1. *Tolerance versus truth.* The plethora of idols in Athens testifies to a general tolerance of multiple religious beliefs and practices in the ancient world. Rome became upset with foreign religions only when they were perceived as disturbing peace and security and denigrating Roman supremacy. One could choose from a great smorgasbord of gods with their different specialties, and many believed that there was safety in numbers. The relative disinterest in doctrine lessened the potential for theological friction. In one papyrus fragment the writer says, "I pray to all gods,"[9] and an inscription says, "We magnify every god."[10]

Tolerance is also a prime virtue in many parts of the modern world. The danger is that it can lead to mushy relativism. In the ancient world, Christians and Jews were different from everybody else because of their religious intolerance. Christians know that much that passes for gold is only dross. Not every religious idea is true, and it makes a difference what one believes or does not believe. Christians recognize the blinding, corrupting effects of sin that twist human minds to exchange the truth of God for a lie (Rom. 1:25) and to suppress the evidence for God and fabricate feeble and insidious substitutes.

Christians were labeled "haters of humankind"[11] because they refused to participate in the worship and sacrificial meals to local, traditional gods in pagan temples and the great festivals in towns and cities and therefore refused to participate in the center of social life in the ancient world and the source of great civic pride. Apuleius describes a certain baker's wife in his novel as "an enemy of faith and chastity" because she is a "despiser of all the gods whom others did honor."[12] Since the gods were also deemed to be the ones who preserved the state and order, to reject them would open up the community to divine disfavor and catastrophe.

Some intellectuals scoffed at the religious gullibility of the masses. In Aristophanes's comical play *The Birds*, the birds of Cloud-cuckoo-land blockade heaven so that the whole supply of sacrificial offerings from earth is cut off and the starving gods are compelled to come to the birds to seek peace at any price. The satire, says T. W. Manson, "kills the popular religious beliefs by ridicule, but it offers nothing in their place." What Manson says of the prophets is true of Christianity: it offers "the showing of a more excellent way." He writes, "In the white heat of prophetic zeal and insight all the baser elements are burnt away, and only the pure metal of a wholly spiritual religion is left. . . . Real religious reform comes through the really religious."[13]

2. *The incompatibility of paganism and Christianity.* Paul gives an exposition of the relationship between the creator God and his creation in order to defend himself against the charge that he is introducing some new deity. Some have noted that this sermon is quite different from Romans 1:18–32, which gives a far more disparaging picture of pagan idolatry. Paul's address to the Areopagus council is more confrontational and biblical than is commonly recognized. Though he may seem to utilize Stoic and Epicurean categories, his arguments are thoroughly grounded in Scripture. It would be wrong to think that one can start with contemporary pagan culture and philosophy and arrive at Christian theological truth. The two are fundamentally incompatible.

Paul does not begin by condemning the Athenians for their idolatry. He recognizes that his listeners are believers of one sort or another with some kind of commitment, so he approaches them as one who stands with them on common ground—created by God for fellowship with God. He uses language that his audience understands, but the use of common vocabulary does not mean that he shares their worldview. He challenges their views on creation, providence, and life after death from the biblical perspective.[14] He is interested not in winning debates but in sharing his faith so that he might win converts. He hopes to provoke curiosity that will elicit further questions and conversion. Some mock. Some remain undecided. Some believe.

3. *In Paul's day, people yearned for "salvation," but not the salvation that we understand as "deliverance from this world and safe passage to the next."*[15]

Salvation was viewed as connected to blessings for this earthly life. People "wanted divine benefits, not enlightenment—health, wealth, protection and sustenance, not moral transformation. . . . In short, they wanted religion to serve them on their own terms—not to change them, but to exalt them."[16] Most religious inscriptions are dedicated to gods who heal diseases and give riches.

Many believed that death leads to nothingness. Many tombstone inscriptions read, "I was not. I was. I am not. I do not care."[17] Such fatalism led people to want to live life now to the fullest: "Eat, drink, and be merry" (cf. 1 Cor. 15:32). The use of the "I" in the inscriptions, however, might suggest that the persons do care and want to continue after they are dead. Christianity offered the promise of resurrection, a promise not offered elsewhere. The God who created us and sustains us enters into a covenant relationship with us and delivers those who believe in Christ from the clutches of death.

Illustrating the Text

We're called to preach truth, not bow to the idol of tolerance.

Applying the Text: Athens was a tough place to preach the gospel. Immersed in learning, many on the Areopagus council thought that they had seen and heard it all, and so they sneered at Paul and his message. Many parts of the world today are little different. Christians frequently become minority dissenters amid a hostile culture. They can expect to be thought of as strange, have people laugh in their face, and even face the danger of death. Their ultimate goal is not to make Christianity culturally respectable but rather to proclaim the truth of the gospel. One does so fully aware that many do not want to hear about repentance or to admit that they must change their benighted worldviews and lifestyles or face God's judgment.

Our goal is to win souls, not arguments.

History: Pyrrhus was the king of ancient Epirus, a Greek state, and came to power in 295 BC. A skilled general, Pyrrhus determined to launch an offensive war against the armies of Rome, aiming to take territory on the Italian Peninsula. He had a series of victories, most famous among these the Battle of Asculum. However, the cost of these victories was almost as great for him as it was for the Roman army that he defeated, and because the Romans had more armies to throw at the invader, Pyrrhus was forced to turn tail in defeat. It is from this king that we inherit the term "Pyrrhic victory," which can also be stated as "winning the battle but losing the war."

Apologetics is important and biblical (see 1 Pet. 3:15), but it is not an end in itself. We don't debate for the sake of debating. We provide answers and reasonable proofs for our faith in order to sway minds and hearts. When this biblical work verges into caustic argumentation, we have started fighting the wrong battle.

In a world that wants easy answers, Christianity offers eternal hope.

Science: Imagine a doctor who preferred to prescribe painless placebos rather than hard medicine. He might save his patients from the pain of treatment, but at what cost? In our world, the medicine of gospel truth can be very hard to swallow, for not only do we proclaim the good news of salvation in Christ, but also we must explain why that salvation is necessary. It is not simply because we're victims of a cruel world and need rescuing. It's not only because we're deceived and misguided, making mistakes along life's way. Each and every person is living in willful rebellion against God. In order to find the healing of forgiveness and reconciliation, we must face the horror of what we have done. That's hard medicine.

Law and Disorder in Corinth

Big Idea

God's promise to protect Paul so that he can stay in Corinth to expand his ministry is fulfilled.

Key Themes

- The emperor's banishment of Jews like Aquila and Priscilla from Rome serves only to spread the gospel throughout the Roman Empire.
- Jews tied to the synagogue are expelled when they commit themselves to Christ, and they face persecution for their faith.
- God steadfastly fulfills promises of protection to missionaries to accomplish God's goals in spreading the good news.

Understanding the Text

The Text in Context

Paul arrives in Corinth, where he will stay for a long period. He continuously preaches and testifies "to the Jews that Jesus was the Messiah" (18:5). Preaching in a hostile world is always dangerous, but the Lord appears to him with a command and a promise, "Do not be afraid; keep on speaking, do not be silent. For I am with you" (18:9–10). Here in Corinth he meets Aquila and Priscilla for the first time. "Their contacts with Paul and their presence in three of the most important centers of early Christianity—Corinth, Ephesus [18:18–19, 26] and Rome—underline their importance in the history of early Christianity."[1]

Interpretive Insights

18:1 *After this, Paul left Athens and went to Corinth.* The Romans had decimated Corinth in 146 BC, but Julius Caesar rebuilt it as a Roman colony in 46 BC. Though the city was geographically in Greece, it was heavily influenced by Roman culture and politics. Situated on the narrow isthmus between the southern and northern parts of Greece, Corinth was a natural crossroad for land and sea travel. It had access to two harbors, one at Cenchreae, six miles to the east on the Saronic Gulf, and the other at Lechaeum, about two miles to the north on the Corinthian Gulf. Its population was a mix of Roman freedmen, indigenous Greeks, immigrants, and transients from far and wide. As the capital of the Roman province of Achaia, it bustled with commercial activity and brimmed with a variety of religious cults.

18:2–3 *There he met a Jew named Aquila, a native of Pontus, who had recently come from Italy with his wife Priscilla.* The first time Rome is explicitly mentioned in the narrative is to explain why Priscilla and Aquila are in Corinth. Jews had been expelled from Rome. Suetonius claims that Claudius (r. AD 41–54) took this action because they "were constantly making disturbances at the instigation of Chrestus."[2] "Chrestus" was a common Latin name and may refer to a particular troublemaker. It may also refer to a controversy between Jews and Jewish Christians over "the Christ," and Suetonius misspells the name. If that is the case, those banished probably are the leaders, which makes it likely that Aquila and Priscilla were "particularly active on the Christian side."[3] It would also reveal that the gospel has already reached Rome.

Aquila and Priscilla, husband and wife, are always mentioned together as a team in the New Testament. Priscilla's name usually precedes her husband's.[4] She may have had higher status as one who was freeborn, while her husband may have been a freedman; or she was more prominent as a leader in the church.[5] They welcomed Paul into their home and business. As leather workers, they would have made tents, canopies, and similar goods. Their trade allowed them to be mobile, and they returned to Rome (Rom. 16:3–5) sometime after Nero allowed Jews to return to the city five years later.

18:4–5 *Every Sabbath he reasoned in the synagogue, trying to persuade Jews and Greeks.* Paul debated in the synagogue on the Sabbath and conveyed the gospel to customers and passersby at his workshop on other days. He prided himself on working with his hands as an artisan (1 Cor. 4:12; 9:6; 1 Thess. 2:9; 2 Thess. 3:6–8). His menial labor comports with an ideal found in rabbinic literature for those who dedicate themselves to the study of the law (*m. 'Abot* 2:2), but some of the Corinthians thought it demeaning. Silas and Timothy probably brought funds from the Macedonians when they arrived (Phil. 4:16), and that also irked some of the Corinthian Christians (2 Cor. 11:7–9).

18:6 *But when they opposed Paul and became abusive, he shook out his clothes in protest.* Stout opposition to Paul in the synagogue spirals into sneering indignities and forces him out. Paul's gesture of shaking his clothes (cf. Neh. 5:13), which is similar to shaking the dust from his feet (13:51), and his sharp words echoing Ezekiel 33:5 mark his public break with the synagogue.

Titius Justus

Roman male citizens normally had three names: a forename (personal name) and two surnames. The name "Titius Justus" consists of two surnames (a *nomen*, designating his clan, and a *cognomen*, derived from various factors that helped to distinguish members belonging to a large clan). It is possible that he is the Gaius whom Paul mentions in Romans 16:23 as the church's and his host in Corinth. "Gaius" was a common forename (Acts 19:29; 20:4; 3 John 1), and "Gaius Titius Justus" would be a complete Roman name. Paul mentions Crispus and Gaius as the two he baptized in Corinth (1 Cor. 1:14).

They are held responsible for their rejection of the salvation offered in Jesus. Paul will shift his attention to a more wide-ranging audience who will be receptive to his message.

18:7–8 *Then Paul left the synagogue and went next door to the house of Titius Justus.* Gentile worshipers of God have responded to the gospel, and staying near the synagogue gives Paul access to others who may join this house church. The proximity of the church probably caused the synagogue leaders to become even more aggravated. Crispus was the leader of the synagogue who initially may have allowed Paul to speak. He was banished when he became a Christian.

18:9–11 *Do not be afraid; keep on speaking, do not be silent.* Paul received personal encouragement during this difficult time from a vision from the Lord. Paul's Macedonian vision had directed him to new territory (16:6–10). The vision here directs him to stay rather than flee from the looming danger. The phrase "I am with you" recalls God's pledge to assist or do battle for his people (Gen. 21:22; 26:3; 31:3, 5; Exod. 3:12; Josh. 1:5, 9; Isa. 41:10; 43:5; Acts 7:9; 10:38). Paul obeys God's command, and God's presence fortifies him to proclaim the gospel in Corinth for a longer period of time than he has stayed anywhere else.

The reference to God's "many people" in Corinth again underscores that gentiles who believe also become the people of God (15:14). Membership is based not on race but solely on the response to the grace of God.

18:12–13 *While Gallio was proconsul of Achaia, the Jews of Corinth made a united attack on Paul.* Paul has incited the wrath of the Jews elsewhere, but the Corinthian Jews bring a formal accusation against him before the highest authority in the land. They may regard his message as blasphemous, but the Christian message created the recent trouble for Jews in Rome, and they may fear similar repercussions in Corinth.[6] Therefore, they may want to distance themselves in Roman eyes from the likes of Paul with his preaching that Jesus is the Messiah. The charge is that Paul induces people to worship in ways that are against the law. The reference to "the law" is ambiguous. They want the governor to think in terms of Roman law and not the law of Moses.

Gallio is the elder brother of the philosopher Seneca, the tutor and later advisor to the future emperor Nero. Achaia was a senatorial province, and the proconsul normally was in office for a year. This incident probably took place in AD 51–52.

18:14–16 *since it involves questions about words and names and your own law—settle the matter yourselves.* Paul does not need to put up any defense as Gallio immediately dismisses the charges. He interprets the law to be the Jewish law, which he dismisses as much ado about nothing, minor disputes over insignificant words and names. The case has no merit under Roman law.

Gallio assumes that Christianity is a faction of Judaism and not a separate religion. Persuading those formerly connected to the Jewish synagogue to worship God differently next door is not a criminal offense. It is an internal Jewish matter that should not concern a Roman proconsul. There has been no riot, and Gallio is uninterested in Jewish differences of opinion over their religion.

18:17 *Then the crowd there turned on Sosthenes the synagogue leader and beat him in front of the proconsul; and Gallio showed no concern whatever.* After the Jews were curtly ejected, the crowd pummels Sosthenes, the synagogue leader. The attackers are not identified. It is unlikely that they are Jews fuming over the mishandling of the case. They already had been driven away. It is more likely that a gentile crowd, having observed Gallio's annoyance, think that they can violently vent their anti-Jewish prejudice with impunity. Luke does not present Gallio as a shining moral light. He is unconcerned about the savagery that the crowd inflicts on Sosthenes in front of his tribunal.

Theological Insights

1. God works to spread the gospel through what initially may appear to be a disruptive setback. The emperor Claudius's capricious expulsion of Jews from Rome resulted in Paul forming a bond and partnership with Priscilla and Aquila that supported his lengthy ministry in Corinth, a key Roman colony.

Acts 18:1–17

Priscilla and Aquila also were instrumental in the instruction of Apollos (18:26). This story again confirms Paul's statement, "We know that in all things God works for the good of those who love him, who have been called according to his purpose" (Rom. 8:28). "All things" refer to the sufferings of Christians who love and serve God in a hostile world (cf. Rom. 5:3–4; 8:18, 35–39).

2. God promised Paul protection from harm so that he can achieve God's mission in Corinth. God does not promise that Paul will not be attacked, however, but only that he will be shielded from injury. Gallio's dismissal of all charges against Paul by his adversaries is not the result of Rome's virtuous justice. God uses a biased official to fulfill the promise. The result is that the local church takes root and grows and the church universal later receives for the ages two powerful letters from Paul to the Corinthians.

Teaching the Text

1. *The gospel can make headway even in places reputed to be dens of iniquity.* Like many cities, Corinth was plagued by moral and social ills. It was not only the capital of Achaia; many regarded it to be the capital of sin and decadence in the Roman world. A writer from the second century explained why he did not go to Corinth: "I learned in a short time the nauseating behavior of the rich and the misery of the poor."[7] Paul recognized both its strategic location at the crossroads of the Greco-Roman world and its desperate need for the gospel.

It is often repeated but wrong to assume that Paul was chastened by his presumed failure in his toe-to-toe confrontation with the philosophers of Athens and decided from then on to preach only the simple message of the crucified Christ (1 Cor. 2:1–4).[8] The speech in Athens should not be interpreted as a philosophical discourse that adopts the philosophical categories of the Stoics and Epicureans. Since some became believers, Athens was not a complete failure, and Paul never wavered in preaching Christ crucified from the beginning of his ministry.

2. *Prophetic denunciations are calls for repentance.* Paul's harsh words against the Corinthian synagogue, "Your blood be on your own heads! I am innocent of it. From now on I will go to the Gentiles" (18:6; cf. 13:46–47; 28:26–28), should not be read as a rejection of Israel and its replacement by gentiles. His words need to be understood in light of Scripture and the prophets' bitter denunciations and threats against the people that are "intended to provoke repentance."[9] Paul confesses to suffering "great sorrow and unceasing anguish" in his heart over the failure of the majority of his people, "those of my own race, the people of Israel," to believe (Rom. 9:1–4). He writes to the Romans to say that he will not venture to Rome just yet but

must return to Jerusalem because he cannot give up on his people because God will not give up on them. Paul is confident that God eventually will turn "godlessness away from Jacob" (Rom. 11:26 [cf. Isa. 59:20]). Consequently, one should not be surprised that when Paul arrives in Ephesus he immediately goes into the synagogue (18:19) or that he hastens back to Jerusalem (18:22). The synagogue in Ephesus receives him warmly and asks him to stay (18:20). A divided response in which some bitterly reject the gospel and some gladly receive it is par for the course whether the audience is Jewish or gentile. Paul's stern warning therefore should not be interpreted to mean that God has forsaken the Jews.

3. *Gallio's decision not to adjudicate the Jewish accusations against Paul may be taken as "the first official recognition in Acts by a Roman governor that Christianity is not a crime."*[10] Nonetheless, one should not praise Gallio for his imagined impartiality in letting Jews settle their own disputes. Like Pilate, who recognized Jesus's innocence before his Jewish accusers, Gallio recognizes that Paul is innocent of the charge. Unlike Pilate (Luke 23:1–25), he does not cave in to their pressure. Instead, his probable anti-Semitism surfaces in his brusque dismissal of the Jews and his tolerance of violence committed against a Jew. Unlike the proconsul Sergius Paulus (Acts 13:12), Gallio is totally indifferent to the Christian message. He simply announces his insufficiency to be the arbiter of theological disputes. How true that is. The Roman justice system and its officials, or any government for that matter, are incompetent judges in such matters. Nor are they to be regarded as Christianity's benevolent protectors. Only God has that role.

Gallio's reaction does teach that Christians owe the world more than arcane theological disputes over "words and names" (18:15).

Illustrating the Text

God's presence is the greatest assurance.

Biography: **Lottie Moon.** Moon was among the first women commissioned by the Southern Baptist Convention as a foreign missionary. She devoted her life to missions in China. In a letter to Dr. H. A. Tupper dated May 10, 1879, she wrote: "In a humble manner you are trying to walk in his footsteps. As you wend your way from village to village, you feel it is no idle fancy that the Master walks beside you and you hear his voice saying gently, 'Lo! I am with you always even unto the end.' . . . When the heart is full of such joy, it is no effort to speak to the people: you could not keep silent if you would. Mere physical hardships sink into merited insignificance. What does one care for comfortless inns, hard beds, hard fare, when all around is a world of joy and glory and beauty?"[11]

Jesus, the one who suffered for us, walks with us in the midst of persecution.

Bible: In Daniel 3, we are told the story of three men willing to die for their faith: Shadrach, Meshach, and Abednego. The king of Babylon had ordered them, along with all his court, to bow down before a statue of himself. When the three refused, they were thrown into a fiery furnace. Looking into the furnace, the king asks, "Didn't we throw three men in there?" "Yes," reply his advisers. The king responds, "But I see four, and one looks like a son of God!" Jesus is with us in the midst of suffering.

God sometimes uses a prophetic rebuke to bring deep conviction, not total condemnation.

Bible: According to 2 Samuel 12, after David sexually took advantage of Bathsheba and orchestrated the death of her husband, Uriah, the Lord sends the prophet Nathan to David. In his wisdom, Nathan approaches David—a man of position and power who has become spiritually blind and callous—with a parable. He narrates a story of a rich man who has stolen the precious ewe lamb of a poor man. In response, David is indignant and shouts out the word of deserved condemnation of the sinner, "The man who did this must die! He must pay" (2 Sam. 12:5–6). But Nathan unveils that the sinner is indeed David and rebukes him, "You are the man!" (12:7). The end result of the rebuke, however, is not condemnation. Nathan advises that there will be devastating consequences for David's sins, but he explains, "The LORD has taken away your sin. You are not going to die" (12:13). This prophetic rebuke was necessary to bring David, the man after God's heart, back to the Lord and to his right mind. David acknowledges, "I have sinned against the LORD" (12:13), and Psalm 51 is the ensuing cry of confession and repentance.

Believers Are Strengthened, and Jews Are Presented with Persuasive Arguments That Jesus Is the Messiah

Big Idea

Other Christians, empowered by the same Holy Spirit, are instrumental in the spread of the gospel and build on the same theological foundation.

Key Themes

- Paul's ministry is controlled entirely by his discernment of God's will.
- Newly formed disciples need strengthening through continued instruction.
- Apollos and Paul continue boldly in their campaign to persuade Jews from the Scriptures that Jesus is the Messiah.

Understanding the Text

The Text in Context

Paul's second missionary journey is completed, and he briefly stops in Ephesus before returning to Antioch and heading out on his third journey, in which he will return to locations where he established churches on his first visit. Ephesus features prominently in this section, and Luke provides vignettes of other important contributors to the spread of the gospel, Priscilla and Aquila, Apollos, and twelve former disciples of John the Baptist.

Interpretive Insights

18:18 *Paul stayed on in Corinth for some time. Then he left the brothers and sisters and sailed for Syria, accompanied by Priscilla and Aquila. Before he sailed, he had his hair cut off at Cenchreae because of a vow he had* *taken.* Luke does not say what kind of vow Paul made. Shaving the head (cf. 21:23–24) is associated with a Nazirite vow described in Numbers 6:1–21. It requires that one's hair not be cut during the period in which the vow is in force. A period of thirty days would have been the minimum length of time.[1] At the end of this time, the hair is cut and presented in the temple as a burnt offering along with other sacrifices. That may explain why Paul does not stay on in Ephesus when asked to do so by the synagogue but quickly heads for Jerusalem. This vow reveals that Paul sees no conflict in maintaining his Jewish piety as a Christian. It supports his later insistence that he has remained faithful to the law (cf. 21:24; 22:3; 24:14; 28:17).

18:19–21 *They arrived at Ephesus.* As a port city, Ephesus was another major commercial center. It was the fourth largest city in the eastern Roman Empire and was the seat of the provincial governor of Asia. Paul relies on God's will to determine what he will be doing. He had been divinely prevented from working there (16:6), but the warm reception that he receives from the Jews of the synagogue who want him to stay longer bodes well for his future ministry there. It will become the center of a long ministry during his third phase of missionary work. Priscilla and Aquila's trade as leather workers facilitates their mobility. They can set up shop anywhere and travel with Paul to Ephesus to help establish the ministry.

18:22–23 *When he landed at Caesarea.* Paul lands at another important seaport and the seat of government for the Roman prefect of Judea. Paul returns to Jerusalem after every mission campaign. Paul has established churches far and wide, but he is not a hit-and-run evangelist. The brief note of his travel itinerary (18:23) to the places where churches have started, presumably, Derbe, Lystra, Iconium, and Pisidian Antioch, stresses his continued pastoral concern for these communities. Paul states that his ambition has always been "to preach the gospel where Christ was not known, so that I would not be building on someone else's foundation" (Rom. 15:20), but "his desire for the new ministry did not lead him to neglect the old."[2] Acts never mentions that when Paul could not travel in person he wrote letters to strengthen his various churches.

18:24–25 *Meanwhile a Jew named Apollos, a native of Alexandria, came to Ephesus.* The narrative briefly shifts from Paul visiting his churches to a new figure. Apollos is introduced as a Jew and native of Alexandria, Egypt, where many Jews lived. Acts does not tell how the gospel reached Alexandria, but apparently Apollos had been instructed there in the way of the Lord. As someone "learned," he would have had a formal education and expertise in rhetoric. He also had been trained in the synagogue and had a thorough knowledge of the Scriptures.

Apollos spoke with "great fervor" ("burning enthusiasm" [18:25 NRSV]); literally, "fervent in the spirit." The definite article before "spirit" in the Greek most logically signifies the Holy Spirit.[3] If so, the Spirit rouses his fervor. He knows the story of Jesus and taught it accurately and therefore must have believed that Jesus was the more powerful one whom John the Baptist prophesied would come. His deficiency is that he knew only the baptism of John the Baptist with its emphasis on repentance and forgiveness of sins (Luke 3:3). He apparently did not fully understand Christian baptism in Jesus's name and that the promised baptism with the Holy Spirit and fire (Luke 3:16) had been fulfilled in the Pentecost event. Before meeting with Priscilla and Aquila, he also would not have been taught Paul's tenet that tied Christian baptism to the death and resurrection of Jesus (Rom. 6:3–5).

18:26–28 *When Priscilla and Aquila heard him, they invited him to their home and explained to him the way of God more adequately.* Christians are to "weigh carefully what is said" in a teaching and worship context (1 Cor. 14:29), and Priscilla and Aquila spotted a flaw in Apollos's teaching. They do not silently stew over his deficiency, attempt to undercut his ministry, or publicly rebuke him to embarrass him. Instead, they communicate their concerns privately to him. To his credit, he willingly accepts their instruction and mentoring. Since he knows the Scripture well, he must conclude that what they teach tallies with Scripture.

Though Paul recognizes that he and Apollos are "co-workers in God's service" (1 Cor. 3:9), they mostly worked independently (cf. 1 Cor. 16:12). The church recognizes Apollos's gifts for ministry, nurtures them, and sends him to Corinth, where Paul had so much trouble with the synagogue. Stephen's opponents "could not stand up against the wisdom the Spirit gave him as he spoke" (Acts 6:10). Likewise, Apollos's success as a formidable debater outstrips his Jewish opponents in the public square. This triumph can only be attributed to the power of the Spirit.

19:1a *While Apollos was at Corinth, Paul took the road through the interior and arrived at Ephesus.* As he had promised, if God so willed, Paul does return to Ephesus and will stay for over two years. It is easy to draw lines across a map tracing Paul's journeys. Those two-dimensional lines ignore the grueling nature of such travel. The foot journey that begins in Antioch (18:23) and ends in Ephesus "was well in excess of 1,000 miles."[4] It is during such journeys that Paul faced the dangers from rivers, from bandits, from hostile Jewish and gentile opponents and false believers, in the city and the wilderness, and at sea that he catalogues (2 Cor. 11:26).

19:1b–4 *There he found some disciples and asked them, "Did you receive the Holy Spirit when you believed?"* It is not clear if these "disciples" are Christians or disciples of John the Baptist. The term "disciple" is used of John's followers in Luke 5:33 and 7:18, but Luke always refers to Jesus's disciples with a definite article: "the disciples." These twelve "believe" but do not believe in Jesus as the one who comes after John the Baptist (13:25) and have not received the Holy Spirit. They may only believe John's call to repentance and his prophecies of coming judgment and a more powerful coming one. They certainly have heard of the Holy Spirit, but they have not heard that John's prophecy that one more powerful than he will come who will baptize with the Holy Spirit and fire (Luke 3:16) has been fulfilled in Jesus. Unlike Apollos, who is not baptized, these disciples are rebaptized "in the name of the Lord Jesus." The incident makes clear that John's baptism is not Christian baptism and is insufficient (Acts 11:16). It also affirms that receiving the gift of the Spirit is the essential mark of a Christian (cf. John 3:5; Rom. 8:9; 1 Cor. 12:3; 1 John 4:13).[5]

19:5–7 *When Paul placed his hands on them, the Holy Spirit came on them, and they spoke in tongues and prophesied.* Now having been baptized in the name of Jesus, they receive the Spirit when Paul places his hands on them as Peter and John did with the Samaritans (8:15–17). They reenact the Pentecost experience of the disciples by speaking in tongues and prophesying, which confirms the reality of the Spirit's presence. This phenomenon should be interpreted in terms of the languages in Acts 2 and not in terms of the unintelligible tongues that Paul seeks to rectify in 1 Corinthians 12–14.

Theological Insights

1. Acts emphasizes that John the Baptist was a great prophet, but he was only a precursor to the Son of God, who came after him (1:5; 11:16; 13:25). Jesus has superseded him in the history of salvation (Luke 16:16).

2. Unlike John's baptism of repentance, baptism "in the name of the Lord Jesus" (8:16; 19:5 [cf. Rom. 6:3; Gal. 3:27]) was possible only after the death and resurrection of Jesus. One not only renounces past sins but also confesses Jesus to be Lord and pledges to serve him.

3. The present age is the age of the Spirit, and Christians are those who have received and are empowered by the gift of God's Spirit when they come to faith.

Teaching the Text

1. *Empowerment by the Spirit is the key to unleashing the gospel's power.* Apollos has impressive academic credentials. He is steeped in knowledge of Scripture, can draw on a reservoir of stories about Jesus, and is adept at delivering spellbinding oratory that burns with enthusiasm. But education, eloquence, and emotion are not the primary ingredients for success in proclaiming the gospel. They might produce only a polished speaking performance and

little more. It might not be God speaking to the people but only a preacher showing off. What is crucial for a message to be God's message is for the preacher to be empowered by the Spirit. Peter and John were "unschooled, ordinary men" (4:13), but, filled with the Spirit, they unleashed the power of the gospel in Jerusalem that the powers that be could not stifle no matter how hard they tried. The word of God often reaches people's hearts despite the preacher's skills or lack of skills. What is required is that the preacher be full of faith and the Spirit.

2. *All believers need to grow spiritually.* Apollos, for all his preaching ability and insight into Scripture and accurate knowledge of Christ's ministry, still needed to grow in his understanding of the faith. He needed further instruction. That is true for all Christians.

The church should not ignore doctrinal error. Priscilla and Aquila handle Apollos's faulty theology well. They do not shout, "Heresy!" They do not try to kick him out of the church. They take him aside privately and give him the instruction that he needed. Nothing in the text suggests that they are as educated as Apollos. They are blue-collar workers. It says something about Apollos's character that he accepts their correction and instruction without resentment. He is not afraid to admit his weaknesses and does not think of himself more highly than he ought to think (cf. Rom. 12:3). Their pastoral instruction contributed to Apollos's dramatic success in Corinth.

3. *Paul instructs the Ephesian disciples of John the Baptist in the same gentle, pastoral manner.* He recognizes that their faith is deficient. He asks them penetrating questions that will make them receptive to further instruction. They respond to this approach because they recognize that Paul is trying to edify them rather than condemn them. They believe in the promises that John had prophesied would soon come true, and Paul shows them how they have been fulfilled in Jesus. They receive more than instruction; they receive the Holy Spirit, who guarantees the truth of the instruction. These disciples of John are now brought into the mainstream of Christian faith. One can infer that, like the disciples at Pentecost who received the Holy Spirit, these twelve disciples of John the Baptist will now become bold witnesses for Jesus.

Illustrating the Text

Talent without the Holy Spirit's empowerment will not produce transformation.

Science: All those who work in the kitchen are chemists, whether they are aware of it or not. As they mix and match ingredients, stir and measure and sample, they are blending different things to make one thing: a flavor, a dish, an experience. Those who cook regularly know that it is not enough to combine a set of ingredients correctly. Essential to the process is proper cooking temperature and time. Why? Because when we heat food, we're doing more than warming it up. We're ushering in the almost alchemical magic of chemistry. One cooking website describes what happens:

> We heat food for many reasons. Actually cooking the food is only one of them. . . . Heating starches changes crystallized starch molecules into gels. Bread becomes stale when the starches crystallize, and warming the bread returns them to their soft gel state, making the bread taste and feel fresh. . . . Heating meat causes the tough collagen connective tissue to denature and soften into a gel. Heating it more causes the other proteins to harden, and we get crisp bacon.[6]

Heating a dish transforms the ingredients and makes something new and delicious. Similarly, it is only when we are filled with the Holy Spirit that our various talents and gifts can become something useful for the kingdom of God.

Understanding of salvation may come in stages.

Testimony: In reflecting on his own journey to becoming a Christian, C. S. Lewis writes, "If I find in myself a desire which no experience in this world can satisfy, the most probable explanation is that I was made for another world."[7] But for Lewis this realization came slowly as his faith evolved from paganism to theism to true Christianity. During this journey, he especially struggled with the incarnation. His understanding moved "from the Absolute to 'Spirit' and from 'Spirit' to 'God'" and finally to the incarnation.[8] Throughout this process, Christians such as J. R. R. Tolkien, Hugo Dyson, and Owen Barfield guided him toward a deeper and more mature understanding of God. Without the influence of these friends, Lewis would not have been able to make the same impact.

The Clash of Gods
Making Waves in a World of Rival Religiosity

Big Idea
What pagan society accepts as normal is often totally irreconcilable with the way of Christ and must be abandoned.

Key Themes
- Allegiance to Christ must be total, and often it will challenge cultural norms. A Christian cannot practice sorcery or worship a pagan god or goddess.
- There is grave danger in misusing Christ's name for one's personal profit or advantage.
- Obedience to the way of Christ inevitably instigates violent resistance from those whose lifestyles and livelihoods are thereby threatened.

Understanding the Text

The Text in Context

Paul takes the road to Ephesus from Corinth. In Ephesus, the word of the Lord will continue to be proclaimed, God will work extraordinary miracles, and the name of the Lord Jesus will be held in high honor. The great Artemis, a god made by human hands, will be exposed as a powerless god whose esteem will wane when people are confronted with the gospel of Christ.

Interpretive Insights

19:8–10 *Paul entered the synagogue and spoke boldly there for three months.* Paul returns to the synagogue and again gets tossed out. His preaching about the kingdom of God would necessarily include an exposition of Jesus's kingly role as Savior and Lord. The synagogue opponents deliberately twist his teaching and libel the character of Christians in order to rouse public animosity against them. Paul sees no point in endlessly crossing swords with them. He leaves.

Paul moves to the lecture hall of Tyrannus,[1] where he teaches a predominantly non-Jewish audience for two years, during which time he could cover in depth Jesus's life, death, and resurrection and the interpretation of Scripture.[2] Since Ephesus was a commercial center, people flooded into the city from all over, and the result is that everyone in the province of Asia heard the gospel (cf. 19:26; 1 Cor. 16:8–9, 19). The synagogue's obstinacy has the effect of broadening the reach of the gospel to gentiles far beyond the city (cf. Rom. 11:11). The churches in Colossae, Laodicea, and Hierapolis (Col. 4:12–16) likely were started by those who came to hear Paul.

19:11–12 *God did extraordinary miracles through Paul.* The miracles and their effect are mentioned only after the emphasis on teaching, but both have their positive effect in spreading the gospel. That people took Paul's sweat handkerchiefs and work aprons suggests that he did not limit his teaching to the lecture hall. He also evangelized in his workplace, where people would find these items and take them. It saves them the effort of trying to transport their sick through the narrow and crowded streets to him for healing. Luke would not want to convey that they had magical properties; it is the power of God that causes the healing. Though the people may not have a sophisticated theological understanding of how this healing happens, they experience God's power and mercy (Luke 6:19; 8:44; Acts 5:15), which encourages them to learn more.

19:13–17 *Seven sons of Sceva, a Jewish chief priest.* Imitation is said to be the sincerest form of flattery, but in the case of the sons of Sceva it is evil.[3] They equate Jesus's name with magical power and invoke it to conjure up his spirit to cast out an evil spirit.[4] Despite the weighty number of seven exorcists (contrast the seven demons Jesus cast out [Luke 8:2; 11:26]), they fail to drive out the demon and end up being flailed by it. Had Jesus or Paul been the exorcist, the demon would have surrendered, but it could easily spot religious fraudsters. To run away naked is to suffer utter public humiliation, which, for believers, adds comic relief to the story.

19:18–20 *Many of those who believed now came and openly confessed what they had done.* Those who believed were already Christians, but they may have been entangled in sorcery practices before coming to faith and had not entirely given them up. Sorcery was pervasive in the ancient world with its witches' brew of practices and ideas. Persons from all levels of society were enchanted by its lures and promises to drive away evil spirits or to fulfill hopes. Suetonius reports that the emperor Nero solicited rites from magi in order to escape the ghost of his mother, whom he had murdered.[5] The mortifying trouncing of the Sceva brothers drives home the perils of sorcery to those who witnessed or heard about it. It impels them to rid themselves of their entire stock of sorcery books and paraphernalia worth an impressive fifty thousand pieces of silver.

19:21–22 *After all this had happened, Paul decided to go to Jerusalem, passing through Macedonia and Achaia.* Luke does not explain why Paul decided to go to Jerusalem. One can infer his reason from Romans 15:25–28. There he explains that he is not coming to Rome straightaway because he thought it necessary to deliver in person the collection from the churches of Macedonia and Achaia for the poor among the saints of Jerusalem. Presumably, he wanted to interpret that this gift signified the bond between gentile and Jewish Christians.

The translation "I must *visit* Rome" (Acts 19:21) may mislead readers. He does not intend to make a holiday stopover. He will head into the dragon's lair, the power center of an empire that brutally dominates the world. There he intends to preach fearlessly the gospel that Jesus, not Caesar, is Lord.

19:23–28 *About that time there arose a great disturbance about the Way. A silversmith named Demetrius, who made silver shrines of Artemis, brought in a lot of business.* Artemis was viewed as the powerful goddess who had wrought marvels and guarded the welfare of the city. Pausanias attributes Artemis's fame throughout the world to the antiquity of the cult, the huge size of her temple (four times larger than the Parthenon and counted as one of the seven wonders of the world), and the eminence and wealth of Ephesus where she was so revered.[6] It was "through economic means the religion of Artemis became an indispensable pillar in the cultural structures and life of Asia, and was therefore a crucial factor in the lives of all individuals whom Christianity hoped to convert."[7]

Once again (cf. 16:16–22), the gospel is bad for pagan businesses. Luke presents a head-on clash between God, for whom Paul has gained converts among "all the residents of Asia" (19:10 NRSV), and Artemis, who is worshiped by "all Asia and the world" (19:27 NRSV). The goddess will lose. The sales figures for devotional souvenirs plummet. These idols perhaps were silver shrines in which statuettes of the goddess were placed in recesses in the houses of devotees or replicas of the temple with her sitting on a throne. The silversmith Demetrius justifiably fears that a complete economic and "cultural collapse" would occur if the Christian movement continues to grow and gain influence.[8] He primarily wants to avert widespread unemployment in the Artemis industry. Religion, business, and patriotism are all intertwined. If the goddess's majesty is scorned, so is the city's honor. The tactic of stirring up the crowd's frenzy by chanting patriotic/religious slogans imperils the Christians.

19:29–31 *Soon the whole city was in an uproar. . . . Paul wanted to appear before the crowd, but the disciples would not let him.* The disciples prudently fear for Paul's life if he were to address a horde of people inflamed by hate and running amok. They and sympathetic officials dissuade him from confronting the crowd. "Officials" translates "Asiarchs" ("leaders of Asia"), who were high-ranking municipal figures. Their concern for Paul's safety shows that the gospel has reached the highest circles. Paul's traveling companions, however, are seized and hauled to the theater, which could hold over twenty-four thousand.

19:32–34 *The assembly was in confusion: Some were shouting one thing, some another. Most of the people did not even know why they were there.* The hubbub is typical of a seething mass of people who allow themselves to be swept along in the passion of the moment. Most had simply joined a mob with no idea what the protest was about. Alexander presumably is pushed forward to represent the Jewish community that feared that they might be tarred with the same brush as the Christians. Presumably, they want him to dissociate the Jews from this Christian anti-idolatry movement. Alexander also might be a Jewish Christian who would defend the Christians against the charges.

19:35–41 *The city clerk quieted the crowd.* The city clerk is the leading city official, who apparently commands respect and mollifies the angry throng. His sole aim is to prevent any further rioting because that would incite the ire of the Romans. The rioters, not the Christians, would be punished for causing the uproar, and the local authorities would be held accountable for failing to control it. He argues that Artemis's and the city's reputations have not been diminished by these men. He repeats the religious party line that the goddess's image fell from heaven. If that is so, they must concede that the Christians' denigration of gods that are made by human hands could not include Artemis. Otherwise, it would contradict their beliefs about Artemis. He points out that these men have not physically desecrated the temple. Finally, if any have suffered financial losses, they can follow due process and press charges in the law court. This speech averts any further violence.

Theological Insights

Luke states, "The word of the Lord spread widely and grew in power" (19:20), which refers to the addition of church members. The wording reveals the belief that the Christian community is integrally tied to the word.[9] The church without the word of the Lord is like a light bulb without electricity.

Teaching the Text

1. *Healing power belongs to God alone.* Luke has no intention of presenting Paul as some supernal holy man and that items that touch his body acquire

magical healing power. The power to heal belongs solely to God, which becomes clear when the healing takes place when Paul is not physically present. In Acts, God works healing in various ways through various servants of the gospel, but these servants are nothing in and of themselves. The accounts of healing are intended to provide material evidence that "the gospel is good for the body as well as for the soul, good for this life as well as for the next."[10]

The account also creates a contrast with those who trade in the religious artifacts associated with Artemis. Paul does not market his sweat cloths, work aprons, and handkerchiefs for profit, claiming that they have healing powers. Had he done so, he would have been no different from the peddlers of magical amulets or idol statuettes sold in the marketplace. No payment is necessary for the healing worked by God. Nothing related to the Christian faith can ever be dispensed as if it were a commodity to be sold. Cultic merchandisers who use the Christian faith as a pretext for personal gain will be judged by God.

2. *Christianity challenges the propensity of human beings to seek magical means to manipulate imagined powers to perform their will. Christianity and sorcery are mutually exclusive, and the black arts must be completely rejected.* Christians can only "trust in the power of God and God's word."[11] The humiliation of the seven sons of Sceva, who tried to appropriate Jesus's name to drive out a demon, is perceived by many of the Ephesian believers as "a defeat of magic in general: magic has become obsolete. . . . The magic books are useless now—emblems of a defeated regime—and so must be burned."[12] The owners of the books were not under any external duress to engage in a book-burning crusade but under internal duress created by their newfound faith. They voluntarily renounce their former ties to sorcery with a public bonfire.

The monetary value of these books is staggering. No one, however, thinks to sell these expensive assets and give the proceeds to pad the churches' budgets or Paul's travel allowance. The Christian faith requires that these books go up in flames in order to prevent them from ever being used again.

The incident with the sons of Sceva also puts a striking twist on how people understood the magical power that supposedly comes from knowing the various names of spiritual beings. These conjurers try to usurp Jesus's name for selfish purposes. The question is not "whether the exorcist 'knows' the name of Jesus, but whether the demons 'know' the exorcist as one who has truly been invested with authority to call upon that holy name."[13] If exorcists have power over demons, it is only because Jesus has given it to them (Luke 10:17–19). It is never a power that they possess, and consequently they can never pass it on to others through the use of rituals and formulas.

It is one thing for a demon to expose someone as a fraud: "Jesus I know, and Paul I know about, but who are you?" (19:15). It is quite another for Jesus to do so in the judgment: "Many will say to me on that day, 'Lord, Lord, did we not prophesy in your name and in your name drive out demons and in your name perform many miracles?' Then I will tell them plainly, 'I never knew you. Away from me, you evildoers!'" (Matt. 7:22–23).

3. *The gospel message does not always bring the peace and tranquility that many imagine it should. Instead, it often creates upheaval.* Christians are never to wreak violence on others. The city clerk affirms that Christianity is not an insurrectionist movement intent on inciting havoc around the world. Their opponents are the ones who cause the uproar. But Christianity does destabilize the status quo that resists God. Christianity is countercultural and does not blithely coexist with pagan culture and values. True Christianity will hurt worldly business that would obstruct or oppose the greater business of the kingdom of God.

The city clerk of Ephesus, therefore, seriously misreads the situation in thinking that Christianity is inoffensive and harmless. It does intend to bring about the demise of worship and values that pervert peoples' judgments, affections, and lives. The clerk does not recognize its power to do so. He does not think theologically. His only interest is the practical matter of averting a riot that will force the Roman overlords to intervene.

Christians do not use violence to vandalize or deface the objects of other people's worship. They only use arguments to expose error, and they rely entirely on the power of God to convince others of the truth. They also do not want to replace Artemis and become the next official religion of Ephesus, because in that case they would be under the thumb of the city and its special interests. Christians want to create a global community of citizens in God's kingdom, not local bands of partisans who yell their heads off at outsiders.

Illustrating the Text

After conversion, Christians must completely reject the black arts and idolatry.

Missions: Shawn Tyler explains the challenge of helping Africans reject the influence of evil spirits and witchcraft: "Responding to the Gospel is the greatest step in an African's move away from the bondage of the spirits. . . . A complete cleansing must take place in the new Christian's home and life. The missionaries and church leaders must lead the new Christian in burning all objects associated with the spirits. Remove and destroy all symbols and charms of witchcraft, shrines, sacrifices, and objects of protection. This may involve digging up buried charms, pulling up special plants, cutting off amulets from the body, ripping out charms sewn into clothing, and uncovering all manner of talismans hidden in the roof, bedroom, kitchen, grain storage, and compound. . . . There is a great need to fill up a person's life with good now that he or she has emptied himself or herself of evil."[14]

Christian faith and pagan practice are mutually exclusive.

Missions: Jim Palmer, a missionary to the Miskito people in Central America, tells of witnessing a baptism by one of the pastors under his charge. A woman came to be baptized wearing an amulet that the people were accustomed to wearing to ward off the evil spirits. His heart sank. Did he not teach the pastor about how animism contradicted the Christian faith? As the woman emerged from the water and came up on the shore, she yanked off the amulet and threw it down into the river. It was a dramatic demonstration that she knew that in Christ she no longer needed to fear the spirits or believe that her life was controlled by fatalism.

Paul Brings Renewal to the Churches

Big Idea

Paul the missionary is also Paul the pastor, who takes great pains to console and to exhort in person the churches that he started across a wide geographical area.

Key Themes

- Encouragement is a key component for helping churches in their Christian growth.
- Speaking the word and breaking bread together are consistent elements of the churches' worship.
- Christians gather on the first day of the week, when they celebrate Christ's victory over death.

Understanding the Text

The Text in Context

Paul stated his intention to revisit Macedonia in 19:21, and after spending almost three years in Ephesus, he returns to the churches that he founded in Philippi, Thessalonica, and Berea. Luke gives only a highly abbreviated account of these reunions and summarizes it as "speaking many words of encouragement" (20:2) both in Paul's farewell to the Ephesians and his return to the Macedonians. Encouragement is addressed to believers and can include offering spiritual comfort and exhortation. Paul's Letters to the Philippians and the Thessalonians model this combination of pastoral reassurance and appeal.

Interpretive Insights

20:1–3 *When the uproar had ended, Paul . . . set out for Macedonia . . . and finally arrived in Greece, where he stayed three months.* "Greece" probably is a reference to Achaia and the churches at Corinth and Cenchreae (Rom. 16:1). Sailing would have shut down during the winter, and presumably he writes his Letter to the Romans during this period (Rom. 16:23). He explains in the letter why he is postponing his visit to Rome and heading for Jerusalem.

Unbelieving Jewish opponents, intent on doing Paul harm and silencing his message, have continually dogged him. Possibly, these enemies were also headed to Jerusalem for Passover and were taking the same ship. They schemed to kill him on the way. Luke provides no details about this new plot that causes Paul to alter his plans. Paul has had many narrow escapes and avoids putting himself in unnecessary danger. Instead of sailing directly to Syria from Greece, he takes an overland journey of around four hundred and fifty miles.

Paul has set his face toward Jerusalem for Passover, and the reference to this plot is reminiscent of Jesus's fateful journey to Jerusalem (Luke 9:51). Passover was also the season when the Jewish leaders hatched their scheme to put Jesus to death (Luke 22:1–2, 7). The parallels are not exact. Paul will not be executed in Jerusalem. But the various warnings that Paul receives may remind the reader that, as in the case of Jesus, God is the one who ultimately controls Paul's destiny, not unholy conspirators. The warnings become a test of Paul's will to go to Jerusalem despite the danger that is in store for him there.

20:4–6 *He was accompanied by Sopater son of Pyrrhus from Berea, Aristarchus and Secundus from Thessalonica, Gaius from Derbe, Timothy also, and Tychicus and Trophimus from the province of Asia.* The names of Paul's seven traveling companions and their cities of origin are not a random list. They represent the success of Paul's mission work in the provinces of Macedonia, Galatia, and Asia. They also give the impression of being a delegation. They likely are representatives of the churches that contributed to the collection (1 Cor. 16:1–4; 2 Cor. 8:16–9:5). This list of names fleshes out Paul's assertion that he fully proclaimed the gospel of Christ "from Jerusalem all the way around to Illyricum" (Rom. 15:19).

Aristarchus is mentioned in 19:29 and 27:2, and in Paul's Letters as his "fellow prisoner" (Col. 4:10) and one of his "fellow workers" (Philem. 24). Tychicus is mentioned as a "dear brother and faithful servant in the Lord" (Eph. 6:21; Col. 4:7) and someone whom Paul sends to other churches (2 Tim. 4:12; Titus 3:12). Trophimus will resurface in 21:29 (cf. 2 Tim. 4:20) as one of the gentiles whom Paul is accused of taking into the temple precincts. The beloved Timothy also travels with Paul, but Sopater, Secundus, and Gaius are mentioned only here.[1] The reintroduction of "we" to the narrative suggests that Luke, assuming that he is this mysterious character who last appeared in 16:17, has rejoined the party. A representative from Achaia is not mentioned. Is Luke their representative, or did they not participate (cf. 2 Cor. 8–9)?

Their seven-day layover in Troas occurred probably because they had to wait for a ship headed to the right port.

20:7 *Paul spoke to the people and . . . kept on talking until midnight.* Breaking bread together on the first day of the week (1 Cor. 16:2), not the Sabbath, suggests that Christians have separated from the synagogue and commemorated the resurrection on this day (cf. Matt. 28:1; Mark 16:2; Luke 24:1; John 20:1–2; 1 Cor. 16:1–2). Since no legal holy day existed in the first century when workers had the day off and there was no standard time for quitting work, there could be no fixed hour for the church to meet. The church gathered on Sunday evenings, and members came when they could and stayed into the night. They do not meet under the cover of darkness but hold their love feast in the light. Breaking bread is reminiscent of Jesus's last supper before his death, which has now become the Lord's Supper (1 Cor. 11:20), and continues the tradition of the Jerusalem church of breaking bread together (Acts 2:42, 46). Speaking "until midnight" provides a concrete example of what Luke means when he reports in 20:2 that Paul spoke "many words of encouragement." The time Paul could stay with them was limited, and he took advantage of what time he had to teach the churches. Paul's stamina to undergo an exhausting travel schedule and to speak through the night is amazing and a testimony to his dedication to his calling and the power of the Spirit.

20:8–9 *a young man named Eutychus . . . fell to the ground from the third story and was picked up dead.* The name "Eutychus" means "lucky" and probably is a slave name. Slaves were given names by masters that expressed their hope for them. His lethal fall from the third floor indicates that the believers had gathered in a room in an apartment building (*insula*) in the city.

20:10–12 *Paul went down, threw himself on the young man and put his arms around him. "Don't be alarmed," he said. "He's alive!"* Eutychus is really dead, not seemingly dead. As Peter raised Tabitha back to life (9:36–42), so Paul brings Eutychus back to life. Throwing himself on the young man and putting his arms around him is similar to what Elijah and Elisha did (1 Kings 17:19–22; 2 Kings 4:34–35) in bringing young men back to life.

Eutychus does not need to be carried back on a stretcher but has fully recovered so that he can be led away. Restored to life, he is restored to the community. The accident does not cause them to cancel worship, and Paul goes back to preaching.

20:13–16 *We went on ahead to the ship and sailed for Assos, where we were going to take Paul aboard. He had made this arrangement because he was going there on foot.* Luke does not explain why Paul chose to go on foot. There are no hints of any threats. Paul also bypasses Ephesus because of his hurry to reach Jerusalem by Pentecost. Perhaps he wishes to avoid any more trouble in that city that might delay him, or the ship that he boarded was not scheduled to stop in Ephesus. More likely, he did not want to be detained by his social obligations to his many friends after spending three years of ministry there. The elders will rendezvous with him in Miletus, thirty miles south.

Teaching the Text

1. *Representatives from the churches where Paul has successfully evangelized travel with him to Jerusalem.* The list of those men accompanying Paul suggests that he was circling back to these churches to take up their offerings to bring to Jerusalem. Paul initially planned to send only emissaries to Jerusalem with the collection (1 Cor. 16:1–4). He later changed his mind, believing that it was necessary for him to deliver the gift in person, probably because he could interpret its symbolic theological significance. He regards it not simply as a handout for the poor of the Lord's people in Jerusalem (Rom. 15:26) but as a material token of the spiritual unity between Jewish and gentile believers. These men are living proof of the gospel's success among gentiles. This symbolic dimension of the gifts from predominantly gentile churches explains why he asks the Romans to pray that the contribution he takes to Jerusalem "may be favorably received by the Lord's people there" (Rom. 15:31). If Jewish believers accept the gift from uncircumcised gentile believers, it demonstrates that they also accept them as brothers and sisters in Christ.

While Paul highlights the collection project in his letters (Rom. 15:25–32; 1 Cor. 16:1–4; 2 Cor. 8–9), Luke, for whatever reason, does not emphasize this aspect of Paul's ministry that compels him to go to Jerusalem despite the perils that he will face there.[2] Luke only alludes to it in passing in 24:17, "After an absence of several years, I came to Jerusalem to bring my people gifts for the poor and to present offerings." Luke is intent on showing that Paul is faithful to his Jewish heritage in his desire to be in the Holy City for Passover. His failure to provide a clear motivation for the journey to Jerusalem "has the effect of heightening the resemblance to Jesus' own journey. The gathering of these 'disciples' (named in pairs), and the 'sending of them on ahead' provide a mirror image of Jesus' gathering and sending on of his emissaries ahead of him on the way to Jerusalem (Luke 9:1–6; 10:1–12)."[3] Paul undergoes the same doom-laden journey to Jerusalem as Jesus did. In the Gospel, Jesus is the one who warns his followers about the coming sufferings that he will endure in Jerusalem. In Acts, others warn Paul of the dangers and try to persuade him to abandon his plans. The journey narrative that follows presents Paul as an intrepid disciple who denies himself and takes up his cross daily to follow in Jesus's footsteps (cf. Luke 9:23).

2. *Paul was not a maverick apostle; he was engaged in team ministry.* Luke's story focuses so much on Paul, his preaching, his travels, and his various scrapes with antagonists that the prominence of team ministry can easily be

overlooked. Paul is not a lone maverick carrying the gospel to the world. He is surrounded by a cloud of partners and supporters. As one who identifies himself in all humility as a slave of Christ, it would have been highly inappropriate for him to have disciples. He did have a large number of associates. Earle Ellis counts "some 100 names, often coupled with a score of assorted titles," in Acts and Paul's Letters who are in some way linked to the apostle.[4] Though Paul travels off on his own in this section, he rarely is portrayed as working alone. He is not a "super-apostle" (2 Cor. 11:5) who thinks he can do all things through his own superpowers. He does all things through Christ, who strengthens him (Phil. 4:13), and with others who support, fortify, and partner with him in his work. Success in ministry can always be traced to God's miraculous grace and a team effort. Many on the team often barely get mentioned or go unnamed, but they are crucial to the success of every endeavor.

3. *The power of the resurrection is evident in the miraculous raising of Eutychus to life after he fell to his death*. Paul preached for an extended time, but Luke does not portray the apostle as somehow culpable for Eutychus's fall from the window (despite contemporary jokes about long-winded sermons). The reason for the young man's sleeping and falling lies elsewhere. The otherwise unnecessary mention of the many lamps, which would be burning olive oil, serves to shift the blame from Paul's lengthy speaking to the lengthy time that Eutychus has been exposed to the sleep-inducing effect of the lamp smoke while he was perched in the window.

At Qumran, one could be excluded from the assembly for thirty days for falling asleep (1QS 7:10), but no blame is attached to Eutychus for dozing off. Unlike the sudden deaths of Ananias and Sapphira, who attempted to deceive the Holy Spirit by falsifying their donations to the church, there is no lesson to be learned from Eutychus's fall to his death. It is not a warning against falling asleep in the church service. Ananias and Sapphira were guilty; Eutychus is not. Worn out from his work during the day, his gradual falling asleep in a crowded, smoky room is understandable.

The fall to his death also should not be interpreted symbolically to mean that outside the church is death or as an illustration of what happens when one fails to obey Paul's injunction to keep constant watch (20:28). The account is intended to show that God grants Paul the miraculous power to bring Eutychus back from the dead when he wraps his arms around him. The power of the resurrection is present not only in Paul's words. Tragedy is averted. The community returns to break bread together, and Paul continues to speak until daybreak.

Miraculously thwarting death certainly comforts believers, but sometimes death is not miraculously overcome. Terrible events can occur in Christian gatherings, but believers never despair. Paul's exclamation, "Don't be alarmed.

He's alive!" is similar to the angel's assurance to the women who came to Jesus's tomb, "Don't be alarmed. . . . He has risen!" (Mark 16:6). Because of Jesus's resurrection, in trying times when miracles have not happened, Christians still "do not grieve like the rest of mankind, who have no hope" (1 Thess. 4:13). They find solace in good times and in bad from their trust in the God who raises the dead.

Illustrating the Text

Encouragement is a necessary ministry.

Christian History: From 1789, William Wilberforce made repeated efforts to introduce bills to Parliament to ban the slave trade, but he faced continuous opposition. Knowing of Wilberforce's discouragement, John Wesley wrote to encourage him (it was Wesley's last letter before his death). In a letter dated February 24, 1791, Wesley wrote: "Unless God has raised you up for this very thing, you will be worn out by the opposition of men and devils. But if God be for you, who can be against you? Are all of them stronger than God? O be not weary of well-doing! Go on, in the name of God and in the power of His might. . . . That He who has guided you from youth up may continue to strengthen you in this and all things is [my] prayer."[5] Despite being on his death bed, Wesley believed that Wilberforce needed his encouragement once again. Six days after this letter, Wesley passed away.

Quote: Dietrich Bonhoeffer. Bonhoeffer exhorts, "God has willed that we should seek and find His living Word in the witness of a brother, in the mouth of man. Therefore, the Christian needs another Christian who speaks God's Word to him. He needs him again and again when he becomes uncertain and discouraged, for by himself he cannot help himself without belying the truth. He needs his brother man as a bearer and proclaimer of the divine word of salvation. He needs his brother solely because of Jesus Christ. The Christ in his own heart is weaker than the Christ in the word of his brother."[6]

Gospel ministry and teamwork are inseparable.

Christian Biography: Billy Graham is a world-renowned evangelist, spiritual advisor to American presidents, and one of the most admired persons in the world and considered as the "Greatest Living American" according to Gallup polls, but Billy Graham has never separated from his two coworkers, Cliff Barrows and George Beverly Shea. "*The Team* is a term that has always permeated the Graham organization. . . . But it all started with team followership in the inner core, and that started with Billy himself." Cliff Barrows shares, "[Billy Graham] is a friend of the team. He spoke of the team and team activities as 'ours,' not as 'me and mine.'"[7]

Paul's Bittersweet Farewell Exhortation at Miletus

Big Idea

Paul recaps his mission and how he has carried it out with integrity. He has declared to both Jews and Greeks that they must turn to God in repentance and have faith in the Lord Jesus.

Key Themes

- Paul has been faithful in fulfilling his ministry calling to proclaim the gospel to Jews and Greeks.
- Paul shows no concern for his personal safety because his ultimate concern is to spread the gospel and to finish the course that God has set before him.
- Paul is constrained to go to Jerusalem, placing his trust completely in God, who controls his destiny.

Understanding the Text

The Text in Context

Luke summarizes Paul's ministry in an emotional farewell speech, the only speech delivered to Christians in Acts. In reflecting on his ministry, Paul's speech sets up a model of gospel ministry. He also shows his readiness to endure the sufferings to follow.

Interpretive Insights

20:17–19 *From Miletus, Paul sent to Ephesus for the elders of the church.* That Paul summons the elders of the church in Ephesus to Miletus indicates that this speech is specifically meant for church leaders. They are firsthand witnesses and can testify to the truth of what he says about his ministry with them. The speech is not Paul's defense against critics but an exhortation for others to emulate him. The translation "I served the Lord" can be interpreted to mean that he performed the duties of a slave. His service is more than volunteer or part-time service. He is owned by Christ (Rom. 1:1; Phil. 1:1), and he can expect no special reward for his obedience. He can in all humility say that he is an "unworthy servant" who has only done his "duty" (Luke 17:7–10).

Luke does not report every plot carried out against Paul. He covers only the actions by the silversmith to lobby against him in Ephesus and does not mention the plots carried out by his Jewish opponents in the city. Since unbelieving Jews fought against him at every turn, one is not surprised that they surfaced in Ephesus as well (1 Cor. 15:32; 2 Cor. 1:8).

20:20–21 *I have declared to both Jews and Greeks that they must turn to God in repentance and have faith in our Lord Jesus.* In the narrative, Paul has spoken "publicly" in city centers, lecture halls, and governor's residences. "House to house" means not that he went door to door but that he spoke in the household rooms where the churches assembled (1 Cor. 16:19). The message that he preached remained consistent regardless of the venue or the audience, Jew or gentile: "Turn to God in repentance and have faith in our Lord Jesus."

20:22–24 *And now, compelled by the Spirit, I am going to Jerusalem, not knowing what will happen to me there.* Paul switches to future projections of his ministry. He is under the constraint of the Spirit, which is a reminder that the Spirit is still the one in control of this story. The Greek word translated as "compelled" can also mean "bound." Ironically, the man who wanted to bind Christians in chains (9:2, 14, 21; 22:5) is now himself bound by the Spirit to preach a gospel of liberation and will be bound in chains for doing so (24:27). This divine compulsion explains why he ignores the warnings of supporters to abandon his plans to go to Jerusalem because of the dangers. He is certain that he must go but uncertain about what exactly will happen, except that it will bring hardships and chains. He accepts whatever God has in store for him.

The imagery of a "race," expressed with the Greek word *dromos*, recalls 13:25, where that word is used of John the Baptist completing his work (cf. 1 Cor. 9:23–26; Phil. 3:14; 2 Tim. 4:7). Paul intimates that his race is nearing its end. For most of the rest of the narrative, Paul will continue "the task of testifying to the good news of God's grace" as a prisoner.

20:25–27 *Now I know that none of you among whom I have gone about preaching the kingdom will ever see me again.* Others have been prophesying through the Holy Spirit about the danger that lies ahead for Paul. Now, he himself prophesies that his future is fraught with peril. Proclaiming the gospel is hazardous duty, yet he never "hesitates" to preach (20:20). The Greek verb translated as "hesitate" can also indicate that he did not "shrink back" or "keep silent." He does not try "to please people" or flatter them in his preaching or tell people what he thinks they want to hear (1 Thess. 2:4–5). The gospel calls for repentance, and he does not back off from confronting people with the ugly truth of their sin and the certain prospect of God's judgment.

Ezekiel 3:17–18 and 33:7–9 provide the backdrop for Paul's concern about having blood guilt for failing to deliver the whole message from God. God has also appointed him as a "watchman" and given him a word to speak that is not only good news about the forgiveness of sins but also contains a warning: "When I say to a wicked person, 'You will surely die,' and you do not warn them or speak out to dissuade them from their evil ways in order to save their life, that wicked person will die for their sin, and I will hold you accountable for their blood" (Ezek. 3:18 [cf. 3:20]).

20:28 *Keep watch over yourselves and all the flock of which the Holy Spirit has made you overseers. Be shepherds of the church of God, which he bought with his own blood.* The watchman image continues as Paul applies it in his charge to the Ephesian elders. "Keep watch over yourselves" is the same warning that Gamaliel gave to the Sanhedrin, though there the Greek words are translated as "consider carefully" (5:35). Religious leaders first must examine themselves lest they lead their charges to ruin. The backdrop is Ezekiel 34, where the prophet excoriates the shepherds of God's flock for failing to care for the weak, looking after only themselves, and abandoning the flock to predators. The church must be rightly led, or it too will be scattered and lost.

"Overseers" are identical to "elders." "Elder" refers to "age, experience, and wisdom"; "overseer," to the role of leading, managing, and guarding.[1] Overseers are not "overlords," and Paul makes clear that the church belongs to God, not to them. God acquired rights over the church with "his own blood." Some interpret this phrase to mean "his own [Son's] blood" (cf. Eph. 2:13; Col. 1:20; 1 Pet. 1:18–19; Rev. 5:9). The grammar of the text suggests that it refers to God's blood, which gives prominence to how much it cost to redeem the church.

20:29–32 *I know that after I leave, savage wolves will come in among you and will not spare the flock.* Paul warns of external opponents and internal apostasy. Unlike the wolves that come in sheep's clothing (Matt. 7:15), these predators steal into the church undisguised. Paul does not identify how these treacherous teachers distort the truth. The church has been plagued through the centuries by deviant teaching, which, like Satan, who can masquerade as an angel of light (2 Cor. 11:14), poses as enlightened truth. Paul wrote a letter of tears to the Corinthians (2 Cor. 2:4) and spoke of his anxiety for his churches (2 Cor. 11:28), and here he discloses that he has passionately warned the churches of the manifold threats that would sabotage their faith (cf. Rom. 16:17–18). Paul has done all he can do to edify them to secure their inheritance in the age to come.

20:33–35 *I have not coveted anyone's silver or gold or clothing.* Paul never accepted financial support from a church while present with them, but rather maintained himself by making tents (1 Cor. 4:12). It put him on a par with those of relatively low social status who work with their hands, but it kept him from becoming a burden to the people he served (2 Cor. 11:9; 1 Thess. 2:9; 2 Thess. 3:7–9) and prevented money issues from hindering the advance of the gospel (1 Cor. 9:12). He refused to accept support from those to whom he ministered in order to avoid being encumbered by patron-client obligations.

20:36–38 *When Paul had finished speaking, he knelt down with all of them and prayed. They all wept as they embraced him and kissed him.* Paul's hunch that he would never return to Ephesus may or may not have proven true. He admits that he does not know exactly what will happen to him. His letters to Timothy and Titus suggest that he continued his mission work after a first imprisonment in Rome, and he may have returned to the area. He did send Timothy to Ephesus with his instructions for ministry there (1 Tim. 1:3).

Theological Insights

The reference to God's blood in 20:28 reflects high Christology and assumes an intimate association between God's Son and God. C. K. Barrett states, "It was enough for Luke that when Jesus Christ shed his blood on the cross he was acting as the representative of God; he was God's way of giving life, blood, for the world."[2] Robert Gundry comments that in that passage, as in 20:28, "Luke comes close to equating Jesus with God."[3] Jesus is much more than God's representative, however. Luke 22:20 refers to Jesus's blood "poured out for you," and his blood amounts to God's blood because they are so interconnected. This interconnection is evident in Acts when Luke refers to "the grace of God" in 14:26 and to "the grace of the Lord," which refers to Jesus as Lord, in 15:40.

Teaching the Text

1. *Since there were no books in the first century on what is expected of Christian ministers, Paul's life becomes a model for others to emulate.* This speech has striking parallels with his exhortation in 2 Timothy 4:1–8. The purposes are similar. Paul has no intention of boasting about all that he has done, but rather he aims to provide an example of what is expected of ministers.

The unspoken assumption is that the minister's character, manner, and tone should be shaped by the message of Jesus and bear witness to its truth. Paul brought people to repentance and taught them how to walk worthily of the God who has called them into his kingdom and glory. He himself had to live worthily of the gospel in order to show others how to do so. Paul's speech provides a sketch of character traits that are to be expected in a minister and those that are detrimental to ministry.

Paul exhibited sincerity, courage, and loving care for others. He did not isolate himself from his flock but instead invested his life in the lives of those with whom he ministered.

He was not presumptuous, pompous, or domineering; he served with gentle humility (20:19). Humility was not a virtue among the Greeks and was considered to be a trait suitable for the insignificant, weak, and poor. Christians reappraised humility in light of Christ as a virtue that refrains from self-exaltation and the pursuit of public honor. Instead of always looking out for number one, humility leads one to look out for the needs of others first. Those driven by vain ambition to rise through the ranks are no more than hirelings who care nothing for the sheep (John 10:12–13).

Paul's whole being was committed to the message. He faced considerable adversity but was not crushed by it (20:19–20). He held nothing back in determining to share what was good for the audience, even when it risked rousing enmity.

He was obedient to the Spirit (20:22) and bravely confronted hardships and potential death because completing the course that God has commissioned him to fulfill was more important to him than life itself (20:24). He did not flinch when faced with rejection, hardships, or martyrdom.

He did not preach for profit (20:33–35) or to burnish his reputation and enhance his own personal glory. He did not want the audience to respond, "What a great speaker Paul is!" He wanted them to respond, "What a great redeemer Jesus is!" The gospel of God's grace comes free with no strings attached, and Paul is compelled to preach it with no delivery fee.

2. *Paul's speech addresses the minister's role.* Ministry means serving the Lord (20:19). Churches become confused when they regard their ministers as employees who labor only for them. Shepherds work not for the sheep but for the owner of the flock, God. They owe their allegiance only to the one Master and must live in a certain way. The way ministers live can change the way others do.

The gospel is a matter of life and death. Ministry means offering what is profitable and helpful related to salvation (20:20), not pandering to the audience with good advice or tips on how to be happy, well adjusted, and successful in business. The aim of preaching is to bring forth repentance and faith and to edify (20:20–21). It requires witnessing to the grace of God (20:24), but if preaching "neglects to give a warning, the ungodly will die but the watchman bears the guilt."[4] It requires preaching the whole counsel of God.

Ministry means building up the church (20:20). Paul never mentions growth in numbers. Growth is to be measured by the community's sanctification. The term "sanctification" appears for the first time in Acts in 20:32 (cf. 26:18). It reminds the audience that a divine power flows through them from their relationship with Christ and enables them to live a holy life and to abandon the values, attitudes, and practices of their former life.

Paul warns in 2 Timothy 4:3–4, "For the time will come when people will not put up with sound doctrine. Instead, to suit their own desires, they will gather around them a great number of teachers to say what their itching ears want to hear. They will turn their ears away from the truth and turn aside to myths." Ministry requires safeguarding the truth of the gospel and warding off its manifold human misrepresentations.

Ministry also reaches out to the weak (20:35), taking good news to the poor, proclaiming "freedom for the prisoners and recovery of sight for the blind, to set the oppressed free" (Luke 4:18).

3. *Jesus's saying "It is more blessed to give than to receive" does not appear in the Gospels.* It has become a popular verse for stewardship campaigns. In an evil way, it has been used by unscrupulous preachers to urge followers to contribute sacrificially to the preacher on the pretext of extending the ministry. Some misuse this verse to claim that one will receive greater material rewards for giving to a ministry. In the context, Paul uses this saying to refer not to generosity with one's material goods but to sacrificial generosity with one's life. Its meaning is more fully captured by his statement in 2 Corinthians 8:9: "For you know the grace of our Lord Jesus Christ, that though he was rich, yet for your sake he became poor, so that you through his poverty might become rich." As Christ did not withhold anything in giving his life for others, so Paul gave of himself completely to his ministry. His giving meant that he endured hardships, suffered abuse, and supported himself and his companions through manual work (cf. Eph. 4:28). Paul gives of himself to others "for the sake of the gospel," so that he "may share in its blessings" (1 Cor. 9:23).

Illustrating the Text

Spiritual leaders must be Christlike models for others to imitate.

Art: Artists learn by copying great masterpieces. They carefully study the life and works of the artist. They examine how the master artist has used tools, materials, colors, light, and brush strokes to create their works of art, and then the student attempts to do exactly the same. At times, people will purchase the copies, because the replicas are so similar to the original. The student has become like the master, and the student can point to the master as the origin of the work of art.

Church leaders are called to teach truth that transforms, not to pander to people's felt needs.

Quote: Well-known author and bishop in the United Methodist Church William Willimon comments,

> Jesus doesn't meet our needs; he rearranges them. He cares very little about most things that I assume are my needs, and he gives me needs I would've never had if I hadn't met Jesus. He reorders them.[5]

In a culture that markets to people's "felt needs," we're called to preach the only message that can actually impact people's real needs.

Greater blessing comes through laying down our lives than by clinging to our rights.

Biography: **Maximilian Kolbe.** Kolbe was a Franciscan friar who lived in Poland during World War II. He was well known as an evangelist and teacher, helping to found a publishing center near Warsaw. He engaged in international missions, traveling to China and establishing a monastery in Japan. But the act that would cause his name to be remembered did not come through a publishing house or foreign mission field. It came in the squalor of a Nazi death camp, the infamous Auschwitz. After refusing to abandon the Polish town where he was ministering, Kolbe was captured by the Nazis and imprisoned. His great act of selfless heroism came after a group of prisoners were rounded up for execution for a failed escape attempt. As the name of Franciszek Gajowniczek was called, the victim cried out through tears, "My wife! My family!" Without hesitation, Kolbe volunteered to take his place. They took him instead, and he was murdered. Is it any wonder John Paul II called him "the patron saint of our difficult age"?[6]

Run the race in a manner worthy of Christ.

Quote: **Eric Liddell.** Liddell, the Scottish Olympic gold medalist, said, "It has been just a wonderful experience to compete in the Olympic Games and to bring home a gold medal. But since I have been a young lad, I have had my eyes on a different prize. You see, each one of us is in a greater race than any I have run in Paris, and this race ends when God gives out the medals."[7] After his fame as an Olympic gold medal champion, he went to North China to serve as a missionary. He would die in an internment camp there in 1945.

Prepared to Die for the Name of the Lord Jesus

Big Idea

Despite the continual warnings about the dangers awaiting him in Jerusalem, Paul remains undaunted and determined to continue the journey fully knowing that death looms.

Key Themes

- Paul is much beloved by believers far and wide.
- Friends sound the alarm at every stop that Paul risks his life if he shows his face in Jerusalem.
- Paul is obedient to what he discerns through the Spirit as the Lord's will.

Understanding the Text

The Text in Context

It is no surprise that Paul and his companions sought out the disciples in the port city of Tyre. According to Luke 6:17, a large number of people from "the coastal region of Tyre and Sidon" joined others from all over Judea and Jerusalem to comprise the audience for the Sermon on the Plain. Those scattered by the persecution that spilled over from Stephen's death led some to flee as far as Phoenicia (Acts 11:19). Paul and Barnabas passed through Phoenicia on their way to Jerusalem from Antioch and told believers how the gentiles had been converted, and they gladly received the news (15:3). Warnings of the dangers awaiting Paul in Jerusalem surface three times: in 20:22–24, in 21:4, and in 21:10–11. Paul persuades the believers that "the Lord's will be done" (20:14).

Interpretive Insights

21:1–4 *We landed at Tyre, where our ship was to unload its cargo. . . . Through the Spirit they urged Paul not to go on to Jerusalem.* The expression "torn . . . away" (21:1) conveys how close-knit Christians are and how beloved

Paul has become. Christians have become family and part from one another with tears, but part they must when they are under the compulsion of a greater task.

Travelogues were interesting fare to ancient audiences. They could experience vicariously the adventure but also admire the intrepid traveler who undergoes the hardships of travel. Ancient travelers were not able to book passage long in advance but had to wait to hitch a ride for a fare on a ship that was going in the right direction. Conditions on cargo ships were not the best. "And when we had come in sight of Cyprus, leaving it on the left hand, we sailed unto Syria" is a more literal translation of verse 3 and reflects the vivid account of a veteran seafarer.

Believers know "through the Spirit" that enemies will pounce if Paul steps foot in Jerusalem. Some of them may have been refugees from the previous persecution and are concerned for Paul's well-being, so they try to dissuade him from continuing such an ill-fated journey. They infer that he should avoid the city at all costs. The warnings highlight the peril and Paul's courage in proceeding. He resists his fellow believers to obey what he believes is God's will.

21:5–6 *When it was time to leave, we left and continued on our way.* Luke records another emotional leave-taking similar to Paul's departure from Miletus. Paul had not founded the church in Tyre, but this farewell shows that he is widely held in high regard. Praying for him as a group that includes wives and children indicates the inclusive nature of the Christian faith and "enhances the solemn religious character of Paul's journey to Jerusalem."[1]

21:7 *We continued our voyage from Tyre and landed at Ptolemais, where we greeted the brothers and sisters and stayed with them for a day.* These are churches that were started when the persecution in Jerusalem caused Christians to flee the city (8:4; 11:19). Paul (Saul) was one of the ringleaders in the persecution (8:1–3; 9:1–2), and now, ironically, he comes to strengthen these churches. Loveday Alexander writes, "It's fascinating in these last stages of Paul's journey to see how the Way has been spreading like an underground root system in all sorts of unexpected directions."[2]

21:8–9 *Leaving the next day, we reached Caesarea and stayed at the house of Philip the evangelist, one of the Seven.* Philip had four unmarried daughters who prophesied. He is one of the Seven (6:1–7), and the term "evangelist" distinguishes him from the apostle Philip (1:13). After Stephen's death, Philip left Jerusalem during the time of persecution and by the efforts of Paul (Saul) to "destroy the church" (8:1–5). The Christian faith transforms lives and relationships as Philip now welcomes Paul into his home.

Mentioning that Philip's daughters prophesied confirms the prophecy that Peter cited from Joel that "your sons and daughters will prophesy" (2:17).

21:10–11 *a prophet named Agabus came down from Judea.* Agabus predicted earlier that a severe famine would spread over the entire Roman world

(11:27–28), and now he delivers dire warnings concerning Paul's fate. He dramatizes his prophesy by taking Paul's belt and binding his hands and feet. This is what will happen to him if he continues his march to Jerusalem. The binding reinforces what the Spirit has told Paul in every city on the way (20:23). He will be bound by chains in Jerusalem. The Jewish leaders will cause the Romans to arrest him, and their continual pressure on two Roman governors will prevent his release from custody. Eventually he will appeal to Caesar and be transported to Rome under guard.

21:12–14 *Why are you weeping and breaking my heart? I am ready not only to be bound, but also to die in Jerusalem for the name of the Lord Jesus.* Unlike others who plead with Paul not to go up to Jerusalem because of the danger, Agabus simply foretells what will happen. He does not urge Paul to abandon his journey, knowing that Paul will not be deterred.

Paul's response, "The Lord's will be done," recalls Jesus's acceptance of his destiny on the Mount of Olives through prayer (Luke 22:42). It is Paul's friends who want the cup to be removed and to preserve him from danger, but they finally accept the Lord's will. Though Paul's heart is breaking over the grief of his friends, nothing will stop him. He and his companions continue the journey.

Teaching the Text

1. *Taking up a cross to follow Jesus means that suffering for the sake of the gospel is a part of every Christian's destiny.* Paul's destiny has been known since the Lord told Ananias, "I will show him how much he must suffer for my name" (9:16). Paul already has suffered much, but it is not over yet. More is to come. Everyone along the way recognizes the danger that Paul will encounter in Jerusalem, and Paul knows it as well. Paul's friends, however, differ with him about what he should do. The disciples in Tyre urge him "through the Spirit" (21:4) not to continue on. They join others in wanting him to abandon his plans, but Paul will not be dissuaded.

Since they have been informed by the Spirit and by a prophet of the dangers, they urge Paul through the Spirit to call a halt to this perilous venture. It may seem that the Spirit gives contradictory messages, since Paul asserts that he is "compelled by the Spirit" to go to Jerusalem (20:22). Luke does not present this conflict as a contradiction. It results from a different interpretation of what should be done in light of the Spirit's witness that Paul will meet with adversity and incarceration. The conflict highlights how difficult it is to determine what God's will is even when the Spirit unveils the future. Knowing what will happen and knowing what to do are two different things.

The conflict also shows how Paul's resolve to obey the Lord's will is put to the test. It is not Satan who coaxes him to save himself from suffering, but "his own well-meaning friends."[3] Their obstruction does not mean that they are "somewhat weak in faith."[4] They want to protect a revered and extraordinarily successful missionary. But their opposition also draws attention to "Paul's willingness to suffer for the faith."[5] He is unfazed by the danger, and his devotion to his calling will not allow him to retreat or call it quits. Since Paul knows well in advance what will happen to him in Jerusalem, "his arrest and trials are not an unexpected interruption of his plans but a part of what he must face to complete his ministry."[6]

2. *Prophecy in the church.* Philip's daughters join an illustrious group of those who are said to prophesy or are identified as prophets in Luke-Acts: Zechariah (Luke 1:67), John the Baptist (Luke 1:76), and Agabus (Acts 11:27–28; 21:10–11). Prophets are recognized as church leaders along with teachers in 13:1 and 15:32. Prophets proclaim future events, but Paul also uses "prophecy" to refer to strengthening, encouraging, comforting, and instructing the congregations in public worship (1 Cor. 14:3, 31).

Virginity is not a requirement for a prophet. The detail about Philip's daughters being unmarried simply explains why they live with their father. This status also allows them to devote themselves entirely to their role as prophets (cf. 1 Cor. 7:25–35). Luke takes for granted that God speaks with prophetic authority through women, beginning his Gospel with the celebrated speeches of Elizabeth (Luke 1:41–45), Mary (Luke 1:46–55), and Anna (Luke 2:36–38). It is therefore curious that the daughters are silent in the text. But what would they prophesy that Luke would want to include? The narrative focuses only on the warnings of the dangers that lie ahead for Paul in Jerusalem. If Luke were to include prophecies from them that were related to something other than that issue, it would be off point. If he records them reiterating the warnings that others have uttered, it would make the sudden appearance of Agabus, who traveled from Judea to meet with Paul, and his dramatic enacted prophecy seem superfluous. The omission of any prophecy from these female prophets, therefore, should not be taken as a slight.

Mentioning that they were prophets highlights the "godly influence" of their father,[7] offers a balance between female and male prophets, and affirms that Joel's prophecy that "your sons and daughters will prophesy," cited by Peter at Pentecost (2:17), has been fulfilled. Later, Papias, the bishop of Hierapolis, mentions Philip's daughters as having moved to his city.[8]

Illustrating the Text

Personal safety cannot hinder one's resolution to obey the call of God.

Christian Biography: **Alexander Duff.** Duff was the first overseas missionary of the Church of Scotland to India. He was almost shipwrecked twice before arriving in Calcutta in 1830. He shared the gospel with many people, including introducing Christian ideals to high-caste Hindus, established schools within his churches and missions, and changed the educational system of India. He left India in 1863 to share about the mission work there. During one of the lectures, he grew faint and became ill. His friends insisted that he should discontinue his mission work. Fearing that he may die, they implored, "If you go back, you will die!" He responded, "I will die if I don't go back," and continued, "Will any of you young men or women give your lives to carry the gospel of Christ to India? If you won't, then I will go back that they may know that in England there is one man who cares for their souls."[9]

Quote: C. S. Lewis. Lewis wrote, "I didn't go to religion to make me happy. I always knew a bottle of Port would do that. If you want a religion to make you really comfortable, I certainly don't recommend Christianity."[10]

Christians are called to persevere.

Quote: **Winston Churchill.** During World War II, Winston Churchill uttered these words that would be long remembered: "Never give in, never give in, never, never, never—in nothing, great or small, large or petty—never give in except to convictions of honour and good sense." The greater context of those words adds more weight to their meaning:

> But we must learn to be equally good at what is short and sharp and what is long and tough. It is generally said that the British are often better at the last. They do not expect to move from crisis to crisis; they do not always expect that each day will bring up some noble chance of war; but when they very slowly make up their minds that the thing has to be done and the job put through and finished, then, even if it takes months—if it takes years—they do it.[11]

May Churchill's words about the British be true of every Christian.

Whether or not we understand where God is taking us, we're always called to obey his directions.

Human Experience: Anyone who has ever learned how to rappel knows something about trust and obedience. The instructor walks you through the steps, explains the knots, and shows you how to control your descent. Eventually, you have to stand at the edge of the cliff and lean back and into the rope. You have to trust it to hold you, even though you've never done anything like this before. Obedience and trust are intimately linked. If we trust the Lord, it is much easier to follow him into the future. Why? Because we know that he will hold us, no matter what.

Paul Meets James and the Elders in Jerusalem

Big Idea
Jewish Christians who believe in Jesus as the Messiah continue to be Jews and can remain faithful to their Jewish customs.

Key Themes
- James and the elders rejoice and praise God for the advance of the gospel among gentiles.
- Paul is viewed suspiciously by other Jewish Christians who believe rumors that he would have them turn their backs entirely on the law.
- James and the elders believe that Paul can refute the misrepresentations of his preaching by having him publicly participate in sacrificial rites in the temple.

Understanding the Text

The Text in Context

The leaders of the church in Jerusalem were persuaded by Peter that gentiles can receive the Spirit and be baptized and then praised God for granting them "repentance that leads to life" (11:1–18). After the testimonies of Peter, Paul, and Barnabas, and with James's leadership, the Jerusalem Council rejected the demand from the believers belonging to the party of the Pharisees that gentiles must be circumcised and keep the law of Moses if they are to be saved and included in restored Israel (15:1–31). These issues have been settled. This third meeting with the leaders in Jerusalem raises other issues that Luke intends to show are also resolved. Are Jewish Christians to abandon their Jewish manner of life or may they continue to practice Jewish piety? Is Paul's successful mission among the gentiles an anti-Jewish movement? Is circumcision, which makes Jews distinct as a special people in covenant with God, to be completely ditched?[1] This incident reveals that the answer to these questions is a resounding no (cf. Rom. 3:1–2, 28–31).

Interpretive Insights

21:15–17 *After this, we started on our way up to Jerusalem.* The decision has been made, and Paul, escorted by other disciples, makes tracks for Jerusalem. He and his companions board in the home of Mnason. Mnason, like Barnabas, was a native of Cyprus. His name is possibly a Greek spelling of a Hebrew name, "Manasseh" or perhaps "Menachem." Luke does not say where Mnason resides, perhaps in Jerusalem or on its outskirts. Housing would have been in short supply in Jerusalem and its vicinity during the Passover season. Mnason, like Barnabas, who owned a field, apparently is wealthy enough to have a home large enough to accommodate the entire party. Luke does not name every host where Paul stays. When persons are named, it is likely that they served as eyewitness sources (Luke 1:2). As an early disciple, Mnason may have been in the first group of converts and a source for some of the events that Luke records.[2]

The situation has completely changed from the time when the disciples in Jerusalem sought to keep their distance from Paul (9:26). They receive him gladly as one of the brothers and sisters.

21:18–20a *The next day Paul and the rest of us went to see James.* Paul reports on the successes of his mission among the gentiles in detail, "one by one" (21:19 NRSV). He takes no credit for what has happened. The glory goes to God, who works through the ministry of missionaries. Attributing the success to God, what "God had done," is another reminder that it is God's will for gentiles to come to faith in Jesus and that they need not become circumcised.

The passage follows a pattern similar to when Paul appeared with Barnabas before the apostles and elders of the church in Jerusalem in chapter 15. He is welcomed (15:4), and he recounts what God has done through him among the gentiles (15:12). James agrees that gentiles need not be circumcised and become Jews in order to be saved, and he issues a decree as a resolution to the problem (15:19–20). What is different from that visit is that the elders now praise God when they hear of the conversion of gentiles. No one insists, "The Gentiles must be circumcised and required to keep the law of Moses" (15:5). That issue has been resolved, but they must decide another issue. Some enemies now claim that Paul encourages Jews who become Christians to give up keeping the law.

Luke does not mention the elders' reception of the charitable gifts and offerings that Paul brought for his nation (24:17). Introducing the issue of the collection would only divert attention from Luke's main focus, which is Paul's arrest, defense, and imprisonment. The account of these events constitutes over one-fourth of Acts. One can infer, however, that when James and the elders glorify God at news of the response of gentiles to the gospel, they also gladly accepted any gifts that Paul brought from the gentile churches.

Acts 21:15–26

21:20b–22 *You see, brother, how many thousands of Jews have believed, and all of them are zealous for the law. They have been informed that you teach all the Jews who live among the Gentiles to turn away from Moses.* Great success has occurred among the gentiles who have believed the gospel, but the phrase "how many thousands of Jews have believed" is a reminder that great missionary success has also occurred among the Jews. Luke records the numbers growing from three thousand (2:41) with daily conversions (2:47) to about five thousand (4:4). Despite many Christians fleeing Jerusalem to escape persecution (8:1), Jews have continued to come to faith in the city. The Greek word *myrias* can mean "ten thousand" or, as in the English word "myriad," a very large number. The leaders have been too busy baptizing people to take time for an accurate tally.

James and the elders receive Paul as their "brother." Others regard him as a renegade missionary whom they believe dissuades Jews from living "according to our customs" (2:21). Rumors have it among both believing and unbelieving Jews that Paul rejects the requirement of circumcision and strict observance of the Mosaic law not only for gentiles but also for Jews. Luke does not identify the source of the reports. Had they come from his Judaizing opponents in Galatia, or from his Jewish enemies in Ephesus, or from elsewhere?

Readers know how unfair this picture is. Paul had Timothy circumcised (16:3), took a Nazirite vow (18:18), and rushed to Jerusalem to arrive in time for Pentecost (20:16). Nevertheless, Paul's mission was more open to association with gentile Christians than perhaps many Jerusalem Christians would have deemed risk free. And nonbelieving Jews regarded him as a treacherous scoundrel leading the people astray (cf. Deut. 13:13).

21:23–24 *There are four men with us who have made a vow. Take these men, join in their purification rites and pay their expenses.* The elders know that the rumors flying about are untrue and suggest a way to correct these false impressions. Paul can publicly rebut the cooked-up charges by joining four men in their purification rites and paying for their sacrifices in the temple. Luke does not identify the nature of the vows the men had made and the rites they must perform. It is a matter of indifference, but the shaved heads suggest that the four men took Nazirite vows dedicating themselves to God for a set period of time. This required abstaining from wine, avoiding corpse defilement, and offering sacrifices at the conclusion of the period (Num. 6:2–21). If the four men each had to offer what is prescribed in Numbers 6:14–17—a male lamb, a ewe lamb, and a ram, together with grain and drink offerings and unleavened bread—the cost of paying these expenses would have been substantial.

21:25 *As for the Gentile believers, we have written to them our decision that they should abstain from food sacrificed to idols, from blood, from the meat of strangled animals and from sexual immorality.* It may seem strange that the elders would need to remind Paul about this letter that was sent to the gentile churches with these restrictions, since he was present when the decision was made and was part of the delegation that delivered the letter to the believers in Antioch (15:22). For Luke, the reprise of this apostolic decree serves as a reminder to readers that although the gentile converts need not undergo circumcision in order to become a part of the restored Israel that accepts Jesus as Savior and Lord (15:16–18), they cannot remain idolaters. Paul's participation in the Jewish rites in the temple is a corollary to that decision. It confirms that just as gentile Christians can continue to live as gentiles, Jewish Christians can continue to live as Jews.

21:26 *The next day Paul took the men and purified himself along with them.* Paul follows through on the elders' suggestion. Entering the sanctuary required ritual purification; having come from foreign lands, Paul would have to undergo ritual purification on the third and seventh days before entering the temple.[3] Undergoing this ritual cleansing exhibits his adherence to conventional Jewish piety (cf. Luke 2:22). These purification rites would have taken place in the baths outside the wall of the Temple Mount, between the western and eastern Huldah Gates.

Teaching the Text

1. *Some complain that James and his colleagues imprudently put Paul in jeopardy with their plan to debunk the accusations that he was hostile to Judaism.* When Paul enters the temple, he becomes easy prey for his enemies. F. F. Bruce writes, "If their scheme was well-intentioned and put forward in all good faith, they could not so easily be absolved from responsibility for Paul's exposure to danger and loss of liberty."[4] Some go even further and claim that this plot was hatched with hostile intent. This conjecture is an unnecessarily cynical reading of the text. Luke does not intend for any blame to be laid at the feet of James and the elders because of what happens to Paul in the temple. Well-intentioned plans often go awry. Paul mentions nothing to them about the prophetic warnings he has received and that he needed to be more covert. In this case, Paul's ensuing arrest will accomplish God's plan for Paul. Paul has risked his life again and again to bring the gospel to the gentile world. Luke now shows Paul's readiness to risk his life "to demonstrate his support of Christian Jews who want to live according to the law and share in the temple worship."[5]

2. *Paul's willingness to risk his life in order to disprove the rumors about his teaching shows that Christian Jews may continue to be "zealous" (21:20) for the traditions of the fathers.* In the Letter to the Romans, Paul bristles that his preaching is slandered for promoting lawlessness (Rom. 3:8). Paul has been

attacked in the pagan world for pushing what they perceive as Jewish customs "unlawful for us Romans to accept or practice" (Acts 16:20–21). His Jewish enemies, on the other hand, think that he has gone too far in undermining Jewish distinctiveness and is advocating the abandonment of Jewish customs.

The danger is that zeal for Jewish customs can be easily misdirected. Paul claims that his zeal for the tradition of his fathers was unequaled (Gal. 1:13–14). But God is not interested in muzzle velocity if it is misaimed. Zeal for God must be based on knowledge (Rom. 10:2) that understands that righteousness for both Jews and gentiles comes only through faith in Christ (Rom. 3:22–25). Salvation does not come from one's reliance on obedience to the law (Gal. 3:10–13). Paul regards his past life as an example of misdirected zeal (22:3–5). His fanatical loyalty to Judaism led him to attempt to wipe out what he considered to be an insidious delusion that proclaimed a crucified man as the Messiah of Israel and the Son of God. It is the same misguided fanaticism that drives his antagonists who will conspire to kill him (23:12–14).

Luke Timothy Johnson notes that the term "zealot" in 21:20 can refer to "not only 'zeal' for observance, but also 'jealousy' for honor to be paid to Torah, and therefore hostility toward any perceived derogation of that honor."[6] The problem centers on the word "perceived." What may be perceived as a derogation of the honor due to the law or to God may instead be a derogation of one's own honor or status. Much persecution that purportedly stems from a loyalty to one's religious beliefs actually stems from a desire to protect one's own special religious status and a desire to preserve the status quo that keeps others out.

3. Paul makes accommodations to foster unity in the church and to promote evangelism. Paul does not support the four men's sacrifices in order to win over nonbelieving Jews (cf. 1 Cor. 9:20). Instead, "Paul acts with a spirit of accommodation in order to preserve the unity of the church."[7] The concern is to avoid causing unnecessary offense to faithful Jewish Christians. What Paul does is analogous to Jesus's instructions to Peter regarding the temple tax (Matt. 17:24–27). Jesus offers Peter a means, miraculous to be sure, that enables him to pay the temple tax for the two of them, even though Jesus deems it unnecessary, so as not to cause offense. Likewise, Paul has no intention of unnecessarily provoking conflict that would hinder the Jerusalem church's evangelism among devout Jews or that would dampen the faith of Jewish Christians. His decision to follow through on the leaders' plan is not capitulation but conciliation.

Acts makes clear that the church is to include both gentiles and Jews. Gentile Christians do not need to become Jews, and Jewish Christians do not need to become gentiles. For the rest of the narrative, Paul loudly protests to the crowds and to Jewish and Roman authorities that as a believer in Christ he has been and remains a loyal Jew.

Illustrating the Text

We should never confuse godly zeal with guarding our own turf.

Movie: *The Bridge on the River Kwai*. In this film Alec Guinness plays Lieutenant Colonel Nicholson, the senior officer among prisoners in a Japanese prison camp in Burma during World War II. The camp, presided over by Colonel Saito, is strategically located on the Burma Railway line. Saito informs the POWs that they will be working to construct a bridge to span the River Kwai. The bridge will allow the important rail line to be used to provide needed resources for the Japanese war effort. Initially, Nicholson resists, but at one point he mistakes the soldiers' efforts to sabotage the building of the bridge as shoddy workmanship that will reflect poorly on the reputation of their countrymen. Because of this, he orders the men to build a first-class bridge. When commandos appear to destroy the bridge, Nicholson actually tries to stop them, until he realizes that his misguided drive for national pride almost helped the enemy in their cause of winning the war.

The good intentions of our hearts must never become so clouded that we lose sight of what is really important. Being zealous for the Lord should not be confused with or twisted into the protection of our own turf. We might think that we are protecting something valuable, when in fact we are lifting our agenda over the Lord's. The priority should always be for God first and us a distant second.

In the interest of bridge building, we should be willing to sacrifice our preferences.

Biography: **Nelson Mandela.** Mandela is considered by many people to be one of the greatest negotiators in history. In his effort to win justice for the people of South Africa, Mandela had to find the right times to fight and the right times to compromise. In his biography of Mandela, *Bargaining with the Devil: When to Negotiate, When to Fight*, Harvard Law School professor Robert Mnookin writes,

> He rejected the simple-minded notion that one must either negotiate with the Devil or forcibly resist. He did both. He was willing to make concessions, but not about what was most important to him. With respect to his key political principles, he was unmovable.[8]

Although Christians should never compromise with the devil, we should always seek ways to build bridges with one another. All too often, we view fellowship as a zero-sum game: either you agree with me on everything or we cannot work together. Such should not be our mentality.

Paul's Arrest in the Temple

Big Idea

The doors of the temple are shut to outsiders, which signifies that it no longer can function as the place where God's grace is mediated to all.

Key Themes

- Paul continues to be plagued by Jewish foes who violently resist the gospel's openness to gentiles.
- Once again, a representative of Rome steps in to rescue Paul.
- The preachers of the gospel have nothing to do with violence or rebellions.

Understanding the Text

The Text in Context

The stratagem of Paul publicly participating in redeeming the Nazirite vows of four men in order to show his faithfulness as a Jew backfires. While preparing for the purification ceremony, Paul is grabbed and beaten by a crowd of angry worshipers on a false charge that he deliberately defiled the temple's purity.

Interpretive Insights

21:27–29 *When the seven days were nearly over, some Jews from the province of Asia saw Paul at the temple. They stirred up the whole crowd and seized him.* Trophimus is from Ephesus in Asia, and Jews from Asia recognize him. Since they saw Paul with Trophimus in the city, they mistakenly infer that he brought him into the inner courts and desecrated the temple. Or, they deliberately trump up an explosive charge in order to inflame the crowd.

The sanctuary's dimensions were rather modest and dictated by the Scripture so that it could not be expanded. King Herod decided to increase the temple's grandeur by greatly enlarging the size of its setting. He built an immense plaza to surround the sanctuary. It functioned as a place of trade, business, and teaching. A balustrade was erected to create a boundary between the sacred inner courts and this outer court. Josephus describes it as around 4½ feet high with signs alternating between Greek and Latin that were posted at regular intervals to warn foreigners against crossing the threshold into the holy area. Two stone tablets have been discovered with Greek inscriptions that read, "No foreigner is to enter within the forecourt and the balustrade around the sanctuary. Whoever is caught will have himself to blame for his subsequent death."[1] The summary execution would have been administered by the priestly authorities of the temple. Paul might have been slain had the Romans soldiers not intervened.

The cry "This is the man" might suggest that they were on the lookout for him and had finally nailed him. The charge that he pours scorn on "the law and this place" in his teaching parallels the accusations against Stephen that led to his stoning (6:13–14). An additional charge is tacked on: he denigrates "our people." Their aim is to whip up the crowd to slay Paul.

21:30 *The whole city was aroused.* The whole city is inflamed, as were the Ephesians when cries went up that Paul had denigrated their revered goddess (19:29). They drag Paul from the inner courts to the outer court, where he is encircled by an angry mob. The doors to the temple are shut to keep any other gentiles from possibly entering and defiling it with their unclean presence or to keep the riot from spreading inside. There is no reason to include this extraneous detail unless Luke intends for it to convey a symbolic message that is similar to the tearing of the temple veil at Jesus's crucifixion (Luke 23:45).

21:31–32 *news reached the commander of the Roman troops that the whole city of Jerusalem was in an uproar.* That the Roman soldiers "ran down" implies that they descended the stairs of the palatial fortress Antonia, named by King Herod to honor his friend Marc Anthony. It adjoined the northwest corner of the temple complex and served as a garrison for Roman troops. Josephus reports that soldiers patrolled on the wall above the temple courts and were stationed around the porticoes during festival times, when crowds, easily incited to insurrection, jammed into the temple.[2]

21:33–36 *The commander came up and arrested him and ordered him to be bound with two chains.* In a large show of Roman force, with at least two centurions and their men, the commander tries to snuff out the bedlam before it turns into a full-scale riot. The noise drowns out his attempts to find out what was happening. He has Paul bound (a fulfillment of Agabus's prophecy [21:10–11]) and taken in chains to the barracks, where he can question Paul away from the din. The mob is ready to rip Paul to shreds, and their yelling "Get rid of him" (literally, "Take him [away]") means that they want him killed (cf. 22:22). Those who demanded Jesus's death bellowed the same angry cry (Luke 23:18). In Paul's case, Roman intervention saves him from certain death.

21:37–38 *As the soldiers were about to take Paul into the barracks, he asked the commander, "May I say something to you?"* The commander has no idea who Paul is and suspects that he might be the infamous Egyptian who was associated with the *sicarii* ("terrorists," "assassins," a Latin loanword that literally means "dagger-men"). They engaged in a campaign of terror against members of the Jewish ruling circles who were pro-Roman. Josephus never mentions them doing any violence against the Romans. They stealthily pulled out daggers hidden in their cloaks, stabbed their victims, and melted away into the crowd. The number "four thousand" suggests that Luke uses the term generically for rebels bent on insurrection. The Egyptian false prophet enticed a large number of cutthroats to follow him. He led them into the wilderness and back to the Mount of Olives to stage an attack on the Roman garrison. The governor Felix and his soldiers thwarted that uprising, but the Egyptian escaped. Many feared that he would return to lead another attempted insurgency.[3] The commander initially believes that he has collared a major terrorist. Presumably, Paul's unaccented and proficient Greek indicates that he is not an Egyptian, whom the Romans "typically regarded . . . as uneducated and backward."[4]

21:39–40 *Paul answered, "I am a Jew, from Tarsus in Cilicia, a citizen of no ordinary city. Please let me speak to the people."* Paul never renounces his identity as a Jew (cf. Rom. 11:1; 2 Cor. 11:22; Phil. 3:5). With a note of civic pride, Paul adds that he is not from Egypt but is a citizen of Tarsus in Cilicia. In the ancient world, "one's status and honor were related to one's place of origin."[5] "Citizen" implies more than resident, and it would have been a rare status for a Jew. Paul is not part of the rabble, and the tribune grants him permission to speak, perhaps in hope of quieting the crowd. By speaking their own language, not Greek, Paul hushes the crowd and gives a further sign that he shares their heritage.

Theological Insights

Paul never attacked his people (28:19), contrary to his opponents' accusation. Quite the contrary, he is burdened by their hardening against the gospel and writes that he could wish himself "cursed and cut off from Christ for the sake of my people, those of my own race, the people of Israel" (Rom. 9:3–4a) if only they would believe. The people of God, however, are no longer determined by their ethnic heritage. Gentiles who believe in Jesus also are incorporated into the people of God, much to the chagrin of hardened Jews who militantly resist their inclusion.

Teaching the Text

1. *It is easy to start a riot when religious sensitivities are insulted.* The crowd accepts without any evidence the charge that Paul teaches everyone everywhere

against the people, the law, and the temple and that he must have come to do some mischief. A defiler of the temple deserves the death penalty, and "it is bitter irony that the charge of defiling the temple should be raised at the very moment Paul was ready to complete the Levitical purification ritual."[6] The continual Jewish aggravation with Paul (cf. 9:29; 13:50; 14:2, 19; 17:5–6; 18:12–17) reaches its culmination when the agitators seize Paul.

Luke takes pains to show that Paul has not rejected his Jewish heritage. He is not an agitator causing mayhem; he is a peaceful missionary true to Israel. His Jewish opponents are the radicals stirring up mobs and creating bedlam. They are the ones who try to stamp out the hope of Israel. They are the apostates. They do far more than oppose the people, the law, and the temple. They fight against God (cf. 5:39). They may venerate the temple, but in their misguided zeal they do not submit to the new things that God is doing and do not venerate God's Son. The destruction of the temple in AD 70 will be brought about by impetuous rebels who think that they are fighting for God.

2. *The shutting of the temple doors has symbolic implications.* Joseph Baumgarten makes an important observation: "One of the interesting aspects of Temple ideology is the coexistence of universalist and exclusivist aspirations. Envisioned as a house of prayer for all the nations (Isa. 56:7), the Temple served as the object of pilgrimage and veneration not only for Jews but for countless non-Jewish visitors and admirers. Yet the very structure of the sanctuary and its courtyards embodied strict limitations on the right of access granted to strangers as well as other categories of the populace."[7] Signs around the sanctuary warn non-Jews, "Keep out!" The suspicion that Paul violated this injunction by bringing an uncircumcised gentile into the holy area almost gets him lynched. The architecture of the temple makes it clear that it is *not* a house of prayer for all nations! The note that the temple doors were slammed shut when a near riot ensues is more than a realistic detail. Luke does not care that the temple guardians might have wanted to prevent potential violence from spilling over into the inner courts or to prevent other possible gentiles from encroaching. He is interested in its symbolic significance.

In Malachi 1:6–14, the prophet brings charges against the priests who dishonor God and their vocation by their actions. Their sacrifices are like placing rotten food before an honored guest. God laments, "Oh, that one of you would shut the temple doors, so that you would not light useless fires on my altar! I am not pleased with you, . . . and I will accept no offering from your hands" (Mal. 1:10). As in the days of Malachi, the overlords of the temple do not recognize that God reigns "beyond the borders of Israel" (Mal. 1:5) and that God's name "will be great among the nations, from where the sun rises to where it sets" (Mal. 1:11). The shutting of the temple's doors also signifies that the cultic center of Judaism shut the door on the gospel. The locking of the temple doors "is the sad counterpart to the open doors into the kingdom."[8] F. F. Bruce concludes, "This was the moment when, in Luke's eyes, the temple ceased to fill the role allotted to it in his history up to this point. The exclusion of God's message and his messenger from the house formerly called by his name sealed its doom."[9] The temple cannot have any further significance for God or for the Christian church.[10]

For Luke, the locus of divine forgiveness and salvation has shifted from the temple's altar to the cross of Christ. Nothing can be allowed to stand in the way of anyone who would come to Jesus in faith to receive God's grace (8:36). Paul expresses this conviction in Ephesians 2:13–16: "But now in Christ Jesus you who once were far away have been brought near by the blood of Christ. For he himself is our peace, who has made the two groups one and has destroyed the barrier, the dividing wall of hostility, by setting aside in his flesh the law with its commands and regulations. His purpose was to create in himself one new humanity out of the two, thus making peace, and in one body to reconcile both of them to God through the cross, by which he put to death their hostility."

3. *Since Luke devotes so much attention to Paul's arrest, imprisonment, and defense, he presents the "high point of his career" as "his witness as the imprisoned and suffering servant of Jesus," not as a missionary and pastor.*[11] In his defense, Paul emphasizes that he is on trial for "the hope of Israel" (28:20 [cf. 23:6; 24:15; 26:22–23]). He is a faithful Jew, obedient to the law. What separates him and other Jewish Christians from unbelieving Israel is their belief that Jesus rose from the dead and that Jesus is the fulfillment of prophecies of Scripture concerning the Messiah.

Illustrating the Text

With the shutting of the gates, the temple no longer served its purpose.

Architecture: Independence Hall is considered to be the "birthplace of America" because both the Declaration of Independence and the US Constitution were discussed, ratified, and signed by the nation's founding fathers there. It was the seat of the US government prior to the establishment of Washington, DC, as the new nation's capital. In 1799, the location of government shifted, and the building in Philadelphia no longer was home to the government. Independence Hall holds much history, tradition, and legacy, but it no longer serves the people in the same way as it did prior to 1800. Citizens can always look back at this place to remember all the principles of freedom and democracy that it represents, but today it is only a historic site without power and authority to do what it did before.

Even in the midst of false imprisonment and persecution,
one can be a witness.

History: On April 12, 1963, Dr. Martin Luther King Jr. was arrested in the midst of his campaign against the social and racial injustice occurring in Birmingham, Alabama. He was arrested for coming in to the city as an outsider, inciting civil disturbance, and causing trouble. Even as he was falsely charged, he took the opportunity to continue to preach his message against injustice, penning his now-famous "Letter from Birmingham Jail."

Paul's Defense in the Temple

Big Idea

God called Paul to a universal mission to the gentiles. Paul remains a faithful Jew as a Christian.

Key Themes

- Paul remained a Jew and a champion of God's truth after becoming a Christian.
- The Lord appeared to him again and commissioned him when he was praying in the temple.
- Paul is sent on a universal mission beyond Israel.

Understanding the Text

The Text in Context

The remaining chapters of Acts are devoted to Paul's defense. In this first of six defense speeches, Paul presents himself as a faithful Jew obedient to God. The charge that he has betrayed "our people and our law and this place" (21:28) is groundless. In his later defense speeches, it will also become plain to Roman officials that he is not a rabble-rouser and has not violated Roman law.

Interpretive Insights

22:1–3 *Brothers and fathers, listen now to my defense.* Paul speaks to the crowd in the Hebrew dialect, presumably Aramaic. As a Jew, he addresses them as "brothers and fathers" and presents his case to the crowd as if they were a jury.

Paul was born in Tarsus, probably to a family of some wealth and standing. He was raised in Jerusalem and studied the law under the tutelage of the well-respected rabbi Gamaliel (cf. 5:34). Gamaliel's influence with the Sanhedrin led to the release of Peter and John (5:33–40).

Since more attention is given to Paul's upbringing in Jerusalem than Tarsus, the speech suggests that Jerusalem is primary for understanding his theological background, not the culture of Tarsus. His description of his life as "zealous for God" (cf. Gal. 1:14; Phil. 3:5–6) employs an Old Testament phrase used of Phinehas, son of Eleazar, son of Aaron the priest (Num. 25:13). In righteous indignation, Phinehas impaled an Israelite man and a Midianite woman, a worshiper of Baal, while they were being amorous near the tent of meeting to turn back the wrath of God that would have fallen on the people (Num. 25:1–15). Paul had been no less zealous and no less violent in seeking to protect God's honor and to avert catastrophe befalling the people for perceived infidelity to God.

22:4–5 *I persecuted the followers of this Way to their death.* Paul says that he used to do to Christians exactly what the mob wants to do to him. The leaders who remember his effort during those days are likely to be furious that he became a turncoat.

22:6–10 *I fell to the ground and heard a voice say to me, "Saul! Saul! Why do you persecute me?"* When the risen Lord Jesus appeared to him, Paul (Saul) was converted to the very movement that he so eagerly persecuted. The Lord's query, "Saul! Saul! Why do you persecute me?" Paul's response, "Who are you, Lord?" and the answer, "I am Jesus, whom you are persecuting," appear in all three accounts (9:4–5; 22:7–8; 26:14–15).[1] Unlike the first account of Jesus's appearance (9:3–6), this one includes additional details as told from Paul's perspective. The event occurred around noon, and the light was a blinding "great" light.

The proud and confident Paul is slammed to the ground in the presence of the Lord. The living and exalted Lord Jesus identifies himself with the persecuted, and this encounter changes the direction of Paul's life. The scales were removed from his eyes so that he could see clearly that his zeal was misdirected.

In this account Paul recognizes Jesus as "Lord" and asks, "What shall I do, Lord?" Jesus commands him to get up (cf. Ezek. 2:1–3) and to go to Damascus, where he will receive his orders.

22:11–16 *A man named Ananias came to see me.* Paul does not mention Ananias's misgivings when the Lord told him to go (cf. 9:10–16) and highlights his Jewishness as a devout observer of the law, respected by all the Jews in Damascus. This telling of the story shows that Paul was enlightened not "by a Gentile or by an apostate from the Law" but by a pious Jew.[2]

Ananias's holiness is attested by his authority to cure Paul's blindness with a word. He then delivers Paul's commission from "the God of our ancestors." Readers would know that the commission he receives resonates with the same one that Jesus gave to his disciples (1:8).

Paul shared in the universal guilt of humankind for the crucifixion of the Savior, but he also bore a special guilt for persecuting Christians (1 Cor. 15:9; 1 Tim. 1:13). He readily responds to the command to have his sins washed away through baptism and faith in Christ.

22:17–21 *When I returned to Jerusalem and was praying at the temple, I fell into a trance and saw the Lord speaking to me. . . . Then the Lord said to me, "Go; I will send you far away to the Gentiles."* Paul received further instructions from the Lord while praying in the temple in a "trance." He is commissioned to go to the gentiles. Peter too was praying in a trance when he had a vision that prompted his realization that God would accept repentant gentiles (10:10; 11:5). This account also connects Paul to Isaiah, who received his commission in the temple to "go and tell" (Isa. 6:1–10). Both Paul and Isaiah are told that the people will not accept their testimony. The difference is that Paul is told to leave Jerusalem because of the people's intransigence.[3] Who is "the Lord" who commands him in the temple? The grammatical ambiguity is deliberate and allows the reader to understand that it is Jesus.[4]

The account of this vision means that Paul's universal mission to "all people" (22:15) was not some outlandish scheme that he cooked up on his own but a directive given to him by the exalted Lord in the temple. Whereas Isaiah met resistance at home, Paul meets Jewish resistance in lands far away from Jerusalem. Now, returning to Jerusalem, he faces the full brunt of Jewish hostility to his mission.

22:22–24 *Then they raised their voices and shouted, "Rid the earth of him! He's not fit to live!"* The Jerusalem crowd listens attentively to Paul until he mentions gentiles as recipients of God's blessings (cf. Luke 4:24–30). Outraged, they cry out for him to be put to death. They would stone him as they did Stephen (7:58), but Paul is in the custody of the Romans, so they can only fling dust.

The renewed uproar troubles the commander, who probably could not understand Paul's speech in Aramaic. He orders him to be taken to the barracks so that he can interrogate him. Unlike our modern context, prisoners were not read their rights and could expect flogging as a normal part of their examination.

22:25–26 *Is it legal for you to flog a Roman citizen who hasn't even been found guilty?* Roman citizenship does not provide immunity from prosecution, but Roman citizens were not to be flogged *before* a trial and a conviction. Paul does not openly declare that he *is* a Roman citizen but only offers that it was illegal to scourge one. The centurion's uncertainty about Paul's Roman citizenship compels him to stop and report to his commander. Can this claim be substantiated?[5]

22:27–29 *The commander went to Paul and asked, "Tell me, are you a Roman citizen?" "Yes, I am," he answered.* Paul declares before the commander that he is indeed a Roman citizen. This highest-ranking officer bought his citizenship, and that made possible his appointment to a lofty military position. Paul, however, has higher status than the commander. He is a born citizen.

22:30 *The commander wanted to find out exactly why Paul was being accused by the Jews. So the next day he released him and ordered the chief priests and all the members of the Sanhedrin to assemble.* The commander seeks further clarification about the specific charges from the Sanhedrin.

Theological Insights

1. *God reveals his plan one step at a time.* What the Lord intends for Paul becomes clearer only as he obeys each command. The Lord does not provide us with a complete roadmap of our lives when we submit to his lordship. We never get the whole picture, so that "following God in this earthly life requires walking behind and sometimes feels like plodding through a fog. We can see just far enough to know where to put our feet next, but we have no idea where we are going. We go by faith, not by sight."[6]

2. *Christ emanates the glory of God.* The light's brilliance that causes Paul's temporary blindness is emphasized in this account compared with 9:3. The Greek word translated as "brilliance" in 22:11 is the same word translated as "glory" in 7:2, 55. In 2 Corinthians 4:4–6, Paul describes the believers' conversion from the blindness caused by "the god of this age," who so darkens minds that "they cannot see the light of the gospel that displays the glory of Christ, who is the image of God." He compares conversion to a new creation: "For God, who said, 'Let light shine out of darkness,' made his light shine in our hearts to give us the light of the knowledge of God's glory displayed in the face of Christ" (2 Cor. 4:6).[7]

Teaching the Text

1. *Christianity is the fulfillment of Old Testament promises and the true form of Judaism.* Paul's speeches are a defense both of his own role as a Christian missionary and of the Christian faith. Paul argues that the Way (Christianity) is faithful to and the fulfillment of the hope of Israel. As a Christian Jew par excellence, one who spoke the Hebrew dialect, was "thoroughly trained in the law," was "zealous for God," and was chosen by and obedient to "the God of our ancestors," Paul embodies the truth that Christianity is the legitimate development of Judaism. This argument is made explicit in 24:14–15 and 26:22–23 (cf. Luke 24:25, 44–48). The defense scenes reveal that it is not just

Paul who is on the hot seat for his beliefs and actions. The claims that Jesus is the Messiah and the resurrected and exalted Lord and that God intends to incorporate gentiles along with Jews in the people of God are in dispute. Paul's courtroom evidence provides additional "convincing proofs" (1:3) that bear witness to Jesus as the Christ.[8]

2. *God has the power to transform persecutors into apostles and the harshest critics into believers.* Paul did all in his power under the authority of the high priest and the high council of Israel to rid the nation of this noxious movement that would proclaim a crucified man as the Messiah and the Son of God. The conversion and calling of such a rabid tormentor of Christians shows that God will not "allow Jewish rejection to stand in the way of the world mission."[9]

3. *Paul's transformation affirms the reality of Christ's resurrection.* Some assume that prior to his conversion Paul lived under a cloud of guilt as a Pharisee. One interpreter contends that Paul's "boundless enthusiasm" for Judaism met with disappointment. "The righteousness on which his heart was set stood afar off, mocking his endeavor. Feelings of doubt and disillusionment began to creep in. Was he perhaps on the wrong track after all? Had he accepted a challenge that was beyond his strength? He was missing the mark, and he knew it, and he was unhappy." He felt the law to be "a yoke of bitter bondage" and yearned for deliverance: "Already the first faint yearnings for release had entered the man's soul, the first dim far-off vision of the 'Jerusalem which is above,' which 'is free, the mother of us all.'"[10]

This view is contradicted by Paul's own testimony. He tells the Philippians about his former confidence: "as for righteousness based on the law, faultless" (Phil. 3:6). Prior to his conversion, Paul did not perceive himself to be in a miserable plight from which he needed deliverance. He persecuted the church because he believed that those who were not properly Jewish were a contagion that needed to be exterminated. Nor is there any hint in the text that Paul's conscience was haunted by the death of Stephen, causing him to rethink his persecution of the church and his theology.

If Paul did not come to Christ out of a deep sense of need, if he believed himself to be righteous and did not doubt that what he was doing was right, what caused this dramatic change in the direction of his life? The only explanation from the evidence is that the risen Lord appeared to him. Paul did not begin with a psychological crisis. Instead, he began with Jesus's revelation that caused him to see that his solutions to life were all wide of the mark. The reality of Christ's resurrection caused Paul to reread Scripture, to redirect his life according to God's will, and to reframe all of his theology: Jesus was the exalted Lord, and Jesus died on our behalf and identifies himself with the church.

Illustrating the Text

God can save and transform anyone to be his witness.

Scenario: Abu Bakr al-Baghdadi, the leader of the so-called Islamic State, proclaimed himself the caliph of the Muslim world. The Islamic State committed unthinkable atrocities in Syria, Iraq, and around the world. Imagine, for a moment, waking up tomorrow morning and learning that *this* man has converted to Jesus Christ. This is the kind of conversion that people witnessed in Paul, the former persecutor of Christians and enemy of the Church. Yet, we serve the God who called a persecutor like Paul. If God can reach him, he can reach anyone.

The Christ who was crucified is risen again and changing lives.

Hymn: **"Amazing Grace," by John Newton.** The epitaph on John Newton's tombstone, which he penned, is his testimony: "John Newton, Clerk, once an infidel and libertine, a servant of slaves in Africa, was, by the rich mercy of our Lord and Saviour Jesus Christ, preserved, restored, pardoned, and appointed to preach the faith he had long labored to destroy."[11] Due to his past life as a slave ship captain, he struggled with forgiveness. But he recounted, "I began to understand the security of the covenant of grace, and to expect to be preserved, not by my own power and holiness, but by the mighty power and promise of God, through faith in an unchangeable Saviour. . . . I thought I was, above most living, a fit person to proclaim that faithful saying, 'That Jesus Christ came into the world to save the chief sinners' [1 Tim. 1:15–16]."[12]

"Amazing Grace" [originally titled "Faith's Review and Expectation"]

Amazing grace! How sweet the sound
That saved a wretch like me!
I once was lost, but now am found;
Was blind, but now I see.

'Twas grace that taught my heart to fear,
And grace my fears relieved;
How precious did that grace appear
The hour I first believed.

Through many dangers, toils and snares,
I have already come;
'Tis grace hath brought me safe thus far,
And grace will lead me home.

The Lord has promised good to me,
His Word my hope secures;
He will my Shield and Portion be,
As long as life endures.

Yes, when this flesh and heart shall fail,
And mortal life shall cease;
I shall possess, within the veil,
A life of joy and peace.

The earth shall soon dissolve like snow,
The sun forbear to shine;
But God, who call'd me here below,
Will be forever mine.[13]

Paul's Defense before the Sanhedrin

Big Idea

Paul is shown to be a faithful Jew who risks his life for the hope of Israel.

Key Themes

- The Sadducean high priest and his colleagues in the Sanhedrin are shown to be unjust and opposed to the hope of Israel, the resurrection of the dead. They, not Paul, are the infidels.
- Not all Jews are closed to the gospel. Continuity exists between the church and Pharisaic Judaism in their shared belief in the resurrection. Discontinuity exists over belief in Jesus as the resurrected Messiah and fulfillment of Israel's hope.
- The Romans protect Paul from violence that would halt God's purposes for him.

Understanding the Text

The Text in Context

Fearful of placing Paul, a Roman citizen, in chains, the commander releases him but hauls him before the assembly of the Sanhedrin to face the accusations against him. Paul stands before them and makes a bold defense.

Interpretive Insights

23:1–2 *Paul looked straight at the Sanhedrin and said, "My brothers, I have fulfilled my duty to God in all good conscience to this day."* Paul gets out only one sentence to the Sanhedrin before the high priest, Ananias, orders others to strike him. Josephus gives a less than winsome picture of the high priest, Ananias. He said that he was a great hoarder of money, obtained favor with others through bribery, and had his servants rob lower-status priests of the tithes due them so that some of the older ones who lived off these tithes starved to death.[1]

Paul apparently offends the high priest by addressing the assembly as "brothers," which fails to defer to them as his superiors. He also claims to have a good conscience before God, which implies that God, not this assembly, is his ultimate judge. A good conscience (24:16) entails obedience to God in all matters. In the context, it has to do with his response to his heavenly calling (22:17–21).[2] The high priest finds such a statement to be impudent. If true, it wrecks their case against him.

23:3–5 *Then Paul said to him, "God will strike you, you whitewashed wall!"* Paul is incensed by the violent action that reveals the judge's prejudicial bias. Undaunted and unlike his Lord, who remained silent when struck (Luke 22:63–64), he brashly calls the high priest a "whitewashed wall." The metaphor recalls Ezekiel 13:8–15. There, God denounces false prophets for misleading the people with comforting announcements of peace in a time when there is no peace, which is like building flimsy walls covered with whitewash to make them appear solid. Whitewashing to conceal reality is an apt metaphor for the hypocrite (Matt. 23:27). Ezekiel promises that God will flatten the crumbly wall, and Paul's pronouncement that God will strike the high priest is similar. It is both a prophecy and an oath that invokes God's punishment. The smiting that Paul received from those standing by him is nothing, however, compared to the smiting that God will inflict on these enemies of the gospel (cf. Deut. 28:22).[3]

All astir, bystanders rebuke Paul for insulting the high priest. He backs down only a little by saying that he did not know that Ananias is the high priest. This admission is more an accusation than a confession of ignorance. It implies that no proper high priest would behave as Ananias did. How was Paul to know that he was a high priest?[4] Ananias's behavior makes him "unrecognizable."[5] Paul then shows his Jewish piety by citing the Scripture that commands that one not curse or speak evil of the ruler of the people (Exod. 22:28). Normally, he would respect the high priest, but this high priest is beneath contempt.

23:6 *I stand on trial because of the hope of the resurrection of the dead.* The council was top heavy with Sadducees and had a minority of Pharisees, scholarly laymen devoted to interpreting and applying the law and the development of an oral tradition. Paul sides with the Pharisees in asserting that he is on trial for his belief in the resurrection. He says not that he once *was* a Pharisee, but that he *is* a Pharisee and descended from Pharisees.[6] For Paul, being a Pharisee denotes strict devotion to the law (Phil. 3:5). Jesus said, "Unless your righteousness surpasses that of the Pharisees and the teachers of the law, you will certainly not enter the kingdom of heaven" (Matt. 5:20). For that statement to pack a punch, the righteousness of the Pharisees must have been proverbial and not a sham. Knowing Christ, however, led Paul to the realization that his obedience to the law led not to righteousness but to misdirected pride (Phil. 3:5–9). Nevertheless, Paul never said that he does not "even deserve to be called an apostle" (1 Cor. 15:9) because he once was a Pharisee. He does not reject this background that trained him to be a proficient interpreter of Scripture. He is a devoted Jew who believes in Christ.

23:7–8 *When he said this, a dispute broke out between the Pharisees and the Sadducees, and the assembly was divided.* Paul's confession sets off a theological melee between the Sadducees and the Pharisees. Everything known about the Sadducees stems from Josephus, the Gospels, and the later rabbis, all of which were hostile toward them. All concur that the Sadducees did not believe in a resurrection.[7] The Sadducees found no basis in the Pentateuch for believing in the resurrection and rejected traditions outside the law of Moses. They assumed that personal survival after death comes only through one's offspring and clan. One does not become an "angel" (cf. 12:15) or a "spirit."[8] In Luke 20:27–38, the riddle that they put to Jesus was aimed at making belief in the resurrection look ridiculous. Jesus's response silenced them and won a "well said" from the Pharisaic teachers of the law who heard it (Luke 20:39).

From Luke's perspective, the high priest is a typical Sadducee (Acts 5:17), and his behavior shows him to be unworthy of his office. Sadducees may hold the seats of power, but they do not represent genuine Judaism.[9] If those Jews who do believe in the possibility of resurrection accept what happened with Jesus, they will recognize that "their faith comes to fulfillment in Christianity."[10]

23:9 *There was a great uproar, and some of the teachers of the law who were Pharisees stood up and argued vigorously. "We find nothing wrong with this man."* The teachers of the law who were Pharisees clear Paul of all charges. No one can accuse them of religious disloyalty, teaching against the law (18:13; 21:21, 28), the Jewish customs (21:21), or the Jewish people (21:28), and they absolve Paul. In arguing before the Sanhedrin to let Peter and the other apostles go, Gamaliel, a leading Pharisee, raised a "what if?" question: "If it is from God . . ." (5:39). These Pharisees do the same: "What if a spirit or an angel has spoken to him?" This tactic does not carry the day, since the Sadducees believe that neither is possible.

Comparing the Trials of Jesus and Paul

Jesus's Trial	Paul's Trial
Jesus makes passion journey to Jerusalem (Luke 9:51)	Paul makes passion journey to Jerusalem (Acts 19:21a; 20:22)
A mob seizes Jesus (Luke 22:54)	A mob seizes Paul (Acts 21:30)
Four hearings before authorities:	Four hearings before authorities:
1. Sanhedrin (Luke 22:66–71) 2. Pilate (Luke 23:1–5) 3. Herod Antipas (Luke 23:6–12) 4. Pilate (Luke 23:13–25)	1. Sanhedrin (Acts 22:30–23:10) 2. Felix (Acts 24:1–23) 3. Festus (Acts 25:1–12) 4. Herod Agrippa II (Acts 25:23–26:32)
Jesus is struck and responds with silence (Luke 22:63–64)	Paul is struck and responds with a caustic remark (Acts 23:2–3)
Three declarations of innocence (Luke 23:4, 14, 22)	Three declarations of innocence (Acts 23:29; 25:55; 26:31)
Shout of the crowd: "Away with this man!" (Luke 23:18)	Shout of the crowd: "Away with this man!" (Acts 21:36)

23:10–11 *The dispute became so violent that the commander was afraid Paul would be torn to pieces by them.* The divided council breaks into a jangle of stormy exchanges. Paul might duck the theological ricochets, but many members of the council intend to do him in right then and there. The Roman commander must enter the fray in order to save Paul again from severe injury. Paul is not the rabble-rouser. The Sadducean cabal is a lynch mob.

The necessity of armed intervention by the Romans reveals two things. First, nothing resembling justice could be expected from this lot, and Paul cannot trust his fate to them.[11] Second, God has predestined Paul to bear witness in Rome (23:11). The rescue of the besieged Paul puts him in the hands of the Roman system, which will eventuate in his voyage to Rome and "enable him to bear witness as the Lord desired."[12] The Romans, however, are not to be regarded as Paul's saviors or the epitome of justice. By protecting Paul from the malevolent Jewish leaders, they simply become tools in accomplishing God's will.

Teaching the Text

1. *One need not always be timid and polite in the face of evil.* It seems strange that Luke records "an outburst by Paul for which he must excuse himself."[13] One should not interpret Paul's harsh response as that of a rash hothead, however. Paul's protest scores two important points. First, it highlights that the high priest and his cronies are unjust and have no intention of conducting

a just proceeding. The high priest's conduct disqualifies him as a fair-minded judge and fully merits Paul's indignation. Looking "straight at" or "intensely" (23:1) also recalls Paul looking intensely at Elymas and bitterly accusing him of being "a child of the devil and an enemy of everything that is right" (13:9–10). Through the Spirit, Paul could discern a person's spiritual condition, and he immediately sees through the high priest's hypocrisy.[14]

Second, Paul's citation of Scripture reveals that he respects the office of the high priest. The accusation in 21:28 that Paul "teaches everyone everywhere against our people and our law and this place" does not hold water. The problem is not with Paul but with the conduct of the high priest and his allies, who abuse that office.

2. *The central issue in all of Paul's defense speeches is the resurrection.* He does not bring up the resurrection as a crafty tactic to deflect attention from himself by starting a theological brawl between the Sadducees and the Pharisees. Rather, he makes a "statement of faith," which is "the succinct formulation of the 'main question' of the case against him."[15] If one does not believe in the resurrection, one cannot believe that Jesus is the Messiah and resurrected Lord.

The central issue concerns the hope of Israel and the resurrection, and it continually resurfaces in the rest of the narrative. He will declare before Felix, "I worship the God of our ancestors as a follower of the Way. . . . I believe everything that is in accordance with the Law and that is written in the Prophets, and I have the same hope in God as these men themselves have, that there will be a resurrection of both the righteous and the wicked" (24:14–15). Hopelessly confused, Festus tells Agrippa that he has no idea what the Jews' charges are against Paul, but he surmises that it has something to do with Jesus, a dead man whom Paul says is alive (25:18–19). Paul tells Agrippa that he stands in the dock for the hope that was promised to the Jews' ancestors by God, namely, that the Messiah would suffer and be the first to rise from the dead (26:6–8, 22–23). Before the Jews in Rome, he declares that it is because of "the hope of Israel" that he is placed in chains (28:20). Belief in the resurrection is the center of Paul's preaching. He recognizes: "If Christ has not been raised, your faith is futile; you are still in your sins" (1 Cor. 15:17). In Acts, those Jews who fail to believe that Jesus was raised in fulfillment of the hope of Israel do not belong to Israel and remain ensnared in their sins.

3. *Jesus's resurrection was a bodily resurrection.* The Pharisees allow that a spirit or an angel might have spoken to him after Paul testified that Jesus of Nazareth appeared to him on the road to Damascus in a bright light (22:6–10). Luke's resurrection account, however, emphasizes that the resurrected Jesus was neither a spirit nor an angel. When Jesus appeared to the gathered disciples, they initially thought that it was an apparition from the

spirit world, but the tactile inspection of Jesus's hands and feet confirmed that it was really he and that he was flesh and bone, not some disembodied spirit (Luke 24:39). He walked and talked with them, ate with them, and was touched by them.[16] The one who appeared to Paul on the Damascus road was not an apparition; he was the resurrected Lord.

Illustrating the Text

Christians don't always have to be "nice."

Sermon: "My Strength Is Made Perfect in Weakness," by Dietrich Bonhoeffer. In this sermon on 2 Corinthians 12:9, Bonhoeffer said, "Christianity stands or falls by its revolutionary protest against violence, arbitrariness and pride of power, and by its apologia for the weak.—I feel that Christianity is doing too little in making these points rather than doing too much. Christianity has adjusted itself much too easily to the worship of power. It should give much more offence, more shock to the world, than it is doing. Christianity should take a much more definite stand for the weak than for the potential moral right of the strong."[17]

Jesus's resurrection was a bodily resurrection.

Literature: *The Great Divorce*, by C. S. Lewis. In this imaginative work, Lewis draws a picture of the reality of the resurrection. When the main protagonist enters into the heavenly realms, he is confronted with a new world. He and all the other people who had died and arrived with him were like phantoms or ghosts, but the inhabitants of the new world were "solid people." Flowers were like diamonds. Leaves were too heavy to pick up. Grass penetrated his feet. This new reality was heaven, and they were experiencing the reality of the resurrection and life after death, a life of profound physicality even as it is suffused with spiritual life.

The Vision of God's Purpose for Paul and the Plot against His Life

Big Idea

God's plan is for Paul to testify about Christ in Rome, and human animosity and intrigue do not derail that purpose but instead further it.

Key Themes

- The Lord stands by Paul during his time of trial to give encouragement.
- Jewish fanatics, not Paul, are the ones threatening the law and order in the Roman world.
- Paul is not guilty of any charge deserving death or chains but is transported to the governor for his safety and for a disposition of his case.

Understanding the Text

The Text in Context

The Jewish resistance to Paul's mission (13:45; 14:2–5, 19; 17:5–9; 18:12–16; 19:9; 20:3) continues to gather momentum in Jerusalem. Jews from Asia incited the temple populace to go berserk over Paul's suspected violation of the temple's sanctity. It led to the intervention of the Roman militia and his arrest (21:27–36; 22:22). When Paul appeared before the Sanhedrin, pandemonium erupted requiring the intervention of the Roman commander to rescue him. Paul's bitter opponents do not give up and, with the cooperation of the chief priests, are doggedly determined to liquidate Paul. Once again, the Roman commander must intervene, and he whisks Paul away to Caesarea, where he will become inextricably entangled in the Roman legal process.

Interpretive Insights

23:11 *The following night the Lord stood near Paul and said, "Take courage! As you have testified about me in Jerusalem, so you must also testify in Rome."* One should not assume that Paul thrives on controversy simply because it arose wherever he preached the gospel. Controversy can wear one down, but Paul has weathered it. "The Lord," Jesus, who has risen from the dead, appears to Paul to encourage him for doing well in his testimony before rancorous opponents in Jerusalem. But more is to be done. In all that follows, Paul will be shown to be innocent of political and religious charges. God's concern, however, is not that justice be done and Paul be acquitted of all charges. God intends for Paul to bear witness in Rome.

The Lord does not clarify how or when Paul will get there. He simply issues Paul the next assignment for his mission impossible without filling in the details. Paul had planned eventually to go to Rome (19:21; Rom. 1:13), but it is unlikely that he expected to go there as a prisoner.

23:12–13 *The next morning some Jews formed a conspiracy.* The Romans keep interfering with the passionate intention of militant Jews to do away with Paul, so his opponents boldly decide to resort to covert vigilante action. The unsatisfactory outcome of Paul's hearing before the Sanhedrin leads forty fanatics to swear never to eat or drink until they eliminate Paul. They must assume that they can accomplish the deed within a couple of days.

Their oath is mentioned three times (23:12, 14, 21), and oaths call forth consequences if they are not fulfilled. The Greek verb translated as "bound . . . with an oath" and "taken a solemn oath" implies that they have put themselves under a curse if they fail.

23:14–15 *We are ready to kill him before he gets here.* The chief priests and elders are to be differentiated from the Sanhedrin. The Pharisees on that council would not have consented to the proposed plot, but the temple leadership has been anti-Christian from the beginning. Ironically, when Paul (Saul) was "breathing out murderous threats against the Lord's disciples" (9:1), he went to the high priest to get authorization to take prisoners, and now other radicals are going to the high priest to get authorization to assassinate him.

It would be suicide for these terrorists to try to break into the Antonia Fortress to kill Paul, so they conspire with the chief priests to create a pretext for the Romans to bring Paul outside the prison to the council hall. They plot to assassinate him on the way. They probably plan to have men stationed along the crowded streets rather than let loose a full-scale assault. When the opportunity presented itself, one or more would emerge from the mass of people and lunge at Paul with a dagger.

23:16 *But when the son of Paul's sister heard of this plot, he went into the barracks and told Paul.* To the surprise of most readers, Paul has a married sister with a son who lives in Jerusalem. Paul's young nephew somehow gets wind of the plot and informs him. Family members and friends like Epaphroditus (Phil. 2:25) and Onesiphorus (2 Tim. 1:16–17) would have access to the imprisoned Paul and would provide food and other necessities (24:23). Paul has not been convicted. He is also a Roman citizen with some privileges, and so it is not surprising that this young man might have access to him in custody.

23:17-22 *Then Paul called one of the centurions and said, "Take this young man to the commander; he has something to tell him."* This twist in the plot creates drama. Will a guard listen to a prisoner who tells him to take this boy to the commander with important information? Will the commander pay any attention to a young lad?

Paul is identified as "the prisoner" and probably is infamously so among the soldiers in the barracks. His nephew unveils the entire scheme devised against Paul, and the centurion in charge heeds Paul's demand to take the boy to the commander. The commander also listens and is persuaded to take preemptive action. Everything is to remain hush-hush while he takes countermeasures.

23:23-24 *Get ready a detachment of two hundred soldiers . . . so that he may be taken safely to Governor Felix.* The commander wastes no time and orders half of his contingent of men to prepare to take Paul to the governor on the coast. As the governor's headquarters, Caesarea was the seat of Roman authority in Judea. The governor traveled to Jerusalem only during high feast days in order to suppress potential disturbances. In a time when there was increasing unrest in Judea that will eventually explode into open revolt, the precaution of ordering 470 soldiers to transport Paul to Caesarea is not far-fetched. Forty extemporized assassins would have no chance against 470 battle-tested veterans. Paul also is less vulnerable to an ambush if mounted on a horse along with the cavalry.

23:25-30 *He wrote a letter as follows.* The readers are now informed from the greeting in his letter that the commander's name is "Claudius Lysias." After the greeting, he summarizes the case and why he sends Paul to the governor for a ruling. He paints his actions in the best light, omitting some details. He does not mention that an upheaval occurred in the temple precincts. He did not intervene to protect a Roman citizen but initially thought him to be a terrorist. He had him clapped in chains and ordered that he be scourged during his enhanced interrogation. Only later did he find out that he was a Roman citizen. The preliminary inquiry before the Jewish council did not find him guilty of any violation of Roman law. The plot to kill Paul prompted Lysias to send him under guard to safety in Caesarea under the cover of darkness. He believes that Paul is innocent, but he is a soldier, not a judge. The priestly hierarchy is bent on getting a conviction and a death sentence. If the accusers want to pursue the matter, they must trek to Caesarea and present their case before the governor.

From a Roman point of view, the facts are these. Paul was rescued from a murderous mob. He is a Roman citizen who deserves Roman justice. The inquiry before the Sanhedrin revealed that Paul is accused on matters related to Jewish religious law that did not warrant punishment according to Roman law. Paul's life remains in danger, and his accusers would like to have another chance to bring formal charges against Paul. The conclusion that any fair-minded reader of this letter should draw is that Paul is innocent and his Jewish opponents are frenzied extremists. The result of Lysias's intervention is that Paul is permanently severed from any relationship with Jerusalem and is now embedded in the Roman legal system that will eventually lead him to Rome.

23:31–35 *When the cavalry arrived in Caesarea, they delivered the letter to the governor.* Governor Felix's first question, inquiring about Paul's province, seeks to establish jurisdiction for a Roman citizen. Cilicia, it turns out, falls under the jurisdiction of Syria, which is governed by a Roman legate. Since Felix reports to him, he presumably decides that he can handle the case.

Paul does not get a palatial suite in the governor's official residence, which was Herod's former palace on a promontory by the sea. The praetorium has a place for prisoners to be kept under constant watch.

Teaching the Text

1. *Times of darkness in the Christian life.* The Lord has promised that Paul will testify about him in Rome (23:11), but he is not clear how or if Paul will be extricated from this latest brush with the authorities. Paul's life hangs in the balance. He may have had second thoughts about coming back to Jerusalem and following through with James's plan to win the good opinion of law-honoring Jewish Christians. He may even feel abandoned. When he wrote, "At my first defense, no one came to my support, but everyone deserted me" (2 Tim. 4:16), was he referring to this occasion?

There are times when Christians may feel abandoned by family, friends, colleagues, and even God, but they are not. In the dark of the night when doubts can creep into the soul and crowd out sleep, the Lord stands by Paul to comfort and encourage him. The Lord's word, "As you have testified about me in Jerusalem, so you must also testify in Rome" (23:11), means that Luke understands Paul's defense to be a public witness to God, not a personal self-defense.

The assurance, however, may not be so assuring. In essence, the message is this: "Be of good courage, because you are not going to get off." Through these events God's purposes are being worked out. For the third time, a Roman commander saves Paul's life: from a mob in the temple (21:32–36), from a fracas in the Sanhedrin (23:10), and from a homicidal plot by assassins. Yet

Paul is not released. He remains in captivity. The predictions by the Holy Spirit that his future involves imprisonment (20:23; 21:11) are being fulfilled.

When the Lord told Ananias to go to Paul, he also said, "I will show him how much he must suffer for my name" (9:16). Paul is never given all of the details. He will go to Rome as a prisoner. The Lord does not disclose that it will take two years of imprisonment in Caesarea before it happens. At the time, it seems to be "an apparent disaster, but disasters in Acts have a way of furthering God's own plan."[1] Luke's narrative shows that God's plan for Paul will not be thwarted by temple mobs, terrorists, indecisive and corrupt Roman officials, or forces of nature at sea. Paul will wind up in Rome because God wills it (cf. Rom. 1:13). Servants of the Lord can only respond "The Lord's will be done" (21:14), regardless of the consequences to themselves. They can always be assured that the Lord stands by them through all tribulation and promises to deliver them from death.

2. *Incidental details and the larger purpose of Acts.* Details of family relationships are rare in the New Testament. We know that Jesus had brothers and sisters (Mark 6:3). We know that Peter had a wife and a mother-in-law (Mark 1:30). In this account, Luke lets drop a tantalizing detail about Paul's family without elaborating: Paul has a sister and a nephew.

What was Paul's nephew doing in Jerusalem? Did his mother live there with other members of the family? Was he sent from Tarsus to study how to be a good Jew as Paul had been? Was he or did he become a Christian? How did he get such detailed information of the plot? Did he or other members of his family have connections with the conspirators or the chief priests? Does he want to save more than simply his uncle Paul but an apostle of the Lord? Luke gives no answers.

This detail reveals that Acts is not the story of Paul's life. His family relations are not central to the story. Acts is about how God directs the movement of the gospel in these early days. Paul said that when he became a Christian, he counted all things as loss (Phil. 3:7–8). Did he have to count his biological family as one of the things he considered loss? What is clear from the list of devoted fellow workers in Romans 16 and from the various disciples in Acts who gather to greet and pray with Paul on his way to Jerusalem (20:36–38; 21:4–6, 7, 12–14) and to Rome (28:14–15) is that Christians have a greater family and a support network that extends worldwide as members of God's family.

3. *Violent reprisal has no place in the Christian faith.* Forty zealots swear oaths that they will kill Paul or else. They are like the many religious extremists through the ages who have deceived themselves into believing that they serve and exalt God or the gods through violence (cf. John 16:2). In their dedication to God, the Jewish partisans pledge to fast from food and water until the deed is done. Isaiah, however, harshly condemns those whose religious "fasting ends

in quarreling and strife, and in striking each other with wicked fists" rather than leading to acts of justice and mercy (Isa. 58:3–10).[2] Violence leads only to more carnage. The fanaticism represented by these terrorists will result in the total destruction of the temple and the devastation of Jerusalem within a decade. The hidden message is that Christianity is not a violent movement that will take up the sword against others. Christians will endure being killed by the sword with patient endurance and faithfulness (Rev. 13:14). Their only weapon is their powerful witness to the truth.

Illustrating the Text

Even in our darkest moments, we never stand alone.

Movie: *The Martian.* In this film, based on the novel by Andy Weir, Matt Damon plays an astronaut, Mark Watney, who is part of a team sent to Mars. They are forced to evacuate when a violent storm blows through their site. As the team runs for their ship, Watney is knocked unconscious by a flying piece of debris, which also knocks out his biometric sensors. Without evidence that the lost and unresponsive Watney is still alive, the rest of the team is forced to take off, leaving him behind. Watney faces an intense struggle as he tries to survive on a hostile planet in complete isolation. One of the high points in his experience comes when he is finally able to establish communication with Earth again. In that amazing moment, Watney realizes that he really isn't alone. His plight is now being shared with an entire planet, and someone will now be trying to come and get him.

The greatest news of all is that we are not alone. Christians have the hope of the gospel, that God has not abandoned us. He, in fact, has reestablished the communication that we broke with him through our sin.

The weapons that defend and further Christianity are words of truth, not blades or bullets.

Theology: Over the centuries, Christian theologians and philosophers have developed a theory of "just war." It essentially outlines a set of circumstances under which the civil authority can acceptably become engaged in a military conflict. These conditions include the following: War must be the last resort. Only a legitimate authority can wage war. War can be waged only in response to a wrong suffered, if it has a chance of success, and if it is waged ultimately to win peace. Finally, such a war must not use violence out of proportion to the wrong suffered and must distinguish between combatants and noncombatants. While just war theory outlines what governments may ethically undertake in their capacity as ruling authorities, it never includes the concept of expanding Christianity through warfare.

The Hearing before Governor Felix in Caesarea

Big Idea

The justice denied Paul by Felix will ultimately serve God's purpose for Paul to give witness to the gospel in Rome.

Key Themes

- The chief priests and elders from Jerusalem vigorously pursue Paul's prosecution with false charges.
- Paul defends himself just as vigorously. His accusers present no eyewitnesses and have no case.
- Felix has no interest in pursuing justice and keeps Paul prisoner. He is captivated by Paul and listens to him until he raises issues related to morals and the final judgment.

Understanding the Text

The Text in Context

That Paul was kept under guard by the Roman governor for two years in Caesarea has nothing to do with his guilt for any crime. Felix wanted to listen to Paul's message, hoped to get a substantial bribe from Paul to get an early release, and, failing that, wanted to pander to the Jewish leaders by keeping Paul under wraps.

Interpretive Insights

24:1 *brought their charges against Paul before the governor.* The high priest and leading elders have come in person to Caesarea intent on adding gravity to the charges against Paul and pressure on the governor to decide in their favor. Tertullus, an expert orator, has been hired by the Jewish leaders to prosecute their case. He may or may not be Jewish. He identifies himself with those who seized Paul in the temple, but he distinguishes himself from "the Jews" in 24:5. In 24:9, he is distinguished by Luke from "the Jews" who join in the accusation. The NIV translation has "other Jews" as if he were included in that group, but the word "other" does not appear in the Greek text.

24:2–4 *When Paul was called in, Tertullus presented his case before Felix.* Antonius Felix was procurator of Judea, Samaria, Galilee, and Perea from AD 52/53 to 59/60. He was the former slave of Mark Antony's daughter, the mother of the emperor Claudius. After becoming a freedman, he rose dramatically in the ranks. His brother Pallas served as financial secretary and confidant to the emperor Nero, which did not hurt his own career. The Roman historian Tacitus, perhaps a bit resentful that a freedman could rise to such a high position, says that Felix "practiced every kind of cruelty and lust, wielding the power of king with all the instincts of a slave."[1] Josephus reports that during Felix's tenure the rise of seditious brigands grew worse. Felix conspired to have the high priest Jonathan assassinated by brigands because he continually nagged Felix about his unjust and inept administration. When Festus was sent to succeed Felix, leading Jewish citizens of Caesarea went to Nero to accuse the outgoing governor of mishandling an outbreak of violence between Jews and Greeks in the city. Felix could have faced serious punishment had not Pallas, his influential brother, intervened.[2] This petition to the emperor by Jewish leaders may have led the next governor, Festus, to tread lightly and try to win the high priest's favor.

Tertullus begins his prosecution of Paul by fawning over Felix for his wonderful reform program and fostering peace throughout the land. Because of his lavish praise for an infamously impious governor, readers are predisposed to view Tertullus negatively as a dissembling flatterer. Such exaggeration, however, was normal in attempts to win the favor of a judge in a system in which influence, power, and wealth could bend the rule of law. Tertullus strategically praises Felix for ushering in peace in order to pave the way for his accusation that Paul is a dangerous disturber of the peace.

24:5–9 *We have found this man to be a troublemaker.* Tertullus converts the original religious charges, that Paul taught against the Jewish people and the law (21:28), into more serious civil charges. He labels Paul a pestilent fellow, an agitator throughout the world, a ringleader of the Nazarene sect (as if it were some insidious collection of troublemakers),[3] and, last but not least, a would-be temple desecrater, a serious charge for the Romans that was worthy of the death penalty. He omits any mention of the mob scene in the temple that the Roman commander had to break up. Having declared Felix to be a peacemaker, he portrays Paul as the opposite, someone who stirs up unrest. The implication is that in the interest of preserving the peace Felix should punish Paul.

24:10–13 *When the governor motioned for him to speak, Paul replied.* Paul does not need to hire a rhetorically skilled advocate to defend him, since he can eloquently represent himself. In his introduction, he does not stretch the truth to butter up Felix. He simply states the facts. Felix has been judge over this nation for a long time, and Paul expects a fair trial and to be exonerated if Felix impartially assesses the evidence.

Paul begins his defense by asserting that his accusers do not have a shred of evidence to prove the charges. He came to worship in the temple, not to defile it. He had been in Jerusalem for only twelve days, and part of that time he was under guard. He had no army. He had no interest in staging an uprising.

24:14–16 *I worship the God of our ancestors as a follower of the Way.* Paul continues: he is not a renegade Jew as a follower of the Way. It is not some alien, subversive, underground movement. He believes in the God of Israel and in their holy writings. He also believes in Israel's future hope, the resurrection of the righteous and the wicked. He is a pious man who has a clear conscience toward God and humankind. The resurrection is the fundamental issue behind the entire controversy.

24:17–21 *I came to Jerusalem to bring my people gifts for the poor and to present offerings.* Paul is not a traitor to the faith of Israel, nor is he a rabble-rouser and a menace to society. He demonstrates himself to be devout, as Cornelius is identified for his godliness in giving alms generously to the people (10:2). He was seized in the temple in a ritually purified state after offering sacrifices (21:26). These are not the actions of an insurgent.

What is most important for his case is that the Jews from Asia who made the first accusations are a no-show. The plaintiffs who are present can only offer hearsay evidence because they did not see the fracas in the temple. Paul's point may be summed up this way: "If he had done anything wrong before a crowd of people, the prosecution would be able to bring forward witnesses. There are no witnesses. Therefore, there must be no wrongdoing."[4] By rule of law, the case should be dismissed. Furthermore, the accusers could not reach a verdict of guilty when he stood before the Sanhedrin. The only possible offense that they have witnessed is his shouted declaration before that body that he believes in the resurrection. This confession hardly violates Jewish or Roman law. The Romans could not be troubled by it because they do not perceive how revolutionary the resurrection of Jesus is for the world.

24:22–23 *"When Lysias the commander comes," he said, "I will decide your case."* Felix is informed about the Way, and therefore he must know the truth that it is not a violent faction that threatens public order. Nevertheless, he refuses to clear Paul of the charges and adjourns the case until later. He may delay because he wants more direct information from Lysias, but he is indifferent to issues of justice.

24:24–25 *Several days later Felix came with his wife Drusilla, who was Jewish. He sent for Paul and listened to him as he spoke about faith in Christ Jesus.* Drusilla is the third wife of Felix. Luke does not record her response to Paul, and one wonders why she is introduced. She is the younger daughter of Herod Agrippa I (12:1) and sister to Herod Agrippa II (25:23). According to Josephus, Felix wooed her away from her husband, King Azizus of Emesa of Syria, through the auspices of a Jewish Cypriot posing as a sorcerer.[5] If the audience knows this information, it further discredits his character.

Felix interviews Paul not to gather more facts for the case but out of curiosity about the Christian message. When Paul not only speaks of faith in Christ Jesus but also raises the subject of morals, self-control, and the coming judgment, he directly addresses Felix's greed, lust, and coming doom. The governor becomes alarmed and sends him away. Nevertheless, he continues to see Paul off and on for two years. Paul is not a security risk, but Felix's own security is at risk with the hatred of the Jewish leaders persistently shadowing him.

24:26–27 *When two years had passed, Felix was succeeded by Porcius Festus, but because Felix wanted to grant a favor to the Jews, he left Paul in prison.* Tertullus presented an ingratiating portrayal of Felix's character, but the governor's true colors emerge when he expects a bribe from Paul. Felix is not impressed with Paul's piety in bringing gifts for the poor. Instead, he interprets this gift as an indication that Paul must be sufficiently well off or have friends who could pay for him to let Paul go. He hopes to line his own pockets, but nothing is forthcoming. It is not that Paul is too poor or without friends. Bribery is not the Christian way.

Teaching the Text

1. *Christianity is not a sect but rather the fulfillment of Judaism.* The prosecutor for the Jewish leaders identifies Christianity as a "sect," a term that does not necessarily have a negative connotation. The Sadducees and the Pharisees are also identified in Acts as "sects" (5:17; 15:5; 26:5). The term can refer to a group whose distinctive beliefs set it apart from others. But Paul's admission that he is "a follower of the Way, which they call a sect" (24:14) implies that his opponents want to present the Way as something foreign to the religion of Israel. Luke keeps returning to the theme that Paul is a faithful Jew, faithful to the law and the Scripture's promise of the hope of the resurrection. He is not an apostate; his Sadducean adversaries are. They are an aberrant sect because of their failure to believe in the resurrection. In Jesus's skirmish with the Sadducees over the resurrection, he showed that the resurrection is not some novel idea but is found in the law of Moses (Luke 20:37–38). Jesus argued from the references to the God of Abraham, Isaac, and Jacob that

God did not create these individuals for their souls to lie moldering in a grave and disappear into an empty void at their death. The God of Abraham, Isaac, and Jacob is the God who raised the crucified Messiah from the dead. It is this belief that the crucified Jesus is the Messiah and the first fruits of the resurrection of the dead that separates the Way from other groups in Israel who deny that fact and persecute believers.

The theme that consistently emerges from Paul's defense speeches is that the Way is not "a sect or group within the people of God; it *is* the people of God."[6] Luke's intent is to have Paul's defense speeches do more than simply demonstrate that continuity exists between Christianity and Judaism. Christianity is not merely an offshoot of Judaism. The resurrection of Jesus is the fulfillment of the hope of Israel, and that makes the Christian faith the fulfillment of true Judaism. It is *the* Way that all Israel must follow.

2. *The reference to the resurrection of both "the righteous and the wicked" implies that there will be a final judgment in which the wicked will be judged.* Paul does not tell Felix that as a believer in Christ's resurrection and cosmic lordship he knows that there is a court higher than any Roman court and a judge higher than Caesar or any of his minions. But readers know that God has appointed the resurrected and exalted Jesus as "the judge of the living and the dead" (10:42).

Since judgment is so tied to the resurrection, Paul "strives to have a blameless conscience."[7] He knows that "we must all appear before the judgment seat of Christ, so that each of us may receive what is due us for the things done while in the body, whether good or bad" (2 Cor. 5:10). Christ will examine each person's morals and motives of the heart. Paul therefore lives his life before God such that he and others whom he teaches might discern what is most important in life and be "pure and blameless for the day of Christ" (Phil. 1:10). One should not interpret these statements to mean that one can earn one's own salvation through a good conscience. The virtue of "self-control" that Paul mentions is something that is produced by the Spirit as a fruit of the Spirit (Gal. 5:22–23). It, like righteousness, comes from faith in Christ and walking by the Spirit, not from one's own frantic and futile efforts.

3. *Superficial onlookers versus serious seekers.* Felix has a passing fascination with Paul's explanation of his religious faith. But broaching the topics of morals and a judgment day probably bewilders and offends Felix. The proclamation of the judgment to come is often neglected in modern preaching. For many, the idea of having to face God's judgment seems so "judgmental"! Many people either do not recognize that they are sinners who will be held to account for their sins or do not care to be reminded. Others cannot imagine that a loving God could ever condemn them. It seems so unfair. Did not God create us all with the inalienable right to pursue happiness? Should

we not be able to pursue it however we like? Many do not find happiness in life no matter how hard they pursue it. They may blame their discontent on not getting a fair shake from others and not getting their fair share of things that supposedly make for happiness. It hardly occurs to them that this sense of ennui is caused by their sin and separation from God. When confronted with sin by the preacher or prophet, they often bristle, "What right does God have to condemn me as a sinner? What right does God have to interfere with the way I choose to live my life? It is God who lets me down by not giving me all that I want."

Paul is in a sticky situation, since Felix holds his fate in his hands. He does not use his time with the governor to cajole or smooth talk him to win his favor or to try to negotiate with him in hopes of getting his release. Instead, he morally challenges him with God's requirements of righteousness, self-control, and the judgment that will overtake those who have rebelled against God. Paul's prophetic warnings frighten Felix, but he resists the challenge of the gospel. He puts off making any decision. In the meantime, he deals with his fear by dismissing Paul and distracting himself with worldly hopes of a financial windfall from a bribe.

Illustrating the Text

Christianity is "the Way" for Jews, gentiles—everyone.

Philosophy: Philosophers of religion who subscribe to an "all paths lead to God" ideology sometimes describe the relationship of different faiths by using an Indian folktale: Once three blind men were led to an elephant, a creature they had never encountered before. The first touched the tail. The second touched the leg. The third touched the trunk. Each was asked to describe the elephant. The one who touched the tail said, "An elephant is like a rope." The one who touched the leg said, "No, the elephant is thick and strong, like a pillar." The third replied, "No the elephant is long, rough, and round, like a tree branch." The fourth character in the story is the one-eyed prince, who, though limited himself, has enough "vision" to see that all are partially correct, but all are mistaken. The implication is that the philosophers of religion are the one-eyed princes who see better than any of the others.

The lesson is not so simple, though. There are religions that make diametrically opposing claims, and they cannot both be true. If one claims there is a God and another claims there is no God, one has to be correct, and one has to be wrong. It is not arrogant to say this—this is basic logic—and Christianity should not settle for such a scenario. We proclaim—and should do so boldly—that Jesus is the way, the truth, and the life (John 14:6).

*Every person will have to give an account to God
for the life he or she has led.*

Bible: In Matthew 25:14–30, the parable of the talents, Jesus tells a story in which three servants are each given a sum of money to invest on the master's behalf during his absence. When he returns, the master expects a full accounting. Two of the servants invest wisely and are blessed. The third servant chooses not to invest, so the master takes back the money and casts him out into the darkness. We must note that some of the strongest statements about the reality of judgment come from Jesus. He is the caring Prince of Peace, but he's also the coming Judge. Everyone should invest their life in what is worthwhile, for there will be an accounting.

Many people deal with the fear of judgment by running from God.

Poetry: **"The Hound of Heaven," by Francis Thompson.** In this poem Thompson describes the sinner's attempt to flee God and God's relentless pursuit. Thompson captures with terrible beauty the futility of rebellion:

> I fled Him, down the nights and down the days;
>   I fled Him, down the arches of the years;
> I fled Him, down the labyrinthine ways
>   Of my own mind; and in the midst of tears
> I hid from Him, and under running laughter.
>   Up vistaed hopes I sped;
>   And shot, precipitated,
> Adown Titanic glooms of chasmèd fears,
>   From those strong Feet that followed, followed after.
>   But with unhurrying chase,
>   And unperturbèd pace,
> Deliberate speed, majestic instancy,
>   They beat—and a Voice beat
>   More instant than the Feet—
> "All things betray thee, who betrayest Me."

The Hearing before Governor Festus and King Agrippa and Bernice

Big Idea

Paul came to the decision to appeal to Caesar when it became clear that he would be handed over to be tried again by the Jewish rulers determined to destroy him.

Key Themes

- The Jewish leaders will not let up in their determination to liquidate Paul.
- The new Roman governor Festus takes quick action on Paul's case, but like Felix before him, he would like to oblige the Jewish leaders.
- Paul will never receive a fair trial in Jerusalem, and his appeal to Caesar will take him and his proclamation of the gospel to Rome.

Understanding the Text

The Text in Context

After Paul has endured two years in prison and the governorship has changed hands from Felix to Porcius Festus, the chief priests and the Jewish leaders revive their attacks against Paul, attempting to do away with him once and for all. They seek a favor from Festus asking him to send Paul to Jerusalem, and they plot to have him killed on the way. Caught between his desire to ingratiate himself with the Jewish leaders and his unwillingness to be used as their pawn, Festus decides to transfer Paul to Jerusalem. Paul resists this turn of events and resorts to appealing to Caesar to stand before his court in Rome. Prior to sending him to Caesar, Festus brings Paul before him and his visiting dignitaries, King Agrippa and Bernice.

Interpretive Insights

25:1-3 *Festus went up from Caesarea to Jerusalem, where the chief priests and the Jewish leaders . . . presented the charges against Paul.* Nero appointed Porcius Festus, who belonged to a clan of Roman senators, to serve as procurator of Judea in AD 59/60. Josephus claims that Festus was a conscientious administrator who sought to rid Judea of the increasing plague of deadly brigands and spreading unrest. He died in office in 62.[1]

The chief priests and others of the ruling elite have long memories, and they have not forgotten about Paul. For two years he has been sitting in limbo, and they are still bent on doing away with him. They hope to make headway with the new governor. They adapt the old plan of the forty conspirators to bushwhack Paul while he is being transported between Caesarea and Jerusalem. They want to coax the governor to send Paul back to Jerusalem. Their henchmen would lie in wait for him on the way, take the escorts by surprise, and assassinate him, finally getting their revenge.

25:4-6 *Paul is being held at Caesarea . . . they can press charges against him there.* Felix had left the case of this accused seditionist and temple defiler unresolved. Festus wants to clear his docket of backlogged litigation. He would like to accommodate the Jewish leaders, but he has no intention of being their puppet and does not accept their proposal. If they want to prosecute their case, they must return with him to Caesarea. For Paul, it means that the proceedings will start all over again.

25:7-8 *I have done nothing wrong against the Jewish law or against the temple or against Caesar.* Luke does not rehash the same accusations and defense. The Jewish leaders bring formal charges against Paul but can prove nothing. Paul again defends himself but adds a new wrinkle. Not only has he not infringed Jewish law or polluted the temple, but also he has done nothing to offend Caesar. This statement prepares for his surprising appeal to Caesar that follows.

25:9-12 *"I appeal to Caesar!" . . . "To Caesar you will go!"* After hearing the case, Festus is astute enough to know that the charges are related purely to a religious squabble and do not involve any crime against Roman law. Luke discloses his hidden motives for the audience. Festus wants to ingratiate himself with the Jewish leaders by handing Paul over to them for another trial in Jerusalem. Ostensibly, Jerusalem would be the most appropriate venue to adjudicate a theological matter, and also it would kill two birds with one stone. Festus would rid himself of this nagging case and win the Jewish leaders' good will.

Paul understands the precarious political situation and his legal rights. The governor is likely to cave in to the external pressure from his Jewish adversaries. The governor, despite his immense power, can be press-ganged by the priestly authorities to do what he was not inclined to do, as Pilate was during Jesus's trial (Luke 23:13–25). Paul knows that returning to Jerusalem would be suicide. His vindictive accusers will be his vindictive judges, and they had already decided on the death penalty for him. The danger of an ambush in transit also lurks, and even being set free would be perilous for him because he is a marked man. He is a loyal Roman citizen and decides to appeal to Caesar, who should "hold no terror for those who do right" (Rom. 13:1–6). Festus must be cautious in dealing with a Roman citizen and claims to have no choice except to grant this appeal.

25:13 *A few days later King Agrippa and Bernice arrived at Caesarea to pay their respects to Festus.* Marcus Julius Agrippa II was the son of Herod Agrippa I, who had persecuted the church violently (12:1–23), and the great-grandson of Herod the Great, who ordered the slaughter of the boys two years and younger in Bethlehem and its vicinity (Matt. 2:16). He is also the brother of Felix's wife, Drusilla. When his uncle Herod, king of Chalcis, died, the emperor Claudius gave him his kingdom.[2] He later allowed him to exchange it for the old tetrarchy of Herod Philip, and the emperor Nero awarded him more territory over the years. He defended Jewish causes to Rome, but he was pro-Roman through and through. Vespasian rewarded him for his loyalty during the Jewish revolt by extending his kingdom's borders.[3] He is described as "brilliant, unpredictable, much given to reckless extravagance" and as possessing "both a highly developed sense of self preservation and fine talents as a diplomat."[4] He ruled for forty-seven years, from AD 53 to 100.

Bernice, Agrippa's younger sister, had been married to the same uncle Herod, king of Chalcis, whose kingdom her brother received. After her husband's death, she lived with her brother in what was rumored to be an incestuous relationship that even captured the attention of a Roman satirist.[5] She had a short-lived marriage to King Polemon of Cilicia and then returned to her brother's court. Later, in Rome, she became the mistress of Titus, the Roman general who crushed the Jewish revolt and became emperor in AD 79.[6]

25:14–21 *Since they were spending many days there, Festus discussed Paul's case with the king.* Festus takes advantage of Herod Agrippa's visit to confer with him about Paul. He summarizes the facts of the case that he has been able to untangle for himself. He cites Roman rules of justice and puts his actions in a favorable light. In contrast to Felix, who let Paul languish in prison, Festus moved quickly with his judicial action. He says that he was willing to send Paul to Jerusalem for the trial but says nothing of his motives, which were to gratify the wishes of the Jews, not to see justice done (25:9). From his perspective, the dispute is rooted in Jewish religious rivalries and Paul's claim that a dead man named Jesus is alive. The Greek word behind "religion" in 25:19 probably should be translated as "superstition," a more contemptuous term. It fits his unsympathetic perception of Judaism. Despite his puzzlement and barely hidden disdain, Festus gets it right. The resurrection of Jesus indeed is what it is all about.

25:22–27 *Then Agrippa said to Festus, "I would like to hear this man myself." He replied, "Tomorrow you will hear him."* Agrippa and Bernice's arrival with great pomp and circumstance and a trail of military tribunes and eminent citizens is reminiscent of their father's grandiose pretensions in his royal robes (12:21). Festus tries to weasel out of any responsibility by saying that he found Paul guilty of no capital crime but had no choice when Paul appealed to Caesar. He implies that it is Paul's own fault that he is still incarcerated, and now he must send a report. But what can he say? The prisoner has done nothing worth taking up the time of "His Majesty" (25:26). As Pilate sought help from Herod Antipas concerning Jesus's case (Luke 23:6–12), Festus asks for assistance from Herod Agrippa in drafting his report to the emperor.

Teaching the Text

1. *Paul's innocence and Festus's injustice.* Although he has been convicted of no crime, Paul remains a Roman prisoner. His hearing before Festus reveals once again that none of this conflict has anything to do with Roman law. Readers already know that fair Roman courts attach no importance to such religious matters. With one voice, Gallio, Lysias, Felix, and now Festus recognize that Paul is neither guilty of inciting rebellion nor has done anything to merit prison or death under Roman law (18:14–15; 19:37; 23:28–29; 25:25; 26:31–32; 28:18). From the Roman perspective, the case has to do only with Jewish religious mumbo jumbo that they cannot comprehend (25:19) and lies outside of their jurisdiction. Nevertheless, Paul remains a prisoner. Unlike the Philippian magistrates, no Roman official comes with hat in hand to apologize to Paul for his unwarranted imprisonment (16:35–39).

The Roman law may be just; the execution of it falls short. Paul states that he has done nothing worthy of the death penalty, but he is not afraid of dying (25:11). Yet he has a mission to fulfill and has no desire to become a martyr simply for the sake of becoming a martyr. As a Roman citizen, he has the right to appeal to the emperor before the verdict in the case of a charge with the penalty of death.[7] The governor had wide discretionary power but did not have the authority to issue a death sentence against a Roman citizen, although it was done. Festus could have rejected Paul's appeal.[8] After consulting with his council, he decides to grant it. By doing so, he can sidestep both any blame for putting to death a guiltless Roman citizen and the Jews' ire for not bowing to their demands.

Luke-Acts mentions three Roman Emperors by name: Augustus (Luke 2:1), Tiberius (Luke 3:1), and Claudius (Acts 11:28; 18:2). It is ironic and perhaps fitting that nondescript underlings, Felix and Festus, are named, but the current emperor, Nero, is not. Nero had not yet become the icon of cruelty and evil. He had demonstrated a sense of grandiosity in exaggerating his achievements and talents in brazen attempts to satiate his desire for admiration. It would have been galling to this narcissistic psychopath that he did not even merit a footnote in this history.

2. *God's providence is at work behind the scenes.* Paul might seem to be "the passive pawn of characters and events outside of his control,"[9] but God is the hidden director of events. Paul's opponents are malicious, treacherous, and callous. God has protected Paul from their many plots hatched against his life (9:23, 29; 13:45, 50; 14:2, 5, 19; 23:12–15, 30). Despite human injustice, venality, and enmity, God's promise regarding Paul will be fulfilled: "This man is my chosen instrument to proclaim my name to the Gentiles and their kings and to the people of Israel" (9:15). Paul is protected not because he is Saint Paul, someone special, but because he is a chosen instrument with a special task that he has yet to complete.

3. *Jesus is faithful through trying times.* Paul must have experienced dark moments during this long siege, but Luke does not narrate his frustration or grief (cf. Phil. 2:27). Paul would have been bolstered by the assurance that Jesus stood by him through everything (18:9; 23:11; 26:17–18). That conviction lifted him up so that he could see beyond his own personal crises and view God's greater purposes, God's greater majesty, and God's greater power.

The NIV translation of 25:26 correctly interprets what Festus means when he says that he must submit a report "to His Majesty." The Greek reads "to the lord," and it was not uncommon in the East for the emperor to be called "Lord." Christians can recognize that Festus's biggest problem is that he is reporting to the wrong lord. He earlier referred to the emperor as *sebastos* in 25:21, which the NIV translates "the Emperor." This term means "august," "worthy of reverence." Again, Christians recognize only one ruler who is worthy of reverence and worthy of worship.

Illustrating the Text

We are never the "victim of circumstance."

Science: Every moment of our existence, we are subject to forces beyond our imagination. In the morning, sitting at the table, sipping coffee and eating cereal, we are not at rest. In fact, we are zipping through space at an incomprehensible speed. Our globe revolves at 1,000 miles per hour (mph), circuiting the sun at 66,000 mph, and that sun makes its orbit in the Milky Way at 483,000 mph. If that isn't enough to blow your mind, consider this: the Milky Way itself is ripping through the universe at 1.3 million mph. We are completely unaware of this breathtaking motion, or we take these facts for granted and never give them a second thought. But for just one moment, we should pause and remember the God who set all these forces in motion. He is not the God of the deists who wound up the universe like a clock and then backed off. No, he has numbered the hairs on our heads. His mighty hand, which makes the forces that drive the universe seem minuscule by comparison, is guiding all the events of our lives. And the best news is that this God is good and loving. We are not victims of circumstance; we are under the direction and protection of God.

Everyone serves somebody; the question is whether we're serving somebody worth serving.

Song: "Gotta Serve Somebody," by Bob Dylan. The lyrics of this classic song describe the dilemma faced by every person, whether powerful or weak, rich or poor, famous or unknown. Will we serve the devil, or will we serve the Lord? No matter what, "you're gonna have to serve somebody." In Paul and Festus, we see the two very different outcomes of two people who choose to serve the Lord or another. If appropriate in your context, consider playing this song and/or reading the lyrics.

Paul's Speech before King Agrippa

Big Idea

God commissioned Paul to turn both Jew and gentile from darkness to light, and in continuing obedience to that call Paul turns his defense into an evangelistic appeal.

Key Themes

- God continually presents opportunities for Paul to bear witness to the gospel on a public platform.
- Paul can defend himself eloquently before Roman governors and Jewish kings.
- Paul appeals to his imposing audience to believe in Jesus's resurrection.

Understanding the Text

The Text in Context

Paul defended himself before a mob when he was seized in the temple (22:1–21), before the Sanhedrin (23:1–10), and in front of the Roman governors Felix (24:1–21) and Festus (25:8–11). King Agrippa and Bernice are now favored with Paul's lengthiest defense speech. The speech follows a chiastic pattern:

A Paul is faithful to Jewish tradition (vv. 4–8)
   B Paul formerly persecuted Christians (vv. 9–11)
      C Paul was commissioned by the Lord to witness (vv. 12–18)
      C' Paul served as a witness (vv. 19–20)
   B' Paul now is persecuted as a Christian (v. 21)
A' Paul is faithful to Jewish tradition (vv. 22–23)[1]

Interpretive Insights

26:1–3 *King Agrippa, I consider myself fortunate to stand before you today as I make my defense against all the accusations of the Jews.* Paul directly addresses Agrippa, since he can understand both the Jewish theological issues and the Roman legal niceties. Festus is present (26:24–25, 32), and Paul also wants him to believe, but his speech is aimed at open-minded Jews who believe the prophets.

26:4–8 *The Jewish people all know the way I have lived ever since I was a child.* Paul's past is an open book, and he reasserts his devotion to the law and his Jewish heritage as one who lived according to Pharisaic tradition. He refers to "my own country," "our religion," "our ancestors," and "our twelve tribes." He maintains that he is on trial for believing that God's promises to Israel's ancestors (cf. 13:23, 32–33)—Israel's hope—have been fulfilled in the resurrection. The heart of the matter is the conviction that God raised Jesus from the dead.

26:9–11 *I too was convinced that I ought to do all that was possible to oppose the name of Jesus of Nazareth.* Paul confesses that he formerly was part of the violent campaign to persecute the followers of Christ, whom he now identifies as "the Lord's people." "I cast my vote" does not mean that he was a voting member of the Sanhedrin. It is figurative language that means he gave their death sentences a thumbs-up.[2] He functioned as an enforcer who tracked down believers, not simply in Damascus but in other "foreign cities." Compelling them "to blaspheme" means that he tried to force them to renounce Christ (cf. 1 Tim. 1:13).

26:12–18 *I heard a voice saying to me in Aramaic, "Saul, Saul, why do you persecute me?"* In this third account of his encounter with Jesus on the road to Damascus, Paul omits any mention of Ananias's role, which puts the focus solely on the interaction between himself and the risen Christ. He now includes, besides mentioning that Jesus spoke to him in Aramaic, Jesus's statement "It is hard for you to kick against the goads." The goad is a long, pointed stick used to prod draft animals yoked to a wagon or farm implement. The animal that did not appreciate being jabbed would waste effort by kicking at the stick. Eventually, the animal would learn that it was futile and better to give in to the farmer's control. The phrase was a proverbial expression among philosophers for "the futility of struggling against one's destiny."[3] The image evokes Paul's submission to God's direction and "being pressed into the service of the risen Christ."[4] It was useless for him to try to resist Christ's call to mission.

This account also unpacks more fully the Lord's purpose in calling him. Paul notes that Christ appoints him as "a servant," which recalls Isaiah 42:1–7 (cf. Acts 13:47), from which the imagery of light for the gentiles is drawn. He is sent to turn Jews and gentiles from darkness to light, and "from the power of Satan to God, so that they may receive forgiveness of sins and a place among those who are sanctified by faith in" Jesus (26:18 [cf. Col. 1:13–14]).

The promise of rescue during the mission is also new. That he will need to be rescued means that trouble awaits him in carrying out his commission.

Time and again he has been delivered, surviving stoning (14:19–20), imprisonment (16:19–40), angry mobs (21:27–36), and an attempted assassination (23:12–23). By God's grace, he will survive a shipwreck and a snakebite. Paul uses this promise as part of his defense. Had he been guilty of trying to defile the temple as charged, God would have allowed the throng to kill him, the Sanhedrin to sentence him to death, and the forty fanatics to assassinate him. Instead, God has protected Paul from harm throughout this ordeal.

As a Jew, Agrippa would have been familiar with the concept of Satan as a power opposed to God and the battle between light and darkness. He also would have been familiar with the idea of being sanctified, made holy, which entails being set apart by God to receive an inheritance from God (20:32). What is radically new is the assertion that God intends to deliver gentiles as well as Jews, forgive their sins, and incorporate them with Jews in a holy people.

26:19–20 *So then, King Agrippa, I was not disobedient to the vision from heaven.* Paul has lived in obedience to this heavenly call and continues to serve as a witness before governors and kings. His call for repentance harks back to the beginning of Luke's Gospel and the appearance of John the Baptist. After the quotation from Isaiah 52:10, "And all people will see God's salvation" (Luke 3:6), John demands that his audience "produce fruit in keeping with repentance" (Luke 3:8). "Repentance" refers to a change in one's thinking and orientation that results in a change in one's way of life.[5] Luke particularly emphasizes that repentance has a direct effect on how one deals with others, particularly the downtrodden in society.

26:21 *That is why some Jews seized me in the temple courts and tried to kill me.* Paul the fiery persecutor became the persecuted because of his obedience to this heavenly calling.

26:22–23 *I am saying nothing beyond what the prophets and Moses said would happen—that the Messiah would suffer and, as the first to rise from the dead, would bring the message of light to his own people and to the Gentiles.* Paul's statement about the Messiah repeats almost verbatim what Jesus taught his disciples after his resurrection (Luke 24:46–47). Jesus's death and resurrection are the fulfillment of God's ancient promises to Israel as inscribed in "the Law of Moses, the Prophets and the Psalms" (Luke 24:44).

26:24–26 *At this point Festus interrupted Paul's defense. "You are out of your mind, Paul!"* Festus should be encouraged that the messianic deliverer whom Paul proclaims is one who suffers and dies, not one who leads a rebellion. But he thinks that Paul has gone off the deep end, driven mad by too much study of Jewish writings. To Festus, resurrection and the exaltation of a terrestrial body to a celestial realm are utter nonsense.

Paul responds by saying that his message is not madness but "reasonable," sober truth. "To speak in a corner" was an image used pejoratively by philosophers to disparage those regarded as uneducated, unphilosophical, and secretive.[6] The miracles cannot be denied (4:16), and Christians are not part of a secret society. They proclaim their message from the housetops such that others think that they are turning the world upside down (17:6).

26:27–29 *Then Agrippa said to Paul, "Do you think that in such a short time you can persuade me to be a Christian?"* Paul audaciously pins Agrippa down. If he believes in the prophets, he should be persuaded to believe in Jesus. If he does not believe in Jesus, he does not believe in the prophets and, from Paul's perspective, rejects his religious heritage.

Agrippa is not prepared to take the next step of believing in Jesus as the resurrected Messiah. He puts Paul off by asking if Paul thinks that he can persuade him to become a Christian so quickly. We cannot discern from the written text the tenor of Agrippa's response. Is he responding sarcastically, asking earnestly, or laughing nervously? The word "Christian," however, suggests that it is a negative response. The term was coined by outsiders (11:26) and not as a compliment. Its use in 1 Peter 4:16 suggests that it was applied to those who are despised. King Agrippa would hardly want to join that society. Paul would not wish for anyone to share his chains, but chains are a likely prospect for Christians in this era.

Paul's defense turns into an evangelistic appeal. He does not care if it is a short time or a long time if only Agrippa and others would believe. To become like Paul is to change one's mind about the crucified Christ and to be obedient to God's will.

26:30–32 *Agrippa said to Festus, "This man could have been set free if he had not appealed to Caesar."* The verdict of Agrippa and his court matches that of Lysias (23:29). But they do not have the final say. The wheels of Roman justice have been set in motion, and Festus does not have the will to halt them. Festus brought in Agrippa only to give him advice on what to write in his report to Caesar. He is bound to send Paul to Rome.

It remains unclear what charge Festus attaches to his report when he dispatches Paul to Rome. He cannot write, "This man is mad." The absence of any charge underscores that the Roman legal process is not driving the events. The Lord's promise is being fulfilled: "As you have testified about me in Jerusalem, so you *must* also testify in Rome" (23:11). The testimony of the gospel about a crucified and risen Lord will be brought, appropriately, by an apostle in chains.

Teaching the Text

1. *Paul's defense.* Recapping Paul's defense against the religious and political charges, he first defends his Jewishness. He took a vow and shaved his hair

as a pious man who follows the customs of the fathers (18:18). He specifically identifies himself as a Jew (21:39; 22:3) and talks about "our ancestors" (24:14; 26:6) and "my nation" (26:4; 28:19 ESV), to whom he brought alms. He belonged to the ultraobservant Pharisee wing of Judaism (23:6; 26:5). His preaching to the gentiles is in obedience to a heavenly calling (22:17–21). He personifies the fulfillment of the prophecies that Israel was chosen by God to become a light to the nations.

Second, Paul is not guilty of fomenting social revolution (16:20–21; 17:6–7; 18:13; 19:26–27). He calls Jesus "Savior" (13:23), "Messiah" (17:3), and "Lord" (20:21, 24; 28:31), but he never identifies Jesus as king. Loyalty to Christ does not entail disloyalty to the Roman government. The verdict of all of his trials before Roman officials is "not guilty."

Luke is not simply interested in providing a narrative proving the innocence of Paul. The apostle is an apostle of the Way. Christians are not seditious, intent on leading revolts to establish an earthly kingdom. They will turn the world upside down, but only through a spiritual revolution by the power of God's word.

2. *Three perspectives on Paul's call and conversion.* The three accounts of Paul's call and conversion should not be considered in isolation or regarded as redundant. In this third account, the word "light" appears three times (26:13, 18, 23). The first time it is connected to Christ's appearance on the Damascus road. The second time it is connected to salvation, turning gentiles and Jews from the darkness to the light. The third time it refers to the message of light that is to be preached. The slight variances in the accounts of Paul's conversion and call are instructive. In 9:3, he sees "a light from heaven." In 22:6, it is a "bright light from heaven." In 26:13, it is "a light from heaven, brighter than the sun." In this last account, the light that knocked Paul down to the ground (9:3–4) is described as an intense illumination that also functions to prepare Paul to shine its light among the Jews and gentiles who grope in the darkness under Satan's tyranny (Luke 1:76–79; 2:29–32).[7]

The first account shows Christ's intimate ties to the church that Paul (Saul) persecuted. The second account underscores the continuity of the Christian faith with the Jewish tradition. The third account shows that he also received spiritual illumination. Paul is an example of God's extraordinary grace, which he himself highlights: "God demonstrates his own love for us in this: While we were still sinners, Christ died for us" (Rom. 5:8).

In this last account of Paul's commission, Jesus issues very specific instructions compared to the earlier accounts: "You will be told what you must do" (9:6); "You will be told all that you have been assigned to do" (22:10). The commission is related to the imagery of "light" (26:16–18) and integrally tied to the creation of Israel to be a light to the nations (Isa. 42:6; 49:6; Acts

13:47). As Paul understands it, God illuminated his eyes so that he might illuminate the eyes of others, both Jews and gentiles, with the light of the gospel. A zealous Christ denier becomes a zealous Christ proclaimer engaged in a universal mission.

3. *Proclaiming the gospel while on trial.* Paul begins this discourse by stating that he stands before King Agrippa to make his defense against the Jews' accusations (26:2). At the end, he states that through God's help, "I stand here and testify to small and great alike" (26:22). He moves from defense to proclamation. He does not shrink from shining the gospel's light on those in power. His transition from defense to offense is an illustration of Jesus's promise that the Holy Spirit will teach disciples what to say when they are brought before rulers (Luke 12:11–12; 21:12–15). It also illustrates that "the only real defense available to Paul and to the church as a whole is that of proclamation."[8] Paul does not fear that his proclamation will cause offense and not get him off the hook. He has done nothing deserving of death, but he willingly will accept death as part of carrying out his commission.

Illustrating the Text

The Spirit speaks through his witnesses, even before kings.

Film: *Chariots of Fire.* In this classic movie, Eric Liddell is assigned to run a race on the Sabbath. But Liddell knows where his highest allegiance lies and courageously stands up for his faith, even before the future king of England. Lord Cadogan states, "Hear, hear. In my day it was king first and God after." Liddell responds, "God made countries, God made kings, and the rules by which they govern. And those rules say that the Sabbath is His. And I for one intend to keep it that way." The lords continue to challenge Liddell, but he does not relent. Finally, Edward, Prince of Wales, asserts, "There are times when we are asked to make sacrifices in the name of that loyalty [to country]. And without them our allegiance is worthless. As I see it, for you, this is such a time." But Liddell concludes, "Sir, God knows I love my country. But I can't make that sacrifice."

Only those who are unintimidated by power can witness to power.

Quote: **Oscar Romero.** From his Christian conviction that "it is not God's will . . . for some to have everything and others to have nothing," Romero spoke out against "any and all institutional structures that perpetuated repression of the people."[9] He boldly confessed, "I have no ambition for power, and so with complete freedom I tell the powerful what is good and what is bad. That is my duty."[10] He was killed the next day at the altar during Mass in a small chapel in El Salvador on March 24, 1980.

Our eyes have been opened so that others may see.

Human Experience: Anyone who has flown on a commercial airline knows the drill. Pass through security. Sit at the gate. Wait for your zone number to be called. Finally, pile onto the plane and find your seat. After a few minutes, the flight attendants stand to inform the travelers of safety measures. One part of the presentation always stands out. It goes something like this: "In case of emergency, the oxygen masks may deploy. In such an emergency, be sure to fasten your own mask before helping the person next to you." Once we're safe, we help rescue others. It is what we're called to do, whether we are flying on an airplane or sharing our faith (or both). We have been saved from sin so that we can help to save others.

Storm, Shipwreck, and Shelter

Big Idea

Threatened by storm and shipwreck, Paul is saved so that he might bear witness to the gospel in Rome as God has decreed.

Key Themes

- Paul is marked out as someone with a special mission who will be preserved by God.
- Paul is sturdy, faithful, and courageous because he trusts in God's providence and protection (Ps. 139:9–10), and he conveys that trust to others.
- As God's servant, Paul is an agent of rescue and healing for others.

Understanding the Text

The Text in Context

The vivid account of this sea voyage and shipwreck, including technical seafaring terminology, entertains with its dramatic turns. Audiences have been captivated by shipwreck stories throughout the ages in novels, movies, and news stories. But this account is more than a gripping diversion. Paul's innocence has been confirmed by the Roman governors and King Agrippa, and what seems to be a strange interlude in the story of Paul's progress to Rome provides further confirmation of Paul's innocence. He is under God's protection, and even the forces of nature will not stop his mission. Divine providence intervenes in the nerve-wracking misadventures at sea. Paul, a Roman prisoner, is shown to be a prophet, a man of God who encourages disconsolate shipmates, and a miracle worker.

Interpretive Insights

27:1–8 *When it was decided that we would sail for Italy, Paul and some other prisoners were handed over to a centurion named Julius.* In the other specific references to sea voyages in Acts (13:4, 13; 14:26; 16:11; 18:18, 21; 20:6,

273

13–16; 21:1–3, 6–7), personal narration occurs only in 16:11 and 20:6–21:7. This narration can be attributed to Luke's eyewitness account of a harrowing experience that would have deeply affected him. The "we" also makes clear that when Paul is transported to Rome as a prisoner, he is not alone but was given the privilege of being accompanied by faithful companions. Aristarchus traveled with Paul to Jerusalem (19:29; 20:4) and is mentioned with Luke in Paul's greetings in Colossians 4:10 and Philemon 24. In Colossians, Aristarchus is mentioned as a "fellow prisoner," but there is no indication that he is a prisoner on this journey.

Another honorable centurion (cf. Luke 7:1–10; Acts 10) makes his appearance in the person of Julius. He shows exceptional kindness to Paul by letting him seek help—supplies for the journey and prayerful encouragement—from friends in Sidon when they dock there. Without provisions prisoners could starve on board a ship.[1] Unlike the other prisoners, who most likely have been convicted of crimes worthy of punishment in Rome, Paul has not been sentenced for any crime. He is also known to be a Roman citizen, which may explain why Julius shows partiality toward him. One cannot rule out that the force and grace of Paul's persona also cause the centurion to act favorably toward him.

27:6–8 *There the centurion found an Alexandrian ship sailing for Italy.* There are no commercial passenger ships in this era, and Julius must find a ship headed in the general direction he wants to go. He first secures a trading ship that hugs the coast until heading for Myra, where he knows he can book passage on a ship headed for Italy. An Alexandrian ship would have been carrying grain (27:38), a crucial commodity for Rome. Egypt was a major supplier of grain for Rome. The emperors were so anxious to avoid food shortages in Rome that would lead to instability that captains of the merchant fleet were induced with financial incentives to sail even in the winter.[2] The ship could have belonged to a "special fleet designed and constructed by the Romans expressly to transport grain from Egypt to Italy."[3]

27:9–13 *Much time had been lost, and sailing had already become dangerous because by now it was after the Day of Atonement.* The "Day of Atonement" or "the Fast" (NRSV) occurred in September or October, depending on where it fell on the lunar calendar. Traveling by sea during this season, with its frequent inclement weather, is more than chancy. The risk of storms blowing the ship off course and of constant cloud cover (27:20) and fog that would inhibit navigation make sailing perilous. Paul has experience with maritime disasters, since he already has been shipwrecked three times, once spending "a night and a day in the open sea" (2 Cor. 11:25), and he warns of inevitable calamity if they set sail. The centurion ignores Paul and trusts the judgments of the pilot and the ship's owner. The latter is probably the owner's representative and is motivated more by the opportunity for turning a profit than by safety concerns. They decide to weigh anchor and proceed. Fair Havens apparently did not live up to its name as a suitable place for wintering, and they are imprudently emboldened by a gentle south wind to continue.

27:14–20 *Before very long, a wind of hurricane force, called the Northeaster, swept down from the island.* Fair winds do not last, and a gale force wind, named "Euraquilo," translated as "the Northeaster," soon batters the ship and sweeps it off course. The angry tumult leads the crew to jettison some of the cargo and tackle. They fear being driven into the quicksands off the coast of Africa. Despite these measures the situation remained dire. The "we" (27:20) assumes that even Paul's companion narrating the story has given up hope of surviving.

27:21–26 *Paul stood up before them and said.* Earlier, Paul advised that putting out to sea in the winter goes against common sense (27:10). Now, he does not give advice but a prophecy. Disaster is imminent, but he announces that a divine communication from "an angel of . . . God" assured him that though the ship will be lost, there will be no loss of human life. The angel delivered a divine decree, "You must stand trial before Caesar," that must be fulfilled.

The "angel" may have been Jesus, who appeared to Paul again, but the pagan passengers would not know who he was. When a ship is being whipped about by a tempest, it is not the best time to teach Christology. It calls for reassurance. The passengers and crew would understand about divine messengers who communicate warnings to humans.

27:27–32 *about midnight the sailors sensed they were approaching land.* In the panic of the imminent demise of the ship, the sailors desperately seek to save themselves, ignoring the passengers and prisoners. To save their lives, they surreptitiously prepare to abandon ship in a dinghy and leave the passengers to a watery fate when the ship capsizes or breaks up on the rocks. Paul takes command and warns the centurion, reasoning that their leave-taking would make the situation more dismal, with no professionals to handle the ship. Cutting away the lifeboat may be ill-advised, but it prevents the crew from trying to abandon ship again.

27:33–38 *Now I urge you to take some food. . . . Not one of you will lose a single hair from his head.* Paul seeks to brace his fellow passengers for what is to come. Their hair will get wet, but none will lose a hair on their head, an echo of a biblical image (1 Sam. 14:45; 2 Sam. 14:11 [cf. Luke 12:7; 21:18]). He urges them all to eat. Taking bread, giving thanks to God, breaking it, and eating may be reminiscent of the Last Supper (Luke 22:19), but Paul is not celebrating the Lord's Supper with this mixed company of nonbelievers. Rather, Luke describes a normal meal that follows Jewish practice in giving thanks to God. The three Christians do not withdraw from the others for a private meal; they follow the model of Jesus by conveying God's grace in inviting sinners to participate with them in a meal (Luke 5:30; 15:2). In the midst of extreme danger, Paul sets an example by giving thanks to God, who will save them from this threat.

27:39–44 *In this way everyone reached land safely.* Land is spotted, but the best they can hope for is for the ship to run aground near shore. The soldiers fear that the prisoners in their charge might escape when they swim to the beach. The soldiers would be held responsible and severely punished if any prisoners escape even in the mitigating circumstances of a shipwreck (cf. 16:27).[4] They contemplate summarily killing all the prisoners in order to eliminate that possibility.

The benevolent centurion intervenes and prevents the soldiers from carrying out the carnage, not out of humane concern for the prisoners but because he wishes to save Paul. In this case, the centurion is aligned with God's purposes for Paul.

The entire list of passengers and crew make it safely to land. The number 276 has no special mystical significance, even though it is the sum of the numbers from 1 to 23. The number adds to the wonder that none are lost.

28:1–2 *Once safely on shore, we found out that the island was called Malta. The islanders showed us unusual kindness.* When the bedraggled ship's company gets to shore safely, they are met by the "islanders," which translates a Greek noun transliterated as "barbarians" in some versions. In this context, the term has only a linguistic meaning and refers to those who do not speak Greek. The phrasing of the sentence indicates that the marooned survivors do not expect to be received with such kindness from the natives speaking what sounds to them like gibberish. A natural fear of what natives might do to strangers is expressed in Homer: "Alas, to the land of what mortals have I now come? Are they insolent, wild, and unjust? Or are they hospitable to strangers and fear the gods in their thoughts?"[5] Paul is not on a mission trip, but the natives' warm hospitality, building a bonfire for the sopping wet and freezing passengers, suggests that they would respond receptively to the gospel message.

28:3–6 *Paul gathered a pile of brushwood and, as he put it on the fire, a viper, driven out by the heat, fastened itself on his hand.* Paul is found helping with the chores by picking up bundles of sticks for the campfire. He is bitten by a viper "hanging from his hand" with a solid grip. The natives conclude that this new calamity is ironic proof positive that Paul is guilty of something that merits death. Many believed that the fate of mortals on the sea was controlled by the gods. Paul has escaped death at sea. The gods, however, will not be trifled with and will execute justice on malefactors. Justice is personified as a deity, "the goddess Justice," the daughter of Zeus and Themis. She is the personification of divine law and order. The onlookers assume that "Justice" has finally caught up with Paul. They wait for him to swell up and keel over dead, but nothing happens.

The Maltese natives' opinions of Paul suddenly swing from denigration to adulation. They now regard him as a god for surviving a shipwreck and a snakebite (cf. 14:11–13). Paul is no divine man but only a servant of God who has access to divine power (cf. Luke 10:19) that he uses for others. Paul is not struck down by the goddess Justice but is sustained by the almighty God.

28:7–10 *There was an estate nearby that belonged to Publius, the chief official of the island.* Luke does not record Paul's response to the islanders' adoration. Their high esteem of him results in an invitation to the home of the leading figure on the island. Paul does not bask in this glory, which is owed only to God, but heals Publius's father through prayer. The prayer makes clear that Paul does not possess in himself the power to heal but must rely on God for healing. After this success, Paul proceeds to heal the rest of the sick on the island who came to him. The islanders respond to the miracles by extending their kindhearted hospitality and bestowing on the travelers the supplies they needed for the rest of the journey.

Luke does not narrate that Paul preaches the gospel to them. But the islanders' responses reveal that they are prime candidates to receive it.

Teaching the Text

1. *It is difficult to think of God's providential care when one is in the midst of a maelstrom, regardless of what type of storm it might be, and all seems lost.* This story shows Paul the prisoner almost taking over the running of the ship. He prevents the treacherous desertion of the sailors (27:30–32), assures the despairing passengers of deliverance (27:34), and encourages everyone to eat. Paul is able to do these things because he is buttressed by his faith in God's promises and providence. The ship is blown hither and yon by the wind churning up the sea, but Paul remains convinced that everything is under God's control.

The unsuccessful attempts to control the ship in the storm graphically reveal human helplessness and the inability to direct the desired outcome. The account also reveals that God is in complete control, though the outcome might be surprising. In the midst of pandemonium, it is easy to wonder, "What in the world is God doing?" Believers, however, can draw courage from their trust in the God who unerringly fulfills promises.

2. *Paul is not divine but has divine endorsement.* He does not have the power to calm the wind and the waves, as Jesus did with just a word (Luke

8:22–25). He is, however, close to God. God gives him a vision through a divine messenger that all will be well even when the ship goes down.

Paul's access to divine power notably brings benefits to others. The people on the ship who are saved from death and the people on the island who are cured of their diseases are rescued and restored to health not because they responded to the gospel, as Luke makes no mention of Paul proclaiming the gospel to either group. Rather, they receive this grace because of Paul's faithfulness to God, the benefits of which spills over into their lives. The statement "God has graciously given you the lives of all who sail with you" (27:24) implies that saving all the ship's company was something of a divine favor to Paul. The other prisoners are saved from execution because the centurion wants to save Paul for Rome (27:43), but really it is God's purpose that is being served, not the centurion's. The centurion is interested in fulfilling his duty to deliver his prisoner to Rome in one piece. God has the grander purpose of delivering his servant to present the gospel in the halls of power of the Roman Empire.

3. *Greed and its consequences.* The desire for profit motivated the dicey decision to set sail during a dangerous season for sailing. When disaster strikes, the desperate situation causes the crew to reconsider their priorities. They decide to unload their profits in hopes of saving their lives by ditching the main cargo of grain to lighten the ship so that it can get closer to shore before breaking up (27:38). People make foolish decisions when their lives are driven merely by greed. Life, however, has dramatic ways of changing what one thinks is important.

What the crew does in this story replicates Jesus's frequent enjoinders about what people should do with their property ("mammon") to save their eternal lives (Luke 12:13–34; 14:33; 16:1–31). Some people think that religion is handy for offering comfort in hard times. Christian faith does more than offer comfort. It offers salvation, but it comes with a responsibility. As this ship could not have made it near the shore overloaded with its cargo, so humans overloaded with material possessions will not make it to the eternal shore (Luke 18:18–25). A right relationship with God leads to a right use of material possessions and engenders an attitude of gratitude. It enables one to say grace, as Paul did, even in the darkest of storms.

Illustrating the Text

God is with us and deserves our praise, even in the storm.

Story: I (David) have personally experienced being on the margin of a hurricane while on board a WW II–vintage destroyer in the Atlantic. The waves were enormous, sweeping over the ship. No one was allowed on deck. The frightening experience is seared on my memory. Seeing veteran seamen succumb to seasickness and observing the worry on their faces as the ship ominously tilted back and forth was less than reassuring. The ship's power went off for a moment. Food was neither appealing nor offered. The storm did not last for fourteen days, but when the seas became calmer and one could eat again, I had a renewed sense of awe over the power of the sea and the graciousness of God. The lines of the US Navy hymn, "Eternal Father, Strong to Save," became even more meaningful:

> Eternal Father, strong to save,
> Whose arm hath bound the restless wave,
> Who bidd'st the mighty ocean deep,
> Its own appointed limits keep.

Trust in God, who is strong to save, applies not just to seafaring but to all of life. When the inevitable storms hit, one might experience paralyzing fear, nauseating sickness in the soul, and deep despair. It is then that one should be reminded that God saves us not from storms but through storms. When death inevitably strikes, we trust in God to save us yet again. Therefore, we always live in thankfulness to God—before the storm, in the storm, and after the storm.

One's trust in God produces faith and courage and conveys that belief to all around.

Testimony: Hudson Taylor was a passenger on a ship on his way to China to serve as a missionary. Due to the lack of winds, the vessel was going to move out in the open ocean. The captain approached Taylor to pray for winds. He told the captain that he would only pray for winds if the captain would first put up the sails. But the captain refused for fear of appearing to be crazy. Taylor responded, "I will not ask God to send the winds. If I'm going to pray for wind, I must have enough faith to raise the sails." When the captain finally submitted to Taylor's request, Taylor prayed, and then the winds filled the sails and moved the boat.[6]

God's blessings to faithful believers can benefit others.

Applying the Text: We have been blessed in order to be a blessing. Pastor Rick Warren points out that American Christians, in particular, should understand the ways God has blessed us and how that blessing should redound to a world in need:

> Would you agree that based on the blessings of your life you probably have a greater responsibility than other people in the world? If you live in the United States, I'm sure you'd agree, because it's obvious we've been given freedom that

many people don't have. We've been given opportunities that many people don't have. We've been given material and physical and spiritual abundance that a lot of people around the world simply do not have.[7]

What is one concrete way you are allowing God's material blessing in your life to bless a world in need? What is one practical and specific step God might be calling you to take to make this happen?

The Chained Paul and the Unhindered Gospel

Big Idea

The gospel, which encapsulates the hope of Israel (28:20), has been preached to Jews throughout the empire. The story can end, but the gospel will continue to the end of the age.

Key Themes

- According to Paul's typical practice, he expounds the gospel to Jews.
- God created Israel to be a light to the gentiles. Those who do not believe in Christ and reject that calling are cast off from the people of God.
- The narrative ends, but gospel proclamation does not.

Understanding the Text

The Text in Context

When Paul arrives in Rome, he resumes his role as a preacher to the Jews and, once again, meets with a divided response. The conclusion does not tell us what happens to Paul as he awaits his appeal to Caesar but only that he continues to proclaim the gospel without hindrance to one and all. The closing verses place the emphasis on Jesus (28:23, 31), the Holy Spirit (28:25), and God's salvation and kingdom (28:28, 31).

Interpretive Insights

28:11–15 *And so we came to Rome.* The survivors spend the winter on the island, and the centurion finds another Alexandrian grain ship to continue the journey to Rome when the sailing season opens. The detail that the ship was distinguished by its figurehead of pagan deities, the twin sons of Zeus, who were believed to rescue sailors in peril on the sea, is curious. Presumably, all large ships had some kind of talisman on their prows. Calling attention to this figurehead may remind the reader that while this ship with its idols was safely harbored, Paul's God saved the 276 from a savage storm at sea.

From the southeast coast of Sicily at the port of Syracuse, the ship sails up the coast to Puteoli, the main port for delivering grain to Rome. The rest of the journey will continue on foot along the Appian Way. Christians have spread throughout the empire, and Paul finds them in Puteoli. They extend hospitality to Paul and his companions. Then, Christians from the vicinity of Rome, who heard of his arrival, come to greet Paul at the Three Taverns. This squad of Roman Christians give Paul renewed courage for the journey and reveal the unity of Christians across the world.

Coming to Rome is the fulfillment of a wish Paul expressed long ago (Rom. 15:23, 31–32). More importantly, Rome has been God's goal for Paul.

28:16 *When we got to Rome, Paul was allowed to live by himself, with a soldier to guard him.* Paul is placed under minimal custody. He is allowed to live in rented quarters at his own expense (28:30) and may receive visitors. Paul's "house" (28:30) probably is an apartment room in a tenement building.

28:17–20 *Three days later he called together the local Jewish leaders.* Since Paul is not free to go to the synagogues, he invites Jewish leaders to visit him. This meeting marks the climax of his preaching to the Jews. He summarizes his previous two years as a prisoner, his arrest, his trial, his loyalty to Judaism, and the Roman governors' decisions that he was not guilty.

The Greek text behind "I was . . . handed over," translated more literally as "I was delivered into the hands," recalls Jesus's prediction of his own arrest (Luke 9:44; 18:32; 24:7). The ambiguity allows for God, and not simply the Jews, to be behind this action. God paradoxically has ordained that Paul would become a witness in chains, which accords with the fact that he bears witness to a Savior who was crucified.

The central theme of "the hope of Israel" reappears as the basis for his arrest (23:6; 24:15; 26:6–7). Jewish leaders in Jerusalem have rejected that hope. Will these Jewish leaders in Rome do likewise?

28:21–22 *We have not received any letters from Judea concerning you . . . But we want to hear what your views are, for we know that people everywhere are talking against this sect.* The Jerusalem leaders apparently have not alerted anyone in Rome about Paul. The Roman Jews do know about Christians. People everywhere, presumably Jewish adversaries, are talking against this sect (cf. 17:6). This may be the first time these leaders have heard the gospel preached rather than the rumors.

28:23–24 *Some were convinced by what he said, but others would not believe.* Paul gains a larger audience the next day. He makes his case through his messianic reading of Scripture (cf. Luke 24:45–47) and spends all day expounding texts containing messianic predictions and promises from the Law and the Prophets (cf. 13:15).

Some interpreters, because of the harsh indictment from Isaiah that follows (28:26–27), object that those who were "convinced" did not make a full commitment. The verb "convinced," however, is the opposite of "would not believe." Its use elsewhere in Acts 17:4 implies a decision to accept the message. King Agrippa remained unconvinced and did not believe (26:28). The words from Isaiah are directed not against the whole group but against only those who reject the message. The gospel meets with a divided response throughout Acts. Interpreters often look at this half-empty glass and say that it is entirely empty, implying that the Jews entirely reject the gospel. This reading is mistaken. Some Jews believe; some do not.

28:25–28 *They disagreed among themselves and began to leave after Paul had made this final statement: . . . "Therefore I want you to know that God's salvation has been sent to the Gentiles, and they will listen!"* The Spirit is described as speaking the word of the prophecy that applies not only to Isaiah's generation but also to this current situation. The Spirit's diagnosis is that those who reject God's truth suffer from hard hearts that make them hard of hearing and dim-sighted. They refuse to accept God's plan, laid out in Scripture, to offer salvation to both Jews and gentiles.

The parallels between this incident and Paul's meeting with the Jews of Pisidian Antioch (13:14–50) at the beginning of his mission is instructive.[1] A preliminary positive response to Paul's preaching leads to a request to hear him further (13:42; 28:22), which occurs on the next day (13:44; 28:23). Paul's interpretation of Scripture meets with stout defiance from some (13:45; 28:24). Paul responds with a quotation from Isaiah. At Pisidian Antioch, he cited Isaiah 49:6, that God has made Israel to be a light for the gentiles and commanded that they "bring salvation to the ends of the earth" (13:47). Now, in Rome, the citation from Isaiah 6:9–10 reveals that some Jews refuse to accept this command and reject the mission to the gentiles. Paul now acknowledges that an irrevocable split has occurred, since he refers to "*your* ancestors," not "*our* ancestors" as when previously speaking to Jews (13:17; 22:3; 24:14; 26:6). Those who reject the gospel belong to the line of ancestors who disavow God's purposes and the hope of Israel.

Ironically, Jewish rejection of the gospel results in the widening reach of the gospel to the gentiles. This does not mean that trying to reach the Jews with the gospel is now to be abandoned. After his rejection in Pisidian Antioch, Paul continued to seek to persuade Jews about the gospel. This passage, however, clarifies the seriousness of the division. Those who believe the gospel and accept God's call to be a light to the nations are the true people of God fulfilling God's purpose. Those who do not believe in Christ and reject the inclusion of the gentile believers in the people of God cut themselves off from the people of God (3:23).

28:30–31 *He proclaimed the kingdom of God and taught about the Lord Jesus Christ—with all boldness and without hindrance!* The kingdom of God sums up the preaching of Jesus (1:3). Paul understands it to mean that God has manifested his reign by enthroning Jesus as Lord and Messiah (cf. 2:36) and offering salvation to the world through him. Jesus, not Caesar, is Lord and King. Paul fearlessly proclaims this gospel with Caesar's soldier guarding him.

Luke does not record all that happened during the two years that Paul remained in custody. The end of this period in the narrative is usually judged to be early in AD 62, long before the persecution of the Christians instigated by Nero in 67. Since the Roman officials were tolerant of his "bold" preaching, it is plausible that Paul was released after this period.[2] His response to the prophecies that he would be arrested in Jerusalem and handed over to the gentiles expresses his readiness to die if necessary (20:24; 21:13). The prophecies do not specifically indicate that he would be executed, only that he would face hardships and prison (20:22–23; 21:10–11). They have been fulfilled.

The last word in the Greek text of Acts is an adverb meaning "unhinderedly." That the gospel is proclaimed without hindrance sums up the theme that the word of God is unstoppable. It spreads and grows in power despite crises in the church and opposition from outside (6:7; 9:31; 12:24; 16:5; 19:20). Paul may still be "chained like a criminal," but "God's word is not chained" (2 Tim. 2:9).

Teaching the Text

1. *Why does Acts end where it does?* Luke does not disclose the outcome of Paul's appeal to Caesar. He never mentions the Roman authorities. Was Paul eventually released and able to fulfill his desire to go to Spain (Rom. 15:24, 28)? Was he executed? Multiple answers have been given to explain what seems to be an abrupt and anticlimactic conclusion (cf. Mark 16:8). Some believe that Luke-Acts was written as Paul awaited his hearing before Caesar. Others claim that Luke wrote long after Paul's death and planned a third volume that was not completed or was lost. Still others contend that Luke stopped at the right place. Had he continued with his history, he would have needed to record the executions of Jesus's brother James in Jerusalem and of Peter and Paul in Rome, Nero's blistering persecution of the church in Rome, and the destruction of Jerusalem after the Jewish revolt. This series of dramatic calamities might undermine the theme of the gospel advancing without hindrance. John Chrysostom offered another interpretation: "The author conducts his narrative up to this point, and leaves the hearer thirsty, so that he fills up the lack by himself through reflection."[3]

Though Luke's second volume is titled "Acts of the Apostles," it is the story not of Peter or of Paul but of the gospel's advance through Spirit-empowered witnesses. Peter appears in Acts 1–15 and then completely drops out of the narrative. It is not because Luke has no information about what happened to him but because his purpose lies elsewhere. The ending serves Luke's purpose and shows Paul testifying about Jesus to Jews in Rome as he testified to Jews in Jerusalem, just as the Lord promised would happen (23:11). Jews throughout the empire have been given a chance to respond (Rom. 10:18), to become what God intends for Israel to be, a blessing to the nations (Gen. 12:1–3; Isa. 12:2–4; 49:6; Ezek. 47:22–23).

The Jews are not the villains of the piece, though some Jews as well as some gentiles act villainously. By rejecting their calling, some Jews tragically cut themselves off from the people. Many Jews, however, do respond. All of the missionaries in Acts are Jews who become the light to the world by preaching the gospel. Luke's work ends, therefore, with the fulfillment of the predictions with which it began. Salvation will come to the gentiles through the direct intervention of God (Luke 2:30–32). The quotation from Isaiah 6 in Acts 28:26–27 should be taken as a warning for the Jews to repent, not simply as a pronouncement of their fate. Even if they have been pruned from the olive tree because of their obduracy, they can be grafted into the tree again if they do not persist in unbelief; Acts confirms that God is all-powerful and able to graft in even dead branches and bring them to life again (Rom. 11:22–23).

We need not resort to views that claim that the promises to Israel are still in reserve or that God has two chosen peoples, the church and a dormant Israel. What later became known as Christianity is the fulfillment of Israel's hope and purpose. Christianity has no holy land, no temple, no national borders, and no narrow ethnic identity. Acts shows how this identity develops and why the church is no longer part of what is known as Judaism.[4] The Jews who have not become believers in Jesus as Lord and Messiah refuse to listen and repent, reject the Law and the Prophets and their calling to be a light to the gentiles, and have cut themselves off from the people of God.

2. *Christianity is not a closed book, and the story does not end in Rome.* Rome is the heart of the empire, but it is not "the ends of the earth" (1:8). That phrase, "the ends of the earth," means the same thing as "all nations" in Luke 24:47, as the citations of Isaiah 49:6 in Luke 2:32 and Acts 13:47 (see also 26:23) show.[5] The phrase "denotes both geographical and ethnic universalism."[6] It refers to the inhabited world (Isa. 45:22; 48:20; 62:10–11). Consequently, Rome is only a way station as the Spirit and the gospel message move on with unrelenting power. Instead of the Roman army going to the ends of the earth to subjugate peoples, the gospel goes to liberate and save them.

Illustrating the Text

The church is defined by the gospel, not by one culture, historical period, or human tradition.

Church History: Throughout church history, people have gathered as the church to worship God in different venues and with different styles, but the one sustaining factor is the gospel of Jesus Christ. In the early church, Christians daily met in people's homes. During the time of persecution, believers met in tombs and catacombs to lift up the name of God. With the gaining popularity of Christianity, the body of Christ gathered in magnificent edifices and cathedrals. The body of Christ continues to meet in places such as these as well as in warehouses, office spaces, stadiums, teepees, huts, and out in the open fields. Also, the body of Christ sings songs of Scripture, testimonies, and history in a variety of ways, through hymns, old-time spirituals, rock music, sign language, and poetry. Some are fortunate to sing out loud, and some must sing silently only in their hearts as they are imprisoned and persecuted for their faith. Worship may incorporate different styles and formats, but the church is not defined by culture, human tradition, or preference and style, but by the gospel and believers committed in faith to the Lord Jesus Christ by his grace and mercy.

Many are determined to not believe.

Novel: *Dead Beat*, by Jim Butcher. In *Dead Beat*, part of the Dresden Files series, Harry Dresden, the wizard detective, converses about history with the medical examiner, Butters. Butters denies that people are afraid of the truth, especially if it is fearful. Dresden argues, "Look at history. How long did the scholarly institutions of civilization consider Earth to be the center of the universe? And when people came out with facts to prove that it wasn't, there were riots in the streets. No one wanted to believe that we all lived on an unremarkable little speck of rock in a quiet backwater of one unremarkable galaxy. The world was supposed to be flat, too, until people proved that it wasn't by sailing all the way around it. . . . Time after time, history demonstrates that when people don't want to believe something, they have enormous skills of ignoring it altogether."[7]

The church is still going to the ends of the earth.

Science: During spring and summer, plants produce millions of pollen particles in hopes that they will find a fertile resting place. Even in places like Antarctica, a barren and frozen land where little can grow and temperatures often reach into the negative 100s, pollen has been found. The fine grains of life continue to spread and be carried by wind and water currents that lift pollen into the air and carry it across the oceans until it is found on the highest mountains, in the most barren of desserts, and at the bottom of the deepest oceans. In the same way, the gospel that bears life must be found everywhere. The gospel is continuing to be spread to bring life to people at the ends of the earth, despite resistance, environmental hardships, persecution, and formidable obstacles. Jesus compared the gospel to a seed that is scattered and lifted by the currents of the Spirit to the ends of the earth.

Necessity of the unhindered witness.

Quote: **Elie Wiesel.** In response to the fears of the Holocaust being forgotten, Wiesel shared: "I've given my life to the principle and the ideal of memory, and remembrance. I know that my generation of course is a kind of endangered species. We are less and less. . . . So, look, my generation has become a witness, has been a witness, and now the question of course is—very often I think about [this]—one day the last survivor will be gone. I don't want to be that one. Because the idea to be the *last*, with all the memories, and all the spoken and unspoken ideas, and words, I don't want to be that one."[8] Wiesel understood the importance of being a witness with first-hand experience. He is not merely sharing a story but guarding a trust. In light of people who deny the historicity of the Holocaust (as people do the resurrection), his witness was crucial.

In Greek, the last word of the book of Acts is the word "unhinderedly." Beyond the realm of understanding, scope, and dreams of the early Christians and in spite of persecutions; sufferings; opposition of social, political, and religious leaders; and every type of racial, cultural, geographical, and linguistic hindrance, the gospel has "unhinderedly" continued to this day to each of us. According to the will of God and filled with the Holy Spirit, we too are called to share the good news of Jesus Christ and the kingdom of God and to be his witnesses to the ends of the earth until he returns unhinderedly.

Notes

Introduction to Acts

1. Goodspeed, *Introduction to the New Testament*, 187–88.

2. Thornton (*Der Zeuge des Zeugen*, 200) presents evidence that had the author not been present as an eyewitness of these events, he would have been considered in the ancient context to be a liar.

3. See Garland, *Luke*, 21–24.

4. Ibid., 24.

5. Ibid., noting Strelan, *Luke the Priest*, 106.

6. For a list of proposals, see Green, "Acts," 16.

7. See Jervell, *Luke and the People of God*.

8. Cf. Acts 2:39; 3:25–26; 5:31; 7:5, 17; 10:36; 13:23, 32–34; 26:6–7.

9. Troftgruben (*A Conclusion Unhindered*, 27) contends that Paul's quotation of Isa. 6:9–10 to the Jewish leaders in Rome is intended to be a warning to bring about repentance rather than a total repudiation of Israel.

10. Marshall, "Acts," 514. Cf. Acts 3:18, 24; 10:43; 17:2–3; 18:28; 24:14; 26:22–23.

11. Ibid., 518.

Acts 1:1–11

1. Marshall, *Acts*, 55–56.

2. Robinson and Wall, *Called to Be Church*, 31–32. Cf. Exod. 24:12–18; 2 Esd. 14:23–45; *2 Bar.* 76:2–4.

3. Acts 1:8, 22; 2:32; 3:15; 5:32; 10:39, 41; 13:31.

4. Keener, *Acts*, 1:723.

5. Marshall, *Acts*, 59–60.

6. The language of ascension would have been familiar from the account of Elijah ascending in a fiery chariot and whirlwind (2 Kings 2:11) and Enoch ascending in a whirlwind (*1 En.* 39:3). Ovid (*Metam.* 14.805–851) describes Romulus, the founder of Rome, ascending into heaven, so the imagery would have been familiar in the Greco-Roman world.

7. Robinson and Wall, *Called to Be Church*, 34.

8. Maile, "Ascension in Luke-Acts."

9. Carver, *Acts*, 16.

10. C. K. Barrett, *Acts*, 1:64.

11. Henri J. M. Nouwen, "A Spirituality of Waiting: Being Alert to God's Presence in Our Lives," *Weavings* 2.1 (1986), 9–10.

12. A. W. Tozer, *Of God and Men* (Harrisburg, PA: Christian Publications, 1960), 35.

13. John Wesley, *Rev. John Wesley's Journal* (London: John Jones, 1809), 280.

Acts 1:12–26

1. Twelftree, "Prayer and the Coming of the Spirit," 276.

2. Foakes-Jackson and Lake, *Beginnings of Christianity*, 4:13.

3. Wall, "Acts," 50. Cf. Josh. 7; 2 Sam. 20:4–13; 2 Macc. 9:1–10; Josephus, *J.W.* 7.11.4 §453. Acts records others suffering divine punishment for their sins. Ananias and Sapphira (5:1–11) and Herod Agrippa I (12:23) die; Elymas (13:6–12) is blinded; and the sons of Sceva (19:13–16) are overpowered and beaten by an evil spirit.

4. Johnson, *Literary Function of Possessions*, 180.

5. Tannehill, *Shape of Luke's Story*, 52.

6. Peterson, *Acts*, 129.

7. Zwiep, *Judas and the Choice of Matthias*, 172.

8. Garland, *Luke*, 607.

9. *Chasing Shackleton*, PBS.org, accessed October 13, 2016, http://www.pbs.org/program/chasing-shackleton/.

10. J. Oswald Sanders, *Spiritual Leadership: Principles of Excellence for Every Believer* (Chicago: Moody, 1994), 44.

Acts 2:1–13

1. In the Old Testament it is called "the Festival of Harvest" (Exod. 23:16), "the Festival of Weeks" (Exod. 34:22; Deut. 16:10; 2 Chron. 8:13), and "the day of firstfruits" (Num. 28:26).

2. Josephus (*Ant.* 17.10.2 §254) describes tens of thousands of men gathering at the feast.

3. *b. Shabb.* 88a; *b. Pesah.* 68b; *Exod. Rab.* 31.

4. Philo, *Decal.* 33, 46.

5. Fitzmyer, *Acts*, 233–34; Wedderburn, "Traditions and Redaction in Acts 2.1-13."

6. See, for wind, 2 Sam. 22:11, 16; Job 37:9, 10; 38:1; Ezek. 13:13; for fire, Exod. 3:2; 13:21–22; 19:18; 24:17; 40:38; Isa. 10:17; Heb. 12:29.

7. Philo, *Drunkenness* 146–47.

8. Keener, "Power of Pentecost," 63; cf. Keener, *Acts*, 1:840–45.

9. Krodel, *Acts*, 77.

10. Gilbert, "List of Nations."

Acts 2:14–47

1. Van de Sandt, "Fate of the Gentiles," 57.

2. See Judg. 3:10; 11:29; 1 Sam. 10:10; 19:23; Luke 1:35; 3:22.

3. Schnabel, *Acts*, 136.

4. Kilgallen, "Use of Psalm 16:8–11," 49.

5. C. K. Barrett, *Acts*, 1:151.

6. Tannehill, *Shape of Luke's Story*, 85.

7. Andersen, "Meaning of ΕΧΟΝΤΕΣ ΧΑΡΙΝ ΠΡΟΣ."

8. Keener, "Power of Pentecost," 71.

9. C. K. Barrett, *Acts*, 1:139.

10. Rowe, "Acts 2.36."

11. Keller, *David I*, 218.

12. C. S. Lewis, *Problem of Pain* (New York: Macmillan, 1962), 61.

13. Roger E. Olson, "Water Works: Why Baptism Is Essential," *Christianity Today*, July 30, 2014, http://www.christianitytoday.com/ct/2014/july-august/water-works-why-baptism-is-essential.html.

Acts 3:1–26

1. Hamm ("Acts 3:1–10," 312–13) argues that "the lame man leaping is a sign of the salvation of the whole people."

2. Stott, *The Spirit, the Church, and the World*, 91.

3. Peterson, *Acts*, 172–73.

4. Ibid., 169.

5. Heimerdinger, "Unintentional Sins in Peter's Speech," 271.

6. Spencer, *Acts*, 48–49.

7. Bruce, *Acts* (1973), 113.

8. Paul argues that Christ is the seed of Abraham, and becoming sons of Abraham is something that they could receive only through Christ (Gal. 3:6–9, 16).

9. Samuel is assumed in this passage to be the first of the prophets.

10. Fitzmyer, *Acts*, 284.

11. O'Connor, letter dated July 12, 1957, in *Habit of Being*, 229.

12. F. Olin Stockwell, *Meditations from a Prison Cell* (Nashville: Upper Room, 1954), 36.

13. Ernan Norman, *Jesus Only: Rediscovering the Passion of Primitive Godliness* (Bloomington, IN: WestBow, 2011), 74.

Acts 4:1–31

1. Marrow, "*Parrēsia* in the New Testament," 443.

2. Jeremias, *Jerusalem in the Time of Jesus*, 160–63.

3. Josephus, *Ant.* 20.9.1 §199.

4. The term "men" (*andres*) used here excludes women, so the number of believers was greater than five thousand, further demonstrating the church's incredible growth.

5. Josephus, *Ant.* 20.9.1 §198.

6. Kraus, "'Uneducated', 'Ignorant', or Even 'Illiterate'?".

7. Keener, *Acts*, 2:1163.

8. C. K. Barrett (*Acts*, 1:236–7) shows that, to a Greco-Roman audience, their bold answer conveys that they are upright men.

9. Corrie ten Boom, *The Hiding Place* (Grand Rapids: Chosen Books, 1996), 123.

10. Rudolf Wentorf, *Paul Schneider: Witness of Buchenwald*, trans. Daniel Bloesch (Vancouver: Regent College Publishing, 2008), 363.

11. E. H. Robertson, *Paul Schneider: The Pastor of Buchenwald* (London: SCM, 1956), 125.

12. Quoted in Peter Kreeft, *Christianity for Modern Pagans, Pascal's Pensées Edited, Outlined and Explained* (San Francisco: Ignatius, 1993), no. 310, p. 265.

Acts 4:32–5:11

1. Luke 6:20, 24; 12:16–21, 33; 14:33; 16:13, 19–31.

2. Krodel, *Acts*, 25.

3. Johnson, *Literary Function of Possessions*, 198.

4. McCabe, *How to Kill Things with Words*, 28.

5. Cf. Rom. 15:26–28; 1 Cor. 16:1–3; 2 Cor. 8:1–9, 15; Gal. 2:10.

6. Malina and Pilch, *Acts*, 46–47.

7. Witherington, *Acts*, 210.

8. The Greek verb translated as "keep back" is used to mean "embezzle." It occurs in Joshua 7:1 (LXX) in the account of Achan, who brought God's

wrath against Israel for greedily looting the spoils of war that were devoted to the Lord (Josh. 7:1–26).

9. Jervell, *Die Apostelgeschichte*, 196.

10. Some, like Mary the mother of John Mark, kept their property (Acts 12:12–13).

11. Schnabel, *Acts*, 285.

12. Polhill, *Acts*, 158.

13. Spencer, *Acts*, 58.

14. Pelikan, *Acts*, 151.

15. *Best of Andrew Murray*, 193–99.

16. Krodel, *Acts*, 119.

17. Demosthenes, *Con.* 41.

18. Harrill, "Divine Judgment against Ananias and Sapphira," 355.

19. Ibid., 361.

20. Voltaire to Mme. d'Épinal, Ferney, December 26, 1760, in *Oeuvres Complètes de Voltaire: Correspondance*, vol. 9 (Paris: Garnier Frères, 1881), letter # 4390, p. 124.

21. Margaret and Daniel Partner, *A Cloud of Witnesses: Readings on Women of Faith* (Grand Rapids: Fleming H. Revel, 2000), 12–13.

22. John W. De Gruchy, *Dietrich Bonhoeffer: Witness to Jesus Christ* (San Francisco: Collins, 1988), 182.

Acts 5:12–42

1. Strelan, "Gamaliel's Hunch," 65.

2. Fitzmyer, *Acts*, 336.

3. Peter Tomson ("Gamaliel's Counsel," 601) shows that his position accords with proverbs found in *'Abot de Rabbi Nathan* 46.

4. Ibid., 603.

5. Dietrich Bonhoeffer, *Creation and Fall; Temptation: Two Biblical Studies* (New York: MacMillan, 1959), 104.

6. W. Ian Thomas, *The Saving Life of Christ and the Mystery of Godliness* (Grand Rapids: Zondervan, 1988), 162.

7. Esther Ahn Kim, *If I Perish: Facing Imprisonment, Persecution, and Death, a Young Korean Christian Defies the Japanese Warlords* (Chicago: Moody Press, 1977), 133, 134, 27–28.

Acts 6:1–7

1. Capper, "Palestinian Cultural Context," 353.

2. Witherington, *Acts*, 251.

3. Ferguson, "Laying on of Hands," 252.

4. Marshall, *Acts*, 126.

5. A. W. Tozer, *The Next Chapter after the Last* (Camp Hill, PA: Christian Publications, 1987), 82–83.

6. Dennis W. Bakke, *Joy at Work: A CEO's Revolutionary Approach to Fun on the Job* (Seattle: PVG, 2005), 56.

7. Francis A. Schaeffer, *No Little People* (Wheaton: Crossway, 2003), 25.

8. J. Hudson Taylor, *A Retrospect* (Chicago: Moody, n.d.), 27.

Acts 6:8–7:50

1. Luke shows the spuriousness of this charge in Acts 15:20–21; 16:13; 21:20–21, 26.

2. Summaries of Israel's history are found in Josh. 24; Neh. 9:7–27; Pss. 78; 105; Ezek. 20:5–44.

3. Polhill, *Acts*, 190.

4. Longenecker, "Acts," 343.

5. Cf. Lev. 26:1; Pss. 115:4; 135:15; Isa. 2:8; 37:19; 46:6; Mic. 5:12; Acts 17:23–24.

Acts 7:51–8:3

1. Hamm, "Tamid Service in Luke-Acts," 229.

2. Ps. 47:9; Isa. 2:3; 19:23; Jer. 3:17; Zech. 8:21.

3. Pss. 22:27; 86:9; Isa. 66:18; Zech. 2:10–11; 8:22.

4. Quoted in John W. Doberstein, introduction to Dietrich Bonhoeffer, *Life Together* (New York: Harper & Row, 1954), 13.

5. William H. Willimon, *Acts*, Interpretation (Louisville: John Knox, 1988), 86–87.

6. Joanna Walters, "'The Happening': 10 Years after the Amish Shooting," *Guardian*, October 2, 2016, https://www.theguardian.com/us-news/2016/oct/02/amish-shooting-10-year-anniversary-pennsylvania-the-happening.

7. Elisabeth Elliot, *Through Gates of Splendor* (1957; Wheaton: Tyndale, 2005).

8. Olive Fleming-Liefeld, *Unfolding Destinies: The Ongoing Story of the Auca Mission* (Grand Rapids: Discovery House, 1998), 234–35.

Acts 8:4–25

1. Wall, "Acts," 134.

2. Haenchen, *Acts*, 303. See Justin Martyr, *1 Apol.* 26.3; *Dial.* 120.6.

3. Spencer, *Portrait of Philip in Acts*, 40.

4. Garrett, *Demise of the Devil*, 77.

5. Spencer, *Portrait of Philip in Acts*, 49.

6. Seccombe, "New People of God," 359.

7. Garrett, *Demise of the Devil*, 72.

8. Irenaeus, *Haer.* 1.23.

9. Klauck, *Magic and Paganism*, 23.

10. John C. Maxwell, *The 360 Degree Leader: Developing Your Influence from Anywhere in the Organization* (Nashville: Thomas Nelson, 2011), 104.

11. *Merriam-Webster's Collegiate Dictionary*, 11th ed., s.v. "simony."

12. *The Anatomy of Simon Magus, Or, the Sin of Simony Laid Open* (London: W. Bower, 1700), 6.

Acts 8:26–40

1. Parsons, "Isaiah 53 in Acts 8," 116–18.

2. Spencer, "The Ethiopian Eunuch," 158.

3. Lightfoot, *Galatians*, 291.

4. Garland and Garland, *Flawed Families of the Bible*, 223.

Acts 9:1–30

1. Elaine Prevallet, "Carrying in the Body the Death of Jesus," *Weavings* 17, no. 5 (2002): 21–22.
2. Headlines and article quoted in Charles W. Colson, *Born Again* (Old Tappan, NJ: Chosen, 1976), 166–67.
3. Ibid., 146.
4. Ibid., 150.

Acts 9:31–43

1. The pairing appears in the Gospel of Luke in the angelic annunciation to Zechariah (1:11–20) and then to Mary (1:26–38); the praise of God in the temple for the child Jesus by Simeon (2:25–35) and Hannah (2:36–38); the illustrations in Jesus's sermon at Nazareth, the widow of Zarephath (4:25–26) and Naaman the Syrian (4:27); the first healings, a demoniac (4:31–37) and Peter's mother-in-law (4:38–39); the healing of a loved one, the centurion's slave (7:1–10) and the son of the widow from Nain (7:11–17); the parable of the two debtors, one who owed a lot and one who owed a little, applied to Simon the Pharisee and the woman who was a sinner (7:36–50); the lesson on serving, the merciful Samaritan (10:25–37) and Mary and Martha (10:38–42); the parables related to prayer, the urgent host and the reluctant neighbor (11:5–8) and the persistent widow and the wicked judge (18:1–8); the parables of the hidden kingdom, the man who sowed a mustard seed (13:18–19) and the woman who hid leaven in some meal (13:20–21); those who were healed on the Sabbath precipitating a controversy, a daughter of Abraham (13:10–17) and a man with dropsy (14:1–6); the parables of joy over recovering what was lost, the man who had a hundred sheep (15:3–7) and the woman who had ten coins (15:8–10); the illustrations concerning the coming of the Son of Man, two men in one bed (17:34) and two women grinding grain at the same place (17:35); the characters Jesus encounters on the way to his crucifixion, Simon of Cyrene (23:26) and the daughters of Jerusalem (23:27–31); and those informed of Jesus's resurrection, the women at the tomb (23:55–24:11) and the men on the road to Emmaus (24:13–27).
2. John Calvin, *Commentary upon the Acts of the Apostles*, vol. 1, trans. Henry Beveridge (Edinburgh: T&T Clark, 1859), 306.
3. Martin Luther, *Luther's Explanatory Notes on the Gospels*, ed. E. Mueller, trans. P. Anstadt (York, PA: P. Anstadt, 1899), 93.
4. Charles Spurgeon, "A Revival Promise," sermon delivered on January 11, 1874, http://www.ccel .org/ccel/spurgeon/sermons20.ii.html.

Acts 10:1–48

1. Tacitus, *Ann.*1.8.
2. Tertullian, *Apol.* 16.

3. Tannehill, *Narrative Unity of Luke-Acts*, 2:140.
4. Stott, *The Spirit, the Church, and the World*, 192.
5. Kilgallen, "Clean, Acceptable, Saved."
6. Witherington, *Acts*, 356.
7. Talbert, *Reading Acts*, 95.
8. Corrie ten Boom, *Prison Letters* (Old Tappan, NJ: Fleming H. Revell, 1975), 89.
9. Dietrich Bonhoeffer, *Life Together* (New York: Harper & Row, 1954), 48–49.

Acts 11:1–18

1. C. K. Barrett, *Acts*, 1:501.
2. Johnson, *Acts*, 201.
3. Barclay, *Paul and the Gift*, 488–89.
4. Bock, *Acts*, 409.
5. Wall, "Acts," 171.
6. Noël Piper, *Faithful Women and Their Extraordinary God* (Wheaton: Crossway, 2005), 158–59.

Acts 11:19–30

1. Cf. Exod. 9:3; 1 Sam. 5:6; 6:9; 1 Chron. 28:19; Isa. 59:1; 66:2, 14; Ezek. 1:3; Luke 1:66; Acts 4:30; 13:11.
2. Gaventa, *Acts*, 179–80.
3. Reggie McNeal, *Missional Renaissance: Changing the Scorecard for the Church* (San Francisco: Jossey-Bass, 2009), 24.
4. Krish Kandiah, "The Church Is Growing, and Here Are the Figures That Prove It," *Christian Today*, March 5, 2015, http://www.christiantoday.com /article/a.growing.church.why.we.should.focus.on .the.bigger.picture/49362.htm.
5. Tara Isabella Burton, "Middle Eastern Christians Flee Violence for Ancient Homeland," *National Geographic*, December 29, 2014, http://news.national geographic.com/news/2014/12/141229-syriac-chris tians-refugees-midyat-turkey/.
6. Mark Ellis, "Missionary Died Thinking He Was a Failure; 84 Years Later Thriving Churches Found Hidden in the Jungle," Godreports (blog), May 19, 2014, http://blog.godreports.com/2014 /05/missionary-died-thinking-he-was-a-failure-84 -years-later-thriving-churches-found-hidden-in-the -jungle/.

Acts 12:1–25

1. For another account of his reign, see Josephus, *Ant.* 19.6.1–19.9.1 §§292–354.
2. *m. Sanh.* 7:3; 10:4; Bock, *Acts*, 425.
3. Bruce, *Acts* (1990), 282.
4. It is odd to mention the name of the maidservant. Perhaps she is the source for this incident.
5. Schnabel, *Acts*, 542.
6. Josephus, *Ant.* 19.8.2 §§343–50.
7. Krodel, *Acts*, 214.

8. Stott, *The Spirit, the Church, and the World*, 213.

9. *New World Encyclopedia*, s.v. "Alexander VI," accessed December 6, 2016, http://www.newworldencyclopedia.org/entry/Alexander VI.

10. Irina Ratushinskaya, "Believe Me," in *Pencil Letter* (New York: Alfred A. Knopf, 1989), 76.

11. Helen Roseveare, *Give Me This Mountain* (Fearn, Scotland: Christian Focus, 2006), 157–58.

12. J. B. Fowler Jr., *Illustrating Great Words of the New Testament* (Nashville: Broadman, 1991), 14.

Acts 13:1–12

1. If he comes from North Africa, is he the Simon from Cyrene who carried Jesus's cross (Luke 23:26; Mark 15:21)?

2. Keener, *Acts*, 2:1990.

3. Spencer, *Acts*, 137.

4. Holmes, "Luke's Description of John Mark," 68.

5. Byrskog, *Story as History*, 279.

6. Peterson, *Acts*, 379.

7. Krodel, *Acts*, 229.

8. Cicero, *Div.* 2.90.

9. Klauck, *Magic and Paganism*, 48.

10. Haenchen, *Acts*, 395–96.

11. Garrett, *Demise of the Devil*, 84.

12. Rosalind Goforth, *How I Know God Answers Prayers* (New York: Harper & Brothers, 1921), 16.

13. "Missionary Mindset: Samuel Zwemer," East-West Ministries International blog, January 12, 2016, http://www.eastwest.org/blog/missionary-mindset-samuel-zwemer/.

14. "About Us," Life After God, http://www.lifeaftergod.org/about-us/.

Acts 13:13–52

1. His departure has been attributed variously to homesickness (since he goes to Jerusalem rather than to Antioch), a loss of enthusiasm, onset of fear or illness, resentment that Barnabas is no longer in charge, and resistance to the mission to the Gentiles. All of these reasons are purely speculative.

2. The Greek verb translated as "prosper" can also mean that God "exalted" or "made great." The people's cruel bondage in Egypt goes unmentioned.

3. Hunter, *To Change the World*, 258.

4. Lamin Sanneh, *Summoned from the Margin: Homecoming of an African* (Grand Rapids: Eerdmans, 2012), 238.

5. Ibid., 97, 101.

6. Ruth Rosen, *Testimonies of Jews Who Believe in Jesus* (San Francisco: Purple Pomegranate, 1992), 296.

Acts 14:1–28

1. Hansen, "Galatia," 384–85.

2. Schnabel, *Acts*, 603.

3. C. K. Barrett, *Acts*, 1:669.

4. Rowe, *World Upside Down*, 19.

5. Ovid, *Metam.* 8.611–724.

6. Breytenbach, "Zeus und der lebendige Gott."

7. Tannehill, *Narrative Unity of Luke-Acts*, 2:180.

8. Johnson, *Acts*, 256.

9. Parsons and Culy, *Acts*, 282.

10. Clark, "Role of the Apostles," 184.

11. Spencer, *Acts*, 149.

12. Wall, "Acts," 199.

13. Christian, "Seven Deadly Sins of Messaging," 35.

14. Amy Carmichael, *If* (Fort Washington, PA: Christian Literature Crusade, 1994), 33.

15. John Stott and Christopher J. H. Wright, *Christian Mission in the Modern World*, updated ed. (Downers Grove, IL: InterVarsity, 2015), 74–75.

16. Oliver Maksan, "Coptic Catholics Consecrate First Church in Sinai, against Backdrop of Martyrdom," Catholic News Agency, February 20, 2015, http://www.catholicnewsagency.com/news/coptic-catholics-consecrate-first-church-in-sinai-against-backdrop-of-martyrdom-77670/.

Acts 15:1–35

1. Dahl, "'A People for His Name,'" 326.

2. Cf. Ps. 96:7–8; Isa. 2:2–3; 25:6; 56:6–7; 66:23; Jer. 3:17; Mic. 4:1–2; Zech. 14:16.

3. Bauckham, "James and the Gentiles," 167.

4. Arnold, *Acts*, 360.

5. Wedderburn, "The 'Apostolic Decree.'"

6. Witherington, *Acts*, 462.

7. Parsons and Culy, *Acts*, 295.

Acts 15:36–16:15

1. "Phrygia and Galatia" is better rendered as "Phrygian-Galatia," indicating one region, not two, and refers to South Galatia (Keener, *Acts*, 3:2324–30).

2. Polhill, *Acts*, 345.

3. Marshall, *Acts*, 277.

4. Witherington, *Acts*, 484.

5. Schnabel, *Early Christian Mission*, 2:1153. Mary Smallwood states, "The characteristic feature of a Diaspora community was the synagogue, a term denoting primarily the organized group rather than the building, often known also as a 'prayer house', in which it met for worship" (*The Jews under Roman Rule*, 133).

6. Witherington, *Acts*, 490.

7. Fernando, *Acts*, 431.

8. Jervell, *Die Apostelgeschichte*, 409.

9. Ibid., 413.

10. A. W. Tozer, *The Best of A. W. Tozer* (Grand Rapids: Baker, 1978), 72–73.

11. Mary Brogi, "Gladys Aylward: The Small Woman with a Big Heart for China," Washington University Bible Fellowship, accessed October 12,

2016, http://washingtonubf.org/Resources/Leaders/GladysAylward.html.

Acts 16:16–40

1. Trebilco, "Paul and Silas," 52. See also Trebilco, *Jewish Communities*, 127–44.

2. Trebilco, "Paul and Silas," 64.

3. Twelftree, "Jesus and Magic," 52.

4. Suetonius, *Claud.* 25.4.

5. Rapske, *Paul in Roman Custody*, 119.

6. Ibid., 118, citing Cicero, *Leg.* 2.8.19. Circumcision was also considered to be barbaric (cf. Tacitus, *Ann.* 15.44).

7. Wright, "Earthquakes in Ancient Palestine."

8. Rapske, *Paul in Roman Custody*, 204.

9. Bruce, *Acts* (1973), 323.

10. On prison conditions, see Rapske, *Paul in Roman Custody*, 195–225, 308–9.

11. Tertullian, *Mart.* 2.

12. See Rapske, *Paul in Roman Custody*, 134.

13. "Human Trafficking/Involuntary Servitude," Federal Bureau of Investigation, https://www.fbi.gov/investigate/civil-rights/human-trafficking.

14. Joe Carter, "9 Things You Should Know About Human Trafficking," The Gospel Coalition, August 8, 2013, http://www.thegospelcoalition.org/article/9-things-you-should-know-about-human-trafficking.

15. Shared Hope International, "The National Report on Domestic Minor Sex Trafficking: America's Prostituted Children," May 2009, http://sharedhope.org/wp-content/uploads/2012/09/SHI_National_Report_on_DMST_2009without_cover.pdf.

16. Kevin Porter, "Saeed Abedini: 10 Prisoners Came to Christ in First Year of Imprisonment," *CP World*, February 27, 2016, http://www.christianpost.com/news/saeed-abedini-10-prisoners-came-to-christ-in-first-year-of-imprisonment-158775/.

Acts 17:1–15

1. Manus, "Luke's Account of Paul in Thessalonica," 28.

2. Schnabel, *Acts*, 703.

3. Hardin, "Decrees and Drachmas at Thessalonica," 30.

4. Malherbe, *Social Aspects of Early Christianity*, 97.

5. Ciampa, "'Examined the Scriptures'?" 540.

6. Gaventa, "'Turning the World Upside Down,'" 114.

7. Schnabel, *Acts*, 709.

8. Arnold, *Acts*, 383.

9. R. H. Tex Williams, "World Bible School: A Timely Tool for African Evangelism," in *100 Years of African Missions: Essays in Honor of Wendell Broom*, ed. Stanley E. Granberg (Abilene, TX: ACU Press, 2001), 159–60.

10. George MacDonald, *Discovering the Character of God* (Minneapolis: Bethany House, 1989), 74.

Acts 17:16–34

1. Van der Horst, "Altar of the 'Unknown God,'" 1455.

2. Xenophon, *Mem.* 1.1.1; Plato, *Apol.* 24b.

3. Winter, "On Introducing Gods to Athens"; Schnabel, *Acts*, 728–29. Dionysus is identified as a member of that council in 17:34.

4. Keener, *Acts*, 3:2603.

5. Rowe, *World Upside Down*, 31.

6. The Stoics believed that human affairs were controlled by the immovable decree of blind fate.

7. Edwards, "Quoting Aratus."

8. The Epicureans believed that the gods were completely detached from human affairs.

9. P.Oxy. 1766 (18).

10. *SIG* 1153.

11. Tacitus, *Ann.* 15.44.

12. Apuleius, *Metam.* 9.14.

13. Manson, *Teaching of Jesus*, 148n1.

14. C. Kavin Rowe concludes that Stoicism and Christianity "are—and remain—different and competing languages about the truth of the world" ("Grammar of Life," 50).

15. Savage, *Power through Weakness*, 27.

16. Ibid., 34.

17. *IG* 14.2190; *CIG* 6745.

Acts 18:1–17

1. Murphy-O'Connor, "Prisca and Aquila," 40.

2. Suetonius, *Claud.* 25.4.

3. Haenchen, *Acts*, 538.

4. Acts 18:18, 26; Rom. 16:3; 2 Tim. 4:19.

5. Gaventa, *Acts*, 255.

6. Winter, "Gallio's Ruling," 214.

7. Krodel, *Acts*, 341, citing Alciphron, *Epistles* 3.60.

8. Broneer, "Corinth," 78.

9. Koet, "Close to the Synagogue," 397.

10. Fitzmyer, *Acts*, 630.

11. Lottie Moon, *Send the Light: Lottie Moon's Letters and Other Writings*, ed. Keith Harper (Macon, GA: Mercer University Press, 2002), 89.

Acts 18:18–19:7

1. *m. Naz.* 3:1–5.

2. Polhill, *Acts*, 395.

3. Ibid., 396; Tannehill, *Narrative Unity of Luke-Acts*, 2:232–33; Schnabel, *Acts*, 784–85. Paul uses this phrase in Rom. 12:11, where the NIV renders it as "spiritual fervor," but the RSV as "aglow with the Spirit."

4. Polhill, *Acts*, 396.

5. Marshall, *Acts*, 305.

6. "The Effects of Heating," Your Mother Was a Chemist, http://kitchenscience.sci-toys.com/heating.

7. C. S. Lewis, *Mere Christianity* (Nashville: Broadman & Holman, 1999), 120.

8. C. S. Lewis, *Surprised by Joy: The Shape of My Early Life* (Orlando: Harcourt & Brace, 1956), 237.

Acts 19:8-41

1. The name "Tyrannus" may have been attached to the hall because he lectured there, or he may have owned the building.
2. James Dunn maintains that Paul's lectures were a foundation for his letters, which "should not be seen as simply off-the-cuff compositions in response to particular questions" (*Beginning from Jerusalem*, 769).
3. "Sceva" is a Latin name, which he may have adopted living in the Diaspora. It would explain why his name does not appear in any known list of high priestly families.
4. Hans-Josef Klauck (*Magic and Paganism*, 100) provides examples of ancient magical spells that have been discovered using the name of the God of the Hebrews and the name of Jesus to drive out demons.
5. Suetonius, *Nero* 34.4.
6. Pausanias, *Descr.* 4.31.8.
7. Oster, "The Ephesian Artemis," 34.
8. Rowe, *World Upside Down*, 46.
9. Kodell, "The Word of God Grew," 518.
10. Gundry, *Commentary on the New Testament*, 539.
11. Witherington, *Acts*, 578.
12. Garrett, *Demise of the Devil*, 95.
13. Ibid., 93.
14. Shawn Tyler, "The Gospel and the Spirits," in *100 Years of African Missions: Essays in Honor of Wendell Broom*, ed. Stanley E. Granberg (Abilene, TX: ACU Press, 2001), 358–59.

Acts 20:1-16

1. The uncircumcised Titus (Gal. 2:1–5), who factors prominently in Paul's plan for the collection (2 Cor. 8:6–24), never appears in Acts.
2. Luke also never mentions that Paul wrote letters to his churches.
3. Johnson, *Acts*, 357–58.
4. Ellis, *Prophecy and Hermeneutic*, 3.
5. "Wesley to Wilberforce: John Wesley's Last Letter from His Deathbed," *Christianity Today*, accessed October 13, 2016, http://www.christianityto day.com/history/issues/issue-2/wesley-to-wilberforce. html.
6. Dietrich Bonhoeffer, *Life Together* (New York: Harper & Row, 1954), 23.
7. Harold Myra and Marshall Shelley, *The Leadership Secrets of Billy Graham* (Grand Rapids: Zondervan, 2005), 45, 47.

Acts 20:17-38

1. Schnabel, *Acts*, 845.
2. C. K. Barrett, *Acts*, 2:977.

3. Gundry, *Commentary on the New Testament*, 527.
4. Lövestam, "Paul's Address at Miletus," 3.
5. "Preaching Past TiVo: Do You Tell the Whole Truth to People Who Want Only Certain Parts?," Leadership Forum interview with John Ortberg, Doug Pagitt, Efrem Smith, and William Willimon, *Christianity Today*, Summer 2006, http://www.chris tianitytoday.com/pastors/2006/summer/12.57.html.
6. "Biography," St. Maximilian Kolbe, accessed September 20, 2016, http://www.saintmaximilian kolbe.com/biography/.
7. Matthew P. Kinne, *Fathers of Influence* (Colorado Springs: Honor Books, 2006), 67.

Acts 21:1-14

1. Johnson, *Acts*, 369.
2. Alexander, *Acts*, 160.
3. Tannehill, *Narrative Unity of Luke-Acts*, 2:262.
4. Conzelmann, *Acts*, 178.
5. Ibid.
6. Tannehill, *Narrative Unity of Luke-Acts*, 2:266.
7. Keener, *Acts*, 3:3092.
8. Eusebius, *Hist. eccl.* 3.39.
9. J. B. Fowler Jr., *Illustrating Great Words of the New Testament* (Nashville: Broadman, 1991), 187.
10. C. S. Lewis, *God in the Dock* (Grand Rapids: Eerdmans, 1970), 58.
11. Winston Churchill, "Never Give In," speech delivered at the Harrow School, October 29, 1941, The Churchill Centre, http://www.winstonchurchill .org/resources/speeches/1941-1945-war-leader/never -give-in.

Acts 21:15-26

1. Tannehill, *Narrative Unity of Luke-Acts*, 2:268–69.
2. Keener, *Acts*, 3:3111.
3. Witherington, *Acts*, 649.
4. Bruce, "Church of Jerusalem," 660.
5. Tannehill, "Narrator's Strategy," 256.
6. Johnson, *Acts*, 374.
7. Talbert, *Reading Acts*, 185.
8. Robert Mnookin, *Bargaining with the Devil: When to Negotiate, When to Fight* (New York: Simon & Schuster, 2010), 135.

Acts 21:27-40

1. Schürer, *History of the Jewish People*, 2:222n85, 285n57. Josephus describes this warning and that the Romans gave the leaders the right to kill anyone who goes beyond the partition (*J.W.* 6.2.4 §§125–26; *Ant.* 15.11.5 §417).
2. Josephus, *J.W.* 5.5.8 §§243–44.
3. Josephus, *J.W.* 2.13.5 §§261–63; *Ant.* 20.8.6 §§169–72.

4. Keener, *Acts*, 3:3178.

5. Neyrey, "Luke's Social Location of Paul," 267.

6. Krodel, *Acts*, 407.

7. Baumgarten, "Exclusions from the Temple," 215.

8. Stagg, *Acts*, 224.

9. Bruce, "Church of Jerusalem," 659.

10. Fitzmyer, *Acts*, 697.

11. Krodel, *Acts*, 399.

Acts 22:1-30

1. In 9:7, the men traveling with Paul "heard the sound but did not see anyone." In 22:9, they saw the light but did not hear the voice. In 22:9, the NIV translates that they did not "understand the voice" following the classical Greek usage in which hearing with the object in the genitive case means hearing without necessarily understanding. They heard the voice but did not comprehend the private conversation with Paul, since Jesus was speaking only to him. The main point is that Jesus's appearance was not a private vision but a public event that others witnessed.

2. C. K. Barrett, *Acts*, 2:1040.

3. Joseph Fitzmyer (*Acts*, 709) notes that "far away" recalls Isa. 57:19 and echoes Peter's speech in 2:39.

4. Marguerat, "Saul's Conversion," 149–50.

5. Adams, "Paul the Roman Citizen," 325.

6. Garland and Garland, *Flawed Families of the Bible*, 27.

7. Schnabel, *Acts*, 904.

8. Trites, "Importance of Legal Scenes," 284.

9. Tannehill, *Narrative Unity of Luke-Acts*, 2:272.

10. Stewart, *A Man in Christ*, 83–84.

11. William E. Phipps, *Amazing Grace in John Newton: Slave-ship Captain, Hymn Writer, and Abolitionist* (Macon, GA: Mercer University Press, 2001), 239.

12. John Newton, *The Works of the Reverend John Newton* (London: S. Hamilton, 1822), 96.

13. "Faith's Review and Expectation," *The Olney Hymns*, book 1, no. 41, in *The Life of John Newton, Written by Himself; with Continuation by the Rev. Richard Cecil. To which Are Added, The Olney Hymns. In Three Books.* Edinburgh: Johnstone and Hunter, 1853.

Acts 23:1-10

1. Josephus, *Ant.* 20.9.2 §§205–10.

2. Tannehill, *Narrative Unity of Luke-Acts*, 2:285.

3. Ananias was later hunted down and assassinated by Zealots at the outbreak of the war against Rome (Josephus, *J.W.* 2.17.9 §§441–42).

4. Marshall, *Acts*, 364.

5. Johnson, *Acts*, 397.

6. The phrase in Greek reads, "a son of Pharisees." C. K. Barrett offers that it could also "represent the Semitic use of 'son of,' describing essential character: Paul claims to be the quintessential Pharisee, and thus that it was essentially Pharisaism that he was contending for" (*Acts*, 2:1063).

7. See Josephus, *J.W.* 2.8.14 §165; *Ant.* 18.1.4 §16; *b. Nid.* 70b.

8. Viviano and Taylor, "Sadducees, Angels, and Resurrection."

9. The Sadducees were wiped out when the temple and Jerusalem were destroyed after the revolt against Rome.

10. Conzelmann, *Acts*, 192.

11. Haenchen, *Acts*, 642.

12. Johnson, *Acts*, 408.

13. Tannehill, *Narrative Unity of Luke-Acts*, 2:286.

14. Witherington, *Acts*, 687.

15. Schnabel, *Acts*, 928.

16. Garland, *Luke*, 971.

17. Dietrich Bonhoeffer, *Collected Sermons of Dietrich Bonhoeffer*, trans. Douglas W. Stott (Minneapolis: Fortress, 2012), 169.

Acts 23:11-35

1. Alexander, *Acts*, 172.

2. Noted by Spencer, *Acts*, 214.

Acts 24:1-27

1. Tacitus, *Hist.* 5.9; *Ann.* 12.54.

2. Josephus, *Ant.* 20.8.5–9 §§160–82.

3. "This is the only place in the New Testament where 'Nazarene' is used to describe Christians. It was a term applied to Jesus himself (2:22)" (Marshall, *Acts*, 395).

4. Hogan, "Paul's Defense," 83.

5. Josephus, *Ant.* 20.7.2 §§141–43.

6. C. K. Barrett, *Acts*, 2:1104.

7. Haenchen, *Acts*, 655.

Acts 25:1-27

1. Josephus, *J.W.* 2.14.1 §§271–72; *Ant.* 20.8.9–11 §§182–94; 20.9.1 §§197, 200.

2. Josephus, *Ant.* 19.9.2 §§360–62; *J.W.* 2.12.1 §223.

3. Josephus, *Ant.* 20.9.7 §§219–22.

4. A. A. Barrett, *Caligula*, 34.

5. Juvenal, *Sat.* 6.156–60.

6. Suetonius, *Tit.* 7.

7. Tajra, *The Trial of St. Paul*, 140.

8. Rowe, *World Upside Down*, 82–83.

9. Johnson, *Acts*, 422.

Acts 26:1-32

1. Gaventa, *Acts*, 339.

2. See Keener, "Three Notes on Figurative Language," 44.

3. Arnold, *Acts*, 464.

4. Fitzmyer, *Acts*, 759.

5. Nave, *Role and Function of Repentance*, 145.

6. Malherbe, "'Not in a Corner.'"

7. Marguerat, "Saul's Conversion," 152.

8. Gaventa, *Acts*, 348.

9. C. K. Robertson, *A Dangerous Dozen* (Woodstock, VT: Skylight Paths, 2011), 141.

10. Oscar Romero, *The Violence of Love: The Pastoral Wisdom of Archbishop Oscar Romero* (San Francisco: Harper & Row, 1988), 242.

Acts 27:1–28:10

1. Rapske, *Paul in Roman Custody*, 270.

2. Rapske, "Travel and Trade," 1248.

3. Hirschfeld, "Ship of Saint Paul."

4. Rapske, *Paul in Roman Custody*, 271.

5. Homer, *Od.* 6.119–21.

6. J. B. Fowler Jr., *Living Illustrations* (Nashville: Broadman, 1985), 109.

7. Rick Warren, "The Four Laws of God's Blessing," Pastor Rick's Daily Hope, May 21, 2014, http://rickwarren.org/devotional/english/the-four-laws-of-god-s-blessing 814.

Acts 28:11–31

1. Polhill, *Acts*, 541.

2. Later church tradition claims that Paul was released and went to the "extreme limit of the west" (*1 Clem.* 5:5–7). He was beheaded during Nero's reign when he returned to Rome for a second time (Eusebius, *Hist. eccl.* 2.22.1–2; 2.25.5–8; Tertullian, *Praescr.* 36; *Acts Paul* 10; *Acts Pet.* 3.1).

3. John Chrysostom, *Hom. Act.* 55.

4. Jervell, *Die Apostelgeschichte*, 627.

5. Pesch, *Die Apostelgeschichte*, 1:70.

6. Moore, "'To the End of the Earth,'" 398.

7. Jim Butcher, *Dead Beat,* The Dresden Files 7 (New York: Penguin, 2005), 53.

8. Rob Verger, "Nobel Laureate Elie Wiesel on His Fear of Being the Last Holocaust Witness," *The Daily Beast*, August 27, 2012, http://www.thedailybeast.com/articles/2012/08/27/nobel-laureate-elie-wiesel-on-his-fear-of-being-the-last-holocaust-witness.html.

Bibliography

Adams, Sean A. "Paul the Roman Citizen: Roman Citizenship in the Ancient World and Its Importance for Understanding Acts 22:22–29." In *Paul: Jew, Greek, and Roman*, edited by Stanley E. Porter, 309–26. Pauline Studies 5. Leiden: Brill, 2008.

Alexander, Loveday. *Acts*. Daily Bible Commentary. Peabody, MA: Hendrickson, 2006.

Andersen, T. David. "The Meaning of ΕΧΟΝΤΕΣ ΧΑΡΙΝ ΠΡΟΣ in Acts 2.47." *New Testament Studies* 34 (1988): 604–10.

Arnold, Clinton E. *Acts*. Zondervan Illustrated Bible Backgrounds Commentary 2. Grand Rapids: Zondervan, 2002.

Barclay, John M. G. *Paul and the Gift*. Grand Rapids: Eerdmans, 2015.

Barrett, Anthony A. *Caligula: The Corruption of Power*. New Haven: Yale University Press, 1989.

Barrett, C. K. *A Critical and Exegetical Commentary on the Acts of the Apostles*. 2 vols. International Critical Commentary. London: T&T Clark, 2004.

Bauckham, Richard. "James and the Gentiles (Acts 15.13–21)." In *History, Literature, and Society in the Book of Acts*, edited by Ben Witherington III, 154–84. Cambridge: Cambridge University Press, 1996.

Baumgarten, Joseph M. "Exclusions from the Temple: Proselytes and Agrippa I." *Journal of Jewish Studies* 33 (1982): 215–25.

Bock, Darrell L. *Acts*. Baker Exegetical Commentary on the New Testament. Grand Rapids: Baker Academic, 2007.

Breytenbach, Cilliers. "Zeus und der lebendige Gott: Anmerkungen zu Apostelgeschichte 14.11–17." *New Testament Studies* 39 (1993): 396–413.

Broneer, Oscar. "Corinth: Center of St. Paul's Missionary Work in Greece." *The Biblical Archaeologist* 14 (1951): 77–96.

Bruce, F. F. *Acts of the Apostles: The Greek Text with Introduction and Commentary*. 2nd rev. ed. Grand Rapids: Eerdmans, 1973.

———. *Acts of the Apostles: The Greek Text with Introduction and Commentary*. 3rd rev. ed. Grand Rapids: Eerdmans, 1990.

———. "The Church of Jerusalem in the Acts of the Apostles." *Bulletin of the John Rylands University Library of Manchester* 67 (1985): 641–61.

———. "Paul's Apologetic and the Purpose of Acts." *Bulletin of the John Rylands University Library of Manchester* 69 (1987): 379–93.

Byrskog, Samuel. *Story as History, History as Story: The Gospel Tradition in the Context of Ancient Oral History*. Wissenschaftliche Untersuchungen zum Neuen Testament 123. Tübingen: Mohr Siebeck, 2000.

Capper, Brian. "The Palestinian Cultural Context of Earliest Christian Community of Goods." In *The Book of Acts in Its Palestinian Setting*, edited by Richard Bauckham, 323–56. The Book of Acts in Its First Century Setting 4. Grand Rapids: Eerdmans, 1995.

Carver, William Owen. *The Acts of the Apostles.* Nashville: Sunday School Board, Southern Baptist Convention, 1916.

Christian, Elizabeth. "The Seven Deadly Sins of Messaging." *Communitas: Journal of Education beyond the Walls* 11 (2014): 34–36.

Ciampa, Roy E. "'Examined the Scriptures'? The Meaning of ἀνακρίνοντες τὰς γραφάς in Acts 17:11." *Journal of Biblical Literature* 130 (2011): 527–41.

Clark, Andrew C. "The Role of the Apostles." In *Witness to the Gospel: The Theology of Acts,* edited by I. Howard Marshall and David Peterson, 169–90. Grand Rapids: Eerdmans, 1998.

Conzelmann, Hans. *Acts of the Apostles: A Commentary on the Acts of the Apostles.* Translated by James Limburg, A. Thomas Kraabel, and Donald H. Juel. Edited by Eldon Jay Epp with Christopher R. Matthews. Hermeneia. Philadelphia: Fortress, 1987.

Dahl, Nils A. "'A People for His Name' (Acts 15:14)." *New Testament Studies* 4 (1958): 319–27.

Dunn, James D. G. *Beginning from Jerusalem.* Vol. 2 of *Christianity in the Making.* Grand Rapids: Eerdmans, 2009.

Edwards, Mark J. "Quoting Aratus: Acts 17,28." *Zeitschrift für die neutestamentliche Wissenschaft und die Kunde der älteren Kirche* 83 (1992): 266–69.

Ellis, E. Earle. "The End of the Earth' (Acts 1:8)." *Bulletin for Biblical Research* 1 (1991): 123–32.

———. *Prophecy and Hermeneutic in Early Christianity: New Testament Essays.* Grand Rapids: Eerdmans, 1978.

Fellows, Richard G. "Renaming in Paul's Churches: The Case of Crispus-Sosthenes Revisited." *Tyndale Bulletin* 56 (2005): 111–30.

Ferguson, Everett. "The Laying on of Hands in Acts 6:6 and 13:3." *Restoration Quarterly* 4 (1960): 250–52.

Fernando, Ajith. *Acts.* NIV Application Commentary. Grand Rapids: Zondervan, 1998.

Fitzmyer, Joseph A. *The Acts of the Apostles: A New Translation with Introduction and Commentary.* Anchor Bible 31. New York: Doubleday, 1998.

Foakes-Jackson, F. J., and Kirsopp Lake. *The Beginnings of Christianity: The Acts of the Apostles.* 5 vols. Grand Rapids: Baker, 1979.

Garland, David E. *Luke.* Zondervan Exegetical Commentary on the New Testament 3. Grand Rapids: Zondervan, 2011.

Garland, David E., and Diana R. Garland. *Flawed Families of the Bible: How God's Grace Works through Imperfect Relationships.* Grand Rapids: Brazos, 2007.

Garrett, Susan R. *The Demise of the Devil: Magic and the Demonic in Luke's Writings.* Minneapolis: Fortress, 1989.

Gaventa, Beverly Roberts. *The Acts of the Apostles.* Abingdon New Testament Commentaries. Nashville: Abingdon, 2003.

———. "'Turning the World Upside Down': A Reflection on the Acts of the Apostles." In *Shaking Heaven and Earth: Essays in Honor of Walter Brueggemann and Charles B. Cousar,* edited by Christine Roy Yoder et al., 105–16. Louisville: Westminster John Knox, 2005.

Gilbert, Gary. "The List of Nations in Acts 2: Roman Propaganda and the Lukan Response." *Journal of Biblical Literature* 121 (2002): 497–529.

Goodspeed, Edgar J. *An Introduction to the New Testament.* Chicago: University of Chicago Press, 1937.

Green, Joel B. "Acts of the Apostles." In *Dictionary of the Later New Testament and Its Developments,* edited by Ralph P. Martin and Peter H. Davids, 7–24. Downers Grove, IL: InterVarsity, 1997.

Gundry, Robert H. *Commentary on the New Testament: Verse-by-Verse Explanations with a Literal Translation.* Peabody, MA: Hendrickson, 2010.

Haenchen, Ernst. *The Acts of the Apostles: A Commentary.* Translated by Bernard Noble and Gerald Shinn. Philadelphia: Westminster, 1971.

Hamm, Dennis. "Acts 3, 1–10: The Healing of the Temple Beggar as Lucan Theology." *Biblica* 67 (1986): 305–19.

———. "The Tamid Service in Luke-Acts: The Cultic Background behind Luke's Theology of Worship (Luke 1:5–25; 18:9–14; 24:50–53; Acts 3:1; 10:3, 30)." *Catholic Biblical Quarterly* 65 (2003): 215–31.

Hansen, G. Walter. "Galatia." In *The Book of Acts in Its Graeco-Roman Setting,* edited by David W. J. Gill and Conrad Gempf, 377–96. The Book of Acts in Its First Century Setting 2. Grand Rapids: Eerdmans, 1994.

Hardin, Justin K. "Decrees and Drachmas at Thessalonica: An Illegal Assembly in Jason's House (Acts 17.1–10a)." *New Testament Studies* 52 (2006): 29–49.

Harrill, J. Albert. "Divine Judgment against Ananias and Sapphira (Acts 5:1–11): A Stock Scene of Perjury and Death." *Journal of Biblical Literature* 130 (2011): 351–69.

Heimerdinger, Jenny. "Unintentional Sins in Peter's Speech: Acts 3:12–26." *Revista Catalana de Teología* 20 (1995): 269–76.

Hengel, Martin. *Acts and the History of Earliest Christianity.* Translated by John Bowden. Philadelphia: Fortress, 1979.

Hirschfeld, Nicolle. "The Ship of Saint Paul: Historical Background (Part I)." *The Biblical Archaeologist* 53 (1990): 25–30.

Hogan, Derek. "Paul's Defense: A Comparison of the Forensic Speeches in Acts, *Callirhoe,* and *Leucippe and Clitophon.*" *Perspectives in Religious Studies* 29 (2002): 73–87.

Holmes, B. T. "Luke's Description of John Mark." *Journal of Biblical Literature* 54 (1935): 63–72.

Hunter, James Davison. *To Change the World: The Irony, Tragedy, and Possibility of Christianity in the Late Modern World.* New York: Oxford University Press, 2010.

Jeremias, Joachim. *Jerusalem in the Time of Jesus.* Translated by F. H. and C. H. Cave. London: SCM, 1969.

Jervell, Jacob. *Die Apostelgeschichte.* 17th ed. Kritisch-exegetischer Kommentar über das Neue Testament 3. Göttingen: Vandenhoeck & Ruprecht, 1998.

———. *Luke and the People of God: A New Look at Luke-Acts.* Minneapolis: Augsburg, 1972.

Johnson, Luke Timothy. *The Acts of the Apostles.* Sacra Pagina 5. Collegeville, MN: Liturgical Press, 1992.

———. *The Literary Function of Possessions in Luke-Acts.* Society of Biblical Literature Dissertation Series 39. Missoula, MT: Scholars Press, 1977.

Keener, Craig S. *Acts: An Exegetical Commentary.* 4 vols. Grand Rapids: Baker Academic, 2012.

———. "Power of Pentecost: Luke's Missiology in Acts 1–2." *Asian Journal of Pentecostal Studies* 12 (2009): 47–73.

———. "Three Notes on Figurative Language: Inverted Guilt in Acts 7.55–60, Paul's Figurative Vote in Acts 26.10, Figurative Eyes in Galatians 4.15." *Journal of Greco-Roman Christianity and Judaism* 5 (2008): 41–49.

Keller, W. Phillip. *David I: The Time of Saul's Tyranny.* Waco: Word, 1985.

Kilgallen, John J. "Clean, Acceptable, Saved: Acts 10." *Expository Times* 109 (1998): 301–2.

———. "The Use of Psalm 16:8–11 in Peter's Pentecost Speech." *Expository Times* 113 (2001): 47–50.

Klauck, Hans-Josef. *Magic and Paganism in Early Christianity: The World of the Acts of the*

Apostles. Translated by Brian McNeil. Minneapolis: Fortress, 2003.

Kodell, Jerome. "The Word of God Grew: The Ecclesial Tendency of Λόγος in Acts 1,7; 12,24; 19,20." *Biblica* 55 (1974): 505–19.

Koet, Bart J. "As Close to the Synagogue as Can Be: Paul in Corinth (Acts 18,1–8)." In *The Corinthian Correspondence,* edited by Reimund Bieringer, 397–415. Bibliotheca Ephemeridum Theologicarum Lovaniensium 125. Louvain: Leuven University Press; Peeters, 1996.

Kraus, Thomas J. "'Uneducated', 'Ignorant', or Even 'Illiterate'? Aspects and Background for an Understanding of *AGRAMMATOI* (and *IDIŌTAI*) in Acts 4.13." *New Testament Studies* 45 (1999): 434–49.

Krodel, Gerhard A. *Acts.* Augsburg Commentary on the New Testament. Minneapolis: Augsburg, 1986.

Lightfoot, J. B. *St. Paul's Epistle to the Galatians: A Revised Text with Introduction, Notes, and Dissertations.* 4th ed. London: Macmillan, 1874.

Longenecker, Richard. "Acts." In *The Expositor's Bible Commentary,* vol. 9, edited by Frank E. Gaebelein, 207–573. Grand Rapids: Zondervan, 1981.

Lövestam, Evald. "Paul's Address at Miletus." *Studia Theologica* 41 (1987): 1–10.

Maile, John F. "The Ascension in Luke-Acts." *Tyndale Bulletin* 37 (1986): 29–59.

Malherbe, Abraham J. "'Not in a Corner': Early Christian Apologetic in Acts 26:26." *Second Century* 5 (1985–86): 193–210.

———. *Social Aspects of Early Christianity.* Philadelphia: Fortress, 1983.

Malina, Bruce J., and John J. Pilch. *Social-Science Commentary on the Book of Acts.* Minneapolis: Fortress, 2008.

Manson, T. W. *The Teaching of Jesus: Studies of Its Form and Content.* 2nd ed. Cambridge: Cambridge University Press, 1951.

Manus, Chris U. "Luke's Account of Paul in Thessalonica (Acts 17,1–9)." In *The Thessalonian Correspondence,* edited by Raymond F. Collins, 27–38. Bibliotheca Ephemeridum Theologicarum Lovaniensium 87. Louvain: Leuven University Press; Peeters, 1990.

Marguerat, Daniel. "Saul's Conversion (Acts 9, 22, 26) and the Multiplication of Narrative in Acts." In *Luke's Literary Achievement: Collected Essays,* edited by C. M. Tuckett, 127–55. Journal for the Study of the New Testament: Supplement Series 116. Sheffield: Sheffield Academic, 1995.

Marrow, Stanley B. "*Parrēsia* in the New Testament." *Catholic Biblical Quarterly* 44 (1982): 431–46.

Marshall, I. Howard. "Acts." In *Commentary on the New Testament Use of the Old Testament*, edited by G. K. Beale and D. A. Carson, 513–606. Grand Rapids: Baker Academic, 2007.

———. *Acts*. Tyndale New Testament Commentaries 5. Downers Grove, IL: IVP Academic, 1981.

McCabe, David R. *How to Kill Things with Words: Ananias and Sapphira under the Prophetic Speech-Act of Divine Judgment (Acts 4.32–5.11)*. Library of New Testament Studies 454. London: T&T Clark, 2011.

Moore, Thomas S. "'To the End of the Earth': The Geographical and Ethnic Universalism of Acts 1:8 in Light of Isaianic Influence on Luke." *Journal of the Evangelical Theological Society* 40 (1997): 389–99.

Murphy-O'Connor, Jerome. "Prisca and Aquila." *Bible Review* 8 (1992): 40–51.

Murray, Andrew. *The Best of Andrew Murray*. Grand Rapids: Baker, 1991.

Myrou, Augustine. "Sosthenes: The Former Crispus (?)." *Greek Orthodox Theological Review* 44 (1999): 207–12.

Nave, Guy D., Jr. *The Role and Function of Repentance in Luke-Acts*. Academia Biblica 4. Atlanta: Society of Biblical Literature, 2002.

Neyrey, Jerome H. "Luke's Social Location of Paul: Cultural Anthropology and the Status of Paul in Acts." In *History, Literature, and Society in the Book of Acts*, edited by Ben Witherington III, 251–79. Cambridge: Cambridge University Press, 1996.

O'Connor, Flannery. *The Habit of Being: Letters of Flannery O'Connor*. Edited by Sally Fitzgerald. New York: Farrar, Straus & Giroux, 1978.

Oster, Richard. "The Ephesian Artemis as an Opponent of Early Christianity." *Jahrbuch für Antike und Christentum* 19 (1976): 24–44.

Parsons, Mikeal C. "Isaiah 53 in Acts 8: A Reply to Professor Morna Hooker." In *Jesus and the Suffering Servant: Isaiah 53 and Christian Origins*, edited by William H. Bellinger Jr. and William R. Farmer, 104–19. Harrisburg, PA: Trinity Press International, 1998.

Parsons, Mikeal C., and Martin M. Culy. *Acts: A Handbook on the Greek Text*. Baylor Handbook on the Greek New Testament. Waco: Baylor University Press, 2003.

Pelikan, Jaroslav. *Acts*. Brazos Theological Commentary on the Bible. Grand Rapids: Brazos, 2005.

Pesch, Rudolf. *Die Apostelgeschichte*. 2 vols. Evangelisch-Katholischer Kommentar zum Neuen Testament. Zurich: Benziger; Neukirchen-Vluyn: Neukirchener Verlag, 1986.

Peterman, G. W. *Paul's Gift from Philippi: Conventions of Gift Exchange and Christian Giving*. Society for New Testament Studies Monograph Series 92. Cambridge: Cambridge University Press, 1997.

Peterson, David. *The Acts of the Apostles*. Pillar New Testament Commentary. Grand Rapids: Eerdmans, 2009.

Polhill, John B. *Acts*. New American Commentary 26. Nashville: Broadman, 1992.

Rapske, Brian M. *The Book of Acts and Paul in Roman Custody*. The Book of Acts in Its First Century Setting 3. Grand Rapids: Eerdmans, 1994.

———. "Travel and Trade." In *Dictionary of New Testament Background*, edited by Craig A. Evans and Stanley E. Porter, 1245–50. Downers Grove, IL: InterVarsity, 2000.

Robinson, Anthony B., and Robert W. Wall. *Called to Be Church: The Book of Acts for a New Day*. Grand Rapids: Eerdmans, 2006.

Rowe, C. Kavin. "Acts 2.36 and the Continuity of Lukan Christology." *New Testament Studies* 53 (2007): 537–56.

———. "The Grammar of Life: The Areopagus Speech and Pagan Tradition." *New Testament Studies* 57 (2011): 31–50.

———. *World Upside Down: Reading Acts in the Graeco-Roman Age*. Oxford: Oxford University Press, 2009.

Sandt, Huub van de. "The Fate of the Gentiles in Joel and Acts 2: An Intertextual Study." *Ephemerides Theologicae Lovanienses* 66 (1990): 56–77.

Savage, Timothy B. *Power through Weakness: Paul's Understanding of the Christian Ministry in 2 Corinthians*. Society for New Testament Studies Monograph Series 86. Cambridge: Cambridge University Press, 1996.

Schnabel, Eckhard. *Acts*. Zondervan Exegetical Commentary on the New Testament 5. Grand Rapids: Zondervan, 2012.

———. *Early Christian Mission*. 2 vols. Downers Grove, IL: Intervarsity, 2004.

Schürer, Emil. *The History of the Jewish People in the Age of Jesus Christ (175 B.C.–A.D. 135)*. Revised and edited by Geza Vermes, Fergus Millar, and Matthew Black. 3 vols. Edinburgh: T&T Clark, 1979.

Seccombe, David. "The New People of God." In *Witness to the Gospel: The Theology of Acts*, edited by I. Howard Marshall and David

Peterson, 349–72. Grand Rapids: Eerdmans, 1998.

Smallwood, E. Mary. *The Jews under Roman Rule: From Pompey to Diocletian*. Studies in Judaism in Late Antiquity 20. Leiden: Brill, 1976.

Spencer, F. Scott. *Acts*. Readings: A New Biblical Commentary. Sheffield: Sheffield Academic Press, 1997.

———. "The Ethiopian Eunuch and His Bible: A Social-Science Analysis." *Biblical Theology Bulletin* 22 (1992): 155–65.

———. *The Portrait of Philip in Acts: A Study of Roles and Relations*. Journal for the Study of the New Testament Supplement Series 67. Sheffield: JSOT Press, 1992.

Stagg, Frank. *The Book of Acts: The Early Struggle for an Unhindered Gospel*. Nashville: Broadman, 1955.

Stewart, James S. *A Man in Christ: The Vital Elements of St. Paul's Religion*. New York: Harper, 1935.

Stott, John R. W. *The Spirit, the Church, and the World*. Downers Grove, IL: InterVarsity, 1990.

Strelan, Rick. "Gamaliel's Hunch." *Australian Biblical Review* 47 (1999): 53–69.

———. *Luke the Priest: The Authority of the Author of the Third Gospel*. Aldershot: Ashgate, 2008.

Tajra, Harry W. *The Trial of St. Paul: A Juridical Exegesis of the Second Half of the Acts of the Apostles*. Wissenschaftliche Untersuchungen zum Neuen Testament 2/35. Tübingen: Mohr Siebeck, 1989.

Talbert, Charles H. *Reading Acts: A Literary and Theological Commentary on the Acts of the Apostles*. Rev. ed. Reading the New Testament. Macon, GA: Smyth & Helwys, 2005.

Tannehill, Robert C. *The Narrative Unity of Luke-Acts: A Literary Interpretation*. 2 vols. Philadelphia: Fortress, 1986–90.

———. "The Narrator's Strategy in the Scenes of Paul's Defense: Acts 21:27–26:32." *Forum* 8 (1992): 255–69.

———. *The Shape of Luke's Story: Essays on Luke-Acts*. Eugene, OR: Cascade, 2005.

Thornton, Claus-Jürgen. *Der Zeuge des Zeugen: Lukas als Historiker der Paulusreisen*. Wissenschaftliche Untersuchungen zum Neuen Testament 1/56. Tübingen: Mohr Siebeck, 1991.

Tomson, Peter J. "Gamaliel's Counsel and the Apologetic Strategy of Luke-Acts." In *The Unity of Luke-Acts*, edited by Jozef Verheyden, 585–604. Bibliotheca Ephemeridum Theologicarum Lovaniensium 142. Louvain: Leuven University Press, 1999.

Trebilco, Paul R. *Jewish Communities in Asia Minor*. Society for New Testament Studies Monograph Series 69. Cambridge: Cambridge University Press, 1991.

———. "Paul and Silas—'Servants of the Most High God' (Acts 16.16–18)." *Journal for the Study of the New Testament* 36 (1989): 51–73.

Trites, Allison A. "The Importance of Legal Scenes and Language in the Book of Acts." *Novum Testamentum* 16 (1974): 278–84.

Troftgruben, Troy M. *A Conclusion Unhindered: A Study of the Ending of Acts within Its Literary Environment*. Wissenschaftliche Untersuchungen zum Neuen Testament 2/280. Tübingen: Mohr Siebeck, 2010.

Twelftree, Graham H. "Jesus and Magic in Luke-Acts." In *Jesus and Paul: Global Perspectives in Honor of James D. G. Dunn for His 70th Birthday*, edited by B. J. Oropeza, C. K. Robertson, and Douglas C. Mohrmann, 46–58. Library of New Testament Studies 414. London: T&T Clark, 2009.

———. "Prayer and the Coming of the Spirit in Acts." *Expository Times* 117 (2006): 271–76.

Van der Horst, Pieter W. "The Altar of the 'Unknown God' in Athens (Acts 17:23) and the Cult of 'Unknown Gods' in the Hellenistic and Roman Periods." In *Aufstieg und Niedergang der Römischen Welt* (Berlin: de Gruyter, 1989), II.18.2, pp. 1426–56.

Viviano, Benedict T., and Justin Taylor. "Sadducees, Angels, and Resurrection (Acts 23:8–9)." *Journal of Biblical Literature* 111 (1992): 496–98.

Wall, Robert W. "Acts." In *The New Interpreter's Bible*. Vol. 10, *Acts, Introduction to Epistolary Literature, Romans, 1 Corinthians*, edited by Leander E. Keck, 3–368. Nashville: Abingdon, 2002.

Wedderburn, A. J. M. "The 'Apostolic Decree': Tradition and Redaction." *Novum Testamentum* 35 (1993): 362–89.

———. "Traditions and Redaction in Acts 2.1–13." *Journal for the Study of the New Testament* 55 (1994): 27–54.

Wiedemann, Thomas E. J. "Slavery." In *Civilization of the Ancient Mediterranean: Greece and Rome*, edited by Michael Grant and Rachel Kitzinger, 1:575–88. New York: Charles Scribner & Sons, 1988.

Winter, Bruce W. "Gallio's Ruling on the Legal Status of Early Christianity (Acts 18:14–15)." *Tyndale Bulletin* 50 (1999): 213–24.

———. "On Introducing Gods to Athens: An Alternative Reading of Acts 17:18–20." *Tyndale Bulletin* 47 (1996): 71–90.

Witherington, Ben, III. *The Acts of the Apostles: A Socio-Rhetorical Commentary.* Grand Rapids: Eerdmans, 1998.

Wright, G. Al, Jr. "Earthquakes in Ancient Palestine." *Biblical Illustrator* 16 (1990): 35–37.

Zwiep, Arie W. *Judas and the Choice of Matthias: A Study on Context and Concern of Acts 1:15–26.* Wissenschaftliche Untersuchungen zum Neuen Testament 2/187. Tübingen: Mohr Siebeck, 2004.

Contributors

General Editors
Mark. L. Strauss
John H. Walton

Associate Editors, Illustrating the Text
Kevin and Sherry Harney

Contributing Author, Illustrating the Text
Adam Barr

Series Development
Jack Kuhatschek
Brian Vos

Project Editor
James Korsmo

Interior Design
Brian Brunsting

Cover Direction
Paula Gibson
Michael Cook

Index

Aaron, 71, 235
Abraham, 8, 21, 40–41, 70–71, 74, 76, 80, 107, 140, 143, 155, 256–57, 290
Achaia, 185–88, 199, 204–5
Acts
  audience, 3
  authorship, 2–3
  dating, 3
  ending, 2, 3, 285, 287
  provenance, 3
Aeneas, 100–103
Agabus, 120–21, 218–20, 229
Agrippa I, 53, 124–28, 228–29, 250, 256, 262, 289, 292
Agrippa II, 96, 244–45, 256, 260, 262–63, 266, 268–69, 272–73, 283
Alexander, 200
Alexander (of the high priest family), 44
Alexander the Great, 63
Alexandria, 77, 119, 192
almsgiving, 38–39, 106, 110, 255, 270
amulets, 201–3
Ananias (apostle), 9, 88, 95, 110, 219, 235, 251, 267
Ananias (high priest), 241–42, 296
Ananias (husband of Sapphira), 10, 50–54, 153, 208, 289
angels, 5, 7, 16, 22, 28, 57, 59, 73, 76, 81, 88–89, 106, 108, 110, 113, 121, 124, 126–27, 129, 131, 209, 243, 245, 275
Antioch, 2, 51, 64–66, 118–20, 122, 124, 132, 138–39, 141, 146–47, 152, 154, 160, 191–93, 217, 225, 283
Antiochus Epiphanes, 107, 113

Apollos, 188, 191–95
apologetics, 10, 175, 182
apostasy, 72, 155, 174, 212, 231
  Christianity as, 8, 38, 256
apostles, as the judges of the twelve tribes of Israel, 14, 20
Aquila, 184–85, 187–88, 191–93, 195
Areopagus, 177–78, 180–82
Aristarchus, 3, 163, 172–73, 205, 274
Artemis, 197, 199–202
ascension, 1–2, 5, 13, 16–17, 19, 30, 32, 58, 289
Asia, 77, 161–62, 192, 198–200, 205, 228, 247, 255
astrology, 134, 136
Athenians, 178, 181
Athens, 2, 171, 177, 179–80, 182, 188
atonement, 23–24, 39

Babylon, 72, 74, 190
baptism, 14, 30–31, 33, 35–36, 84–86, 88, 90–91, 102, 109–10, 112, 114, 116, 139, 162, 186, 193–94, 222, 224, 236
  of John the Baptist, 194
  ritual, 107
  in the Spirit, 25
  water, 14
Bar-Jesus. See Elymas
Barnabas, 11, 50–51, 53–54, 65, 96, 118–20, 124, 126, 132–34, 136, 138–41, 145–49, 153–54, 159–60, 163, 217, 222–23
Barsabbas, 21, 51
belief, 40, 85, 148, 172, 232, 238, 241–43, 245, 257
Berea, 171, 173–74, 177, 204–5
Bereans, 173, 175–76

Bernice, 124, 260, 262–63, 266
Bithynia, 161–62
blasphemy, 70, 77, 79, 135, 146, 186, 267
body of Christ, 109, 111, 286
breaking of bread, 33, 204, 206, 208
bribery, 11, 48, 241, 253, 256, 258

Caesarea, 91, 105, 113, 115, 127, 192, 218, 247, 249–51, 253–54, 261–62
calling, for Israel, 8, 41, 135, 174, 281, 285
Cenchreae, 185, 191, 204
centurion, 100, 105, 108–9, 121, 135, 229, 236, 249, 273–76, 278, 281
Christians, as name for followers of Jesus, 120
chosen people, 8, 143, 285
church of God, 94, 97, 212
Cilicia, 77, 160, 230, 250, 262
circumcision, 26, 71, 107, 113, 115–16, 119, 142, 152–56, 159–61, 163, 222–25, 294
Claudius Lysias, 249–50, 255, 263, 269
collection, 199, 205, 207, 223, 295
Colossae, 198
commission, 5, 15, 21, 64–66, 94–97, 132, 147, 214, 234–36, 266–67, 270–71
conversions, 33, 84–85, 97, 102–3, 114, 119, 144, 166–67, 173, 181, 224, 237
    of Cornelius, 100, 112
    of Gentiles, 115, 119, 223
    of jailer and his household, 168
    of Paul, 94, 97, 110, 134, 238, 270
Corinth, 2, 27, 184–88, 191, 193, 195, 197, 204
Cornelius, 7, 41, 88–89, 91, 100, 102, 105–10, 112–16, 132, 153, 255
courage, 43, 45, 48, 61, 165, 214, 218, 248, 250, 273, 277, 279, 282
court, 17, 45, 58, 89, 130, 167, 178, 190, 200, 228–29, 238, 257, 260, 262, 269
covenant, 5, 26, 155, 182
    with Abraham, 8
    of circumcision, 71, 116
    with the fathers, 40, 74
    with Israel, 153, 155, 222
    new, 23, 26
    old, 23
coworkers, 142, 159–60, 164, 178, 209
creation, 146, 180–81
Crispus, 186–87
cross
    of Christians, 22, 58, 77, 79, 86, 207, 219
    message of, 34
crucifixion, 1, 43, 76, 91, 174, 229, 236
Cyprus, 51, 118–19, 126, 132–33, 160, 218, 223
Cyrene, 77, 119, 132

Damascus, 95–96, 120, 235, 245–46, 267, 270
David, 6, 32, 45, 72, 74, 139–41, 154, 190
defilement, 106–7, 224, 228–29, 231, 255, 261, 268

Demetrius, 199
demons, 58, 83–84, 128, 156, 169, 198, 201–2
Derbe, 3, 144–45, 160–61, 192, 205
devil, 48, 132, 134–35, 153, 227, 245, 265
diaspora, 7, 21, 25, 33, 63, 70, 293
Dionysius, 180
Dorcas, 100, 102
Drusilla, 256, 262

early church, 1, 5, 11, 35, 43, 57, 84, 98, 121, 156, 286
Egypt, 70–71, 139, 150–51, 192, 230, 274
elders, 120, 149, 153–54, 207, 210, 212, 222–25, 248, 253
Elijah, 102, 133, 206, 289
Elisha, 84, 102, 206
Elymas, 53, 133–36, 245, 289
encouragement, 51, 101, 119, 147, 163, 186, 204, 206, 209, 223, 247–48, 250, 273–74
ends of the earth, 2, 4–6, 10, 13, 15–16, 73, 77, 82, 142–43, 164, 283, 285–87
Ephesus, 2, 25, 162, 184, 189, 191–93, 197–99, 202, 204, 206, 210–11, 213, 224, 228
Epicureans, 178, 181, 188, 294
Ethiopian eunuch, 7, 10, 78, 88–93, 109–10, 115–16
Eutychus, 206, 208
eyewitness, 15–16, 19, 223, 253, 274, 289

famine, 71, 120–21, 218
Felix, 11, 230, 244–45, 249–50, 253–58, 260–64, 266
Festus, 3–4, 244–45, 254, 256, 260–69
forgiveness, 33–34, 77, 79–81, 96, 101, 114, 140, 149, 232
    by God, 8, 75, 78–79, 84, 268
    of sins, 2, 23, 31, 38, 41, 45, 59, 106, 110, 112, 138, 140, 143, 145, 147, 193, 212, 267
freedman, 69, 185, 254
fulfillment
    of Isaiah, 39–40, 72, 88, 90–92, 94, 97, 142, 164, 236, 251, 267–68, 283, 285, 289
    of Israel's hope, 4, 84, 245, 256–57, 267, 285
    of the word of God, 5–6, 8–9, 21, 23, 32, 37–40, 57, 70–72, 90, 103, 108, 114, 133, 140–42, 154, 164, 195, 220, 232, 237, 243, 268–70, 277

Galatia, 161, 205, 224, 293
Galilee, 20, 100, 125, 127, 133, 254
Gallio, 4, 186–89, 263
Gamaliel, 50, 60, 133, 212, 234, 243
Gerizim, 71, 83
God
    Acts of, 8
    calling, 8, 11, 17, 41, 97, 132, 164–65, 174, 206, 210, 220, 238, 242, 267–68, 270

judgment of, 22, 50, 52–53, 129, 182, 201, 212, 242, 257

kingdom of, 4, 5, 14–16, 22, 61, 76, 84–85, 117, 149–50, 157, 170–71, 196–97, 202, 284, 287

plan of, 30–32, 39, 135, 164, 225, 247, 251, 283

promises of, 5, 70, 75, 77, 103, 267, 277

purposes of, 7, 15, 23, 30–31, 39, 115, 140–42, 154, 175, 177–78, 241, 250, 253, 276, 278, 283

revelation, 40, 89, 105, 108, 176, 237

God-fearers, 107–10, 113–14, 138–41, 166, 169, 172, 174

God-worshipers, 7, 162, 186

grace, 8, 34, 48, 69, 77, 81, 91, 95, 97–98, 110, 120, 122, 140–41, 145, 147, 153, 155, 157, 160, 163, 175, 186, 208, 211, 213–15, 228, 232, 239, 268, 270, 274, 276, 278, 286

Greco-Roman culture, 3, 54, 106, 119, 173, 188

heavens, 4–5, 13, 16–17, 20, 26, 32, 39, 45–46, 58, 76, 79, 83, 95, 106, 135, 169, 174, 181, 200, 242, 246, 259, 268, 270

as circumlocution for God, 16

Hellenists, 63–65, 67, 78, 85–86, 121

Herod Agrippa I. *See* Agrippa I

Herod Agrippa II. *See* Agrippa II

Herod Antipas, 125, 133, 244, 263

Herod the Great, 228–29

Hierapolis, 198, 220

high priests, 43–44, 58, 79, 95, 238, 241–45, 248, 253–54

Holy Spirit
    age of, 194
    baptism of, 14, 25, 84, 114, 193
    coming of, 9, 13–15, 17, 20, 22, 25–28, 53, 82, 102, 108–9, 115–16, 121
    conflict with Satan, 52–53
    continuing Jesus's ministry, 13
    conviction by, 46
    creation in, 116
    descending of, 16, 25
    directing mission, 9
    encouragement of, 101, 149
    enemies of, 50
    filling of, 9, 26–27, 44, 46, 64, 76, 96, 114, 119–20, 155, 158, 195–96, 287
    fruit of, 9, 257
    gift of, 9, 19, 59, 85, 108, 109, 113–16, 121, 153, 194
    inspiration of, 28, 31–32, 45, 59, 70, 219
    leading of, 5, 13, 16–17, 19, 30, 47, 66, 85, 88, 91, 114, 132–33, 135, 152–54, 162, 174, 211, 214, 219, 257, 283
    movement of, 72, 75, 113, 285, 287
    opposing, 54
    persuasion by, 175, 211
    pouring of, 9, 16, 27, 30–31, 57, 114, 153

power of, 9, 13, 15, 26–27, 43, 46–47, 66, 77, 79, 84, 101, 112, 118, 141, 191, 193–95, 206, 284

predicting by, 219, 251

presence of, 17, 22, 26, 40–41, 50, 194

promise of, 31

receiving, 7, 9, 85, 109–10, 115–16, 133, 194–95, 222

regeneration by, 84

reliance on, 57

resisting, 75, 135

sending by, 133

sending of, 16

speaking of, 115

Spirit of Jesus, 162–63

teaching of, 175, 271

testing, 53–54, 84, 208

transformation by, 33

wisdom by, 193, 217–18, 245

work of, 2, 9, 120, 157, 281

work of God in, 172

hope of Israel, 4, 8, 231–32, 237, 241, 245, 257, 267, 281–83

hospitality, 108–9, 137, 159, 162, 166, 168, 173, 276–77, 282

humility, 67, 208, 211, 214

hymns, 81, 168–69, 239, 279, 286

Iconium, 144, 146–47, 161, 192

idolaters, 7, 154, 156, 225

idolatry, 26, 71–72, 113, 146, 154, 156, 158, 161, 179, 181, 200, 202

idols, 11, 53, 72, 143, 154, 156, 158, 172, 177–80, 199, 224, 281
    sacrifices to, 107, 154, 156, 168, 224
    worship to, 106, 119, 128, 148, 180–81, 197, 199, 202, 235

ignorance, 39, 41, 44, 148, 177, 179, 242

Illyricum, 205

imprisonment, 41, 49, 62, 78–79, 124, 131, 167–68, 170, 213, 216, 219, 223, 232–33, 249, 251, 263, 268, 286. *See also* jail; prison

incarnation, 13, 27

inheritance, 51, 139, 212, 268

injustice, 31, 233, 263–64v

Isaac, 39, 71, 74, 76, 107, 256–57

Israel, history of, 69–72, 75, 139–40, 142

Israelites, 5, 39, 71–72, 139, 235

Jacob, 15, 39, 74, 76, 107, 164, 189, 256–57

jail, 59, 128–29, 148, 166, 169–70, 233. *See also* imprisonment; prison

jailer, 7, 116, 166, 168–69

James (apostle), 75, 83, 124–25, 128

James (brother of Jesus), 6, 14, 127, 153–54, 222, 225, 250, 284

Jason, 173

Jerusalem
  as beginning point of mission, 1, 2, 4, 6, 15,
    64, 77, 82–83, 121, 152
  Christians, 58, 122, 199, 207, 223–24
  church, 69, 77, 112, 114, 118–20, 124, 127,
    152–53, 160, 206, 222–23, 226
  council, 7, 152, 155–56, 159–60, 222
  destruction of, 44, 252, 284
  as heart of Judaism, 4
  leaders, 222, 282
  as location, 2, 7, 15, 19, 25, 28, 31–32, 51,
    58, 65, 67, 69–70, 72, 75, 77–78, 83–84, 86,
    88–89, 94–96, 100–101, 108, 118, 120, 122,
    124–26, 138–40, 145, 153, 161, 173, 189, 192,
    195, 199, 205–7, 210–11, 217–20, 222–24,
    234–36, 238, 244, 247–51, 253, 255, 260–62,
    269, 274, 282, 284–85
  as place of worship, 89–90
  priests, 148
  synagogues, 70
  temple, 69
Jesus
  as author of life, 39–41
  baptism of, 16, 25, 108
  court trials, 79, 125, 262
  cross of, 32, 77, 79, 90, 92, 97, 115, 128, 213, 232
  as deliverer, 71, 139, 268
  as God's anointed, 9, 108
  as judge of the living and the dead, 9, 257
  as messiah, 5, 7, 10, 17, 30–32, 37, 39–41, 74,
    77, 82–84, 90, 96–97, 119, 139, 143, 154, 172,
    175, 184, 186, 191, 222, 226, 232, 238, 241,
    245, 257, 268–70, 284–85
  ministry of, 3, 6, 14–15, 19–20, 23, 25, 39, 44,
    58, 64, 85, 108, 133, 136, 195
  name of, 31, 33, 37–39, 44, 46, 60, 84, 96, 132,
    166–67, 193–94, 198, 201, 267
  preaching of, 14, 84
  prophecy of, 20, 45
  as prophet like Moses, 5, 8, 39–41, 71
  as redeemer, 61, 172, 214
  as righteous one, 39–41, 71, 75–76
  as savior, 59, 111, 138–40, 172, 197, 225, 236,
    239, 270, 282
  speech of, 25
Jewish council, 238, 242, 244, 248–49
Jewish leaders, 7, 43–44, 59, 96, 125, 138, 141,
  173, 186, 205, 219, 235, 244, 253–54, 256,
  260–61, 282
John (apostle), 37–38, 40, 43–46, 59, 65, 77–78,
  83–85, 101, 116, 119, 124, 126, 133, 148,
  194–95, 234
John Mark, 51, 133–34, 139, 159, 293
John the Baptist, 5, 14, 25, 33, 116, 125, 191,
  193–95, 211, 220, 268
Jonah, 105, 117
Joppa, 100–102, 105, 110, 115, 117

Joseph (of the Old Testament), 71, 80, 164
Joseph Barnabas. See Barnabas
Joseph Justus Barsabbas, 51, 54, 71, 134
Josephus, 3, 44, 76, 125, 127, 228–30, 241, 243,
  254, 256, 261, 290, 295
Judaism, 4, 6–7, 26, 38, 64–65, 76, 82, 88, 91–92,
  97, 100, 107, 109, 113, 115, 119, 132, 140–41,
  143, 162, 167, 187, 225–26, 232, 237–38, 241,
  243, 256–57, 263, 270, 282, 285
Judas (Jewish leader), 154
Judas Iscariot, 10, 19–23, 51, 149
Judas the Galilean, 60, 127
Judea, 15, 28, 72, 77, 82–83, 100–101, 114, 125,
  152, 192, 217–18, 220, 249, 254, 261, 282
judgment, 23, 28, 34, 42, 92, 117, 127, 140, 177,
  180, 194, 202
  of the nations, 31, 33, 253, 256–59
justification, 116, 140–41
Justin, 83

kingdom
  of Israel, 5, 13–14, 28, 39
  of God, 4, 5, 14–16, 22, 61, 76, 84–85, 117,
    149–50, 157, 170–71, 196–97, 202, 284, 287

lame man, 2, 37–39, 45, 101, 103, 145
  significance of healing, 38, 103
Laodicea, 198
Last Supper, 20, 206, 275
law, 5, 25–26, 45, 60, 70–71, 76–77, 90, 110,
  120, 125, 138, 141, 153, 156, 164, 185, 187,
  192, 222–26, 229, 231–32, 234–35, 237–38,
  242–43, 245, 247, 254, 256, 267
Law and the Prophets, 8, 40, 139, 282, 285
leadership, 9, 19–21, 23–24, 44, 63, 65–68, 86,
  124, 127, 133, 149, 152–54, 157, 160, 163–64,
  185, 202, 210, 212, 215–16, 220, 222, 224,
  226, 282
legalism, 98, 157
Levites, 51, 132
light
  to the Gentiles, 6, 15, 112, 142, 164, 267, 281,
    283, 285
  from heaven, 95, 135, 235, 237, 245, 270
  of the nations, 6–8, 13, 15, 40, 114, 133, 135,
    138, 141, 143, 270, 283, 285
lordship, 16–17, 47, 97–98, 108, 237, 257
Lord's Supper, 206, 275
love, 16, 32, 50, 62, 78, 93, 96, 99, 107, 122, 147,
  150, 179, 188, 206, 270–71
Lucius, 132
Luke-Acts, 3–4, 89, 108, 110, 220, 264, 284
Lydda, 100–102
Lydia, 9, 162, 169
Lystra, 144–45, 147, 160–61, 192

Macedonia, 161–62, 164, 171–72, 199, 204–5
Macedonian vision, 161, 164, 171, 186

magic, 28, 42, 53, 83, 196, 201

Manaen, 132–33

martyrdom, 1, 69, 75, 77–79, 81–83, 107, 118, 128, 145, 214, 263

Mary (mother of Jesus), 7, 19–20, 220

Mary (mother of John Mark), 126

Matthias, 21

mercy, 22, 44, 166, 179, 198, 239, 252, 286

Mesopotamia, 70

ministers, 64, 67, 93, 101, 103, 123, 173, 176, 213–14

ministry, 20–21, 23, 65–66, 103, 136, 175, 192–93, 208, 210, 214–15
  of Apollos, 193
  of the distribution of food, 82
  evangelistic, 88
  to the Gentiles, 132
  gospel, 210
  of John the Baptist, 139
  of missionaries, 223
  of Paul, 8, 113, 120, 147, 163, 177, 184, 187–88, 191–92, 207, 210–11, 213, 215, 220
  of Peter, 100
  preaching and teaching, 63–64
  team, 207
  of the word, 67

miracle, 2, 9–10, 17, 20, 28, 30–31, 33, 37–41, 43–45, 58, 69, 71, 77, 82, 84–85, 100–104, 128–29, 135–37, 144–46, 148, 168, 197–98, 202, 208–9, 226, 269, 273, 277

missionary journeys, 119, 139, 160, 191, 193

Mnason, 223

money, 10–11, 21, 37–38, 41, 48, 50–54, 61, 68, 84–85, 117, 121, 157, 213, 241, 259

monotheism, 107, 133, 167

Moses, 8, 31, 68, 70–72, 89–91, 133, 161
  books of, 83
  customs of, 76
  law of, 26, 71, 108, 141, 153–55, 187, 222–24, 243, 256, 268
  preaching of, 154
  prophecy of, 5

Nazarene sect, 254, 296

Nazareth, 25, 31, 38, 44, 141, 245, 267

Nazirite, 192, 224, 228

Nicanor, 64

Nicolas, 64–65

Niger, 132–33

obedience, 2, 5, 8, 20, 40, 45, 57, 59–62, 65–66, 69–71, 86, 88, 95–96, 106, 110, 113, 117, 186, 197, 211, 214, 217–21, 234, 237, 242, 266, 268–70
  to the Jewish tradition, 6
  to the law, 26, 153, 155, 226, 232, 243

observance of the law, 107, 125, 224, 226

overseers, 59, 212

paganism, 7, 71–72, 86, 95, 98, 107, 127, 134, 148–49, 156, 162, 166–68, 172, 178, 181, 196–97, 199, 202–3, 226, 275, 281

parable, 5–6, 47, 51, 117, 190, 259

Parmenas, 64

peace, 24, 100–101, 104, 108, 114, 149–51, 165, 167, 173, 180–81, 202, 232, 240, 242, 252, 254, 259

Pentateuch, 243

Pentecost, 2, 7, 9, 18–20, 22, 25–29, 34–35, 39, 46, 53, 76, 95, 109, 114, 153, 193–95, 206, 220, 224, 290

Perea, 125, 254

persecution, 1, 7, 10, 43, 47–48, 50, 52, 57, 60–62, 75, 77–78, 81–83, 96–97, 101, 118, 121, 125, 130, 133, 141, 145, 166, 170, 173, 184, 190, 217–18, 224, 226, 233, 238, 284, 286–87

Pharisee, 8, 60, 97, 112, 120, 125, 133, 222, 238, 241–43, 245, 248, 256, 267, 270

Philip, 9, 64–65, 67, 82–85, 88–91, 93, 115, 125, 133, 218, 220, 262

Philippi, 2, 106, 162, 166, 170–71, 174, 204

Phinehas, 94, 235

Phoenicia, 217

Phrygia, 161, 293

piety, 54, 192, 222, 225, 242, 256

Pilate, 39–40, 140, 174, 189, 244, 262–63

Pisidian Antioch, 138–39, 192, 283

places of worship, 73, 162, 173

poor, 9, 11, 44, 51–52, 54, 66–68, 102, 106, 120, 122, 167, 188, 190, 199, 207, 214–15, 255–56

possessions, 10, 50, 53–55, 68, 70, 81, 131, 158, 169, 278

prayer, 9, 17, 19–22, 25–26, 28–29, 33, 37, 41, 43, 46–47, 66–68, 77, 80, 93–94, 98, 102, 105–6, 110–11, 123, 126, 129–33, 135–36, 149, 151, 160, 162, 165, 168, 209, 218–19, 231, 234, 236, 277

preaching, 2, 6–8, 28, 30, 37–38, 45–46, 58, 63–67, 77–78, 83, 85–86, 91, 96–97, 103, 108, 112, 125, 133, 137, 142, 144, 148, 154–55, 161–63, 170–74, 184, 195, 214, 228, 257, 270, 281–85
  of the apostles, 63, 65
  of Barnabas, 134, 139, 141, 147, 155
  of the church, 1
  of the gospel, 6, 37–38
  of John, 65, 101, 139
  of Jonah, 105, 117
  of Judas, 155
  about Moses, 154
  of Paul, 96, 120, 134, 139, 141, 147, 153, 155, 178–79, 184, 186, 188, 192, 197, 199,

206–8, 211, 214, 222, 225, 245, 248, 270, 277, 281–83
of Peter, 7, 33, 65, 101, 108, 112, 115–16
of Philip, 84–86
of Silas, 155
predictions, 251, 282, 285
prejudice, 26, 64, 92, 108, 115–17, 187, 242
Priscilla, 184–85, 187–88, 191–93, 195
prison, 2, 48, 59–60, 79, 99, 111, 124, 126, 128–31, 135, 148, 167–68, 170, 227, 243, 248, 256, 260, 262–63, 284. *See also* imprisonment; jail
prisoner, 48, 69, 80, 84, 168–69, 205, 211, 215–16, 227, 236, 248–51, 253, 263, 273–78, 282
proconsul, 132–35, 186–87, 189
Procorus, 64
promises to Israel, 8, 97, 267–68, 285
prophecy, 66, 121, 220, 242, 275
of Agabus, 229
of Amos, 154
of Isaiah, 142, 164, 270, 283, 289
of Joel, 9, 31, 57, 109, 218, 220
of John the Baptist, 14, 194
of Scripture, 6, 32, 40, 114, 140, 232
prophets
Christian, 31, 70, 78, 97, 102, 120–21, 132–33, 218–20, 258, 273
false, 53, 121, 133, 135, 230, 242
female, 220
prosecution, 236, 253–55
proselytes, 26, 65, 90–91, 115, 138, 155
proselytizing, 167
punishment, 20, 22, 24, 34, 42, 48, 60, 86, 135, 242, 250, 254, 274, 289
purification, 224–25, 228, 231
purity, 105, 228
Psalms, 91, 268
Pyrrhus, 182, 205

racism, 116–17, 233
redemption, 71, 150
repent, 23, 31–34, 39, 52, 79, 84, 86, 88, 116–17, 148, 150, 160, 177, 179–80, 285
repentance, 2, 6, 9, 30, 33–35, 39–41, 84, 86, 110, 112, 114, 136, 142, 150, 177, 188, 190, 193, 210–14, 222, 268
false, 84
John's baptism and message of, 194, 268
in the name of Jesus, 194
ritual, 73
rescue, 2, 69, 89, 126, 128, 183, 228, 244, 247, 250, 267, 272–73, 278, 281
restoration of Israel, 5–6, 13–16, 19, 21, 23, 28, 39, 154, 164, 222, 225
resurrection, 1, 3, 5, 10, 13, 16–17, 19, 21, 30, 32–33, 39, 45, 77, 84, 91, 94–95, 98, 103, 108, 114, 116, 125–26, 128, 137–38, 140, 142, 145,

155, 175, 180, 182–83, 193, 194, 198, 206, 208–9, 238, 241–43, 245–46, 255–57, 263, 266–69, 287
bodily, 14, 17, 48, 167, 245–46
of the dead, 8, 44, 177, 241–42, 245–46, 257
retribution, 22, 54, 127, 168
Rhoda, 126, 292
righteous, 245, 255, 257
Righteous Judge, 22
righteousness, 42, 91, 97, 108, 135, 141, 175, 180, 226, 238, 242–43, 257–58
ritual, 7, 35, 73, 83, 85, 91, 105, 107, 109, 156, 178, 201, 225, 231
Roman
citizenship, 168–70, 236–37
empire, 4, 7, 15, 184, 192, 199, 278, 281–82, 285

sabbath, 92–93, 113, 138, 140–41, 143, 162, 172, 185, 206, 271
Sadduceans, 43–44, 58–59, 65, 241–45, 256, 296
salvation, 2, 6, 13, 15–16, 18, 30–33, 37–39, 41–42, 45, 53, 59, 82, 94–95, 97, 99–100, 103–5, 108–10, 114–17, 120, 138, 140, 142, 152–53, 155, 161, 164, 167–68, 170, 175, 181–83, 186, 194, 196, 209, 214, 226, 232, 257, 268, 270, 278, 281, 283–85, 290
history, 6, 13, 31, 41, 116, 120, 153
Samaria, 15, 64, 77, 82–84, 100, 103, 114, 116, 119, 125, 254
Samaritans, 7, 69, 71, 82–86, 88, 101, 194
sanctification, 66, 215, 267–68
sanhedrin, 7, 46, 50, 59–60, 76, 79, 96, 212, 234, 237, 241, 243–44, 247–48, 250, 255, 266–68
Sapphira, 10, 50–54, 153, 208, 289
Satan, 20, 23, 50, 52–53, 55, 61, 85, 116, 212, 219, 267–68, 270
scattering of the believers, 78, 82, 86, 118, 121, 175, 217
Sceva, sons of, 218, 221, 289, 295
sect, 4, 38, 47, 254, 256–57, 282
Secundus, 3, 172, 205
Sergius Paulus, 133–36, 189
sermon, 8, 30, 73, 75–76, 78, 103, 108, 138, 140–41, 153, 181, 217
Sharon, 101–2
shipwreck, 1, 220, 268, 273–74, 276–77
shrines, 62, 72, 179, 199, 202
signs and wonders, 8–9, 53, 57, 85, 144–45, 148, 153
Silvanus, 3, 135, 163
silver, 11, 38, 41–42, 61, 179, 199, 213
silversmith, 11, 199, 211
Simeon, 7, 132–33
Simon (sorcerer), 10, 83–87, 103, 133
Simon (tanner), 102, 293

Sinai, 25, 71–72, 150
sinners, 41, 76, 110, 112, 148, 257, 270, 276
slave girl, 11, 166–67
slavery, 69, 71
slaves, 31, 113, 116, 206
    of God, 97, 147, 167, 169, 208, 211
Solomon, 38, 57–58, 72, 74
sorcery, 83–84, 86, 197–99, 201
Sosthenes, 187
speech, 2, 5, 8, 10, 45
    of Agrippa, 127
    of Anna, 220
    of Elizabeth, 220
    of Gamaliel, 60
    of Mary (mother of Jesus), 220
    of Paul, 138, 140, 178–79, 188, 200, 210,
        213–14, 234–37, 245, 257, 266–67
    of Peter, 5, 8, 25, 28, 38–39, 59, 114
    of Stephen, 7, 69, 75–76, 80
Stephen, 7, 54, 64–65, 67, 69–73, 75–80, 82, 96,
    118–19, 121, 133, 145, 147, 193, 217–18, 229,
    236, 238
stewardship, 10, 55, 215
Stoics, 178, 181, 188, 294
Suetonius, 185, 198
suffering, 61–62, 94, 98, 130, 150
suicide, 168, 248, 262
synagogue, 5–6, 38, 69–70, 96, 102, 107, 133,
    138–39, 141, 144, 146, 154, 162, 172–73, 178,
    184–89, 192–93, 197–98, 206, 282, 293
    leaders, 186–87
Syria, 95, 119, 127, 160, 191, 205, 218, 250, 256

tabernacle, 72–73
Tabitha, 100–103, 206
table fellowship, 14, 112, 114, 156
talismans, 202, 281
Tarsus, 77, 101, 120, 230, 234–35, 251
temple, 2, 5–7, 23, 25–26, 33, 37–38, 41, 43–47,
    54, 57–60, 67, 69–73, 75, 79, 90, 92, 96, 106,
    145–46, 154, 156, 192, 199–200, 205, 222,
    224–26, 228–29, 231–32, 234, 236, 247–52,
    254–55, 261, 266, 268, 285, 296
    leaders, 43–46, 54, 57–60, 248, 253
    sacrifices, 23, 38, 41, 59, 93, 106, 125, 192, 224,
        226, 231, 255
    worship, 5, 72, 225
tent
    of David, 6, 154
    of meeting, 235
Tertullus, 253–54, 256
theology, 1, 60, 75, 114, 195, 238
Theophilus, 3–4, 14
Thessalonica, 171–74, 177, 204–5
Theudas, 60, 127

times of refreshing, 8, 39–40
Timon, 64
Timothy, 3, 142, 147, 159–60, 163–64, 174, 185,
    205, 213, 215, 224, 226
Titius, 186
Titus, 52, 142, 164, 205, 213, 262, 295
tongues
    of fire, 26, 29
    speaking in, 25–28, 116, 194
traditions
    Christian, 3, 15, 19, 135, 148
    Jewish, 6, 94, 97, 115, 127, 225–26, 243, 266,
        270
    oral, 242
    Pharisaic, 267
trials, 4, 126, 167–69, 178, 232, 236, 242, 244,
    255, 260–62, 267, 270–71, 275, 282
    of Peter, 125
    of Stephen, 79
tribes of Israel, 14–15, 20–21, 23, 28, 164, 267
Troas, 161, 205
Trophimus, 3, 205, 228
Twelve, 15, 19, 23, 58, 63–65, 136, 148
Tychicus, 3, 205
Tyrannus, 198, 295
tyrants, 47, 61, 125, 127–28
Tyre, 127–28, 217–19

uncircumcised, 75–76, 78, 107, 109, 112, 142,
    161, 164, 207, 231
unclean, 102, 106, 108, 116, 162, 229

voyages, 1, 3, 23, 218, 244, 273

Way, 2, 6, 94, 97, 199, 218, 237, 245, 255–58,
    270
witchcraft, 83, 202
witness, 4–5, 9–10, 15, 17, 32, 34, 43, 46, 77,
    114, 121, 132, 141, 143, 145, 147, 149, 152,
    252, 271, 284–85, 287
    of the apostles, 19, 85, 119
    of the disciples, 13, 15–16, 25–26, 32, 82, 114
    of the early church, 43
    to the ends of the earth, 2, 287
    false, 70, 79
    to the Gentiles, 112
    of Jesus's earthly ministry, 23
    mandate to, 14
    meaning of, 145
    of Paul, 7, 232, 238, 244, 248, 250, 253, 266,
        268, 273, 282
    of Peter, 39, 102
    power to, 28
    qualifications of the Christian witness,
        213–14
    of the resurrection, 19, 21

role as, 21
task of, 17
of the twelve disciples of John the Baptist, 195
witnesses, 10, 15, 17
worship, 26, 66, 69–71, 76–78, 83, 89–90, 134,
    139, 154, 162, 174, 177, 186–87, 193, 204,
    206, 220, 245, 255, 264, 286
worshipers, 5, 7, 64, 119, 162, 186, 228, 235

zeal
    for God, 226, 235, 237
    for the law, 110, 120, 224
    of Paul, 60, 97
    for the traditions, 94, 97, 225–26
zealots, 226, 251